1-97

CHRONOLOGY OF THE

Ancient World

10,000 B.C. to A.D. 799

Companion volumes

CHRONOLOGY OF THE MEDIEVAL WORLD
800 to 1491

By R.L. Storey

CHRONOLOGY OF THE EXPANDING WORLD
1492 to 1762

By Neville Williams

CHRONOLOGY OF THE MODERN WORLD
1763 to 1992, 2d edition

By Neville Williams and Philip Waller

H.E.L. MELLERSH

CHRONOLOGY OF THE

Ancient World

10,000 B.C. to A.D. 799

SIMON & SCHUSTER

A Paramount Communications Company

New York London Toronto Sydney Tokyo Singapore

First published in 1976
and reissued in 1994 by
Helicon Publishing Ltd
42 Hythe Bridge Street
Oxford, OX1 2EP

and in the USA by Simon & Schuster
Academic Reference Division
15 Columbus Circle
New York, New York 10023

Printed and bound in England

Printing number
1 2 3 4 5 6 7 8 9 10

Library of Congress Cataloging-in-Publication Data

Mellersh. H.E.L.
   Chronology of the ancient world, 10,000 B.C. to A.D. 799 / by
H.E.L. Mellersh.
      p.   cm.
   Originally published: London : Barrie & Jenkins, 1976.
   Continued by: Chronology of the medieval world, 800 to 1491 / by
R.L. Storey.
   Includes index.
   ISBN 0–13–326422-X
   1. History, Ancient--Chronology.   I. Title.
D54.5.M45   1994   94-30474
930'.02'02--dc20   CIP

ISBN 0–13–326430–0 (set)
ISBN 0–13–326422–X (v.1.)

Contents

Introduction

Chronology of the Ancient World has been prepared as a companion volume to Dr Neville Williams's *Chronologies of the Modern* and the *Expanding Worlds* and Professor Robin Storey's *Chronology of the Medieval World*. Including as it does the so-called Dark Ages, the book ends at the year A.D. 799, when Charlemagne is about to be crowned in Rome and the "Holy Roman Empire" brought into being. The book begins, with the year 10,000 B.C., the first point at which dates can be given with an accuracy of within 1000 years. We begin therefore with Man's life as a neolithic farmer, and continue with the growth of the great river-valley civilizations, through the Bronze Age heroics of the Mediterranean, to the coming of iron and, after another dark age, the flowering of classical Greece and so to the long leadership of Rome, her slow decline and the passing of her power, first to Byzantium and then to the Saracens.

The arrangement of the book follows as closely as possible that of its predecessors. Each page opening covers a period of time, this in the earlier period being usually a century and later usually a decade. The left-hand page covers what may be described simply as events—the actions of men and dynasties and nations; the right-hand page is in contrast concerned with affairs of the mind, the arts and sciences. On the left-hand pages there is a dividing line between events for which a specific, even if approximate date can be given and events and trends for which a date cannot usefully be given or, if given, must be understood to mark as it were the nucleus of the affair.

The right-hand pages are divided into paragraphs as follows:
  A Politics, Law and Economics
  B Science and Discovery
  C Religion and Philosophy
  D The Arts
  E Literature
  F Births and Deaths

Entries under 'C' (Religion and Philosophy) and 'E' (Literature) include references to the lives and activities of the philosopher, author etc., concerned as well as to his works; 'E' also includes references to the development of writing. In 'F' (Births and Deaths) after a birth the date of death, if known, is given in brackets, and wherever possible after a death the person's approximate age. It will be found that dates of death are more often known than dates of birth.

The practice is continued from the previous volumes of giving headings to the pages, calling attention to the period's most striking events. So also is retained the general principle of giving as far as possible an understandable narrative of events, relying on the index to guide those readers who are using the book to find the answers to specific questions.

Something needs to be said of the accuracy of the dates given. Firstly, to avoid the use of the suffix *c* (circa) we have adopted the system of printing firm dates in bold numerals (**708**) and approximate dates in ordinary numerals (708). Thus in the earlier part of the book, up to about 600 B.C., virtually all dates would have called for the suffix *c* and are here printed in ordinary numerals. After 600 B.C. however, as the better-documented classical age approaches, the majority of dates can be given with certainty and they are therefore printed in bold type.

At this point it should be made clear that the accuracy of dates as a whole in this volume of the series, as well as their preciseness, cannot be as great as those of the other three volumes. Nevertheless a great deal of work has been done to achieve chronological accuracy, and no reader need assume that the dates as a whole in ancient history are unreliable.

Something further should be said of the problems of early dating. It is primarily a matter of interpreting the ancient records, of which so many have been brought to light in the last hundred years or so. These were nearly always given in terms of so-called eponymous years, that is to say the first, second, etc., years of the reign of a king or the term of office of a governor. Astronomy has come to our help here. For instance the Egyptians calculated their year in terms of the helical rising of the star Sothis (Sirius), but they failed to make the necessary allowance for leap-years, thus creating an inaccuracy of a whole year at the end of a period of 365 multiplied by 4, or 1460 years. This fact, however, they recognized in due course, celebrating the return to accuracy; and, as we know that such a return occurred in A.D. 139 or 143, we can calculate back to a previous synchronism and earlier records. Similarly the Assyrian record of a certain governor by the name of Pur-Sagale shows that he witnessed in his term of office not only a revolt but an eclipse of the sun— which we can calculate as occurring on 10 June 763 B.C.

Further help is given by an occasional cross-reference from the records of one civilization to another. Some of these occur in the Egyptian records, which are the fullest in the early times; or, to take a comparatively late example, there is the fact that Alexander the Great makes an appearance as a governor in the records of the city of Miletus.

Accordingly, accuracy is built up by working from the known to the unknown. Help is also given in the earlier periods by such techniques as comparison of pottery styles, stratification in archaeological finds, and the now well-known scientific method of carbon-14 dating.

The carbon-14 technique, however, creates problems. The practice of giving a plus-or-minus limit to such dates, where used, has not been followed here, for the reason that a false aspect of accuracy is thereby given, it not being generally realized that statistically even such outside limits by no means give absolute accuracy. Secondly there is a particular difficulty at the time of writing. It has recently been discovered that the rate of disintegration of the radio-active carbon in organic matter (which is the basis of the calculation) does not appear to have been absolutely constant, as had been previously assumed. This discovery has meant that over a period the old, so-called "raw", carbon-14 dates have had to be corrected, the correction pushing them back farther into the past. The trouble is, however, that the amount of correction cannot as yet be given with any certainty. Contributions to a recent joint symposium between the Royal Society and the British Academy on this subject stressed the limitations at present. Nevertheless, this discovery cannot be ignored, and the current "corrections" have been used in this book.*

As far back as about 1,000 B.C. a date, though having to be stated as not necessarily accurate, is unlikely to be wrong by more than a year or two either way; naturally as we recede farther into the past the margin of error increases, until in the early millennia of Man's history the giving or taking of a few centuries has to be accepted. But by then it is the order of events rather than their exact date that matters.

Before leaving this question of accuracy of dating, it has to be recognized that much work is still being done on ancient chronology, and the present writer is only too aware that his dates, where there is uncertainty, will not always remain the most likely ones. For this reason therefore it is hoped that readers will write in to challenge such dates as they consider inaccurate, so that material for a revised edition may be built up.

Finally a word about the index. This is given in terms of dates and paragraphs (A, B, C, etc.) which method enables a reference to be spotted much more quickly than if page numbers had been used. There are certain other points about the index that need to be known for the best use of it, and the reader should familiarize himself with the preliminary notes on p. 466.

Thanks and Acknowledgements

I should like to thank most sincerely, for their helpful advice and encouragement, both the general editor, Dr Neville Williams and my publisher, Mr John Pattisson, the latter reading not only the text but also the index, thus saving me from many inaccuracies. Also I am deeply grateful for the help and advice given me by Dr Brian Sparkes of the University of Southampton.

I have been helped by the earlier work done by the late Walter Lowther Kemp of whose unpublished Ms. I have been allowed to make use.

Finally, I owe a great debt to Mrs Nora Banfield for carrying through the difficult task of typing from my manuscript, and if possible an even greater debt to my wife for her continual encouragement and forbearance.

Stogumber   H.E.L.M.

28 May 1976

---

* Those interested in the problem of carbon-14 dating are referred to a paper read before the Royal Society by Mr H. Barker of the Research Laboratory of the British Museum (*Phil. Trans. Roy. Soc.*, Lond., A 269, pp. 37/45, 1970) and an earlier article by the same author appearing in Vol. XXXIII (1958), p. 253, of *Antiquity*.

CHRONOLOGY

10,000–5,001 B.C.   In America a paleolithic age is established; in Euro-Asia a mesolithic and a neolithic

10,000   At Folsom, in New Mexico, Amer-Indians have established themselves and leave behind their particular flint tool, a spear-head. They are hunting a kind of buffalo now extinct.

In northern Europe there is beginning the Mesolithic or Middle Stone Age. It is a food-gathering way of life, with fishing and fowling rather than wide-range hunting; it is adapted to new conditions, either a forest or a water-side environment, men being squeezed to the edges, as it were, by the all-pervading forest.

8,000   In the Middle East—where the Mesolithic Age can hardly be said to exist—there is inaugurated the Neolithic Age, (see A and B.)

7,500   The final melting of the ice to approximately modern levels has by now destroyed many land bridges, for instance across the Mediterranean. The separation of the British Isles from the European mainland now occurs.

Approximate date of Mesolithic site in Yorkshire, Star Carr.

7,000   The Amer-Indian, slowly migrating from the north of the double continent, has reached the Straits of Magellan—as is shown by the site there of Palli Aiki.

6,800   Neolithic people are settled at the site of Jericho. Here appears the evidence of settled existence in houses: in fact the first known town is built. (And see A).

At about the same time, or perhaps later, and in a similar type of fertile hill country, appears the village on a tributary of the upper Tigris, at Jarmo. Again there are houses (of pressed earth and with earth-and-reed floors).

6,000   The island of Crete becomes occupied.

5,000   At the edge of the desert and west of the Nile above the delta, mesolithic hunters form a settlement in the district now called the Fayum, a precursor of the Egyptian settlement there.

A. Politics, Law and Economics

10,000/7,000 Economically and materially the mesolithic way of life, where it exists (typically in northern Europe), is to some extent a retrograde step from the previously easy hunting days of the paleolithic. The "kitchen midden" sites (as on the Danish coast) shows a people living close to or on top of a huge refuse dump of the discarded remains of shell fish and to have been living on very little else. (See however B).

8,000   The arrival of the Neolithic Age is caused by the emergence of a new way of life and is justly called the "Neolithic Revolution". This is essentially a change from living upon Nature to co-operating with Nature, and it depends on two fundamental inventions: the domestication of animals and the cultivation of crops. (The earliest domestication of sheep may be nearer 9,000 than 8,000 B.C.).

6,800   The earliest known township of Jericho possesses a protective wall, a sign that organised raiding and warfare has appeared.

B. Science and Discovery

10,000/7,000   The mesolithic way of life produces some important inventions:
  the barbed fish-hook and harpoon (e.g. as at Star Carr in Yorkshire);
  the bow and arrow, with its "microlith" flint tip;
  the flint socketed-axe;
  the woven basket;
  the cooking pot of baked clay;
  the comb;

8,000   The mesolithic culture of Mass d'Azil (near Toulouse) flourishes (and see C).

7,500   The dog is domesticated.

7,000   The neolithic way of life (see A) produces new flint tools: the sickle (microliths fitted along its inner curve), the hoe and a better-made axe. The two latter tools, first growing smooth by use, are later smoothed before use: this smooth rather than flaked surface is the hall-mark of the neolithic as against the paleolithic tool.
    As is shown by the finding of obsidian from the island of Melos in the Franchthi cave on the gulf of Argolis, men are beginning to navigate on the open sea (and see 6,000 B).

7,000/5,000   The invention of the growing of crops probably occurs first in temperate climes where the natural process is both easier and more easily observed: it has not yet spread, for instance, to northern Europe.
    Progress is rapid compared with that of paleolithic times: pottery is improved (though not yet wheel-made); spinning and weaving of flax and then of wool is achieved; corn is ground by pestel and mortar and the art of cooking improved; fermentation is recognized and begins to be controlled, with the result that leavened bread and wine and beer come into existence.

6,000   The occupation of such islands as Crete is another indication (see 7000 B) that there have been created boats capable of being rowed out into the open sea.

C. Religion and Philosophy

6,000   The rock paintings of N. Africa and S.E. Spain (see D) have presumably something of the same magical and luck-bringing import as the paleolithic cave paintings. They differ however in that the human figure is boldly shown, something that the paleolithic artist seemed afraid to do. Some of the human figures appear strange and terrifying—perhaps anthropomorphic gods.

At Jericho human skulls are made into ornamental masks and may show a cult of ancestor worship.

D.   The Arts

10,000   The Amer-Indians of the Folsom culture (see opposite) put much artistic skill into shaping their weapons but do not show the same passion to delineate as their European counterparts.

8,000   The Azilians (see 8000 B) paint pebbles with designs representing highly stylized human figures; these presumably have some magico-religious function.

6,000   In N. Africa (e.g. at Tassili on the edge of the Sahara and at Gafsa or Capsa in Tunisia, the Capsian culture), there begin to appear rock paintings, as also in S.E. Spain, probably by migrants from Gafsa. They usually depict hunting and food-gathering (e.g. honey collecting) and have great vitality—stylized as opposed to the "eidetic" vision of the paleolithic artists. Rock painting continues in Africa throughout history.

5000–4001 B.C.   The foundation on the river-valley civilizations of the Nile and
the Tigris-Euphrates

4800   At Hassuna, west of the upper Tigris appears an agricultural community with well-
built houses.
At Merimde, west of the Nile delta, a neolithic settlement flourishes for a few hundred
years before the encroaching desert kills it.

4500   The fourth of the great neolithic river-valley civilizations is formed on China's
Hwang-ho or Yellow River, the other three being the Nile, the Tigris-Euphrates
and the Indus Valley. The oldest culture is known as Tang-shao, economically
based on millet, pig, goat and dog.

4400   At Tell Halaf in northern Syria appears the Halafian culture, which spreads over a
wide area and as far as the Mediterranean coast (and see D). There is a beginning
in the use of copper.
The Iranian culture at Siyalk begins, an agricultural community that lasts until about
3000 B.C., giving place to Elamite Susa.

4200   The first move is made to occupy the marshland of the twin rivers Tigris-Euphrates,
probably from the Iranian plateau to the east. Townships begin to be formed (see A),
of which the first is traditionally Eridu (and see C). The Sumerian civilization
has begun (though there may have been later influxes of people and the speakers
of the Sumerian language may have been amongst these).
At about the same time settlements begin to appear on the banks of the Nile. The
earliest cultures, probably lasting for the rest of this millennium and perhaps
beyond, are known as the Tasian and Badarian (and see D).

4100   Copper beads are used by the Badarians. The *Chalcolithic* Age may be said to begin
at the end of this millennium, and to continue for the first half of the next. This is
the Age where tools as well as ornaments are made of copper and where copper
tools exist alongside stones ones; and it exists over most of the "Fertile Crescent",
extending from the Nile valley through Palestine and Syria to the Tigris-Euprates
valley.

A. Politics, Law and Economics

In this millennium occurs the founding of the two greatest river-valley civilizations, the Sumerian in the area of the twin rivers, Tigris and Euphrates, and the Egyptian in the Nile valley. They are specialized rather than obvious places in which to settle—there is no local flint for instance. But, once settled, their easy fertility encourages leisure and thought, resulting in specialization in jobs and central control of irrigation. So far the existence of towns and villages has been exceptional; now towns proliferate. There occurs what has been called the Urban Revolution (and see C).

B. Science and Discovery

4400   The Halafians (see opposite) make circular domed buildings that seem to be the ancestor of the later *tholos*.

C. Religion and Philosophy

With the neolithic way of life has come a great deepening of religious feeling, particularly in the belief in the magical connection between the cycle of seed time and harvest and the cycle of human life. This leads to the sacrifice of human lives, particularly of those of the great, so that their death and rebirth in their successor may have beneficial influence. Similarly the Urban Revolution (see A) has led to an increased importance of religion. The typical town is ruled by a priest-king, an intermediary between the people and the god of nature (and of the climate upon whom all depend for their livelihood).

4200   At Eridu (see opposite) the principal deity is Enkidu, God of the Waters.

D. The Arts

4400   The Halafian culture, besides making distinctive polychrome pottery, is skilful in small-scale craftsmanship, making clay figurines, the first known seals, and amulets (in the form of the double axe which will later be the great Minoan symbol).

4200   The Badarian culture produces remarkably fine and delicate pottery, also ivory combs and shapely female figurines.

3900/3600   The Al'Ubaid culture develops in Sumeria, at the head of the Persian Gulf. Land drainage is effected, and boats are used for fishing and fowling.

3600   The Sumerian city of Uruk (biblical Erech) is founded.

3500   Egypt, slowly going through her neolothic development, passes from her Amratian culture to her Gerzian. There are changes in type of pottery and in burial practices, but there is no real cultural break. There are developing however two distinct sites of towns or kingdoms: the Upper, or Delta; and the Lower along the river Nile's narrow strip of ultra-fertility.

3300/3000   The Jemdet-Nasr period in Sumeria shows something more approaching a break in culture than does anything in Egypt, a temporary domination of peoples coming again from the Iranian hills. The new types of pottery and of burial custom disappear at the end of the period with signs of conflagration. Cities in the south multiply. There are signs in Egypt of Sumerian influence (see D).

3100   A king, seeming to be named Namer by the hieroglyphics but traditionally known as Menes, advances from his southern capital of Thinis (Abydos) and overcomes the Lord of the Delta Land. He boasts that he captures 120,000 prisoners, 400,000 oxen and 1442 goats. He creates the so-called First Dynasty of the combined Old and New Kingdoms of Egypt.

The Amer-Indians have by the time of this millennium developed three ways of life in adaptation to their environments. In the north a fishing-hunting culture develops, somewhat similar to the European mesolithic. In the plains on the eastern side of the continent a bison-hunting culture develops, similar to the European paleolithic, the typical "Red Indian" way of life but without the aid of the horse. To the west of the continent's mountain backbone a sparser population exists in harsher conditions; living at first on roots and seeds, they develop their own "neolithic revolution", learning to harvest the gourd and the potato and in particular the Indian corn or maize—a practice that will infiltrate into mid-America, the future home of the Mayas.

During this millenium, or even earlier, the neolithic way of life develops in Northern Europe, Britain included. (Current difficulties in the interpretation of carbon-14 dating—see Introduction—makes the giving of any specific dates inadvisable.) This development may have been either spontaneous or indebted to influence or even migrations from the Mediterranean area.

Sites at Vinca in the Balkans and Koln-Lindenthal on the Rhine seem to show that these early farmers were migratory in a slow way, exhaustion of the soil forcing continued movement to new sites. Pottery at these sites is called Danubian; similarity has been observed in it to pottery from Asia Minor.

Villages are built over, or on the edge of, lakes in the district of modern Zurich in Switzerland. These, placed presumably for protection against man and beast, show an elaborate and successful culture, the main hazard being apparently from fire. This culture lasts into Bronze Age times.

A little later appear sites in Britain of the "Windmill Hill People". These are named after their best known site, near Avebury in Wiltshire. Their settlements, known as Causewayed Camps, show them to be herdsmen rather than agriculturists, and their "camps" may have been only used for seasonal gatherings.

The pottery of the Swiss lake dwellers and also the Windmill Hill people shows some similarity to that of earlier pottery of the Nile Delta.

A. Politics, Law and Economics

3200   In the closed societies of Sumeria and Egypt there appears division of labour; particularly there appears the merchant and the smith, i.e. the worker in metal.

B. Science and Discovery

3500   In Sumeria the first wheels for traction appear—they are solid. Also the first war chariot.

3300   The pictures on Gerzian pottery show that the Egyptians have made great progress in the building of boats, not only sailing boats to make use of the prevailing upstream wind on the Nile but also cabined boats to sail the Mediterranean.

3200   At about this time there begins (and to last for about two millennia) the Bronze Age in the Middle East. In the rest of the world—sometimes by diffusion, sometimes no doubt by separate invention—this age arrives later, mostly in the next thousand years though in some areas, e.g. Australia, not at all. The addition of about 10% of tin to copper in the molten state gives bronze which is a much harder product than pure copper; it is a substance no less durable and much less breakable than flint and a substance too that can be recast and re-used and that has a wonderful brightness and colour. Cutting tools such as the saw come with use (e.g. in Egypt).

3200/3000   The art of writing is invented in both Sumeria and Egypt, the Sumerian cuneiform developing slightly ahead of the Egyptian hieroglyphic. Both develop from the pictogram, via the ideogram and the use of the rebus or pun: e.g. as if the picture of a ham were used also to convey the first syllable of Hamburg. Neither method of writing reaches the alphabetical stage, the signs either remaining as pictograms (with a directive sign to make this fact clear) or at best representing a syllable.

C. Religion and Philosophy

3200/3000   Writing becomes the tool and prerogative of the priests, used not only to keep temple accounts but to record the dynasties and reigns of the "servant of the god", i.e. the king.

D. The Arts

3500   In Sumeria the potter's wheel appears, giving more symmetrical pottery.
In Egypt the Amratian culture produces stone as well as pottery vases and also faience.
A Thracian copper age is producing gold harness decorations at Varna, the oldest gold artifacts in Europe.

3300/3100   The thin flat stones used in Egypt for the grinding of malachite for eye-painting, known as palettes, develop into significant works of art. They sometimes show the beginnings of pictographic and post-pictographic writing and sometimes scenes of inter-city warfare. They show too Sumerian influence, as does also an ivory knife handle depicting the favourite scene of "the master of the beasts", a man or god flanked by tamed lions. The most famous palette is that of Narmer (see 3100) showing him defeating the Lord of the Delta land.

E. Literature

3200/3000   The development of writing and the beginning of its use by kings to record their triumphs enables later scribes to compile lists of dynasties and to create—tentatively and not very accurately—literate history.

9

3000–2501 B.C. Egypt's sphinx and pyramids are erected; Deluge in Sumeria; Indus Valley and Trojan civilizations begin

3000   The neolithic and bronze age culture of Siyalk (see 4400) comes to an end.
       The southern Sumerian cities form some kind of federation under the holy city of Nippur; but it does not last.

2900   The most likely date for the Deluge or Flood commemorated in Sumerian and biblical legend (see 2675 E). Archaeological evidence suggests more than one flood.

2900/2600 The Indus Valley civilization (known as the Harappan) is formed. Its two chief cities are Mohenjo-Daro, in modern Sind, about 250 miles up the river Indus, and Harappa, 350 miles farther upstream on the river Ravi in the Punjab. Considerable Sumerian influence is apperant.

2890   Egypt's 2nd Dynasty is founded.

2800   Supremacy in Sumeria shifts for a while to the more northerly city of Kish; inter-city rivalry becomes endemic and one king after another claims sovereignty over the others. As opposed to the truly Sumerian cities of the south, the northern cities appear to be inhabited by men of a Semitic race.

2750   Likely date for the founding of the first city of Troy, the small but strongly walled fortress of a petty chieftain.

2700   King Enmebaragisi of Kish campaigns successfully against his eastern neighbours the Elamites.
       The Sumerian city of Ur comes into prominence for the first time, under the king Meskalam-dug and the Queen Shub-ad (see C). This prominence, evident archaeologically, may have been shortlived, since it is not reflected in the kinglist.

2686   Egypt's 3rd Dynasty is formed. Zoser, either its first or second pharaoh, builds the first, step-sided, pyramid, at Saqqara. Egypt's "Old Kingdom" is generally considered to begin with this dynasty.

2675   Gilgamesh of Uruk (see E) revolts against Kish.

2613   Egypt's 4th Dynasty is founded by Seneferu, who has the first straightsided pyramid built.

2600   There begins – and some authorities set the date three centuries earlier – the bronze age in Crete, with the so-called Early Minoan period, also called its pre-palace period.

2575   The Pharaoh Khufu (Greek Cheops) builds the greatest of the pyramids, at Giza (see C); his nobles are buried in mud-brick mustabas; alongside the pyramid a separate pit contained a dismantled boat.

2550   The Pharaoh Chephren builds smaller pyramids and sets up the Sphinx.
       In Sumeria another city, Lagash, comes to the fore, under a ruler called Ur-nina (and see D).

2520   The city of Ur rises again, under the king Mes-anni-pad-da.

A. Politics, Law and Economics

2675   Egypt imports cedar wood from Lebanon, and so too apparently does Sumeria: in the legend of Gilgamesh (see E) the penetration of the magical Lebanon forest is a feat entailing much danger—cf Jason and the fleece, (1250). Trade and prospecting not only exist but are heroic occupations.

2575   Cheops sends expeditions into Nubia for slaves and into Sinai for copper and malachite. The pyramid texts, besides forecasting the heavenly success of the dead pharaoh, exult in his lifetime successes and the return of his army with many captives.

B. Science and Discovery

3000   During their early dynasties both Egypt and Sumeria develop systems of numbering (decimal and sexuagesimal respectively), and also some practical geometry acquired in the measurement and parceling out of land.
An Egyptian pictogram of an *ox-drawn* plough is used.
The Egyptian priests calculate a 365 day solar year and observe connection between the appearance of Sirius over the horizon and the flooding of the Nile (crucial for crop-raising); they use their knowledge to enhance their magical powers.
In Sumeria the wheel is in general use for traction (see 1650 B).

2650   The great artist-inventor (cf Daedalus in Crete) of Egypt, Imhotep, flourishes. He is credited with designing the pyramids, also with being a great physician.

C. Religion and Philosophy

2800   The first pre-megalithic Stonehenge is built at about this time. This is a neolithic monument comprising a circular earthwork 320 ft. in diameter with 56 small pits around the circumference (later known as the Aubrey holes). The position of the probably natural "heel stone" outside the circle suggests a connection with sun worship and sun observance (as do the later Stonehenges). Nearby is laid out a 300 yard long *cursus*, perhaps for funeral games.

2600   The royal graves of Ur show a similar belief existing in Sumeria. In the great pit in which Queen Shub-ad is buried there go with her not only great wealth and the beasts that drag her bier but also no less than 74 human beings—drivers, musicians, ladies in waiting etc.—who take poison before they pass into the next world to serve their queen.

2575   In Egypt the building of the pyramids exemplifies the belief in the influence of the great ones after their death and so the need to provide them at their death with all the magnificence possible. The same belief is shown in the painting of scenes on the walls of the nobles' mustaba tombs and in the practice of effigy-making (the word for a sculptor being "he who keeps alive").

D. The Arts

2900   The Sumerian temple-tower or Ziggurat begins to be built. (Chaldean Babylon will continue this practice: hence the biblical Tower of Babel).

D. **The Arts** (continued)

2600   The magnificent grave goods in the royal tombs of Ur include a gold helmet, a harp
        with plaques showing "the master of the beasts" (and see 3300 D), a royal standard
        showing scenes of prosperity, and a donkey mascot above the reign-rings of Queen
        Shub-ad's bier.

2550   Ur-nina, ruler of Lagash, leaves his inscription on the buildings of that city, together
        with the bas-relief of himself and family.

E. **Literature**

2800   A king of Kish called Etana is held in Sumerian legend to have risen to heaven on the
        back of an eagle.

2675   King Gilgamesh (see opposite and A) becomes a legendary hero and has an epic
        written about him. (It is during this search that he meets in the other world the hero
        Uta-nipishtim who tells his story of how he survived the Flood, a story remarkably
        parallel to that of Noah in *Genesis*.)

2650   The Egyptian *Books of Wisdom*, i.e. of religious instruction, are written, one of them
        being credited to Imhotep. Papyrus is used as a writing material.

2600   During the reign of Seneferu is invented (though written down later) the fanciful
        story of the magician Zazamoukh.

F. **Births and Deaths**

2648   Zoser d.

2589   Seneferu d.

2566   Cheops d.

2533   Chephren d.

2500–2251 B.C.   Egypt's Old Kingdom declines; Sargon founds a Sumerian empire; Chinese civilization develops

2500   At Barkaer in Jutland is established, amongst the mesolithic hunters, the first farming settlement. Its pottery is "Danubian".

2494   Egypt's weak 5th Dynasty begins.

2470   Eanatum of Lagash, one of Sumeria's great kings, becomes head of the southern cities, though doubtfully so of Kish and the northern.

2400   The more considerable and prosperous city of Troy, "Troy II" is founded.
A prosperous civilization on the Anatolian plateau, the future home of the Hittites, is growing up. The royal tombs of Alaca Hayuk (in the bend of the Halys River) illustrate this prosperity and a high artistic ability (see C and D).

2370   Kish comes under the rule of a queen described as once having been a barmaid or brothel-keeper.

2345   With the establishment of Egypt's 6th Dynasty, a decline of central authority continues.

2340   Lugal-zaggisi, an ambitious ruler, seeks to revive the old Sumerian League and the holy city of Nippur. He boasts that he rules from the Persian Gulf to the Mediterranean Sea.

2331/15   Sargon, a man of humble origin, having become cup-bearer to the King of Kish, usurps the throne. He builds himself a new capital near Kish which he calls Akkad. He sweeps south, defeats Lugal-zaggisi at the battle of Ugbanda, and makes himself master of all Sumeria—of "Sumer and Akkad", that is to say, and of "the black-headed people". He conquers Elamite Susa and may even have conquered Cyprus.

2276   Sargon dies, while subduing a revolt.

2270   Pepi II comes to the Egyptian throne as a child and is said to rule for over 90 years, finally to see his kingdom lapse into a period of near-anarchy and revolution (known as Egypt's First Intermediate Period).

2500   This is the time of China's legendary—and most benign and exemplary—kings, culminating in the Hsia Dynasty (see 2205).

2350   The great period of the Harappan civilization in the Indus Valley begins (see 2900). It exerts skill in building, town-planning and drainage, and shows a centralized administration and an unprogressive way of life. Its script has not been deciphered and no details of its history are known. (See A, C and D).

A. Politics, Law and Economics

2500   Among the grave goods at Barkaer (see opposite) are both amber beads and copper pendants: evidence of trade, north and south, of these two much-prized substances.

2400   Troy begins to take advantage of her strategic position and to grow rich. (She commands a strip of coast where sea currents probably make the porterage of cargoes necessary for any ship trading with the Euxine or Black Sea.)

2350   The Harappan civilization (see opposite) trades with Sumeria via the Persian Gulf. The city's great central store-houses, its lines of workmen's dwellings, its communal bath house, all indicate a paternal government and a regimented way of life.

2300   Sargon trades for frankincense from the Lebanon and prospects for silver in the Taurus Mountains.

B. Science and Discovery

2470   Eanatum of Lagash erects his Stele of the Vultures, on which is shown the earliest known picture of an ordered formation of armed infantrymen.

2350   The Harappans invent a method of writing, which seems however (like the later Minoan) only of use for such purposes as accounting and tax-gathering. Their use of weights and measures shows great advance.

2300   Sargon brings back from his campaigns "specimens of foreign trees, vines, figs and roses for acclimatization on his own land."

C. Religion and Philosophy

2400   At the time of Egypt's 5th Dynasty, Ptah-hotep, governor of Memphis, writes his "Instructions" to his son—which may be called the first known book of philosophy.
   The royal tombs at Alaca Huyuk (see opposite), though showing a superficial similarity to those of Ur of two centuries earlier, produce evidence of only animal and no human sacrifices.

2300   A holy city called "the Gate of God" exists in Sargon's time: translated into the Semite tongue it becomes later Bab-ili or Babylon. Sargon attributes some of his misfortunes to having violated this holy city, whilst the Babylonians remember the skill of his priests' liver-divinations.
   The Harappan culture does not produce outstanding religious buildings; figurines and seals show a horned god, votive bulls, and scenes possibly of bull-leaping reminiscent of later Crete.

D. The Arts

In Crete the Minoan civilization, still in its Early Period (about 2600 to 2000 B.C.), is beginning to display great skill and exuberance in art, particularly pottery, often of somewhat fantastic shapes. Stoneware and miniature carvings in ivory are made. There is no sign of any sort of monumental statuary. Seal-stones (a clue to the discovery of this civilization) are being used.

D. **The Arts** (continued)

2400   The rich grave goods at Alaca Huyuk include figurines of stags and lions in gold, also battle axes and one dagger in iron.

2350   The Harappan civilization produces a great number of seal stones. A bronze figurine of a dancing girl stands out in a comparative dearth of artistic production.

E. **Literature**

2330   The legend of Sargon's humble origin resembles that of Moses, in that he is set adrift as a baby but found and rescued.

F. **Births and Deaths**

2276   Sargon d.

2250–2001 B.C. Egypt revives; Sargon's empire and Troy II disappear; China and Britain develop

2250 Naram Sin, Sargon's third son, acceding after the short but unsuccessful reigns of his brothers, extends his father's kingdom, both northwards into the city of Mari and the land later to be known as Assyria and also eastwards into Elam and the land later to be known as Persia. He has however to contend subsequently with 17 rebel nations, one of which may have been the Hittites, who are emerging on the Anatolian plateau.

2205 Traditional date for the beginning of the civilization of China (see 2500) with the Hsia Dynasty, founded by Yü the Great. (Another source gives the date as 1989).

2190 The empire of Sargon is swept away by barbarians from the north, whom the Sumerians call the Guti or "the Vipers from the Hills".

2180 Egypt's "First Intermediate Period" (see 2270) begins, to last through Dynasties VII to X, of which little is known.

2150 King Gudea of Lagash achieves fame as a good ruler, although he seems to have ruled under the sufferance of the Guti.

2145 Silbury Hill, the great man-made hill near Avebury, Wilts., is built about this time.

2134 Egypt's XI Dynasty begins a reunification of the country.

2113 Sumeria revives for the last time under the most famous of Ur's dynasties, its Third. Ur-nammu is the founder; and prosperity under him and his descendants, Dungi and Ibi-Sin, lasts for about a century.

2060 The reunion of Egypt is positively achieved by Mentuhotep II of the XI Dynasty. Her "Middle Kingdom" has become established.

2050 Troy II is destroyed, the inhabitants hiding caches of valuables and jewelry (one of which is discovered by Heinrich Schliemann in 1871 and greeted erroneously as "the Treasure of Priam").

A. Politics, Law and Economics
2100   Ur-nammu of Ur's Third Dynasty prides himself on his regard for law and order: "By the laws of righteousness of Shamash forever, I establish justice."

B. Science and Discovery
2150   A life-sized statue of Gudea of Lagash shows a plan of the temple that he builds and also a carpenter's rule. (This last has enabled archaeologists to define the Sumerian digit as one of 16.5 millimetres.)

2100   Ur-nammu standardizes Sumerian weights and measures; he builds a canal, dedicated to the moon god.

C. Religion and Philosophy
2250   Naram Sin, son of Sargon, instals his daughters, probably as high-priestesses, in conquered Mari.
The Egyptian scarab beetle, used as an amulet, begins to appear.

2200   Round tombs for communal burying are built in the Mesara plain of Crete, having similarity with later dynastic tholos tombs (see 1300 D).

2150   King Gudea of Lagash rebuilds a Ziggurat and is later deified.

2100   Ur-nammu builds at Ur a temple to the moon-goddess, with an 80 ft tower.

D. The Arts
2250   In Egypt, tomb pictures tend to give way to models —e.g.of a slave-manned boat— placed in the tomb for the same purpose of ensuring a happy after-life.
In his Stele of Victory Naram-sin boasts of his conquests and shows himself trampling upon his enemies.

E. Literature
2190   The invasion of Sumeria by the Guti and the ensuing confusion is described succinctly in cuneiform records: "Who was king, who was not king?"

2180   Egypt's "First Intermediate Period" is described in a later, 19th Dynasty, papyrus as terrible.

2150   *The Dream of Gudea* and other religious poems are inscribed on clay cylinders found at Lagash.

F. Births and Deaths
2180   Pepi II d (about 90).

2010   Mentuhotep II d.

2000–1801 B.C.   Egypt's and Crete's Middle Kingdoms flourish; the city of
Babylon prospers; the Indo-Europeans spread

2000   Sumeria is invaded from the north by the Amorites led by the king of Mari and from
the east by the Elamites. The city of Ur is invested and its great Third Dynasty
comes to an end, King Ibi-sin being carried away in chains.
Crete's "Middle Minoan" or "Old Palace" Period begins (see D).

1991   Amenemhat I, first pharaoh of the great XII Dynasty, comes to the throne and
completes the re-unification of Egypt begun by the XI Dynasty. A nobleman of
Thebes, he creates a new capital further north, close to the Old Kingdom's
Memphis.

1971   Sensusret (Sesostris) I reigns with his father, Amenemhat I.

1962   Senusret I reigns alone. He wages war in Nubia, probably to protect Egypt against
the negroid tribes which have penetrated there during the First Intermediate
Period. His rule seems to have extended as far as the Third Cataract (see C).

1928   Amenemhat II succeeds his father Senusret I as Pharoah: he is the least famous of his
dynasty and is said to have been murdered by his guard.

1900   In Sumeria—which has relapsed into its old condition of warfare between cities,
with Isin and Larsa the most successful—the new city of Babylon (see 2300 C)
begins to acquire importance.
From the ashes of the unimportant villages known to archaeologists as Troy III, IV,
and V there rises Troy VI with its walls and palace: the finding of horse skeletons
leads to the supposition that the Aryan-speaking Indo-Europeans have arrived from
the north.
The Middle Bronze Age is considered to have begun in the Fertile Crescent.

1897   Senusret II becomes Pharaoh, a peaceful king.

1878   Senusret III becomes Pharaoh, a warlike king who continues military campaigns in
Nubia and also for the first time seeks to extend Egypt's power in Syria.

1842   Amenemhat III, the greatest monarch of the Middle Kingdom, comes to the throne:
"the good god", who benefits Egypt more than any before him and reigns for
45 years. He restores the outpost garrison at the Third Cataract (see 1962).

2000   At the beginning of this Second Millennium B.C., whilst Egypt and Crete are thriving
and Sumeria is awaiting a period of renewed prosperity, there must have begun
disturbances in the great belt of steppe-land north of the Caspian Sea where
Aryan-speaking Indo-Europeans had been leading a nomadic, horse-tending existence for centuries. By 1800 B.C. these have moved southward into Asia Minor,
northern Greece and northern Italy.
From the Mediterranean there spreads a practice of building "megalithic" monuments—see C.
At about the same time there migrates from Spain "the Beaker People", named after
their typical and beautiful vessel the bell beaker. They reach areas in modern
S. Germany, Czecho-Slovakia and England. They are agriculturists; their weapon
is the bow and arrow; and they introduce the use of bronze.

Egyptian engineers and travellers: Lake Moeris and the Autobiography of Sinuhe

A. Politics, Law and Economics

With the XII Dynasty a feudal age is created in Egypt, the Pharaoh ruling with enhanced economic and religious sanction but through the local barony or nomarchs. Increased building and artistic activity within Egypt causes warlike and trade expansion both north and south.

1900   Ugarit, on the Syrian coast, grows in commercial importance.

1842   Amenemhat III exploits the copper and turquoise of Sinai.

B. Science and Discovery

The palaces of Crete (see D) show an incipient engineering skill e.g. in drainage. (And see 1650)

1950   Sinuhe (see C) travels in Syria.

1850   Senusret III's engineers cut a channel 260 ft long and 34 ft wide through the cliffs of the Nile's First Cataract so that his war galleys may pass.

1820   Amenemhat III's engineers create the artificial lake of Moeris in the Fayum (or improve upon an earlier effort), thus helping to control the Nile flood.

C. Religion and Philosophy

2000   The building of megalithic monuments, probably by the spread of an idea rather than of a people, begins along the coasts of N.W. Europe. It comprises the use of great stones, to build either on the one hand chambered barrows or so-called passage graves (e.g. at West Kennett in Wiltshire or New Grange in Ireland), or on the other hand impressive monuments of upright stones of a religious or social or scientific purpose (or all three), such as at Avebury and Stonehenge in England or Carnac in France. The so-called "Stonehenge II," built of blue stones brought from the Prescelly Mts. of S. Wales, has a date by the "corrected" Carbon-14 method, of about 2030 B.C. (The great stone circle at Avebury has no Carbon-14 date available.)

At the destruction of Ur there are reports of heavenly omens and monstrous births, e.g. a sheep brings forth a calf with two tails; at Erech the statue of Ishtar is torn down.

1962   At Kerma, at the Third Cataract, has been found evidence of Egyptian occupation and rule at this time, but also of a native cemetery, with evidence of wives and attendants being buried with a chieftain's body. (cf Queen Shub-ad, 2700).

1950   The autobiography of Sinuhe (see E) shows that the Pharaoh is by now considered virtually a god.

D. The Arts

Crete, in its Middle Minoan Period I and II, blossoms forth, with the use of the potter's wheel, into great exuberance and beauty in the ceramic art, creating the delicate Kamares ware which finds its way to Egypt even to be used by the workman building the tomb of the Pharaoh Senusret II. It delights to copy and make patterns from nature, particularly the life of the sea and seashore.

1900   Palaces are built on Crete, at Knossos, Phaestos, Mallia and Zakro.

2000–1801 B.C.   Egypt's and Crete's Middle Kingdoms flourish; the city of
Babylon prospers; the Indo-Europeaos spread

2000   The Advent of the use of bronze in England leads to the decline of "Grime's Graves,"
the Norfolk site of neolithic flint-mining, where some 300 shafts have been dug into
the chalk.

1900   At the site of Yang Shao in N.W. Honan has been discovered evidence of a Chinese
chalcolithic culture: wheel-made pottery; evidence of domestication of the pig and
dog.

D. **The Arts** (continued)

1900 The tomb of Chnemhotep, Administrator of the Eastern Desert, is built, with wall-paintings of the great man fishing and fowling, and such captions as "how delightful is the day of hunting the hippopotamus."

1840 Egyptian sculpture receives a new burst of vigour under the 12th Dynasty, e.g. in a head of Amenemhat III in black diorite.

E. **Literature**

2000 A "Lament" for the destruction of the city of Ur is written.

1950 The story of adventure appears in Egypt, e.g. the nautical phantasy of The Ship-wrecked Sailor and the more factual *Biography of Sinuhe*, describing his travels abroad and his penitential reappearance before his Pharaoh, Senusret I.

F. **Births and Deaths**

1962 Amenemhat I d.

1928 Senusret I d.

1895 Amenemhet II d.

1877 Senusret II d.

1843 Senusret III d.

1820 Hammurabi b. (–1750 B.C.).

1800–1601 B.C.   **Hammurabi creates the first Babylonian Empire; Abraham leaves Ur; Shang Dynasty, Hittites and Hyksos appear**

1800 Abraham leaves the city of Ur, whose glory has finally and wholly departed. He and his family may well have sojourned in Egypt, along with other wandering Semites.

The Assyrians enter history in a reference to their merchants' activities at the modern site of Kultepe at the eastern end of the Anatolian plateau.

An earlier city of Troy is destroyed by earthquake and is rebuilt, as Troy VII (see 1250).

Neolithic farming reaches the Orkneys in the shape of a settlement of well-built stone huts skilfully protected from the elements, at Skara-Brae.

1797 Amenemhat IV, a nonentity, succeeds to the Egyptian throne—and the Middle Kingdom begins its decline.

1792 Most generally accepted date for the accession of Hammurabi the Great to the throne of the new city-state of Babylon. He creates the first Babylonian Empire and a golden age of peace and prosperity, law and order. A Semite, he may have been descended from the Amorites who had helped to destroy the greatness of Ur III. He extends his empire west to the Mediterranean, east to Elam and north to the land of the as yet unimportant Assyrians; with Egypt he does not clash.

1790 Queen Sebeknefrure reigns as Pharaoh for 4 years when she probably marries the founder of the XIII Dynasty.

1786 Egypt's XIII Dynasty reigns in the north but is not recognized in Thebes; a series of short-lived and unimportant Pharaohs during the rest of the century precedes Egypt's relapse and her Second Intermediate Period.

1760 Hammurabi, meeting trouble towards the end of his reign, destroys the city of Mari in the north.

1750 Hammurabi is succeeded by Samsu-Iluna, whose reign only lasts about a decade before a new people, the Kassites (of Indo-European stock or leadership) make their first entrance into Babylonia.

On the Anatolian plateau a local prince called Anittas is said to have conquered many other local cities, including Hatti or Hattusas, which will in the next few centuries become famous as the capital of the Hittites (see 1650 below). At this time end the activities of the Assyrian merchants (see 1800 above).

1715 Under its king, Shamsi-Adad II, Assyria begins to show military prowess, pressing westwards towards Syria. Nineveh is built.

1700 Egypt's Second Intermediate Period begins. The Hyksos ("The Shepherd Kings" or more correctly "The Hill People"), Bedouin tribesmen, infiltrate into Egypt and gradually take over what control exists. Among these Hyksos may have appeared Israelites, i.e. the biblical Jacob and Joseph.

The first series of Minoan palaces (Knossos, Phaistos and Mallia) are destroyed, probably by earthquake.

1680 King Labarnas unites the hardy people of the Anatolian plateau (whose proper name is unknown) to form the powerful empire of the Hittites (see 2250, and 1750 above).

A. Politics, Law and Economics

1790   Hammurabi erects a bureaucracy to run his empire and, as is shown by his voluminous correspondence, attends personally to detail, such as correcting the calendar. His *Code of Laws* (discovered later at Susa, whither it had been carried by conquering Elamites and now is in the Louvre) is harsh and fits the punishment to the crime, though it protects the rights of women; recognizing an upper class, it expects a higher code of morals therefrom and imposes a higher rate of punishment.

1650   Hattusas, the capital of the Hittites, is formed (or rebuilt—see 1750) at the conjunction of trade routes, east-west and south-north.

B. Science and Discovery

1750   The Babylonians under Hammurabi extend Sumerian mathematical and astronomical knowledge, compiling tables of square and cube roots, being empirically aware of the Pythagorean property of the right-angled triangle and closely observing the risings of Venus (for purposes of omens). It is also apparent, from the harsh laws against them if they fail, that surgeons exist.

1700   By this date the horse may be said to have entered significantly into history. It is introduced with the Kassites into Babylonia and with the Hyksos into Egypt, and is received with enthusiasm by the Mitanni and Hittites in Asia Minor. The horse revolutionizes both transport and—with the chariot—war.

The nations of the Near East begin to adopt the cuneiform script, particularly as a means of international diplomatic communication, some also using the Semitic Babylonian language but others endeavouring to adapt the cuneiform signs to their own language—the Hittites doing both.

There begins to spread westwards at this time a cattle and horse rearing people of the Ukraine and northern Turkey. They are Aryan-speaking and their typical weapon is the battle axe, after which they are usually known, "the battle-axe people". They finally reach Scandinavia; and there occurs then a curious reversal of usual practice, the bronze axe of their original culture being copied more primitively in stone.

1650   Not until about now does the wheeled vehicle appear in Egypt.

C. Religion and Philosophy

1790   Hammurabi separates priestly and civil jurisdiction, with decreased power to the former. As king, he styles himself no longer as a god but as "the favourite of the gods".

D. The Arts

1780   Knossos has acquired skill with faience inlay, the most famous example being the so-called Town Mosaic, showing houses of considerable sophistication, some three storeys high.

1700–1600   The Middle Minoan III or New Palace I period begins.

E. Literature

1790   Hammurabi uses the old Sumerian language for ritual and prayers, perpetuating it for Babylon's use, as the Romans used Greek.

1650   The new Minoan palaces begin to be built on the sites of the old ones, together with a new palace on the eastern tip of Crete at Zakro.

Hattusilis I, son of Labarnas, makes of Hattusas the great Hittite stronghold and begins a southward and eastward expansion. This stronghold, when completed, possesses a 30 ft wall of 4 miles circumference.

1640/1600   The Hyksos kings in their capital, Avaris, are increasingly at war with the true Egyptian princes at Thebes, and the latter, under their rulers Sekenre I, II and III, gradually gain the upper hand.

1620/1600   The Hittite king Mursilis I, following Hattusilis, strikes south and captures first Yamhad (Aleppo) and then Babylon. His success is short-lived however: he returns home to be murdered (1590), and Kassite Babylon resumes its quiet trading prosperity.

The 18th Century B.C. is one of trends rather than ascertainable events, as follows:

The Egyptians are going through a time of turmoil under the Hyksos: the names of Hyksos "pharaohs" are known but little else. The Babylonians (as the inhabitants of the Land of the Two Rivers must now be called) are, under Kassite rulers, relapsing into unimportance though not necessarily failing to retain a commercial prosperity. The Assyrians and the Hittites are beginning to be heard of. The Minoan civilization is recovering from the first of its major natural disasters before creating its greatest "New Palace Period".

The Indus Valley civilization is coming to an end before invaders who, with little doubt, must have been the peoples of Indo-European stock who later write the Vedas. The "coolie-lines" (see 2350 A) are growing more slum-like.

Greece possibly receiving further infiltrations of Indo-Europeans is beginning to discover its Mycenaean civilization.

The Amorite city of Alalakh (Tel Atchana on the Orontes river) experiences a period of prosperity.

From about this century, with the gradual introduction of the use of bronze into N.W. Europe—see 2000—the typical barrow or tumulus in this area (including Britain) becomes the round barrow rather than the neolithic or megalithic long or chambered barrow. The use of round barrows continues into the Iron Age.

E. Literature (continued)

1625 Hattusilis I summons his assembly of aristocrats to hear his adoption of Mursilis as his successor in place of his unsuitable nephew (whose mother "bellows like an ox" at the news). This speech is reported in a style of great naturalness and spontaneity.

F. **Births and Deaths**

1797 Amenemhat III d.

1790 Amenemhat IV d.

1750 Hammurabi d.

1650 Labarnas, Hittite king, d.

1620 Hattasilis I, Hittite king, d.

1600–1501 B.C.   Egypt's New Kingdom; Minoan New Palace Period; Mycenaean early wealth

1600 The Mycenaean shaft graves probably begin to be built (see below). The four great Minoan palaces (see D) have begun their century-and-a-half of outstanding prosperity (the Late Minoan I or New Palace Period II).

1590 Sekenre III (see 1640) is killed in battle but has become the folk-tale liberator of Egypt from the Hyksos. The Hittite king Mursilis I is murdered and a period of anarchy sets in, with insurrections within and loss of territory without.

1580 The Theban king, Karmose, continues to effect the expulsion of the Hyksos from Egypt.

1575 Amosis becomes Pharaoh and founds Egypt's great Eighteenth Dynasty. He finally destroys the Hyksos in their capital of Avaris and pursues what is left of them into Syria.

1557 The last ruler of China's Hsia Dynasty, the tyrant Chieh, is deposed by the victorious T'ang, who founds the Shang Dynasty. (An alternative but less likely date is 1766).

1550 Amenophis I changes Egyptian policy from that of restoring or maintaining the country's boundaries to that of extending them. Southwards he begins to subdue and colonize Nubia ("Cush"), whilst northwards he reaches the upper Euphrates and possibly penetrates into the lands of the Hittites and of the Mitanni (see below).

1528 Tuthmosis I succeeds Amenophis I; the 18th Dynasty is now well established, and at its capital Thebes experiences a century and a half of greatness.

1525 Telepinus (the last of the Hittites' "Old Kingdom" kings of which anything is known with certainty) achieves some consolidation in a troubled realm, making a treaty with his southern neighbours.

1524 Tuthmosis I brings back the body of the Nubian king head downwards on the prow of his ship, and then sends his armies again to the upper Euphrates to penetrate into the land of the Mitanni.

1510 Tuthmosis II follows his father as Pharaoh. Little is known of him except that he puts down a revolt in Nubia and that he has a formidable wife called Hatshepsut or Hashepsowe, (see following century).

There begins a period when, whilst the Minoan civilization flourishes undisturbed the civilizations of the Fertile Crescent become involved with each other. Egypt begins her New Kingdom, sometimes and significantly known as New *Empire*. A new power, the Mitanni, is beginning to appear: its people are known as Hurrians but its ruling aristocracy speak an Aryan tongue.

In the Aegean, the Greek-speaking invaders (see 2000 B) have penetrated into the Peloponnese, where they begin to prosper and grow rich, evolving a culture which at once is distinctive and yet owes a great deal to the Minoan. This culture, called the Mycenaean after its chief stronghold, Mycenae, is ruled by a dynasty of kings, whose "shaft graves" (discovered by Heinrich Schliemann in 1876 at Mycenae) date from this century (see A and D).

Grave goods at Mycenae, frescoes at Knossos; Stonehenge 1600–1501 B.C. rebuilt

A. **Politics, Law and Economics**

The Minoans are favourably placed on trade routes across the eastern Mediterranean, and their influence, if not their hegemony, extends over the Aegean and to Cyprus and even Sicily. Their new palaces develop into political, economic, administrative and religious centres, containing, too, storehouses and craftsmen's workshops. Their rulers go down into Greek legend as great law-makers – see 1500 A.

The Shaft Graves (see opposite) show by the quality of their grave-goods that the Mycenaean princes are rapidly accumulating wealth.

B. **Science and Discovery**

The horse-drawn war chariot, introduced by the Hyksos into Egypt, becomes the new great fighting weapon (and status symbol for the warlike aristocracy) of the Middle East. The Mycenaeans also use it but not the Minoans.

The Minoan palaces (see opposite A, and D) show great architectural and engineering skill, in (1) the use of "light wells" to give illumination without too much heat from the sun, and in (2) drainage and sanitation, e.g. in the taking away of surplus water by means of natural, parabolic, curves.

The Minoans change from a hieroglyphic script (largely pictographic) to what Arthur Evans called "Linear A". This however is not so elaborate or efficient as the later "Linear B" (see 1450 B); it has not been diciphered and is presumed to have been in the unknown Minoan tongue.

1550   Egyptian medicine, of considerable efficiency before the Hyksos invasion, now makes further advances. Papyri list clinical cases in great detail; the essential controlling power of the brain is for the first time realized.

C. **Religion and Philosophy**

Probably about the end of this century Stonehenge reaches its final form.

1600   The "snake goddess" and other figurines etc found at Knossos and elsewhere in Crete denote a Minoan worship of a "Mother-Earth" goddess. The "bull-leap" fresco at Knossos, together with many similar depictions in metal work and clay, show a great Minoan preoccupation with the bull as a religious symbol, perhaps as impersonating the power of the earthquake. There is also evidence of both human and animal sacrifice on Crete at this date.

1575   The Pharaoh's name, Amosis, signifying "Moon," suggests a temporary Egyptian moon cult.

"The Book of the Dead" appears increasingly in the tombs of the great from the time of the 18th Dynasty. It contains spells and incantations necessary for the person's passage to the other world.

1560   The Kassite king of Babylon, Agum III, retrieves from the Amorites a captured image of the god Marduk.

D. **The Arts**

The four great palaces of Crete, built or rebuilt in this century, show an architectural and artistic skill and sophistication that is to surprise their later discoverers. These are at Knossos, Phaistos (with its "summer residence" at nearby Hagia Triada), Mallia and Zakro. All show a similar general plan, with an open central courtyard and on the one side the official quarters, including both the storerooms and the formal and religious precincts, and on the other side the royal private quarters.

Frescoes are painted particularly on the walls of Knossos palace. These show an art skilful, personal, uninhibited and gay, such as has never appeared before in the cultural history of the past. Figurines, and cups and vases give the same sort of picture.

The Shaft Graves at Mycenae (see opposite and A) show great skill in metal work and weaponry. From this time and for three centuries at least Mycenaean art will show very great Minoan influence (e.g. in style of dress depicted), though subject matter will be Mycenaean rather than Minoan (e.g. hunting and fighting rather than idyllic natural scenes or sport).

E. **Literature**

With the Pharaohs of the New Kingdom there is developed to the full the boastful and euphuistic style of the narratives on the royal monuments—with such phrases as "his majesty raged like a panther".

The autobiography of King Idri-mi of Alalakh (see 1700) shows that city to suffer from both Egyptian and Hurrian interference.

F. **Births and Deaths**

1590 Sekenre III d.
      Musilis I d.

1550 Amosis d.

1528 Amenophis I d.

1510 Tuthmosis I d.

1500–1401 B.C. The battle of Megiddo; the eruption of Thera; cultures in N. Europe and America

1500   Telepinus, the Hittite king, dies and is followed by the forty years reign of four unimportant kings.

An explosion of the volcanic island of Thera (modern Santorin) covers the town of Thera with pumice. Its houses (including a wealth of wall paintings) remain hidden until A.D. 1967.

1490   Tuthmosis II dies and is followed as Pharaoh by his son, the warlike Tuthmosis III, at present under the thumb of his stepmother Queen Hashepsowe.

1488   Probable date by which Queen Hashepsowe has established herself as Pharaoh, assuming the double crown of Egypt, dressing as a man and even wearing the Pharaoh's ritual wooden beard.

1488/69 Queen Hashepsowe, with the help of her chief favourite Senenmut, concentrates on internal progress rather than foreign conquest (see A and D).

1469   Hashepsowe dies and Tuthmosis III comes into his own, reigning for another 33 years.

1468   Tuthmosis III advances northwards to defeat the petty Palestine princes under the Prince of Kadesh. This he does at Megiddo. (This is not either of the biblical battles of Megiddo, for which see 1125 and 609).

1460   A new dynasty appears in the land of the Hittites with King Tudhaliyas II. The "Hittite Empire" dates from this accession, but for the rest of this century this king and his two successors are doing little more than struggle against surrounding enemies under the tutelage of the Mitanni.

1457   Tuthmosis III in his eighth campaign reaches the height of his success by crossing the upper reaches of the Euphrates and temporarily defeating the Mitanni, possibly with Hittite help. (This is the farthest point that Egyptian armies will reach for nearly 800 years.)

1450   The Mitanni however are by no means crushed, and at this time carry off a golden gate from the Assyrian capital, Assur.
Many Minoan and Cycladic sites are destroyed, though Knossos survives.

1436   Amenophis II succeeds to the Egyptian throne. He has been trained to be an heroic figure, a great athlete and a great man with horses. In the early years of his reign he parades his strength in Syria; but, having retired with a boasted wealth of booty and prisoners, he leaves the Mitanni influence there undisputed.

1430   Amenophis II apparently settles down to an unwarlike reign.

1420   The Hittites are still suffering from invasion from all quarters.

1413   Tuthmosis IV becomes Pharaoh.

1406   Tuthmosis IV goes on his sole recorded campaign – to put down revolt in Nubia.

Writing is used for Egyptian boasting and Minoan accounting 1500–1401 B.C.

A. Politics, Law and Economics

1550–1450   At Boghagköy, in the central uplands of Asia Minor some hundred miles from the sea, and at the site of the Hittite capital Hattusas, have been found codes of law, most of which are thought to date from this period. Though the blood feud is recognized as being above the law, the laws themselves show as somewhat superior to Hammurabi's (see 1790 A) in that there is less accent on "fitting" and harsh punishment. The only capital offences are for rape, unnatural sexual intercourse, defiance of the authority of the State, and disobedience on the part of a slave–whose lot however is fairly well cared for.

      Similarly the laws of the Minoans date from about this time, or earlier. Nothing is known of these–except that the mythical Rhadamanthys became a legendary lawgiver.

1460   The scenes in the tomb of Rekhmire, vizier to Tuthmosis III at Thebes show 'tribute" (i.e. trade goods) being brought in; included are some from Crete, carried by people who are called Keftiu and are obviously slim-waisted Minoans.

      In the same tomb (and also those of other viziers) there is laid down the duties of this particular office, duties that may date back to the Middle Kingdom. Egyptian laws are also referred to in the statement that the Vizier sits in court with the forty rolls of the law open before him; these rolls have however never been discovered.

1450   The scenes portrayed in Queen Hashepsowe's funerary temple (see D) depict great activity in shipping and trade–across the Mediterranean Sea, from a port on the Red Sea, and up the Nile. Hashepsowe also boasts how much gold she uses in the decoration of her buildings. Egypt is in fact acquiring a reputation for wealth and the possession of gold — see 1370 E.

B. Science and Discovery

1468   Tuthmosis III hunts elephants on the river Orontes: thus the Syrian elephant must then have been reasonably prolific; it lasts at least until Roman times.

1450/1400 At Knossos the Linear B script succeeds the Linear A (see 1600 B). Linear B is an early form of Greek. Not so flexible an instrument as current cuneiform or Egyptian hieroglyphics, it seems to have been used only for administration purposes — accounting, ration-issues, lists of personnel, tallies of tax receipts in kind, etc. These documents (incised on clay but also probably written on papyrus) show signs of agricultural prosperity – especially in the number of sheep.

C. Religion and Philosophy

1500   In India the period of the Vedic hymns and religious rituals may be said to begin (and see 800 C).

1480   Queen Hashepsowe has scenes painted in her temple attributing to her a divine origin.

1469   On his way to achieving full powers Tuthmosis III enlists the help of the Theban priesthood: from this date may be said to grow this priesthood's power, culminating in the usurpation by Hrihor (see 1095). From now onwards decisions of state are made increasingly by means of priest-directed oracle.

1405   Amenophis III becomes Pharaoh. Egypt, through trade and conquest and the exploitation of Nubian gold, has become fabulously rich and the new Pharaoh does little campaigning but is content to rest on his gilded laurels.

      Bronze-using cultures flourish in this and the following century in England (Wessex) and in S. Germany and Denmark. They are pastoral rather than agricultural—the climate is becoming drier—and they are ruled by a warrior-type aristocracy as are the Mycenaeans. Unlike the Mycenaeans however their method of burial of chiefs and their families is cremation, the remains being placed in urns and interred in cemeteries—hence the so-called Urnfield culture, which continues into the Iron Age.

      In America neolithic skills develop parallel to those in the Old World: weaving, basket-making, pottery-making, the building of houses and the formation of villages; the rise of a priesthood. Skills that never develop in America until the coming of the white men are the use of iron, of the wheel, of the plough, of money.

      The Mitanni, a people whose own records have not been discovered, dominate the scene in Asia Minor and Syria.

1450   The great eruption on Thera island (see 1450 A) having seriously weakened but not destroyed the Minoan civilization, a Mycenaean dynasty begins to establish itself in Knossos. Much of the glory is departing from Crete but by no means all its prosperity. (See B and also the next century.)

      Cyprus, already influenced by Minoan culture, receives an influx of Mycenaeanized Minoans at about this time.

C. Religion and Philosophy (continued)

1450/1400 Signs of religiosity in Crete are shown by the Linear B tablets, where rations of grain go to "Potnia, the Lady", i.e. the Earth-Mother goddess, as well as to human beings.

1413 A stele of this year tells how the prince Tuthmosis has received promise of kingship (as Tuthmosis IV) if he will free from sand the great Sphinx of Giza (see 2550).

1405 From the time of Amenophis III at least (as disclosed by the presence of mummified bulls) there grows up the popular cult of Apis, the sacred bull, recognized and chosen as a god, whose birthday is a great celebration (see Cleopatra, 51 C).

D. The Arts

1480 Queen Hashepsowe builds her magnificent funerary temple within the cliff semi-circle at modern Der el-Bahri, with its colonnades of white limestone (see B and C).

1460 The Vizier Rekhmirē has his tomb built (see also A), the scenes on its walls having been excellently preserved into modern times.

1450 With the appearance of the Mycenaeans at Knossos (see opposite) there begins to appear also the so-called "Palace style" in pottery, more formal and less uninhibited.
The use of glass (for ornament but not for windows) appears in Egypt.
On a sarcophagus at Hagia Triada, in Crete are painted funerary scenes which seem to show the Minoans, under Mycenaean domination, to be resistant to change in their forms of art.

1413 Tuthmosis IV erects at Thebes the tallest known obelisk (105 feet high)—now in Rome.

E. Literature

1460 As a counterblast to the usual Egyptian boasting there is the advice given to a young officer, Amenemope, probably of the time of Tuthmosis III, enlarging on the dangers and hardships of campaigning.

F. Births and Deaths

1490 Tuthmosis II d.

1469 Queen Hashepsowe d.

1440 Tudhaliyas II, Hittite king, d.

1436 Tuthmosis III d.

1413 Amenophis II d.

1405 Tuthmosis IV d.

1400   Further destruction occurs in Crete, caused by either the final eruption on the island of Thera and supplementary earthquake locally, or further Mycenaean invasion, or, just possibly, revolt against the Mycenaean rule.

Tudhaliyas III comes to the Hittite throne and rules for a further twenty years of difficulty and impotence.

1395   Traditional date for the founding of the Chinese city of An Yang (see 1300).

1380   Both the Babylonian and the Mitanni kings are allied by royal marriage to Egypt. (In the El-Amarna Letters—see E—the former complains that he is receiving insufficient "gifts" from Egypt or, later, that another Egyptian bride might be sent and that it really will not matter if in fact she is not of royal blood since no one will know the difference.)

The Assyrians, at present vassals to the Mitanni, begin to interfere in Mitanni politics.

Suppiluliumas, the Hittites' greatest king, comes to the throne. He begins by strengthening his capital city and prepares for his main task, which is to destroy the power of the Mitanni.

1370   Suppiluliumas crosses the Euphrates and attacks the kings of the Mitanni and of Kadesh, whom he defeats, though not decisively. He extends his kingdom to the Lebanon and the Syrian town of Alalakh.

Amenophis III in his closing years—as is shown by the El-Amarna Letters (see E)— is failing to protect and support his regents in Syria and Palestine against their enemies (which include the Habiru, either merely "bandits" or possibly the Hebrews).

1367   Amenophis III dies and is succeeded by his son under the name of Amenophis IV.

1363   Amenophis IV changes his name to Akhneten, builds for himself a new capital, Akheteten, "The Horizon of Aten", (half way between Thebes and Memphis), and institutes a religious and cultural revolution (see C, D and E).

1360   Akhneten totally neglects his empire and continues the later policy of his predecessor in refusing all help to his governors in Syria and Palestine.

1355   Akhneten—it appears possible—puts away his wife Nefertiti in disgrace.

1350   The king of the Mitanni, Tushratta, having sought alliance with Egypt and been let down, is deposed and assassinated by a faction who have sought help from Assyria. Mitanni power is waning, and Assyria's rising.

Akhneten dies and is succeeded as Pharaoh by a boy, Smenkhare, who spends his 3-year reign at the new capital Akheteten.

The fortress of Tiryns, second only to Mycenae in strength, is built by the Mycenaeans.

1347   Another boy king ascends the Egyptian throne. He changes his name from Tutankhaten to Tutankhamen and returns to Thebes—the "religious revolution" is over and the new capital is left to crumble.

A. Politics, Law and Economics

1400   Ship sheds excavated at Kommos, near Phaistos on the southern coast of Crete, dating from this time, suggest that there was a commercial shipping fleet, trading with Egypt and the eastern Mediterranean.

1370/50   The El-Amarna letters (see E) show the naivety and crudity of the diplomatic exchanges of the Powers. They also show the vast hoards of gold that Egypt has, or is believed to have, accumulated.

1363   Akhneten's religious revolution has its political aspect, a struggle against established priestly domination.

1350   A shipwreck from this period, found at Ulu Burun (near Kas in southern Turkey), included metal objects (copper and tin), amphoras, ebony, ivory, bronze weapons and tools, cylinder seals from the Near East, a gold scarab from Egypt, and pottery from Cyprus. It may have been heading for Mycenae, and illustrates the nature, purpose, and organisation of international trade in the late Bronze Age.

1339   The fact of Egypt's wealth is supported by the magnificent grave-goods of Tutankhamen, a youthful and comparatively unimportant king. (Tutankhamen's tomb, exceptionally unrobbed, is opened by Howard Carter in 1923.)

1339/5   The priest Ay, on becoming Pharaoh and in restoring the old ways, also restores the laws — and sees that they are obeyed.

1308   Seti I has a care for his gold-miners in Egypt's eastern desert, ensuring them a water supply.

B. Science and Discovery

1339   Amongst the grave-goods in Tutankhamen's tomb is placed an iron dagger, probably a gift of the Hittites who are already developing iron-smelting techniques. There is also in Tutankhamen's tomb a chariot, dismembered and stacked in a way described in both Homer and in the Linear B script.

C. Religion and Philosophy

1390/70   In building Queen Tiye's (see D) pleasure-lake, the barge to sail on it is called "The Aten gleams", showing that the cult of the *Aten*, the sun's disc, is not entirely new when Akhneten adopts it.

1363   Akhneten institutes his religious revolution in changing the worship of Amun-Re to that of the Aten (see immediately above, and E below), a monotheistic religion but one embodying no great moral teaching.

D. The Arts

1400   In Crete the period Late Minoan III, or Post Palace I, begins and with it some Mycenaean influence appears, e.g. the depiction of a military helmet on an amphora.

1390/70   Amenophis III has his palaces built, including two colossi of himself and a large pleasure-lake for his wife, Tiye. A new fashion appears of inscribing narratives on scarabs instead of on the walls of tombs.

1340 Suppiluliumas defeats and ends the power of the Mitanni, capturing Carchemish and making Syria his dependancy. He fails however to make of the Mitanni a buffer state between himself and the rising power of Assyria, the latter absorbing the lands of the Mitanni.

1339 Tutankhamen dies.
The power of the Hittites is shown at this time by the fact that Tutankhamen's widow, Ankhesnamun, sends two letters to their king Suppiluliumas suggesting that one of his sons should be sent to become her husband (and so Pharaoh). A son is sent but is apparently murdered by Haremheb (see 1335 below). The high priest Ay becomes Pharaoh, presumably marrying Ankhesnamun.

1339/7 Plague having carried off Suppiluliumas; his son Mursilis II consolidates his empire and defeats a western foe, called the Arzawa.

1335 The army commander Haremheb (who may have carried on the government at Thebes during Akhneten's experiment) becomes Pharaoh and repairs the damage done by his three weak predecessors.

1330 Syria, encouraged by Haremheb, revolts against the Hittites, but unsuccessfully.

1320/9 Haremheb, secure on the throne of a revived and renewedly orthodox Egypt, spends his last years in sponsoring rebuilding at Thebes (see D).

1309 Egypt's "Keeper of the Horse" founds its 19th Dynasty, calling himself Rameses I.

1308 Seti I succeeds as Pharaoh; he campaigns against the Hittites in Syria but makes little headway.

1306 Muwatallis accedes to the Hittite throne, finding it stable but facing a rising threat from a revived Egypt.

Whilst the Egyptians and Hittites and Mitanni are fighting in Syria, its coastal towns, Tyre and Sidon and Byblos, are thriving as trading cities: from this time at least the title Phoenician may be given to their inhabitants.

The Mycenaeans must during this century have been increasing their wealth and nursing their warlike spirit, though it is probably not until the beginning of the next century that there comes into power the dynasty of Atreus (to which belongs the King Agamemnon made famous by Homer).

Israelites are probably beginning to infiltrate into Palestine (but see 1235). Jericho, apparently deserted since Hyksos times, is rebuilt and prospers.

1380/40 In the reign of Suppiluliumas there is the first Hittite reference to people of consequence called the Ahhiyawa, generally thought to have been the Homeric *Achaiwoi* or Achaeans, that is to say the Mycenaean Greeks.

D. The Arts (continued)

1363/5 Under Akhneten there occurs also an artistic revolution, the delineation of royalty and important persons becoming less formal and more natural, at times almost caricature. A religious but human touch is that of the rays from the sun's disc ending in beneficent hands touching the people below. The building of the new city of Akheteten is ambitious but shows signs of shoddy and hurried workmanship.

1339 In Tutankhamen's tomb (and see B) there are at least three items of great artistic significance: a wooden chest, the panels of which show the Pharaoh in battle behind his prancing chariot horses (not historically accurate for this particular pharaoh); the throne-panel showing Ankhesnamun endearingly touching her husband; and the scene on an ivory chest of the young Ankhesnamun and Tutankhamen picking flowers.

1320 Haremheb begins the Hypostyle Hall at Karnak (which Rameses II is to complete), probably being responsible for the avenue of ram-headed sphinxes.

E. Literature

1370/50 The "El-Amarna" correspondence takes place between the rulers of the Fertile Crescent civilizations, Egyptian, Babylonian, Hittite, Mitannian, Assyrian and Syrian, and is written in Babylonian cuneiform, the diplomatic language of the age, on tablets found in 1887 at Tell el-Amarna. They are written in polite language as from one brother potentate to another, but they embody close bargaining for the diplomatic exchange of daughters in marriage and of "gifts", particularly of gold— of which Egypt has, in the eyes of the rest, so much that it is to her "as dust". The later correspondence includes complaints by the Egyptian regents in Syria that the Pharaoh is neglecting them.

1363/50 At some time after changing his name, Akhneten composes his Hymn to the Sun. This famous hymn, which Psalm 114 strikingly resembles, proclaims the beneficent power of the "beginner of life".

F. Births and Deaths

1400 Hattusilis d.

1367 Amenhophis III d.

1350 Akhneten d. (41).
      Tushratta d.

1347 Smenkhare d.

1339 Tutankhamen d. (18).
      Supilluliumas d.

1335 Ay d.

1308 Haremheb d.

1306 Mursilis II.

1300–1201 B.C.   Battle of Kadesh; fall of Troy; exodus of the Jews; founding of An Yang; rise of the Assyrians

1300 (or possibly up to 100 years earlier—see 1395)   The great city of the Shang Dynasty is founded: An Yang on the Huan river, north of the Hwang-ho. The traditional founder is the tribal chief Pan-Keng. Archaeological digging from the beginning of the 20th century has shown that the traditional claim for a great city is justified, and that a brilliant but barbaric culture exists for two and a half centuries—see D and E.

    Pharaoh Seti I restores law and order in Syria and advances to Kadesh, where he confronts the Hittites but does not seek battle with them. The young Crown Prince, later to be Rameses II, appears to have accompanied his father on his campaigns and in the latter's final years to have acted as co-regent.

1290   Rameses II, called the Great, becomes Pharaoh. He builds the city of Pi-Ramesse (Biblical Raamses, see 1235 below), and prepares for a confrontation with the Hittites.

1285   The battle of Kadesh on the Orontes is fought between Egypt under Rameses the Great and the Hittites under Muwatallis. Each side has its allies, those on the Hittite side being possibly the Lycians and the Homeric Dardanians (i.e. Trojans). Rameses is surrounded but extricates himself with personal bravery. Hittite records show however that the battle is not the Egyptian victory that Rameses claimed but, rather, a draw, the Hittites being subsequently able to advance further.

1276   With the Accession of Shalmaneser I, Assyria emerges into the first of its three periods of power. Shalmaneser strikes north and west, taking Carshemish but leaving Babylon to his successor.

1275   Hattusilis III comes to the Hittite throne. The rising might of Assyria draws him and Rameses II closer together.

1269   A treaty of peace and mutual protection is signed between the Hittites and Egyptians.

1257   Shalmaneser dies.

1256   The eldest daughter of Hattusilis III is given in marriage to Rameses II, thus sealing the alliance.

1250   Tudhaliyas IV comes to the Hittite throne, an unwarlike and religiously-minded king: the Hittite empire is declining.

1250/40   Most likely date for the war of the Mycenaeans against the Trojans (the war of Homer's *Iliad*). At this time there is another Hittite reference to the Ahhiyawa, their king being described as of equal rank to the Hittite king.

1249   Babylon falls temporarily to the Assyrians.

1235   Most likely date for the *Exodus* of the Israelites from Egypt: almost certainly in the reign of Rameses II, though possibly earlier. The Israelites leave after having helped to build the city of Pi-Ramesse on the Delta (see 1290). They are led by Moses (who has a fabled rescue at birth similar to Sargon's), and are given their laws (see A and C).

A. Politics, Law and Economics

1300–1250   The Minoans during this century, though all glory has disappeared from their palaces, show considerable building activity, e.g. additions at Hagia Triada and Tylissos.

The Mycenaeans have a maritime trade as big as or bigger than the Minoans a couple of centuries earlier, extending into Syria in the east and probably as far as the British Isles in the west. Each Mycenaean lord has his treasure house and exerts diplomatic influence by the exchange of "gifts".

1272   Litigation over land-ownership, as described on a scribe's tomb, shows the equality, in Egypt, of men and women before the law.

1250   The Trojan War and the Hittite references to the Ahhiyawa lead to the supposition that the Mycenaeans, besides punishing woman-stealing (of Helen), are seeking, by warlike means, commercial advantages in the control of the entrance to the Black Sea.

1235   The Laws of Moses (including the Ten Commandments) show some similarity to Hammurabi's, for instance in their harsh insistence of appropriateness of punishment—"an eye for an eye".

In this century the medium of exchange throughout the Middle East is silver and the unit of weight is the Babylonian *shekel*, at 8.4 grammes, 60 *shekels* going to the *mina*.

B. Science and Discovery

1300   In the Shang city of An Yang the culture of the silk worm and the making of silk has begun. There has also been introduced, possibly from the west by Hunnish tribes, the horse (see C). The great use of omens (see E) shows that the Chinese method of writing has by now considerably developed, there being already about 2000 separate characters. Advances are also made in astronomy, in recording of eclipses, and in calculating the length of the year and the seasons.

1275/50   The Hittites are beginning to be known as producers of iron: King Hattusilis III tactfully temporizes when a neighbouring power, probably Assyria, asks for a supply.

C. Religion and Philosophy

1300   At An Yang the kings are buried with their chariots but also with a considerable number of attendants (comparable with contemporary Tutankhamen but, so far as human sacrifice goes, with Queen Shub-ad of a millennium and a half earlier). There is great use of bronze chalices in their religious practices (see D) and of omens and oracles (see E).

Minoan art during the century shows a loss of light-heartedness but an increase in religious content, there being a plethora of crude votive offerings. Somewhat similarly crude votive offerings appear at Mycenae.

Egyptian tombs no longer display happy scenes of everyday life but rather the perils to be faced in the life hereafter.

1275–50   The Hittite king, Hattusilis III, shows a remarkable religious and political conscience in publishing his "autobiography". In this he justifies himself for deposing the son of the previous king, his brother, in favour of himself and seeks the protection of his patron goddess, Ishtar.

1230   Danger is growing for Egypt in Rameses II's declining years—from the Libyans west of the Delta.

The Mycenaeans and their allies, on returning from their wars in or around Troy, meet internal trouble (see below).

1224   Rameses II dies and Meremptah succeeds him. Meremptah puts down disorder in Syria and Palestine and there is reference on a stele of his reign to the Israelites (the only known Egyptian reference).

1219   Meremptah achieves a victory over the invading Libyans, who are helped by the "Peoples of the Sea" (see below). This is an attempted migration rather than an invasion.

1214–1202   Meremptah dies, an old man, and is followed by a 20-year period of five relatively unimportant pharaohs and of internal unrest. The last of these, and the last of the 19th Dynasty, is a woman, Twosre—the only Queen, besides Hashepsowe, to be buried in the Valley of the Kings.

1207   Renewed fighting between Assyria and Kassite Babylon.

1300   In the area N. of the Alps and particularly in the basins of the Rhine and upper Danube, there develops a culture of mixed farming, with a more efficient use of bronze which is helped by trade with the Mediterranean area. These people are horse users, and their chiefs possess fine swords. Here is the cradle of the Celts.

1250   The second half of the century sees the beginning of the disintegration of the Mycenaean culture. It is significant that on their return the Homeric heroes meet with internal trouble and the stories of their dynasties end. Also the struggles of Egypt, at this time and in the ensuing century, against the "Peoples of the Sea" show a general increase of turmoil and movement and unrest in the Mediterranean area. The Peoples of the Sea seem to have been essentially displaced persons seeking new homes.

C. Religion and Philosophy (continued)

1250/20 The stone reliefs found at the sanctuary of Hattusas and probably raised by King Tudhaliyas IV, show the official Hittite pantheon (of "a thousand gods") to have been headed by a Weather God, Sharma, and a Sun goddess. At Alaja Huyuk a king and queen are shown worshipping a sacred bull.

1249 The Assyrians carry off the effigy of Marduk from Babylon.

1235 The Commandments of Moses are shown, like Hammurabi's, to be god-given, but show also a deeper conception of deity; Jahweh however is a tribal god, though even the Egyptians, it is held, will have to be ruled by him. It is while Moses is being given the Commandments that Aaron (his elder brother) persuades the Israelites to worship the golden calf.

D. The Arts

In this final century of their greatness the Hittites show very considerable artistic ability, from monumental rock-carvings to small gold figurines. There is a rock carving of King Tudhaliyas IV being protectively embraced by the god Sharma; there are beautiful belts and head-circlets of pure pale golds, replicas of the sacred stag in bronze and electrum. One sculpture shows musicians playing the lute and bagpipes.

In Egypt, in spite of the material success of the 19th Dynasty, art is deteriorating.

1300 Outside the walls of Mycenae the tholos or beehive tombs are being built. The chief of these is attributed to Atreus, the founder of the dynasty to which the Homeric kings, Agamemnon and Menelaus, belong. Having some similarity to earlier tombs at Ugarit in Syria, they are also thought by some to connect with the megalithic monuments of western Europe (see 2000 C). They show considerable architectural skill.

The Shang culture at An Yang, besides showing architectural skill in rammed-earth building and ceramic skill with near-porcelain, demonstrates a phenomenal skill in bronze casting, making a variety of urns or "chalices", which, it is thought, are used in religious services, each type having a different function.

The Thracian bronze age is producing gold bowls (as discovered at Vulchitrun).

1291 The Hypostyle Hall at Karnak (see 1320 D) shows not only the Pharaoh magnificent in his chariot behind prancing steeds but also Seti I with a couple of prisoners under each arm.

1290/24 Rameses II (Shelley's Ozymandias) sets up enormous and boastful statues of himself, including those at Abu Simbel. His chief wife receives a magnificent tomb in the "Valley of the Queens", west of Thebes.

1260 There begins the last phase of Minoan culture, Late Minoan IIIb or Post Palace Period III (see 1300 E above).

E. Literature

1300 "Linear B" tablets found at Mycenaean Thebes and at Tiryns are thought to date to about this time, thus bridging the gap between those at Knossos and Pylos (see 1450 B and 1200 E).

At An Yang writing is put to the use of making enquiries of the oracle. Questions are written on bone or tortoise-shell and cast into the fire: the pattern of the ensuing cracks gives the answer.

1256 The diplomatic Egyptian-Hittite marriage (see opposite) is described in the Egyptian account in an extremely tendentious manner — as an offering to appease the wrath of the Egyptian King and God.

1250 The legend of Jason and the golden fleece may emanate from a Mycenaean sea-venture into the Black Sea of about the same time as their greater venture to Troy (see opposite). The practice of catching river-gold in a sheep's fleece may indicate a real search for gold behind the legend.

1219 The descriptions of the victory of Meremptah over the Libyans and the Peoples of the Sea refer to Egypt's "great joy": they commemorate a very real national victory and deliverance.

F. Births and Deaths

1291 Seti II d.

1282 Muwatallis d.

1257 Shalmaneser I d.

1250 Hattusilis III d. (53).

1224 Rameses II d. (about 85).

1220 Tudhaliyas IV d.

1214 Meremptah d.

1200–1101 B.C. The Peoples of the Sea and the Dorian Greeks; the fall of the Near East civilization and the rise of the Chinese

1200   Probable date for the first arrival of the Dorian Greeks (or at least a new group of Greek speakers) in the Peloponnese, to be followed during the remainder of the century by the destruction of the Mycenaean palaces: Mycenae itself, Tiryns (probably caused by earthquake) and Pylos (where the Linear B tablets appear to tell of the struggle – see E).

1195   Probable date (if the biblical "forty years in the wilderness" is accepted) of the death of Moses and of the entrance of the Israelites into Palestine under their military leader Joshua. They cross the Jordan and capture Jericho.

1194   Probable date for the destruction of Alalakh (see 1370) by the Peoples of the Sea.

1190   The last recorded Hittite king comes to the throne, Suppiluliumas II; despite his name, he can do nothing to revive the failing glory of the Hittites, whose records end with him. (But see Neo-Hittites in 10th century.)

1184   Egypt's Twentieth Dynasty begins.

1183   Traditional date for the end of the Trojan War (but see 1250-40).

1182   Rameses III, Egypt's otherwise inconsiderable 20th Dynasty's most important king, becomes Pharaoh.

1177   Rameses III beats off a renewed attack by the Libyans.
        Rameses III spectacularly defeats the People of the Sea (see 1219 and 1250), who are checked in their major sweep into the Nile Delta and the Palestine and Syrian coasts.

1173   Kassite Babylon finally ends, after the best part of a century of intermittent war with Assyria (see 1276). It is the Elamites however who give the *coup de grace* (it being, no doubt, now that they carry off the stele on which are written Hammurabi's laws — see 1790 A).

1171/66 Rameses III again beats off the Libyans. After this however success seems to leave him: some attempts to recreate a Syrian empire are abortive and he ends his reign with trouble at home (see C) and a harem conspiracy over the succession.

1166   Rameses III is followed by a series of short-lived pharaohs, all called Rameses.

1150   Probable date at which the biblical Samson flourishes.

1146-23 Babylon under its new "Pashē" dynasty experiences a short revival of military importance under Nebuchadnezzar I (not to be confused with the biblical "King of the Jews" 605-561). This king defeats the Elamites but fails before the Assyrians.

1125   There is fought the second great battle of Megiddo, in which the Israelites, called to arms by their "Judge", the prophetess Deborah, defeat the Canaanites under their general, Sisera (see also A, C and E).

1124   In the reign of Rameses IX, the High Priest is shown on the monuments as of equal height with the Pharaoh, i.e. of equal power.

The boasting and the deeds of Rameses III and Tiglath-Pileser I   1200–1101 B.C.

A. Politics, Law and Economics
1125 At the battle of Megiddo the Canaanites, according to the biblical account, have 900 chariots of iron.

1115 Tiglath Pileser I does much for the economy of Assyria, repairing all the "water-machines", storing grain and increasing the flocks and herds.

B. Science and Discovery
1174 Rameses III's account of his victory over the Peoples of the Sea (see E) states that a net across the river-mouth ensnares the enemy.

1115–1110 Tiglath Pileser, a great hunter, kills Syrian elephants and also a "nakhiru, which they call a horse of the sea", off the Syrian coast. He is also something of a naturalist, collecting wild animals, including the Egyptian gift of a crocodile, and experimenting with the breeding of ibex and deer.

C. Religion and Philosophy
1174–51 In their efforts to unite, the 12 tribes of Israel meet at the sanctuary of Shiloh. Rameses III builds his palace and temple at Medinet Habu (see D and E).

1150 In the reigns of the weak pharaohs after Rameses III the Theban priesthood probably possesses the chief power. It is however unable to prevent the robbery of graves, which continues throughout all times of weak control in Egyptian history.

D. The Arts
1174 The walls of the temple and palace at Medinet Habu, built by Rameses III, give a vivid picture of his naval battle against the Peoples of the Sea.

E. Literature
1200 In China appears, probably in this century, *The Book of Changes*, or *I Ching*, a dissertation on divination.
  At Pylos in the Peloponnese (legendary home of the Homeric Nestor) the Linear B tablets extend their function of ration indents and so forth to a series of military and naval dispositions—perhaps in an effort to stay the invasion of the Dorian Greeks (see opposite). According to a Greek legend, the Heraclidae, that is to say the descendants of Hercules, having been turned out from Tiryns, return with the Dorians to wreak their vengeance.

1174 With the reliefs of Rameses III's temples (see D) goes a boastful account of his victory over the Peoples of the Sea, which is also vivid: "As for those who reached my boundary, their seed is not. Their hearts and their souls are finished into all eternity."

1125 The Song of Deborah (*Judges* 5) tells of the defeat of Sisera (see opposite)—"the stars in their courses fought against Sisera"—and his assassination by Jael.

1115 The Assyrian account of Tiglath-Pileser's victories foreshadow the full horror of later accounts: as boastful as the Egyptian but, unlike them, revelling in ruthlessness and cruelty.

1122   Traditional date (which however may possibly be 75 years too early) for the end of China's Shang Dynasty and the beginning of her Chou Dynasty (see opposite). This is said to have been founded by Kings Wên and Wu.

1115/1110   Tiglath-Piliser I (not the biblical king, who is No. III) comes to the Assyrian throne and, taking full opportunity of the fact that all the neighbouring powers are weak, rounds off his country's first period of power by a series of military campaigns coupled with sound and enlightened administration (see A to C). He strikes north-west into the Taurus mountains, relieves the pressure of a combination of petty princes on his province of Kummukh (Roman Commegane) and meets and defeats the remnants of the Hittites. He also reaches the Mediterranean coast and extracts tribute from the Lebanon and Byblos and Sidon.

This century sees the end of the Bronze Age in the Middle East and the Aegean and the beginning of a Dark Age, at least in the latter area. The turmoil caused by the People of the Sea may have been caused by renewed pressure, from the north, of Indo-European tribes; and, as the century progresses, these tribes, in particular Phrygians and Dorian Greeks, penetrate into Asia Minor and Greece.

The twelve tribes of Israel are struggling to establish themselves in Palestine, against the Canaanites and later the Philistines, and are being ruled by their Judges, national heroes who also help to keep them on the strait course of their monotheistic religion.

1122   This is the orthodox date—perhaps nearly 100 years too early—for the inception of China's Chou Dynasty, becoming, for at least three centuries, stable and prosperous, the opposite of the Dark Age period into which the Near East and Aegean are relapsing. China for the first time is knit, though loosely, into one feudal kingdom.

F. Births and Deaths

1195   Moses d. (at a biblical age of 120).

1170   Joshua d. (or later, at a biblical age of 110).

1166   Rameses III d.

1125   Sisera d.

1103   Nebuchadnezzar I d.

1100–1001 B.C.   **Dorians in Crete, Libyans in Egypt, Philistines in Canaan, and wandering Semites in Assyria and Babylonia**

1100   The Dorians spread to Crete. The Minoans—after three centuries of Mycenaean domination during which they have by no means lost their identity—finally come to the end of their distinctive civilization. Such crude, small townships as Karphi, south of Mallia, show that for a few generations the Minoans flee before the invaders to live in the hills. The dispossessed Mycenaeans (see 1200) retire partly into Arcadia, but largely into Attica and Athens itself. They also begin the so-called Ionian migration into the Aegean coastline of Asia Minor. To the southern corner of this coastline the Dorians themselves migrate. Cyprus at this time, or even earlier, receives Greek immigrants.
Civil war rages in Egypt, with Libyans and also Nubians taking part.

1095   In the reign of Rameses XI the priesthood, in the person of Hrihor, finally take over the power of the pharaohs, creating a theocracy at Thebes.

1087   Rameses XI dies, the last of his name and the last of the 20th Dynasty, Egypt after his death falling apart into a new form of double kingdom. The 21st Dynasty begins with Smerdes, ruling from Tanis in the north whilst Hrihor and his descendants rule, more or less undisturbed, at Thebes in the south.

1080   Assyria's plight (see below) is worsened by famine, flood and plague.

1076   Tiglath-Pileser I dies.

1075   The Israelites suffer from the Midianites but are brought back to strength of purpose by their "Judge", Gideon (see B and C).

1050   The Israelites reach the lowest point in their struggle with the Philistines, (see 1200), the Ark of the Covenant being captured (see C).
Samuel becomes ruler of Israel, the last of the Judges.

1030   Samuel achieves a temporary victory over the Philistines.

1025   Saul is made King of Israel, and saves his country from the Amalekites (in the Negeb). Agag, king of the Amalekites, is spared by Saul but is assassinated by Samuel, as fitting sacrifice in a holy war.

1020   Saul is for a while successful (with the help of David) against the Philistines.

1016   David, a heroic figure at Saul's court and, by one biblical account, already annointed king by the aged Samuel, so arouses the jealousy of Saul that he has to flee. For 6 years he lives the life of an outlaw, at one time allying himself with the Philistines.

1010   Saul and his son Jonathan are defeated and slain by the Philistines at the battle of Mount Gilboa (and see E). David becomes king of Judah.

A. Politics, Law and Economics

In the last third of the century there is a struggle among the Israelites, between those who want to continue as a theocracy and those who want to be like other nations with a king. The latter win.

1091   The timber of the Lebanon is still being exploited (see E).

1020   Goliath, the Philistine, is armoured with bronze (biblical brass) but armed with iron.

B. Science and Discovery

1075   The Syrio-Palestinian Semitic peoples are developing a true alphabetical script.
The camel is brought out of the Arabian desert by the Midianites who use it as a war-steed in attacking the Israelites.

1050   The Philistines seem for a while to be able to deny the use of iron to the Israelites; but, by the time of Saul and David, never able to follow up fully their advantage, they are on the way to final defeat. David has his warriors taught the use of the bow.

C. Religion and Philosophy

1075   Gideon cures the Israelites of the temptations of a less austere worship, that of Baal.

1050   In an effort to overawe and conquer the Philistines, the Israelites send out from Shiloh the Ark of the Covenant, accompanied by the two sons of Eli, the High Priest. It is captured and its sanctuary, Shiloh, is destroyed; after 7 years however the Philistines return the Ark, as bringing them Plague. Samuel (his grandson being christened Ichabod, The Glory Has Departed) stages a religious revival.

D. The Arts

The art of the Minoans, which the Mycenaeans for so long have poorly copied, disappears: in the fresco entirely, in pottery to a formal patterning, to develop into the *Geometric* style.

E. Literature

1091   An Egyptian named Wenamun (as shown in the Medinet Habu papyri) is sent on a mission to the Phoenician coast, to collect timber from Lebanon for his god and his king, and receives most unmannerly treatment, finding that both king and god are of small account compared with their standing in the past.

1010   David laments Saul and Jonathan—"How are the mighty fallen!" (II Samuel IV. 19–27).

F. Births and Deaths

1087   Rameses XI d.

1076   Tiglath-Pileser I d.

1040   David b. (–970 B.C.).

1010   Saul and Jonathan d.

1003   David, having defeated the faction of Saul, becomes king of a united Israel and Judah; he defeats the Jebusites and from their city creates his new capital, the city of David, Jerusalem.
The Philistines attack him and he wins two battles over them.

Both Assyria and Babylonia in this century are suffering from inroads of wandering Semites, sometimes called Aramaeans; even the Assyrians, relapsing into a dark-age period of which little is known, are apparently fighting for their very existence.
The Phoenicians are beginning to create a colonial empire, Tarshish and Gades being founded. Similarly the Israelites, left alone for a while by their powerful neighbours, are succeeding in their efforts to develop from a collection of tribes into a united people and to dominate Palestine.

1027   Archaeologically revised date for the beginning of China's Chou Dynasty (see 1122).

1050   The Phrygians (see 1200) found their city of Gordion (some 100 miles west of modern Ankara) and establish themselves as the main successors to the Hittites.

1000/970   David, coming to the combined throne of Israel and Judah, probably in 1003, continues on the throne, undisturbed by any outside power but not undisturbed at home, until his death. The chief events of his reign (to which exact dates cannot be given) are:—

David brings the Ark of the Covenant to his new city, Jerusalem, dancing before it in ecstasy but to the disgust of his wife Michal (daughter of Saul). He appoints priests to attend it and composes for them a song to sing (see E). As a "man of war" however, he is not allowed by the prophet Nathan to build a temple at Jerusalem. David becomes prosperous and subdues his enemies "from Dan to Beersheba", including the Edomites, whom he nearly exterminates. During the Ammonite war he has Uriah the Hittite (see below) "put in the forefront of the battle" so that he can have Bathsheba as a wife. (Her second child is Solomon.)

Internal troubles henceforth begin. Absalom murders his half brother for incestuous rape of his sister, flees the court, is forgiven by David, but then revolts against him. David in turn has to flee Jerusalem. Finally Absalom is defeated, slain—and lamented. Further revolts and wars bring David's reign to a close, with a pestilence, taken by David as divine retribution for his effrontery in seeing how many fighting men he can muster, and with great preparation for the temple that he is not allowed to build.

970   Solomon comes to the throne of Israel and Judah, and marries the daughter of Pharaoh (which one, unknown).

966   Solomon, with the help of the Phoenician king, Hiram of Tyre, and of his Lebanon cedar-wood, begins to build the Temple at Jerusalem.

959   The Temple is completed and Solomon proceeds to build palaces for himself and wife.

950   Solomon's further building is finished, and he and Hiram of Tyre exchange gifts, whilst Pharaoh makes a present of the town of Gezer, which he has earlier sacked.

945   In Egypt Libyan chieftains, already in the country and calling themselves chiefs of the Meshwash, take control and, in the person of Shoshenk I, begin the 22nd Dynasty. They rule from the Delta, whilst Thebes remains no more than a religious centre, with however considerable power still exerted by the priesthood.

At about this time must have occurred the visit to Solomon of the Queen of Sheba (South Arabia). Solomon begins to collect his vast harem of foreign women and to please them with a proliferation of idolatories.

934   King Assurdan II of Assyria begins the revival of that country.

931   Solomon dies, and the combined kingdom of Israel and Judah begins to disintegrate. He is succeeded by his son Rehoboam.

925   The Pharaoh Shoshenk I (biblical Shishak) stages a military expedition into Palestine, penetrates into Jerusalem and takes away the treasures in the temple and royal palaces.

A. Politics, Law and Economics

980   David's census, which takes over 9 months, shows there to be, of "men that drew the sword, 800,000 in Israel and 500,000 in Judah."

970   Solomon, receiving the gift from his God of an understanding heart, judges between the harlots as to whose baby has survived (I Kings 3).

960   In order to build his temples and palaces, Solomon raises a levy of workmen and begins to over-tax his people.

950   Solomon and Hiram equip a fleet to obtain the gold and sandal-wood of Ophir (? S. Arabia or possibly India).

945   Evidence of trade between Israel and S. Arabia is shown by the Queen of Sheba's train of camels bearing spices, gold and precious stones.
Solomon shows regard for the convention that the horse and chariot is a status symbol. The Bible credits him with stabling for 40,000 horses, and archaeological excavation (at Megiddo) has unearthed at least 450.

B. Science and Discovery

970/31   Solomon is credited with being able to "speak of Nature" (I Kings IV, 33).

C. Religion and Philosophy

1000/970   On the journey of the ark to Jerusalem the driver of the ox-cart on which it rested touches it to steady it, and for this act, according to the Bible (II Samuel VI, 7), he is struck down dead.

960   Solomon's temple is designed more to Canaanite standards than Jewish (and is later to be called an abomination by Ezekiel).

945   The ruling priesthood at Thebes is depending increasingly on the answering of questions by oracle (cf China, 1300 E).

931   Solomon dies with a great reputation for "wisdom", i.e. philosophy (see E).

D. The Arts

Pottery in Greece is, as in Crete, of the angular-patterned, "Geometric" style.

960   Solomon's temple is made of ashlar stone and with liberal use of gold. It is however smaller than his palace, a matter of 90 by 30 feet (taking the cubit at 18 in) against 150 by 75 feet.

E. Literature

Both the "Homeric" poems of Greece and the *Vedas* of India are being recited and carried down from one generation verbally to another (see 900 and 800 E respectively).
By this century the Phoenicians (among other Semitic peoples) have acquired their alphabet.

925/14   Rehoboam, Solomon's son, is faced with discontent from his people and with many enemies, including Hadad of Edom (supported by Egypt). The result is the split into a double kingdom, of Israel (or the Ten Tribes) in the north under Jeroboam, with its capital at Samaria, and of Judah (hence "the Jews") in the south, with its capital at Jerusalem.

911   Assyria's revival is continued with King Adad-nirari II, who forcefully pacifies Babylon and defeats the Aramaeans and also the Urartu (later the Vannic civilization, see 840).

During this century there develops in Syria the Neo-Hittite civilization, with its centre at Carchemish. It pays tribute to Syria but at the time of the biblical Uriah (see 1000–970) is prosperous. Egypt during its 21st, 22nd and 23rd Dynasties suffers two centuries of confusion and rebellion, with occasional upsurges of interference in the Near East, where its reputation, though lessened, is still considerable. Assyria is quiet until at least the end of the century. The Israelites therefore, with the help of the Phoenicians, are left to develop their brief period of political significance and economic greatness. The Greeks, presumably proliferating but hardly yet to be considered emerged from their Dark Age, continue to migrate across the Aegean Sea.

1000   Primitive settlements exist on the site of Rome.
A bronze-age Celtic settlement (see 1300) is established at Halstatt (30 m. S.W. of Salzburg): the presence of salt is the primary attraction.

E. **Literature** (continued)

970 King David leaves behind him his great reputation as a poet, 73 of the Psalms being credited to him.

931 King Solomon leaves behind a great literary reputation, centring on "wisdom". Ascribed to him are the biblical Proverbs, Ecclesiastes, the Song of Solomon, and Psalms 72 and 127.

F. **Births and Deaths**

990 Solomon b.

970 David d. (70).

931 Solomon d. (59).

924 Shoshenk I d.

913 Rehoboam d.

908 Jeroboam d.

889   Israel emerges from a period of strife with the now separate and stronger kingdom of Judah; Omri is chosen as king.

Assur-nasir-pal II, one of Assyria's great conquerors, comes to the throne.

880   Omri establishes the Israelite capital at Samaria.

877   Omri's son, Ahab, comes to the throne of Israel. He marries Jezebel, a Phoenician and worshipper of Baal.

876   In a great campaign Assur-nasir-pal II marches westward, reaches the Mediterranean and conquers Syria, founding the fortress of Harran from which to administer the country. He appears to leave the Jews alone, but extracts tribute from the Phoenicians. On his way he subdues neo-Hittite Carchemish.

Jehosaphat comes to the throne of Judah, and "walks in the ways of the Lord". His daughter marries Ahab's son, thus patching up an alliance between Israel and Judah. He brings some peace and prosperity to Judah.

870/55   Elijah denounces Jezebel and Ahab and foretells a 3-year drought, which occurs (and in Phoenicia also). He confounds the prophets of Baal (who are afterwards massacred) and brings rain. He denounces Ahab for plotting the death of Naboth in order to possess his vineyard.

859   Shalmaneser III comes to the Assyrian throne and finds a powerful combination of Canaanite and Syrian states allied against him under the leadership of Adad-idri (Ben Hadad of the bible) the Syrian king at Damascus.

855   Shalmaneser III claims a victory over the federation under Adad-idri at the battle of Karka, probably on the Orontes.

854   The mantle of Elijah falls upon Elisha, who proceeds to prophesy the death of Ahab and has a dashing army captain named Jehu annointed as future king.

853   Ahab, in spite of having sent a large contingent to the battle of Karka, now dies fighting Adad-idri of Syria. Jehosaphat, being persuaded reluctantly to join him, escapes with his life.

842/836   Jehu massacres the royal families of both Israel and Judah (including Jezebel), though the seed of David does survive in Judah in the person of Jehoash. Jehu reigns in Israel. He pays tribute to Assyria (see D).

841   The oppressive Chinese King, "Li" is dethroned and there follows the Kung Ho or Public Harmony regency.

840   The city of Van (on the southern shores of the lake of that name, south of Mount Ararat) is founded by King Sarduris I and the Vannic kingdom (called Urartu by Assyria and Ararat by the Jews) withstands the might of Assyria for over a hundred years.

834   The Medes, an Indo-European people, are first mentioned in the Assyrian records.

831   An Assyrian general claims a victory over the King of Urartu (Van).

A. Politics, Law and Economics

870/40   The Phrygians (see next page), by reason of the Midas legends, have apparently access to a source of gold.

The political influence of Elijah and Elisha is considerable, including (as with Samuel) the power of king-making.

876/51   Jehosaphat sends Levites, with the book of the law, to teach in the cities of Judah; he also appoints Judges in the larger (walled) towns. He builds ships to trade with Ophir, but they are wrecked.

B. Science and Discovery

Phrygian pottery shows soldiers armed with spear and round shield, grieves and helmets, remarkably similar to those shown on early Greek vases.

840   Vannic metallurgy (being near to Taurus mountain mines) reaches a high standard; a fine bronze gryphon has been found.

C. Religion and Philosophy

The religion of the Phrygians (see next page) leaves, like its music, an impression on Greece and, later, Rome. Its mother-goddess is Cybele and its male attendant-god Atys; and it is rather more than usually orgiastic.

870/40   Elijah and Elisha have enormous moral power as well as political. They make it clear to the kings of Israel and Judah that what matters is not economic prosperity but rectitude and obedience to the one god.

840   The sacred tree of the Vannic kingdom is the vine, which the king plants with great ceremony.

D. The Arts

The music of the Phrygians (see next page) is sufficiently famous to have left its impression upon classical Greece: in the great use of the flute and in the legend of Midas judging a musical contest between Pan and Apollo and being rewarded with ass's ears for his pains (which he hides under his tall Phrygian cap).

879/24   Both Assur-nasir-pal II and Shalmeneser III build themselves palaces at Calah or Nimrud (which Sir Henry Layard is to excavate in the 19th century). The most outstanding features are colossal carvings of winged bulls and reliefs showing royal lion-hunts and battle scenes. (Assyrian relief-carving is to reach its height later—see 668 D.) An obelisk shows Jehu paying tribute to Assyria.

E. Literature

In this century the art of writing is developed in India, merchants introducing the Phoenician alphabet.

The Greeks are beginning to copy the Phoenician alphabet (see 1000 E) and to evolve their own.

870/40   The stories of Elijah and Elisha are told in I Kings 17 to II Kings 13.

827/800   The Chinese drive the nomadic Huns out of their domains. This may have set in motion a movement of their western neighbours, the Scythians, which becomes apparent in the next two centuries.

824/811   Shamshi-Adad V succeeds to the Assyrian throne and spends two years in putting down internal revolt, having ignominiously to ask for help from Babylon. He then extends his boundaries east and south, being at war with Babylon but largely leaving Palestine alone. Babylon is humbled.

811   Adad-nirari III succeeds to the Assyrian throne, but his mother Sammu-ramat exerts the real power. These two are the probable originals of the legendary Semiramis and Ninus.

802   Adad-nirari III is successful in Syria before having to face Vannic aggression. He invests Damascus.

The use of iron is spreading into Europe, particularly at Halstatt (see 1000).
The Etruscans begin to infiltrate into N. Italy in this century, probably coming from the East.
The Phrygians (see 1050 and 655) reach the height of their prosperity in this century, under their kings with the dynastic title of Midas.

841   With the Kung Ho regency authentic chronology in Chinese history begins; there follows a feudal age, until the arrival of the Han dynasty.

F.   **Births and Deaths**

877   Omri d.

859   Assur-nasir-pal d.

854   Elijah d.

853   Ahab d.

851   Jehosaphat d. (60).

843   Jezebel d. (see II Kings IX, 30).

824   Shalmaneser III d.

814   Jehu d.

811   Shamsi-Adad V d.

810   Elisha d. (probable date).

790   A treaty is made between Assyria and Babylon, the former regarding herself protectress of the latter.

783   Adad-nirari III dies and there follow three inconsiderable kings in Assyria and a time of weakness.

In Egypt, which is still experiencing troubled times and lack of strong central government, the Pharaoh, Shoshenk III, having reigned for 52 years, is followed by one called Pemay, "the cat." At this time the 23rd Dynasty is existing concurrently with the 22nd.

776   Traditional date for the first recorded victor in the pan-hellenic games, the Olympiad, held every four years and having a political and economic and social significance as well as a genuine athletic and competitive one (a keeping fit for war). This is the first certain date in Greek history.

771   The original Chou Dynasty of China ends with the deposing of its king Yu and the shifting of the capital city. For another five centuries the Chou Dynasty will continue but it will be a much looser confederacy of often warring barons under a head who is little more than a religious symbol "the King of Heaven".

765/50   The Israelite prophet Amos *floruit* (See C).

754   Beginning of the *Ephoi* list at Sparta (a board of five overseers or rulers).

753   Traditional date for the founding of Rome by Romulus, and year from which all subsequent Roman events are dated: "AUC, ab urbe condita". It is not such a reliable date as the Greek one above, though by now Latin-speaking tribes exist in Italy, arriving probably from further east, with Etruscans to their north and Greek "colonial" city states about to be founded to their south.

751   Piankhi, an Ethiopian, advances north from Napata, makes war with the 24th Dynasty in the Delta and founds Egypt's seventy-year-long 25th, Ethiopian, Dynasty, restoring the country sufficiently for it to meet later and with some success the impact of Assyria (see 700–651).

Greece, after the violent times of her migrations in the generations after the final collapse of the Mycenaeans, is beginning a different form of movement overseas, the voluntary foundation of new cities along the mid-Mediterranean and Aegean coasts; this movement is caused by increased prosperity and the pressure of population.

B. Science and Discovery
763   An eclipse of the sun is noted in the Assyrian archives.

C. Religion and Philosophy
800   In India the period of the production of the metaphysical prose-works called the Upanishads begins. The religion brought by the Indo-Europeans, later to be called Hindu, has become well established, with the great accent on the ceremony of sacrifice carried out by the priest or *brahman*.

765   During the next 30 years Amos and Hosea flourish. They are the first authors of written prophecy and they denounce the public immorality and social injustice of Judah. In face of the Assyrian menace they announce their nation's obligation to righteousness and warn of Jehovah's punishment if it fails to meet it: there begins to appear the concept of not merely a national god but also a Lord of Hosts, a righteous god of all peoples.

D. The Arts
The Neo-Hittite reliefs at their fortress at modern Karatepe show a dancer and musicians, one with a double pipe.

E. Literature
The monuments at Neo-Hittite Karatepe give accounts in both Hittite and Phoenician writing (thus making the former decipherable).

F. Births and Deaths
783   Adad-nirari III d.
Shoshenk III pharaoh, d.

750–701 B.C.   **Greece colonizes; the kingdoms of Israel, of Van, and of the Neo-Hittites collapse**

747 Nabonassar becomes king of Babylon; is anti-Assyrian.

745 An Assyrian by the name of Pul comes to the throne and assumes the title of Tiglath Pileser III. He revives his country and resumes her conquests.

745/34 Greek colonization continues (see 800). Within this period are traditionally founded colonies at Cumae in Italy, at Poseideion on the Orontes, at Syracuse and Naxos in Sicily.

733 Israel and Syria, with some backing from Van and the Neo-Hittites, form a confederacy against Assyria, which King Ahaz of Judah refuses to join. Tiglath Pileser III comes to the support of Ahaz and invades Syria and northern Israel. He extinguishes the Syrian monarchy, sets up a puppet king, Hosea, in Israel, and deports the leading citizens of the Galilee area.

733/01 Isaiah and Micah, prophets of Judah, flourish (see C).

728 Tiglath Pileser III establishes full suzerainty over Babylon and declares himself its king.

725 Taking no notice of the exhortations of the prophet Isaiah of Judah, Hoshea, king of Israel seeks support from Egypt and revolts against Assyria. The Israelite capital city of Samaria suffers a 3 year siege.

722 Samaria falls and a wholesale deportation into Mesopotamia of Israelites is made, to the number, it is said, of 27,290, their place being taken by Assyrian colonists. This signals the end of Israel as a nation and the so-called Captivity of the Ten Tribes; Israel becomes the land of the Samaritans. (Judah meanwhile, under King Hezekiah, remains inviolate.)
After a recurrence of dynastic turmoil, a new king comes to the Assyrian throne, calling himself Sargon II. Having completed the pacification of Samaria, he turns his attention north and east to the Neo-Hittites and the kingdom of Van.

720 Greek colonization in southern Italy (to be known as Magna Graecia) continues with the founding of Sybaris.
The Dorian Greeks in the south and west of the Peloponnese, i.e. the Spartans, fight to gain control of the rich Messenian plain, once the property of King Nestor of Pylos—see 1200 E.

717 The Neo-Hittite Carchemish falls to the Assyrians.

716 Shabako, brother of Piankhi, becomes Pharaoh and finishes the task of re-uniting Egypt preparatory to meeting the might of Assyria.

715 Traditional date for the accession of Rome's first king after Romulus and Remus, Numa Pompilius (and see C).

714 Sargon II defeats the Vannic army and seizes its king's treasure, thus ending the prosperity and historical significance of Van or Urartu. The vacuum created allows Scythians and Cimmerians, to the north of the Black Sea, to move south.

A. Politics, Law and Economics

750   In Greece the concept of the City State is growing: common gods, and common law, administered from a fixed place (and see B).

721   Assyrian law (as illustrated by fragments of stele that have survived) is harsh and owes little to Hammurabi: e.g. 'If a woman has had a miscarriage by her own act, when they have prosecuted and convicted her, they shall impale her on stakes without burying."

720/715   In an interval between the reigns of the Ethiopian pharaohs, the Pharaoh known to the later Greeks as Bocchoris the Wise reigns. He is credited with reforming the laws.

B. Science and Discovery

750   With the development of the Greek city-state (and its need for defence) develops also the idea of ranging heavily armed infantrymen in close order behind a wall of shields: the *hoplite* formation.

705   Hesiod in his *Works and Days* shows the current efficiency of good farming.

Sennacherib, in his frieze of the transport of one of the colossi adorning the gateways of his palace, shows his personal interest in a great engineering feat. He also dams a river in order to rebuild the ancient and neglected Nineveh, and introduces the cotton plant into his country.

C. Religion and Philosophy

733   The collapse of Israel having brought the great enemy, Assyria, to the very gate of Judah, there arise the prophets Micah and Isaiah to announce their warnings and denunciations. Both regard Assyria as the necessary instrument of God's displeasure if the people will not mend their ways, but Isaiah is by no means without hope, nor can he conceive of Jerusalem not surviving—hence his later uncompromising advice to Hezekiah to defy the Assyrians. (And see E).

721   The religion of Assyria, in this year that begins a near-century of four great reigns, seems to have been, rather more than usually for these times, one of fear and magic and propitiation and omens. The principal god, Ashur, appears usually within the symbol of a winged disc, which symbol is carried into battle, preferably in the king's own chariot.

715   Numa Pompilius, Rome's first king, is also traditionally the founder of their religious observances.

705   Hesiod, with Homer, is said to have "given the Greeks their gods".

D. The Arts

In Greece the "Geometric" style of pottery is giving place to more lively styles e.g. of stylized warriors—Greece is approaching her artistic renaissance and learning anew from the East. At Athens the Dipylon vases show elaborate funeral processions and other signs of growing wealth and civilization.

710   In Babylon a revolt against Assyria places King Merodach-Baladan (his biblical name) on the throne.

709   Defeated by Assyria, the Neo-Hittite kingdom comes to an end.
       In Cyprus (where pre-Dorian rather than Dorian influence seems to have followed the Minoan) a chieftain is shown on a monument as paying tribute to Assyria.

705   Sennacherib succeeds to the Assyrian throne, and opportunity is taken by the vassal states and enemies of Assyria to stage a general revolt—led by the king of Babylon and supported by the Pharaoh of Egypt. Hezekiah of Israel is approached and agrees to join the revolt, hoping for support from Egypt and contrary to the advice of the prophet Isaiah.

703/01   Sennacherib reacts energetically and Babylon is defeated. He then turns west, into Palestine, defeating an Egyptian army that has advanced so far, and taking the city of Lachish as well as "forty-six walled cities".

D. **The Arts** (continued)

730 A Greek myth credits a Phrygian musician by name Olympus with inventing the enharmonic scale of quarter tones.

703 The Assyrian army being particularly skilled at such operations, Sennacherib has its feats at the siege of Lachish recorded in stone.

E. **Literature**

The Assyrian monuments and archives give a most detailed account of the doings of the Assyrian king — sin this century a year by year account. Their boasting is distinctive in its accent on frightfulness: it is creating a new use for literature, the installing of terror.

750 Homer, a Greek of Asia Minor, about whom little is known, is born at about this time. His birthplace is most probably Smyrna or the island of Chios. Most scholars accept that he is the author of both the *Iliad* and the *Odyssey*.

733/01 The prophecies of Isaiah are recorded and are later given pride of place in the Old Testament books of prophecy. (They comprise *Isaiah* chapters 1 to 39.)

705 Hesiod, the Boeotian poet and farmer, *floruit*, writing his *Works and Days*, of practical and ethical advice, and his *Theogony*, giving an account of the origin of the world and the birth of the Greek gods.

F. **Births and Deaths**

730 Piankhi (Pharaoh) d.

727 Tiglath-Pileser III d.

723 Ahaz d.

705 Sargon II d.

702 Merodach-Baladin king of Babylon d.

700   Sennacherib, continuing his Palestine campaign, boasts that he has Hezekiah, King of Judah, cut off and shut up in Jerusalem "like a caged bird". He send his commander-in-chief and an army to the walls of Jerusalem demanding capitulation. Hezekiah, with Isaiah's moral support, defies the Assyrian general, who retires. This miraculous salvation of Jerusalem is credited by Isaiah (see E) to a visitation of plague upon Sennacherib's army (supported to an extent by Herodotus); the Assyrian records suggest that Sennacherib has to hurry home to meet internal trouble. Hezekiah ends by paying considerable tribute to Sennacherib; but he has saved Judah from the fate of Israel (see 722).

692   The Chaldeans, with Elamite support, defy Assyria and seize the throne of Babylon.

689   Taharka (biblical Tirhakah), a son of Piankhi the Ethiopian, becomes Pharaoh.
Babylon, temporarily unsupported by Elam (suffering from dynastic trouble) is besieged by Sennacherib, who takes and sacks the city, which has now become a stronghold of the dangerous Chaldean party.

681   Sennacherib is assassinated by his sons. Civil war follows but Esarhaddon, one of his sons, gains control. (See A).

680   Esarhaddon, who has married a Babylon wife, rebuilds Babylon, but not without local opposition.

676   Esarhaddon, in a continued policy of expansion, conducts a campaign in Arabia, extracting tribute and then retiring.

675   Esarhaddon, recognizing Egypt, with its great fame, as the real enemy to his ambitions, invades that country and reduces the fortresses of the Delta.

673   As a subordinate operation Tyre is besieged by the Assyrians, who however fail to invest it.

671   Assyria renews its attack on Egypt. The Pharaoh Taharka is defeated but escapes to Ethiopia. Esarhaddon appoints local rulers, including Necho of Sais, and retires to deal with home affairs.

670   Gyges (to Assyria "Gugu") comes to the Lydian throne and begins to build up that country to power and wealth.

669   Esarhaddon, setting out for Egypt again, dies at the fortress of Harran. The Pharaoh Taharka returns to Egypt and re-occupies Memphis.

668   Assur-bani-pal succeeds to the Assyrian throne, as that country's last great king. He concludes a treaty with Tyre, which Esarhaddon has been unable to capture: the Phoenician coastal cities acknowledge Assyrian overlordship.

667   In his first Egyptian campaign Assur-bani-pal finally turns Taharka out of Memphis, re-appoints pro-Assyrian governors everywhere and retires.

664   Tanuatamun succeeds Taharka as Pharaoh and re-occupies Memphis. Assyria's puppet king, Necho of Saïs, rebels and is taken away temporarily as captive to Nineveh.

A. Politics, Law and Economics

683   In Athens the office of *archon* (ruler) is made annual.

681   The assassination of Sennacherib exemplifies the perennial Assyrian trouble: there is no political mechanism wherewith to achieve continuity after the death of a king.

670/52   Gyges of Lydia establishes his wealth in Greek eyes by sending rich gifts to Delphi (see also C). In the eyes of later Greeks Gyges is the typical *tyrannos*.

660   The new-founded Ethiopian city of Meroe has the economic advantage of access to iron.

B. Science and Discovery

700   At Jerusalem Hezekiah builds his tunnel (still existing) to bring water from outside the city walls to the pool of Siloam within.

668/31   The library accumulated by Assur-bani-pal at Nineveh (and see E) shows Assyrian achievements in science: medical treatises, including prescriptions and diagnosis and treatment of disease; tablets of multiplication, lists of plants; astronomical and astrological tables; treatise on glass-making.

C. Religion and Philosophy

668/31   Assur-bani-pal's library includes prayers and hymns, incantations and omens.

670   The reputation of Delphi is already established as a centre for seeking the inspiration and advice of the gods—see A above.

D. The Arts

The "Dedalic" style of art (credited by Diodorus to Daedalus) appears in Crete. It includes free-standing statuary.
In this half century the Etruscans create their own script, probably learnt from the Greeks.

673   An Assyrian monument shows some wishful thinking as to the conquest of Tyre by depicting Esarhaddon holding in his hand cords attached to rings through the lips of the king and god of that city.

668/31   The scenes of royal lion-hunts decorating the palace of Assur-bani-pal show Assyrian art at its peak, and with rather less attention to warlike scenes; also excellent work in bronze and ivory.

660   Under the 26th, Saïte, Dynasty, Egyptian sculpture, conservative and uninspired since the 19th Dynasty, makes a conscious revival, trying to return to the strength and simplicity of the Old Kingdom.

E. Literature

700   The Assyrian demand for surrender outside the walls of Jerusalem (see opposite) and the ensuing scene, as described in 2 Kings 18, provides a classic example of the Jews' faith and the lack of understanding of it by their enemies.

663   In his final Egyptian campaign Assur-bani-pal claims to have penetrated to Thebes and to have carried away vast booty; the Egyptian record however (see E) claims a victory for Tanuatamun. Nevertheless this Pharaoh does soon retire to his native Ethiopia (i.e. modern Sudan), there to found the city of Meroe, a city that will continue something of Egyptian culture into the 4th century A.D. Assur-bani-pal also retires from Egypt, to meet trouble from invading Cimmerians.

660   There occurs the first recorded Greek naval battle between Corinth, at present probably the most thriving city-state on the Greek mainland, and her colony Corcyra (Corfu).
    Gyges of Lydia is threatened by the Cimmerians and asks for help from Assyria; with or without its help he succeeds in pushing the barbarians back. He ceases to be pro-Assyrian.

658/1   Another Saïte prince (see 671), possibly Necho's son, by name Psammetichus the First, seizes the opportunity to throw off the Assyrian yoke and to found Egypt's 26th (Saïte) Dynasty. He is helped by mercenaries (whom Herodotus calls "bronze-clad").

655   The aristocratic family of the Bacchiadae, rulers of Corinth, are expelled.

653   The Medes (see 834) fail in an attack on Nineveh.

652   The Cimmerians, returning, capture the Lydian capital, Sardis, and kill Gyges. In an effort that helps to exhaust them, the Assyrians manage to defeat the Cimmerians and to throw them back northwards—to be absorbed by the Scythians.
    Babylon's puppet king, in spite of being the brother of Assur-bani-pal, is persuaded to join a coalition against Assyria.

651   Assyria retreats from Egypt for the last time, in order to meet trouble nearer home.

    The rulers of the old civilizations, Egypt, Babylon, Assyria, war amongst themselves without fully realizing the threat from new peoples of different race, Cimmerians, Scythians, Phrygians, Medes, Lydians, Ionian Greeks.

700   At about this date the city of Tartessus (biblical Tarshish) comes to power under Iberian chiefs, having thrown off the rule of its founder, Tyre. A kingdom is founded under the legendary Arganthonius ("Silver Man") and prospers, with the help of the local mines, for about 150 years.
    The Celts begin to settle in Spain and a few reach England.

670   Argos, under King Pheidon, is at the height of its power, though soon to decline. Mycenae and Tiryns are under her control and at about this date achieve a temporary defeat of Sparta.

660   A Mongolian people begin to enter Japan, probably coming through Korea; they oust the aboriginal Ainus (coming probably from Siberia). This is also the traditional date for Japan's first emperor, Jimmu.

E. **Literature** (continued)

668   Assur-bani-pal in his library collects ancient texts going back to Sumerian times (including the story of Gilgamesh, which includes the Babylonian version of the biblical Flood). He also provides Sumerian grammars.

667   Assur-bani-pal, on the Rassam cylinder (named after the 19th century archaeologist who found it), gives a long list of Egyptian puppet princes and the towns and areas they are meant to rule.

663   The stele of Tanuatamun, contradicting the Assyrian claim to victory (see opposite), and known as the Dream Stele, tells how the pharaoh saw two snakes, on his right and left—interpreted as meaning: "Upper Egypt belongs to thee; take to thyself Lower Egypt!"

F. **Births and Deaths**

694   Hezekiah d.

681   Sennacherib d.

669   Esarhaddon d.

664   Taharka (Pharaoh) d.

652   Gyges d.

650–601 B.C.   Nineveh falls: the death-struggles of Assyria and the rise of Chaldean Babylon

650/30   For the first twenty years of the century the Scythians, raiding southwards on their horses, are a constant source of terror to Assyria, Syria, Lydia and Palestine, though they also keep the Medes in check.

650   At the battle of Babsame on the Tigris the Assyrians manage to defeat the coalition of enemies formed against them.

649   Psammeticus I continues his climb to power and the 26th Dynasty is safely founded. From now on, the influence upon Egypt will come from Greece rather than from the lands of the two rivers, whilst her danger is from Assyria's enemies rather than Assyria herself.

648   Babylon capitulates to Assyria and is once more devastated—to be again rebuilt, on the orders of Ashur-bani-pal.

639/6   Elam, one of Babylon's main supports in the coalition against Assyria, is quelled. Susa is sacked.

637   Josiah comes to the throne of Judah, at the age of eight, his regent being the High Priest.

632   In Athens, Cylon, having gained a victory in the Olympic games, seizes the Acropolis with the intention of making himself Tyrant. Lured away from the altar of Athena, where he has taken refuge, he is put to death.

631   Assur-bani-pal dies, and the disintegration of Assyria's last span of greatness begins: she is over-extended and has no friends.

630   The Minyae, earlier inhabitants of Thera, having quarrelled with the later Dorian inhabitants, set sail and eventually found the colony of Cyrene, in N. Africa.
Nabopolasser, a Chaldean, is appointed by the Assyrians as administrator of Babylon and in his master's name puts down a rebellion. He then rebels himself.
Sparta wages her second Messenian war (and see A).

626   The Assyrians endeavour to oust Nabopolasser but fail; this Chaldean rebel becomes acknowledged king of Babylon, founding his Chaldean dynasty and the city's last and most splendid period of greatness.
The Scythians pour down through Syria and Palestine, helping to weaken Assyria, annihilating the Philistines and reaching the borders of Egypt. They appear to leave Judah alone; but the prophet Jeremiah now comes forward in that country, warning of dangers to come.

625   Periander becomes Tyrant of Corinth; he has a reputation as a philosopher.

623/16   Prolonged and inconclusive war is waged between Assyria and Babylon, with a small Egyptian force either helping Assyria or seeking to defend its country's own interests in Syria.

620   Greek mariners (Phocaeans) settle in Spain near Tartessus, the farthest-west colony.

A. Politics, Law and Economics

The use of stamped coinage (as opposed to a mere standard weight of metal) comes into use in this half-century amongst the trading states and cities of the Asia Minor coast—traditionally introduced by Lydia.

The Etruscans are ruled by a close aristocracy, known to the Romans as the *Lucumones*. A confederacy of twelve states or tribes meets annually near Volsinii (some 50 miles N. of Rome).

650   In Egypt Psammeticus I uses his daughter Nitocris (not to be confused with the Babylonian queen, see 600 F) to gain political power at Thebes, where the 25th Dynasty still reigns. He makes her the god's, (i.e. the Pharaoh's) wife, and she is received with acclaim by the priesthood.

637/608   King Josiah of Judah reissues the Deuteronomic Laws, said to have been found in the Temple.

630   The revolt and second subjugation of the Messenians may well have led at this time to the peculiar harsh laws and customs of the Spartans, creating a dedicated military aristocracy perennially suppressing a subjugated helotry. The Spartans credit their laws and constitution to a mythical Lycurgus, who—like Solon of Athens later—leaves Sparta in voluntary exile so that the Spartans may be the more likely to keep their oath of obedience to his laws.

621   Traditional date for the making of the Draconian Laws for Athens—said to be written in blood, not ink, because death was the punishment for nearly all crimes.

B. Science and Discovery

642   Ancus Martius, Roman king (acceding traditionally on this date), builds a bridge over the Tiber and founds the port of Ostia.

648   The fourth of April is the probable date on which Archilochus (see E) records an eclipse of the sun.

610   Necho II of Egypt fails in an attempt to join the Nile to the Red Sea by canal (see 510 B); he may have sponsored a Phoenician voyage that circumnavigated Africa from East to West (and see Hanno, 490 B).

C. Religion and Philosophy

Egypt, under ever-changing foreign dominations, shows a marked increase in religiosity—in animal worship, and in gifts of land to the temples (and see D).

639/36   The Assyrians in sacking Elamite Susa, destroy its ziggurat and deport the statues of its gods.

637/08   Josiah, King of Judah, in his efforts to revive the Deuteronomic Laws, endeavours once more to purify the Jews' religion, destroying all local sanctuaries in favour of the pure and centralized worship in the temple at Jerusalem.

626   Jeremiah is called to the prophetic vocation as a young man. He sees no hope in formalism and ritual, and prophesies doom unless there is a change of heart. This is the time also of the prophets Zephaniah, Nahum and Habakkuk.

616   Traditional date for the beginning of the Etruscan Tarquins as kings of Rome, the first being Tarquinius Priscus.

615   The Medes under their king Cyaxares, having got the upper hand of the Scythians, now appear on the borders of Assyria.

614   Nabopolasser of Babylon and Cyaxares the Mede sign a treaty, and probably bind it with the marriage of their children.

613   In the usual summer campaign of this year the Assyrian army holds its own against the combined Medes and Babylonians.

612   The Medes persuade the Scythians to join in with them and the Babylonians. Confronted by this triple alliance, Nineveh, after a siege of three months, falls and the Assyrian king perishes in the burning capital. A general, calling himself Assuruballit, assumes the kingship and takes up a new stand at Harran.

611   His allies the Medes temporarily retiring, Nabopolasser harries the country round Harran but cannot take the fortress itself. The Phoenician coastal cities (see 668) regain some measure of independence.

610   Necho II follows Psammeticus I as Pharaoh.

609   The Assyrian garrison at Harran, with an Egyptian contingent to support it, is threatened by a renewed coalition of Babylonians and Medes. The garrison flees, leaving Harran undefended.

608   The Assyrians under Ashuruballit try to recapture Harran, but fail and fade out of the records. The victorious Medes turn upon their temporary ally the Scythians, who retire to their own lands and never again penetrate into the lands of the Fertile Crescent.

      Pharaoh Necho II, seeing the chance to fill the vacuum left by Assyria, and to re-assert Egypt's traditional sway over Syria, sends his full army north. King Josiah of Judah, still considering himself Assyria's vassal, meets the Egyptians single-handed at Megiddo and is slain. (It is this battle of Megiddo that enters Jewish conscience sufficiently to give its name to the prophetic world-battle of Revelations, "Har" or the Mountain of "Megiddo", Armageddon.)

605   The Egyptians are finally defeated near Carchemish, the Babylonian army being under the command of the Crown Prince Nebuchadnezzar. Later in the year (September) Nebuchadnezzar succeeds to the throne.

604/02   The people and towns of the old Assyrian empire acknowledge Nebuchadnezzar, the Chaldean of Babylon, as their new master. Only Phoenician Askelon, and Jehoiakim, king of Judah, are exceptions. Askelon is destroyed. Jehoiakim relies on the strength of Egypt, against the advice of Jeremiah, the prophet.

601   Egypt for a while is able to withstand the might of Nebuchadnezzar's army, throwing it back from her borders.

C. Religion and Philosophy (continued)

608   Pharaoh Necho II sends a thank-offering for his victory at Megiddo to the shrine of Apollo at Miletus (having made use of Ionian mercenaries).

D. The Arts

In Egypt in this half century there is, in sculptures, reliefs, etc., a nostalgic copying of Old Kingdom styles.

E. Literature

648   Archilochus of Paros (see B) flourishes, one of the earliest of the Greek lyric poets, who come from the islands and the Asia Minor coast towns more often than the mainland. One of his lampoons, against the family which would not let him marry their daughter, is said to have led to suicides in the family. Another makes fun of Spartan heroics.

626   Jeremiah, before the Captivity (see 597), warns his countrymen in an invective full of phrases that have become part of the legacy of European literature. *Lamentations* as well as the Book of *Jeremiah* is attributed to him.

625   Alcman, the Spartan lyric poet, *floruit*. Part of his *Parthenion*, or choir-song for maidens, survives.

      About this time also lives another poet and musician, Arion, a singer to the lyre who is said to have converted the Dionysiac *dithyramb* into a trained chorus. From this time probably dates the Greek system of *modes*, 8-note scales.

612   The prophet Nahum rejoices at the fall of the "bloody city" of Nineveh.

F. Births and Deaths

639   Solon b. (—559*c*.).

636   Thales b. (—546*c*.).

631   Assur-bani-pal d.

630   Most probable date for the birth of Zoroaster: perhaps 10 years later and possibly at 800 or even 1000 B.C.

610   Psammetichus I d.

608   Josiah d. (37).

605   Nabopolasser d.

650   The Etruscans, having established themselves in northern Italy, seek to infiltrate into the Campania district; Rome, on the Tiber, to an extent bars their way.

A second wave of Greek colonization creates city-states around the Black Sea, Megara and Miletus being the chief mother-cities.

The Halstatt people (see 1000) learn to make use of iron and blossom forth as the great Celtic, Iron Age, culture of northern Europe. The burials of their chiefs become grand affairs, the dead man in his four-wheeled chariot with his weapons around him. Trade and influence spread to them up the Rhone and the Danube; swords are of iron or iron models copied in bronze.

600   Nebuchadnezzar, having over-reached himself in Egypt, retires to recuperate and re-equip his army.

Massilia (Marseilles) is founded by the Phoenicians of Asia Minor.

Athens fights Lesbos (Mytilene) for Sigeum, a promontory controlling the Hellespont (see A).

599   Syracuse, once a "colony" or city-state founded from the mainland (see 745) itself founds another city in Sicily, Camarina.

Nebuchadnezzar campaigns again and defeats the nomad Arabs of Syria.

598   King Jehoiakim of Judah, ignoring the warnings of Jeremiah, allies himself with Egypt. He is removed from the throne by Nebuchadnezzar and Jehoiachin placed in his stead. The latter proving not much more satisfactory, Nebuchadnezzar, in the autumn, advances on Jerusalem, destroying Lachish on the way.

597   In January Jerusalem is besieged, and in March it falls. One of Jehoiakim's sons, renamed Zedekiah, is set on the throne of a city depleted but not destroyed, while Jehoiachin and the leading men and craftsmen are deported into Babylonia. Daniel is a child amongst them.

596   Sparta, by now the most powerful Greek city, arbitrates on the long dispute and war between Athens and Megara over the ownership of the island of Salamis. Athens is awarded the prize.

595   Nebuchadnezzar puts down a palace revolt.

In Egypt Necho II is succeeded by Psammeticus II, who however continues a defensive policy, except for a foray into Nubia.

595   In Athens, Solon, increasing in popularity, advocates the first "sacred" war, to protect the pilgrims to the shrine of Apollo at Delphi against the Phocians (in whose territory Delphi lies).

594   Solon is called upon to mediate between contending factions in Athens and is appointed archon with unlimited powers. He uses them with great effect, providing Athens virtually with a set of laws and a constitution (see A).

593   Solon, so that Athens may settle down to obey his laws undisturbed, leaves to go on his travels. (On these he is said by Herodotus, to have met and given philosophic advice to King Croesus of Lydia.)

592/1   Athens, left without Solon, does try to regard his laws, but tends nevertheless towards the sort of unrest that leads to the appearance of a "tyrant".

Carthage (founded, traditionally from Tyre, some 200 years earlier) is increasing in prosperity and is beginning to occupy Sicily.

In Greece the future great rivals Sparta and Athens are acquiring their characteristic roles, the one as the closed military power of the Peloponnese, the other as the politically free (but no less aggressive) trading and maritime city-state.

In northern India, history begins to emerge with some certainty. Tribes are settling down into either monarchies or republics, the former concentrated in the Ganges plain and the latter in the foothills of the Himalayas and the Punjab. The monarchy of Magadha (N.W. of modern Calcutta) is gradually coming to the fore.

China begins a period of great literary and philosophic activity, which continues until almost the end of the Chou Dynasty.

A. Politics, Law and Economics

600   The Athenians' first overseas venture, the capture of Sigeum (see opposite) is for trading reasons, and in rivalry with her near neighbour Megara (which city is soon left behind in the great Greek rivalry).

595   In the Sacred War to protect the pilgrims to the shrine of Apollo, help is sought for and given by an early form of Greek co-operation, the Amphictyonic League of Anthela (near to the pass of Thermopylae.) Members agree not to destroy each other's cities or cut off their water supply (and see C).

594   In Athens Solon puts a stop to slavery for unpaid debt and makes a compulsory reduction in all debts. Other results of Solon's year of office are:—
the first steps in democracy by the opening of the Assembly to the lowest classes;
the codification of the law;
the democratization of the law courts and the avoidance of professionalism by a system of appointment to office by drawing of lots amongst all citizens.

B. Science and Discovery

Chaldean or Neo-Babylonian science shows considerable progress beyond that of Hammurabi's time (see 1750 B) or even of Assyrian (668 B). In medicine, though much is a matter of priestly incantation, surgeons not only perform operations but have some idea of the prognosis of a disease; they have also wisely—in view of earlier legal penalties—formed themselves into a professional body. Though largely used for astrological purposes, Chaldean astronomy becomes famous: the sky is divided into zones, and the signs of the Zodiac, as well as the names of many constellations, are now invented, and remain. So too are invented and remain the 7-day week and the 24-hour day. Chaldean mathematics invents a system partly decimal and partly sexagesimal; it also for the first time invents the "position concept", the magnitude of a numerical symbol depending on its relative position as written: this is something which is lost and does not reappear until after the end of the classical world of Greece and Rome.

In this half-century the Greeks probably invented the trireme, a ship with three banks of oars.

C. Religion and Philosophy

600   The commonest sacrifice amongst the people of the emerging Indian kingdoms (see opposite) is of the horse, a special horse being permitted to wander at will, the king claiming all the territory over which it wanders.
The Roman Forum ceases to be used as a cemetery.

597   Jeremiah, in his vision of the good and bad basket of figs, puts his faith in the Jews deported to Babylon rather than in those left behind.

595   The Greek Sacred War (see opposite and A) brings into lasting fame Cleisthenes of Sicyon. Marrying his daughter into the aristocratic Athenian family of the Alcmaeonidae, he has as his grandson a more famous Cleisthenes (see 510 A).

D. The Arts

Nebuchadnezzar finds time to rebuild to its most famous and splendid state the city of Babylon, giving it its terraced or "hanging" gardens. Chariots can pass each other along the walls, and its towers are of bronze. Bas reliefs of bulls and dragons are overlaid with bright enamels. The Euphrates is bridged within the city, the Queen, Nitocris, being, according to Herodotus, responsible for this feat.

This is the period when the influence of Near Eastern motifs and subjects is most felt in Greek art, especially in Corinth.

Corinthian pottery is increasing in skill and is being exported (but see 510 A).

594 Solon encourages foreign craftsmen to settle in Athens.

E. Literature

600 At Mytilene on the island of Lesbos there flourish the lyric poets Sappho and Alcaeus.

600 In China appears *The Book of Odes* or *Of Poetry*, an anthology going right back to Shang times, with the principal theme of human love.

592 Ezekiel begins to prophesy.

F. Births and Deaths

598 Jehoiakin of Judah d.

595 Necho II, Pharaoh, d.

590 King Cyaxares of the Medes makes war on Lydia.

589 Apries (biblical Hophra) becomes Pharaoh: he is young and belligerent.

589/8 There are two years in Athens with no archon—i.e. "anarchy".

588 Zedekiah rebels and the Babylonian army besieges Jerusalem again.
Apries sends a naval expedition up the coast, and for a couple of years gains control of the Phoenician coastal towns.

587 Apries advances overland into Palestine and Nebuchadnezzar breaks off the siege of Jerusalem to meet the threat. Apries ignominiously retires, proving Egypt to be once more a broken reed so far as the Jews are concerned.

586 The siege of Jerusalem is renewed (see 597 A), and the city falls, this time to be completely destroyed. Zedekiah flees but is captured at Jericho, and has to witness the death of his sons before being blinded. This is the end of Judah as a nation, 136 years after the end of Israel. With the captivity in Babylon there enter "the Jews".
Nebuchadnezzar also lays siege to Tyre, a desultory affair that lasts 13 years. Sidon however falls to him.

585 With the help of Babylon, peace is sealed between the Medes and Lydia by a royal marriage (and see B).

584/3 In Athens the archon Damasias attempts to convert his office into a tyranny but after 2 years fails.

581 Cyrus, later to be the founder of the Persian Empire, and known as Cyrus the Elder, is born.

To this decade may be assigned the deeds and successes of Tarquinius Priscus, who traditionally reigns from 616 to 578 B.C. and who does much to make Rome powerful and prosperous, quelling the Sabines and other Latin tribes.

A. Politics, Law and Ecomonics

582 Strengthened by its management by the Amphictyonic League (see 595 A) the Delphic Oracle grows in importance and security. In this year there begins at Delphi the four-yearly holding of the Pythian Games. Cleisthenes of Sicyon the first to win the chariot race—something to give him increased political fame as well as athletic.

B. Science and Discovery

590 The welding of iron is, according to Herodotus, invented about this time, the king of Lydia (father of Croesus) presenting a welded salver to Delphi.

Rome under Tarquinius Priscus increases its buildings and lays down its drainage system.

585 An eclipse of the sun (probably on May 28th) sees a drawn battle and the end of the war between Lydia and the Medes.

C. Religion and Philosophy

590 At this date Zoroaster—assuming his birth to be at 630 B.C.—converts a King Hystaspes (not necessarily the father of Darius). Essentially, Zoroaster reforms rather than invents the Persian religion, converting a form of polytheism, that is not unlike the Indian Vedic form, to the worship of a single god, the "Wise Lord" or Ahura Mazda.

585 Thales of Miletus *fl.*, pioneer of Greek rational thinking. He is said to have predicted the eclipse of this year (see B).

D. The Arts

590 The Etruscan kings, great builders, introduce the use of the arch into Roman architecture.

E. Literature

The Greek alphabet is spreading to the Etruscan and Latin tribes of Italy.

589 Greek mercenaries, fighting for Psammeticus II, leave an inscription behind on the leg of the statues of Rameses II at Abu Simbel.

581 According to the legend, repeated by Herodotus, Cyrus (see opposite) is the scion of a noble Persian family and of the daughter of King Astyages of the Medes. There is also the familiar legend that a prophecy of greatness puts his life in danger but that he is saved and reared by a peasant.

F. Births and Deaths

581 Cyrus the Elder of Persia b. (−530).

580 Greeks found the city of Acragas (Agrigentum) in Sicily. At about the same time other Greeks (Dorians, some from Rhodes Is, under an adventurer called Pentathlus) endeavour to oust the Carthaginians from their N.W. corner of the island.

578 Servius Tullius becomes king of Rome (and see A and B).

575 Alyattes, king of Lydia, unmolested by the Medes, experiences a prosperous reign; he ends a long war with the Ionian cities, Miletus in particular, in which city he builds two temples to Athena.

573 Tyre submits to Nebuchadnezzar, after its 13 year siege.

571 Solon, having returned to Athens from his travel, stirs up enthusiasm for a final effort to win Salamis.

Little is known of the last twenty years of Nebuchadnezzar's reign; the story that he goes mad is confined to the Bible; his own inscriptions however refer to a four-year suspension of interest in public affairs.

Similarly there has survived no contemporary account of the Jewish captivity in Babylon (but see E on Ezekiel). The Book of Daniel, written about 165 B.C., tells of the deeds of that hero and there is no reason to doubt his historicity.

In Athens regional rivalry exists: "Men of the Plain": the "Men of the Coast".

A. Politics, Law and Economics

578   Servius Tullius, reigning by tradition for 43 years, organizes Rome as a soldier-state, dividing all citizens into "classes" according to their material worth and basing on this not only taxation but their rôle in the Army, those who can afford so to equip themselves being in the cavalry, i.e. knights.

B. Science and Discovery

578   Servius Tullius proceeds during his reign to fortify Rome with its first wall (or bank and ditch).

C. Religion and Philosophy

572   Control of the Olympian festival passes to the Elians. The games and festival are assuming an importance in the Greek world.

D. The Arts

580   A statue of a pair of twins is made and signed by "Medes", presumably Polymedes of Argos, and set up at Delphi: it owes something to Egyptian tradition but is a step towards the freedom and naturalness of the best classic Greek statuary.

E. Literature

Ezekiel continues his prophesying in captivity, seeing in Nebuchadnezzar the divine instrument of chastisement but making nevertheless promises of restoration.

F. Births and Deaths

578   Tarquinius Priscus d.

570   Pharaoh Apries seeks to help the Libyans to destroy the Greek city of Cyrene (see 630) but fails and loses his throne. Amasis, a man of the people, succeeds, after a short civil war. Amasis increases the prosperity of Egypt, marries a Cyrenean, earns the title of a phil-Hellene, and develops the Delta town of Naucratis.

570   Athens finally succeeds in winning the island of Salamis from Megara, the young Pisistratus gaining fame by being on the expedition.
Phalaris becomes tyrant of the Greek city of Acragas in Sicily and is reputed to have gained control, by cruel methods, of most of the island.

568   Amasis has a skirmish with Babylonian forces. However, neither Nebuchadnezzar nor his successors seem to have seriously contemplated a full-scale conquest of Egypt.

565   Nebuchadnezzar builds a defensive wall north of Babylon, presumably against his one-time ally, the Medes.

562   Nebuchadnezzar dies and is succeeded by Amelmarduk, who is said to have ruled without law or restraint. He shows mercy however to King Jehoiachin of Judah by releasing him from prison and having him to dine at the king's own table.

561   In Athens Pisistratus earns for himself a reputation and a bodyguard (see A).

A. Politics, Law and Economics

570   Naucratis (see opposite) becomes a thriving port, almost wholly Greek.
First Greek coinage is minted at Aegina by c. 570.

561   Pisistratus, hero of the victory over Megara at Salamis, takes his first step to power
by a demagogic ruse, showing his wounds to all at the Agora and saying they are
inflicted by his enemies and the enemies of the people.

B. Science and Discovery

570   Anaximander is credited with having produced the first map (and see 500 B).

C. Religion and Philosophy

570   Anaximander, philosopher of Miletus *fl.* (and see B). He continues Thales' speculation as to the fundamental reality and speaks of the four elements, earth, air, fire
and water, emanating from some one thing more fundamental.

566   The festival of the Panathenaea (as depicted on the Parthenon frieze) is said to have
been held for the first time.

E. Literature

Aesop, a freed slave of Samos, *fl.* He may have left nothing in writing but he leaves
behind a reputation as a teller of fables; some of these are later put into verse by
Socrates.

568   Eugammon of Cyrene, poet, *fl.* In his *Telegony* he completes the Homeric story of
Odysseus.

F. Births and Deaths

570   Apries, Pharaoh d.

562   Nebuchadnezzar d.

560 Pisistratus becomes Tyrant of Athens.
Croesus becomes king of Lydia and embarks upon a policy of expansion, until his sway extends along all the Asia Minor coast as far as the mouth of the R. Halys (but see 547).

560 A Phocaean colony is founded at Alalia (or Aleria) in Corsica.

559 Neriglissar succeeds to or possibly usurps the Babylonian throne, having won the hand of Nebuchadnezzar's daughter.
Cyrus becomes king of Anshan, a southern province of what is later to be called Persia (see below).

559/6 Under the rule of Pisistratus, Miltiades the elder founds an Athenian colony in the Thracian Chersonese, the northern shore of the Hellespont.

557 Neriglissar campaigns in Cilicia to defend this part of his empire.

556 Neriglissar dies and is succeeded by the last of the Chaldean or Neo-Babylonian kings, Nabonidus, a Syrian, Nabonidus having deposed the previous king's son, who has held the throne for less than 3 months. The Medes take the opportunity to seize and hold northern Syria and the old Assyrian fortress of Harran.
Nabonidus makes a pact, against the Medes, with Cyrus of Anshan.

556 Pisistratus is forced into exile.

555 Nabonidus invests Harran (see C).

554 Nabonidus, advancing into the Lebanon, falls ill. Belshazzar is made regent at Babylon.

554 Phalaris, the Tyrant of Acragas, is overthrown by a popular rising headed by a man called Telemachus.

553 Cyrus begins his three-year struggle against Astyages, King of the Medes. Meanwhile Nabonidus, apparently not realizing where his danger lies, marches south on an expedition against Teima, a city in the Arabian desert about 100 miles E. of Akaba. Here he stays, for as much as twenty years, intent apparently on forming a new capital city in a safe spot. Babylon is left to the care of Belshazzar.

A. Politics, Law and Economics
560 Croesus, King of Lydia, reigning for 14 years, achieves a lasting reputation for wealth: his country—as are too the Greek cities on the Asia Minor coast—is well situated for trade between East and West. The Greek cities find it worth while to pay tribute to Croesus but are living in a precarious situation.

C. Religion and Philosophy
554 Nabonidus, of Syrian origin, restores the temple of the Moon God at Harran, destroyed by the Medes. At Babylon the priests are affronted by their king's unorthodox religious predilections.

D. The Arts
553 Nabonidus, on capturing Teima (see opposite) rebuilds the city on a scale comparable to Babylon. He also restores the Ziggurat at Ur.

F. Births and Deaths
560 Siddhattha Gautama (later to become the Buddha) b. (–480c).
Amelmarduk d.

559 Solon d. (80).

556 Simonides of Ceos, poet, b. (–467).

554 Phalaris of Acragas d.

553 Zoroaster d. (77).

551 Confucius b. (–479).

550–541 B.C. Cyrus, as king of the Medes and Persians, conquers Croesus and also the Ionian cities

550 Cyrus wins the Median throne and spends the next two years in consolidating his position (as king of the combined Medes and Persians).

550/49 Pisistratus returns to Athens but is almost at once forced into exile again.

547 Cyrus, ready for expansion, crosses the Tigris and reaches the Halys, where he fights a drawn battle with King Croesus of Lydia.

546 Croesus retires to his capital, Sardis, for the winter and sends for help from the Babylonians (who are theoretically the Medes' allies) and also from Egypt and Sparta. Cyrus however follows up rapidly, and Sardis falls. Croesus is probably spared, and Herodotus tells the story of how, having earlier met Solon, he is saved from immolation by quoting the wise Greek's philosophy.

545 The Greek cities of Asia Minor (Ionian etc.) are forced to accept Persian suzerainty, being allowed however freedom to trade so long as they pay tribute. The Phocaeans however, "pioneer navigators of the Greeks", refuse to submit and remove themselves to Corsica where they reinforce the colony of Alalia or Aleria (see however 535).

541 Cyrus becomes master of Syria, by bribery and propaganda rather than fighting.

---

550 In this decade the Babylonian Empire, having been powerful for little more than half a century, seems to be quietly losing its power, with Prince Belshazzar in Babylon and King Nabonidus trying to make an important city out of Teima.
Celts begin to arrive in Ireland, and to a small extent in Scotland and England (see 480).

Rome thrives and is enlarged under Servius Tullius; the Halstatt culture spreads

A. Politics, Law and Economics

To this decade may be assigned the political successes of Rome's second Etruscan king, Servius Tullius (by tradition 578-534). He begins an alliance with his neighbours in the shape of a Latin League, and is reputed to have given a modicum of political power to the Roman Assembly of the Plebs (there already being a Senate of elders to advise him).

550 First coinage minted by Corinth and Athens.

C. Religion and Philosophy

550 Anaximenes, philosopher of Miletus, *fl.*

550 The temple of Artemis (Diana) is built at Ephesus.
Probably by this date the biblical books, Kings I and II, have been written.

542 Siddhattha Gautama, living the easy life of a minor Bengal prince, marries.

D. The Arts

550 The Halstatt skill in weapons and distinctive mode of decoration (reminiscent of Scythian) spreads through N.W. Europe.

548 The rebuilding of the sanctuary of Apollo at Delphi is begun, it having been burnt down. Most of the Greek cities contribute but chiefly the Alcmaeonidae family of Athens.

E. Literature

Theognis of Megara, elegaic poet and author of "Maxims", *fl.*

F. Births and Deaths

550 Anacreon (poet) b. (-465).

547 Anaximander d. (63).

Chaldean Babylon falls to Cyrus the Persian; the Etruscan
Tarquinius Superbus becomes the last king of Rome

540 Cyrus defeats the Bedouin sheikhs around Teima. Nabonidus is forced to leave his new capital and to face Cyrus along the protective wall that Nebuchadnezzar has built. He fails to hold it.

Pisistratus returns to Athens once more and remains Tyrant until his death.

540 Polycrates becomes tyrant of Samos, defying Persia, allying himself with Egypt, and building up a fleet of 100 ships (and see B, D and E).

539 Rebellion has broken out in Babylon, and the city is in no state to withstand a siege. The Greek account speaks of feasting, and the Bible (Daniel, Ch. V) tells of the writing on the wall. The Euphrates is partially diverted and Cyrus' army achieves an easy victory.

In October, probably the 29th, Cyrus triumphantly enters Babylon. The Persian Empire takes over from the short-lived Babylonian (and absorbs the kingdom of the Medes).

538 Cyrus occupies Jerusalem and allows all the Jews in Babylon who wish to do so to return to their native land. (And see C and E).

535 The Carthaginians, allied on this occasion with the Etruscans, defeat the Greek Phocaeans in a naval battle off their colony in Corsica, Alalia (or Aleria—see 545)—which is abandoned.

534 Traditional date for the accession of the last of Rome's Etruscan kings (and the last of all her kings) Tarquinius Superbus (the Proud or Arrogant). He begins by putting to death many senators and revoking his predecessor's concessions to the Plebs. He reigns for 24 years.

533 Cyrus crosses the Hindu Kush and receives tribute from the Indian cities of the Indus valley. According to Herodotus he there forms his twentieth satrapy of Gandhara—which is later to supply some mercenaries for the Persian war against Greece.

Cyrus the Persian begins to create the most efficient empire to date and to bring relative peace to a long-time warring Middle Eastern world.

A. Politics, Law and Economics

Pisistratus' tyranny in Athens is remarkable for its respect for law and constitutional procedure, and in its encouragement of agriculture and trade (see also C, D and E).

540   King Bimbisara rises to power in the Ganges kingdom of Magadha (see 600), controlling trade with the delta ports and building roads.

535   The Carthaginian victory of Alalia (see opposite) gives her command of the western Mediterranean and the ability to close the Straits of Gibraltar to the merchants of Tartessus (see 700), this native city now declining in prosperity. At the same time the Greeks (see 620) leave Spain.

B. Science and Discovery

Polycrates of Samos employs Eupalinus of Megara to build him an aqueduct. Pisistratus of Athens also has waterworks constructed, possibly by the same engineer.
Xenophanes (see C) observes fossil imprints and correctly interprets them.

C. Religion and Philosophy

540   Xenophanes, Greek Eleatic philosopher of Asia Minor, *fl.* He is an opponent of anthropomorphism and polytheism—"Men have made God in their own image."
Athens, under Pisistratus, takes over the Ionian religious festival on the sacred island of Delos. She also develops her Pan-athenaean festival, (see 566 C).

539   Daniel, according to the biblical account, manages to remain popular and in high office after Persia takes over from the Chaldeans in Babylon.

538   The second prophet named Isaiah (see E) sees hope for the Jews in the restoration by Cyrus.

D. The Arts

540   The Athenian black-figure pottery is at its height. Names are known of potters and painters, e.g., Exekias and his "Achilles and Ajax playing draughts".
Polycrates of Samos has a temple built to Hera on his island.
At Athens Pisistratus builds a new temple to Dionysus at the foot of the Acropolis. He also begins to build the temple of Olympian Zeus (to be finished by Hadrian), and also restores the temple of Athena Polis on the Acropolis, the sculptors working for the first time in marble.

537   At Jerusalem Zerubbabal begins the restoration of the Temple.

534   In Rome Tarquinius Superbus builds a Temple of Juno on the Capitol.

E. Literature

540   Pisistratus has Homer's *Iliad* and *Odyssey* written down. He also helps to lay the foundation of Greek tragic drama by founding the new festival of "the Great Dionysia".
Anacreon, poet, *fl.* at the court of Polycrates.

E. **Literature** (continued)

538 The writings on the second Isaiah (see E) eventually appear in the single Biblical book of Isaiah (see 733 E), chapters 40 to 55.

F. **Births and Deaths**

540 Mahavira (founder of Jainism) b.

534 Servius Tullius d.

530–521 B.C.   Athens continues under tyranny; Egypt suffers temporary
Persian invasion

530   Cyrus leads an expedition against the Massagetae (Asiatics from around the Sea of
Aral) and is killed.

529   His son Cambyses succeeds him. The Persian Empire has now been firmly established,
and this date is considered its foundation date.

529/26   Dynastic troubles result in the death of Cambyses' brother Smerdis (or Bardiya).

527   Hippias and Hipparchus, sons of Pisistratus, continue the latter's Tyranny in Athens
(and see E).

526   Pharaoh Amasis is succeeded by Psammetichus III.

525   Cambyses invades Egypt, wins the stubbornly fought battle of Pelusium, and besieges
and invests Memphis. Egypt passes into the Persian Empire under Persian kings
(the 27th Dynasty).
Polycrates of Samos fails to come to Egypt's aid. He sends a fleet to aid the Persians
but sees to it that it will not function by manning it with men who hate him. This
fleet turns back and attempts a revolution. It receives Spartan and Corinthian aid
but fails.

525/22   During his three-year stay in Egypt Cambyses meets successive failures: expeditions into the western desert and into Ethiopia fail, and his Phoenician sailors (see
A) refuse to fight against their fellow countrymen the Carthaginians. Cambyses'
ensuing anger is said to have driven him mad.

522   On his way home to quell an usurper to the throne, Cambyses dies.

522   Polycrates is lured to the mainland, captured by the Persians and crucified.

521   After dynastic trouble, Darius I becomes King of Persia. There are revolts in Babylon
and other parts of the Persian Empire.

A. Politics, Law and Economics

The Phoenician coastal towns (Sidon now taking the lead from Tyre) help to provide the Persians with both a mercantile marine and a fighting navy.

527   The cities of Magna Graecia indulge in a destructive rivalry that makes their influence in Italian history minimal. At this time Sybaris and Croton (later at war) combine to suppress Siris.

B. Science and Discovery

530   Pythagoras, of Samos, *fl*. Besides announcing his theorem about a right-angled triangle he develops a whole doctrine of numbers (see C).

C. Religion and Philosophy

530   Pythagoras of Samos is a mystic as well as a mathematician: besides insisting that the key to the universe lies in numbers, he preaches immortality and transmigration of souls. He founds a brotherhood in Croton of Magna Graecia, which however the citizens of Croton destroy.
Confucius marries and enters the service of the Duke of Lu.

530   Gautama, at the age of 30, cuts loose from his princely life and becomes an ascetic.

525   The Biblical books Chronicles I and II are probably written now.

524   Gautama, having abandoned the life of strict asceticism, sits under the famous Bo tree at Benares and has a vision of what he must teach. During the next 40 years or so he and his disciples will teach by word of mouth and he will become the Buddha.

522   Cambyses by the time of his death has acquired an evil reputation in Egypt for destruction of her temples and disregard of her religion.

521   The rebuilding of the temple at Jerusalem, having come to a stop, is resumed and completed in the next 5 years.

D. The Arts

The golden age of Athenian vase pottery is about to begin: red figures, left in the natural colour of the clay, on black. Euphronius and Euthymides are known names of artists.

529   At Pasargadae, the new capital city that Cyrus has built in Southern Persia, is erected the dead king's tomb in white marble.

524   The Sybarites build Doric temples at Paestum in Italy.

E. Literature

527   The Athenian Tyrants' court (see 540 A) becomes literary and welcomes the poets Simonides of Ceos and Anacreon of Teos.

F. **Births and Deaths**

530 Cyrus d.

527 Pisistratus d.

526 Amasis, Pharaoh, d.

525 Aeschylus b. (–456).

522 Polycrates d.

522 Cambyses d.
     Pindar b. (–448).

520   Darius puts down the revolt in Babylon.

520   Tarquinius Superbus, by guile, military victories and diplomatic marriage, raises Rome to undisputed head of the Latin League.

519   Darius has to put down a second revolt in Babylon and crushes all resistance (and see E).

514   In Athens a minor revolt led by Harmodius and Aristogiton against the sons of Pisistratus fails, Hipparchus being killed. The result is an increase in the harshness of the tyranny. (See 527)

512   To protect his empire from potential enemies beyond the Bosphorus, Darius invades Thrace (with the help of Greek conscripts from the Asia Minor cities). He crosses the Danube and at least impresses the Scythians, though the expedition is probably not such a failure as Herodotus states. Thrace and Macedonia acknowledge Persian overlordship. Miltiades the Younger, nephew of M. the Elder (see 559) is in charge of the bridge over the Danube and wishes to destroy it and so cut off the Persians.

511   The Alcmaeonidae family of Athens seek help from King Cleomenes of Sparta in getting rid of the sons of Pisistratus.
Aristagoras becomes governor of Miletus, under the Persians (and see 499).

A. Politics, Law and Economics
517 Darius visits Egypt and sets the priests and wise men to a codification of the Egyptian laws, a task which keeps them busy for 15 years.

B. Science and Discovery
515 Darius completes the canal from the Nile to the Red Sea begun by Necho II (see 610 B). He also sends Scylax (a Carian), on a voyage of discovery into the Indian Ocean and the Red Sea, establishing a sea route between India and Persia.

C. Religion and Philosophy
520 The Sibylline Books of Oracles (which remain in Roman possession until A.D. 405) are by tradition purchased by Tarquinius Superbus. The price, at first scornfully refused, is 300 pieces of gold.

517 The Chinese philosophers, Confucius and Lao Tse, are believed to have met. Lao Tse (or Tzu), teaching much as Confucius but more emotionally, writes *Tao Te Ching*, or "The Book of the World Law and its Power." He may have lived 200 years later; he may even be a mythical figure, though the teaching—Taoism—is very real.

D. The Arts
520 The tomb of the princess of Vix (on the Seine) shows great riches, which include cups and wine-mixing bowls from Greece. This exemplifies not only the riches of Celtic chiefs but their desire for beautiful things from the classic world—particuarlly if connected with wine. At Heuneberg, on the Danube, an elaborate Iron Age fort, Greek drinking vessels are similarly imported.

520 Tarquinius Superbus is reputed to have started building the Capitol of Rome, with the help of the spoils of war.

514 Statues are put up in Athens to Harmodius and Aristogiton (see opposite).

E. Literature
519 Darius sets up on the great rock-face of Behistun (on the Ecbatana-Babylon road) an account of his early successes. (The cuneiform writing used is an adaptation of the earlier Babylonian and Sumerian, and the copying of it largely enabled Sir Henry Rawlinson in the 19th century to decipher the cuneiform writing.)

F. Births and Deaths
519 Cratinus, Greek writer of comedies, b. (–422c).

514 Hipparchus d.

514 Themistocles b. (–449).

513 Parmenides b. (–440c).

510   With the help of King Cleomenes of Sparta, the sons of Pisistratus are turned out and Athenian "tyranny" ends. Athens is forced to join Sparta's Peloponnesian League. The Magna Graecia city of Croton finally defeats and destroys Sybaris.
Dorieus, brother of the King of Sparta, having helped in the war between the Magna Graecia cities of Croton and Sybaris, fights the Carthaginians in Sicily.

510   Tarquinius Superbus is banished from Rome (and see E).

507   Cleisthenes (of the Alcmaeonidae family and grandson of Cleisthenes of Sicyon, see 595 C) rises to power in Athens as a champion of Solon's ideas (see A). Cleomenes of Sparta attempts to interfere but has to retire.

506   Cleomenes, to avenge his humiliation of the previous year, organizes a full-scale Peloponnesian invasion of Attica. Corinth cries off however and the whole thing dies. Athens meanwhile demonstrates her new-found power by defeats of the Boeotians and Chalcidians.

504   The exiled King of Rome, Tarquinius Superbus, having failed to win back his throne with the help of the people ov Veii, allies himself with Lars Porsena, king of Clusium (but see 505 A).

501   Aristagoras of Miletus fails in an attack on Naxos on Persia's behalf—and fears the consequences (see 499).

Rome has become a republic. She is experiencing a decade which will never be forgotten (see E), and which will determine her never again to have a king—see 44.

A. Politics, Law and Economics

510   Persia introduces a bimetallic system of coinage.

Athens is increasing her export of pottery (see 530 D) at the expense of Corinth.

509   After the expulsion of King Tarquinius Superbus (but before his final defeat) the Romans set about framing for themselves a republican constitution. The system of twin consulate is now established, also the twin office of quaestors (financial and legal officers). It is the landed aristocracy who have the power, with their Senate of much greater importance than the people's Assembly. The Plebs (all those other than aristocratic families, including the growing commercial class) now begin their long struggle for power (sometimes known as the Struggle of the Orders).

507   The legal and constitutional reforms, put through in Athens by Cleisthenes, ensure for that city her particular form of democracy. The four ancient tribes are abolished and replaced by ten new ones, and all citizens are enfranchised with a personal vote in the popular Assembly.

505   Tarquinius Superbus issues an edict denying citizens the use of iron weapons.

501   Confucius is made Governor of the city of Chungtu and institutes practical reforms.

B. Science and Discovery

Under Darius, the Persians develop a system of roads, the first empire-builders to pay proper attention to this necessity. In particular is built the great Royal Road running from Sardis in Asia Minor to Susa, north of the Persian Gulf, a distance of over 1500 miles and considered a journey of three months for a man on foot. It helps to widen the Greek idea of geography, and on their maps it takes on something of the fundamental importance of our Equator.

C. Religion and Philosophy

510   In the Ganges area, Mahavira, aged about 30, takes up the ascetic life and founds the religious sect of the Jainites.

D. The Arts

509   The Jupiter Optimus Maximus temple is erected on the Roman Capitol.

E. Literature

510/504 By tradition, the prime cause of the expulsion from Rome of King Tarquinius Superbus is the misconduct of his son: the story of Lucretia who, dishonoured, commits suicide and makes her menfolk vow vengeance. Many stories also grow up of the struggle to prevent the hated tyrant's return, including the fight on the bridge into Rome between Lars Porsena and Horatius Cocles, and the attempt and failure of Mucius to kill Lars Porsena and the former's holding of his right hand in the fire to show to his captors that he can endure torture—thus giving birth to his family name, Scaevola or the left-handed.

Revolt of the Ionian cities against Persia; the Maya
civilization begins to form

499   Aristagoras, governor of Miletus (see 511 and 501) induces the Ionian cities of Asia
Minor to revolt against Persia; the pro-Persian tyrant of Mytilene being stoned to
death. Aristagoras seeks help from Cleomenes, King of Sparta (see G), but the
Spartans are too insular to respond.

498   Athens and Eretria (in Euboea) respond to the Ionian plea for help against Persia and
send troops.

498/7   The combined Ionian and mainland Greeks attack Sardis, which is burnt. Retreating to the coast they are met by a Persian force and defeated. Aristagoras flees, and
dies.

496   The Roman king, Tarquinius Superbus, and his ally Lars Porsena, are finally defeated
at the battle of Lake Regillus, near Clusium.

496/3   Thracians and Scythians drive Miltiades the Younger (see 512) from the Chersonese.
He flees to Athens.
Cyprus throws off Persian domination, but a Phoenician-manned Persian fleet re-
stores it.

494   The Ionian revolt against Persia ends with the Persian capture of Miletus and the
defeat of the Greek fleet at the battle of Lade.

493   In the Ganges kingdom of Magadha, King Bimbisara is murdered by his son Aja-
tashatru, who comes to the throne, fortifies his capital city, and increases his
kingdom by force of arms.

492   The Persians under their general Mardonius subdue Thrace and Macedonia, losing
however part of their fleet on the promontory of Mount Athos (Chalcidice).
In Sicily the Greek cities are warring amongst themselves: Syracuse is saved from
being destroyed (by neighbouring Gela) by the intervention of Corinth.

491   Gelon becomes Tyrant of Gela (and see 485).

Darius the Great, King of Persia, never having forgiven the mainland Greeks for
interfering in Asia Minor, sends them a demand for earth and water, the symbols of
submission. Some city-states submit, including Aegina (see A); but Athens and
Sparta maltreat his emissaries, the latter symbolically pushing the Persian herald
down a well.
In this century the Amer-Indians in central America are beginning what is known as
their "formative" period. This lasts for some 8 centuries and develops into the
distinctive culture of the Mayas with in particular its astronomical skills. The climate
has however left little in the way of archaeological evidence behind.
Rome and her Latin allies, throughout the century now to begin, are warring on the
one hand with the Etruscans in the north and on the other with the native mountain
tribes to the south, the Aequi and the Volscians in particular.
Persian influence on her Indus valley province (Gandhara, see 533) is, until the coming
of Alexander, considerable—generally in the ways of religion, and particularly in
the way of coinage. The capital city, Takshashila, becomes known to the Greeks, as
Taxila.

A. Politics, Law and Economics

Roman trade—not much a concern of the landed aristocracy—declines at this time and remains small for the best part of 200 years.

496 Carthage and Rome make a treaty wherein Roman ships undertake not to trade westwards of Carthage and the Carthaginians undertake not to interfere on Latin soil.

494 At the end of a military campaign, the Plebs element in the Roman army retires to the Sacred Mount outside Rome—the so-called "Secession of the Plebs"—and threatens to found a new city. It succeeds in establishing the Tribunate, an office specifically created for its protection.

493 Rome and the Latin League recognize commercial contracts binding throughout their cities. Rome abandons her claim to hegemony over the League.
Themistocles (see 482) becomes Archon of Athens and develops the Piraeus.

491 Aegina fears to lose her Pontic trade and so submits to Persia.

B. Science and Discovery

500 Sushruta, a professor of medicine at Benares, writes in Sanskrit a system of diagnosis and surgery.
Hecataeus of Miletus *fl.* He is a traveller and geographer and writes a text for the map of Anaximander (see 570 B). He advises the Greeks not to rebel against Persia.
The use of iron begins in China; bronze is, however, still the standard metal for weapons in the early Han period, i.e. around 200 B.C.

499 King Cleomenes of Sparta (see opposite) is said to have been shown a map by Aristagoras, but not to have been impressed.

C. Religion and Philosophy

500 Heraclitus, philosopher of Ephesus, *fl.*, his philosophy centring on the proposition "Everything flows".

497 Confucius sets out on his travels as a wandering teacher, moving from court to court amongst the many rulers in a now divided China.

494 The Persians burn down the temple of Apollo at Didyma, a deed out of keeping with their usual religious tolerance.

D. The Arts

Etruscan art flourishes, especially in bronze and pottery, and in monuments on sarcophagi, e.g. as found at Cerveteri.
At Persepolis the structural-columned architecture of the Persians reaches its perfection. Later Persian kings also build palaces here (see 330 D).

E. Literature

500 In India there begin to be compiled the epic poem, the *Mahahharata* and the popular collection of cosmic stories, the *Puranas*, Both gradually grow, over the best part of the next thousand years.

Around the beginning of this century Darius has begun the building of the splendid new capital of the Persians Empire. Known to the Persians as Parsae, and to the Greeks as Persepolis, it lies some 150 miles N.W. of Cyrus's Pasargadae. At the beginning of this century the Carthaginians oust the Greeks from Malta.

E. **Literature** (continued)

499 Aeschylus, aged 25, competes for the first time for the Athenian Tragedy prize but is unsuccessful.

498 First Pindaric ode.

494 The Athenians, profoundly affected by the crushing of the Ionian revolt, fine their poet Phrynichus 1000 drachmae for reminding them of the tragedy in a play of his.

F. **Births and Deaths**

500 Anaxagoras, the Ionian philosopher, b. (-428c).

497 Aristagoras d.

495 Sophocles b. (-406).

493 Bimbisara d.

490   Darius sends his expedition, under Artaphernes and Datis the Mede, across the Aegean, for the purpose of being avenged on the Athenians and Eretrians (see 498). Hippias, the aged ex-tyrant of Athens (see 527) is aboard, hoping to be restored. The city of Eretria is destroyed and Athens is in great danger of the same fate. On Hippias' advice the Persians land in the Bay of Marathon, where they meet the Athenians supported by the Plataeans. Philippides (or Pheidippides) the runner, is sent for help to Sparta, which however arrives too late (see C.)
(late summer). Under the skilful generalship of Miltiades (see 496) the Greeks defeat the Persians at the battle of Marathon. The Persians retire to their ships and sail round to Athens, but decide to return home.

489   Miltiades, after his great victory, leads a naval expedition to Paros, it is said to pay off a private score. He is unsuccessful, and on his return is fined and put in prison—where he dies of wounds received at Paros. His son Cimon is imprisoned, but the fine is finally paid.

488   Theron becomes Tyrant of Acragas in Sicily.

487   Aegina and Athens, for a long time rivals, are at war.

486   Encouraged by the news of Marathon, the Egyptians revolt against Persian rule.

485   Gelon of Gela becomes Tyrant of Syracuse.

485/3   Xerxes succeeds to the Persian throne. He first quells an Egyptian revolt, ruling more harshly and less beneficently than has his father.

483   Xerxes prepares for his great expedition to crush the Greeks, the plan being for a land army to cross the Bosphorus and to skirt round the Thracian and Macedonian coast, with a fleet always nearby in support. To avoid another catastrophe to his fleet (see 492) he has a canal cut through the promontory of Mt. Athos.

482   Themistocles (who has fought at Marathon) secures the ostracism of his opponents, including Aristides "the Just", (who had also fought there) and becomes the political leader of Athens. (And see A).

481   Xerxes arrives at Sardis and begins to build up his great army and navy of invasion. Egypt contributes 481 ships.
There is a Greek defensive congress at Isthmus.

481   In China (see 771) central control further deteriorates: the "period of the Warring States" begins and lasts until 221 B.C.

A. Politics, Law and Economics

487   The archonship at Athens is made an appointment by lot from all the citizens.

483   Themistocles persuades the Athenians to devote the wealth from the new-found silver mines at Mount Laurium to the creation of a fleet.

482   In Athens great use is made at this time of expulsion by majority vote, i.e., ostracism (see opposite).

B. Science and Discovery

490   Hanno, the Carthaginian navigator, makes his famous voyage about this time, though the date is very uncertain and may have been 50 years earlier. The *Periplus* is a Greek translation of what is believed to be his own account, which he had posted up in the temple of Moloch. His intention is to found colonies, and 60 ships and 30,000 people are said to have set out. The armada sails through the Pillars of Hercules and round the coast of Africa, probably reaching beyond Cape Verde and to within 12 degrees of the Equator; it meets "troglodytes" and gorillas.

C. Religion and Philosophy

490   The Spartan delay in sending troops to Marathon is caused by a religious scruple: they must wait until the moon is full. After the battle stories abound that the god Pan caused the panic of the Persians.

490   The Chinese philosopher Mo-ti *fl.*, his teaching being one of love and pacifism.

483   Confucius returns from his wanderings (see 497 C) and devotes himself to the compilation of his Dialogues. He also writes appendices to the "Book of Changes" (see 1200 E).

D. The Arts

490   Nine bronze bells are cast and interred in a tomb in the city of Shou-hsien.
At Aegina in this decade a Doric temple is built (and survives).

489   Out of the spoils from the battle of Marathon the Athenians build a "treasure-house" at Delphi.

E. Literature

486   Comedy becomes part of the City Dionysia (religious festival) at Athens.

484   Aeschylus wins the Athenian Tragedy prize for the first time.

F. Births and Deaths

490   Phidias b. (-432). Pericles b. (-429).

F.   **Births and Deaths** (continued)

490   Hippias d.

489   Cleomenes of Sparta d.
      Miltiades d.

485   Darius I d.

484   Herodotus b. (–424).

480–471 B.C.   Persia's second invasion of Greece; Thermopylae, Salamis and Plataea

480   (Spring) Xerxes watches his huge and polyglot army across the Hellespont.
(August) Under the Spartan king, Leonidas, the Greeks—mostly from the Peloponnese and including a small contingent from Mycenae—await the Persian land force at the pass of Thermopylae. Xerxes, after waiting in vain for the Greeks to retire, attacks. Finally the Greeks are outflanked through treachery, and the Spartans under Leonidas die to a man.
(Sept.) The Persians are checked but Athens is invested and burnt. In the Bay of Salamis Themistocles—with the help of Aristides (returned from ostracism)—tricks the Persian admiral, and the Persian fleet is destroyed by the Athenian; Xerxes watches from the land. The Persian army retires to winter in Thessaly.
The Greek city of Himera in Sicily, in its quarrel with Acragas, enlists Carthaginian help. (See A).

479   Xerxes having left the war to his general, Mardonius, the Persians are defeated at the battle of Plataea. The Greeks are under the command of Pausanias, nephew of King Leonidas of Sparta, with the Athenian contingent under a repatriated Aristides. At sea the Persians are defeated at the battle of Mycale, off the Asia Minor coast. The Ionian cities begin to be rescued from Persian domination.

477   At a battle on the Cremera river the Romans are defeated by the Etruscans—whose power is nevertheless on the wane (see 474 below).

477/6   Pausanias captures Byzantium. Dazzled by success, he aims to become tyrant of all Greece, with *Persian* help.

476   Cimon of Athens now released from prison and gaining in power at the expense of Themistocles, ousts Pausanias and the Spartans, from the area of the Bosphorus. The Spartans, hearing that Pausanias is intriguing with the Persians, recall him. (And see 470 C).

476/71   Under the leadership of Cimon the Confederacy of Delos (see C) continues to fight the Persians and to release the Ionian cities from her domination.

474   Cimon clears the island of Scyros of pirates (and see C).
Hieron, succeeding Gelon as Tyrant of Syracuse, defeats the Etruscans in their efforts to win the Greek city of Cyme in Italy: this may be said to mark the end of Etruscan power.

471   Themistocles, suspected of peculation by the ungrateful Athenians, is ostracized.

---

480   Celts of the Halstatt culture, who have been infiltrating into the island for half a century or so, begin to arrive in Britain in quantity. This is the main Celtic immigration, greatly augmenting and changing the balance of Britain's population. It stems from the Low Countries and northern France, and spreads from S. and E. England well into the Midlands. It is known as Britain's "Iron Age" culture. A It is the Celts' practice to build large forts on commanding ground, sometimes choosing sites on which have been earlier causewayed camps (see 4000); so far these have only one line of earth fortification round them. The Celts tend to farm only on the more easily drained land, but they are good farmers—as is shown at Little Woodbury in Wiltshire. They store their grain in pits, lined with straw, carefully lidded and frequently renewed.

A. Politics, Law and Economics

480   In a shrewd political move Xerxes encourages the Carthaginians to attack the Greeks in Sicily. Under the first of her military leaders to be named Hamilcar, Carthage sends across a large army. With the help of Gelon, tyrant of Syracuse, and Theron of Acragas, the Carthaginians are defeated (see C) at the battle of Himera.

478   Athens is refortified as well as rebuilt after the Persian destruction, in spite of Spartan opposition.

478/7   Sparta having failed in leadership (see 477), there is formed under the leadership of Cimon of Athens the Confederacy of Delos (and see C), an alliance of Greek maritime cities around the Aegean. The contribution of each member, whether in ships or money, is carefully assessed by Aristides.

B. Science and Discovery

480   Sataspes, commanded by Xerxes to circumnavigate Africa, gets only a little way beyond the Pillars of Hercules.

480   Xerxes's engineers (including Egyptians) build two parallel bridges over the Hellespont for his great army to cross.
(2nd Oct.) An eclipse of the sun discourages the Peloponnesian army from following up the victory of Salamis.

475   Parmenides (see C) says the world is a sphere.

C. Religion and Philosophy

480   In India, at the death of Gautama Buddha, the monastic life increases widely, monks and nuns wandering and preaching and seeking alms. Their teaching supplements considerably such education as the brahmans provide.

480   Anaxagoras comes to live in Athens (and see 465 D).
Hamilcar (see A), failing in his sacrifice to Baal to ensure victory, is said to have immolated himself. The Greeks after their victory try unsuccessfully to stop the Carthaginian practice of sacrificing babies to Moloch.

478   Delos, seat of the worship of Apollo (as well as being a a trading centre and something of a slave emporium) is considered so holy that it is safe without having to be fortified and a fitting headquarters for the confederacy (see A) of which Athens is the head.

475   Parmenides (of Elea in Italy) fl., his philosophy being opposed to that of Heraclitus in that he stresses the idea of unchangeability.

474   Cimon, as an act of piety which is immensely popular, brings back the reputed bones of Theseus from his expedition to Scyros.

D. The Arts

478   A monument is raised at Athens to the tyrant-slayers (see 514), to replace the original one looted by the Persians.

D.   **The Arts** (continued)

475   Theron, Tyrant of Acragas, begins to build a row of temples along the city's southern wall—continued after his death.

E.   **Literature**

480   Euripides is born on the day of the battle of Salamsi.
Around the trophy raised at Salamis the young Sophocles leads the chorus of triumph.

478   The biblical story of Esther, of her marriage, to King Xerxes, and of her saving of the Jews from massacre, refers to this time when Xerxes has returned home from his Greek expedition. The historical authenticity of the story is however somewhat in doubt.

474   The *Histories* of Herodotus end their narration with this year.
Hieron of Syracuse sends a bronze helmet to Olympia in commemoration of his victory over the Etruscans (see opposite). Pindar immortalizes the victory in an ode.
The Greek poets Pindar and Bacchylides are flourishing at this time and both visit the rich court of Hieron of Syracuse. Both sing this tyrant's praises for his victories in the Olympic Games. (Pindar celebrates many winners of the Olympic Games.)

472   The earliest extant play of Aeschylus wins the Tragedy prize, the *Persae*, dealing with the Persians at the battle of Salamis. (Aeschylus has fought at Marathon and Salamis).

F.   **Births and Deaths**

480   Leonidas d.

480   Euripides b. (–406).
Protagoras b. (–411).
Gorgias, Sicilian Sophist b. (–385c).
Antiphon (orator) b. (–411).
Gautama Buddha d. (80).

479   Mardonius d.

478   Gelon d.

472   Theron d.

471   (or possibly earlier) Confucius d. (80).

471   Thucydides (historian) b. (–401c).

470 Cimon continues the war against Persia and the building up of the Delian confederacy (and the power of Athens).

469 The island of Naxos wishes to secede from the Delian Confederacy and is blockaded, a high-handed Athenian action resented by the rest of Greece.

468 Sparta, giving up dreams of empire, has to meet trouble nearer home, chiefly from Arcadia with the support of Argos. Argos regains control of Tiryns.

467/6 Cimon carries the war against Persia into Asia Minor and wins the battle of the river Eurymedon—Persia's decisive defeat, though she continues to be an emeny of the Greeks.

465 Xerxes is murdered by his uncle and the head of his bodyguard, Artabanus.

465/3 Athens defeats the fleet of the islanders of Thasos (and see A) and continues to build up her empire.

464 Artaxerxes I (called Longimanus), son of Xerxes, ascends the Persian throne.
Egypt seizes the opportunity to revolt against Persia (and see 459), the revolt being led by Inaros, a Libyan.

464/2 Sparta, though becoming increasingly anti-Athenian, is unable to help the Thasians: she is suffering at home from a severe earthquake and the ensuing revolt of her helots.

463 In Athens the democratic statesman Ephialtes and the young Pericles attempt to get the oligarchic Cimon ostracized for allegedly recieving bribes.
Themistocles, in exile, approaches Artaxerxes—cf the similar approach of the Persians by Pausanias (477). Themistocles hopes to use the Persians to help himself back into power in Athens. He fails but is given by the Persians the satrapy of Magnesia.

462 Cimon, persisting in Athenian friendship towards Sparta, sends military help against the revolting helots. He is told that his help is not wanted.
Argos, taking advantage of Spartan preoccupation, finally conquers Mycenae (which seems to have been temporarily independent of her—see 480). The town below the citadel is destroyed but not the citadel walls. The inhabitants are dispersed, some finding their way into Macedonia.

461 In Athens Ephialtes and Pericles finally procure the ostracism of Cimon, unpopular for his pro-Spartan policy which has obviously failed. Ephialtes is murdered.

A. Politics, Laws and Economics

465   The battle between the fleets of Athens and of the island of Thasos arises from rivalry over trade with the Thracian hinterland and in particular over the ownership of a gold mine.

463/1   Ephialtes, with the support of Pericles, reduces the powers of Athens' Council of the Areopagus (filled with ex-archons and so a stronghold of oligarchy) and transfers them to the people, that is to say to the Council of Five Hundred, the Assembly and the popular law courts. The office of Judge is made a paid one and is recruited by lot from a list to which every citizen can have his name added.

C. Religion and Philosophy

470   Pausanias, convicted of treason by the Spartans, flees to the local temple of Athena for sanctuary. The sanctuary is respected, but Pausanias is starved to death, his dying body being carried out of the temple so that it shall not pollute it.

470   The disciples of Confucius collect and write down his teachings: ethical rather than religious and centring round the golden rule of doing to others as one would be done by.

D. The Arts

470   At about this time is executed one of the bronze statues of winners at the games: that of the charioteer, which still stands at Delphi.

465   The teachers of Pericles are said to have been Anaxagoras the philosopher and Damon the musician.
Scenes of the battle of Marathon amongst others are painted in the "Painted Stoa" of the Athenian market place. The artist is Polygnotus of Thasos, friend of Cimon, assisted by Micon, an Athenian.

463   Polygnotus also paints murals at Delphi, two of them being later noticed by the historian and traveller, Pausanias, depicting the sack of Troy and Odysseus' visit to Hades.

E. Literature

468   At the Dionysia at Athens, (see 540 E) with Cimon as judge, Sophocles (aged 27) wins the prize for Tragedy, beating Aeschylus. The latter retires to the court of Hieron of Syracuse.

467   Aeschylus' *Seven Against Thebes*

F. Births and Deaths

470   Pausanias of Sparta d.

469   Socrates b. (−399).

F. **Births and Deaths** (continued)

468 Aristides d.

467 Hieron of Syracuse d.; Andocides (orator) b.

465 Xerxes d.

465 Anacreon, poet, d. (85).

461 Ephialtes d.

460–451 B.C.   Athens pursues an aggressive policy under Pericles;
Cincinnatus saves the Romans

460   After the ostracism of Cimon, Athens transfers her friendship from Sparta to Argos.

459   The aggressive policy of Athens, now beginning to be controlled by the highly
patriotic Pericles, is such that she has few friends, and finds herself at enmity with
the Peloponnesian city-states as a whole, including the island state of Aegina facing
her across the Saronic Gulf. In spite of this she launches on an ambitious foreign
venture, responding to a call for help from Inaros, the head of the revolt against
Persia in Egypt. This expedition penetrates to Memphis, invests the city, but remains unable to take it.

458   Ezra is sent to Jerusalem by Artaxerxes (see C).
The Romans escape disaster from the Volscians by calling Cincinnatus from his work
at the plough to command their army and take on the office of Dictator (see A).

458/6   After a great effort Athens is victorious over her Peloponnesian enemies, Aegina
being forced to become a member of the Delian Confederacy. A Spartan force,
going to the help of Boeotia in a local dispute, is nearly cut off by the Athenians on
its return (see A). Boeotia too becomes a member of the Confederacy.

456/4   The Athenians suffer a severe defeat in Egypt. Her fleet is defeated, her army
retreats across the Sinai Desert to Byblos before its remnants are rescued, and the
rebel Inaros is crucified.

454   Pericles declares that the Confederacy's treasure at Delos is not safe from the Persian
navy and has it transferred to Athens.

453   Achaea, on the southern shore of the Corinthian Gulf, is made part of the Athenian
Empire.

452/1   The warring Greek city-states are temporarily exhausted, and a 5 year truce is
arranged between Athens and the Peloponnese.

451   The Persian fleet moves to a rebellious Cyprus to restore order. Cimon, who has
returned to favour though not to power in Athens (see 457 A), plans an expedition
to help Cyprus, Pericles being favourable.

In Sicily during this decade and the next a remarkable native leader arises, Ducetius;
he founds many native cities and for a while threatens the Greek cities.

A. Politics, Law and Economics

459 Athens is tempted into her Egyptian venture (see opposite) by prospects of increased trade with that country.

458 Pericles continues Ephialtes' democratizing activities (see 461) by making the archonship a paid office and the lower class of citizens eligible for it.

458 The Romans, who in creating the office of Consul (see 509 A) have made provision for a dictatorship in an emergency, now make use of this power in appointing Cincinnatus (see opposite) to the post.

458/7 The Spartan expedition to Boeotia (see opposite) has the purpose of strengthening the city-state of Thebes against Athens.

457 On the Spartans' return from this expedition the exiled Cimon turns up in the Athenian camp, pleading to be allowed to serve his city again. This request is refused. However, at the ensuing bloody battle of Tanagra, his friends fight so well that he is taken back into favour.
Aegina, on joining the Delian Confederacy, is assessed, with Thasos, for a yearly contribution at 30 talents.

454 The Roman Plebs, suffering from very much the same economic and financial ills that Solon had earlier lifted from the suffering Athenian *polloi*, force the patricians to begin a reform and codification of the law. As a first act, a three-man commission is sent to Athens, to study that city's laws.

451 There is then set up in Rome a Board of Ten, the *Decemviri*, followed by a second board of which half the members are plebeian. These produce the twelve Tables of the Law. (But see 450 A).
An Athenian law is passed giving citizenship only to those born of Athenian parents.

B. Science and Discovery

458 The great double line of Long Wall from Athens to the Piraeus are built.

C. Religion and Philosophy

458 (or possibly sixty years later) Ezra, on being sent by Artaxerxes to Jerusalem, brings with him a further large number of Jewish exiles and also valuable gifts for the temple from both Jews and the Persian king himself. His task is the enforcement of the Jews' own laws. After fasting and prayer he and a chosen committee blacklist those guilty of mixed marriage.

D. The Arts

460/57 The Zeus temple at Olympia is built. On the metopes is shown Hercules holding up the heavens for Atlas, Athene helping him with a cushion.

E. Literature

458 Aeschylus' trilogy, the *Oresteia*, is performed; one part of it, the *Eumenides*, causes excitement because of its implied comment on the reduced role of the Areopagus court (see 463 A).

455 Euripides' first play appears, *The Daughters of Pelias*.
Ion, of Chios, poet and philosopher *fl.*: a friend of both Cimon and Sophocles.

458 Possible date for the Biblical Book of Ezra—unless written later by someone else.

F. Births and Deaths

460 Democritus b. (–361).
Hippocrates b. (–357*c*).

458 Lysias, orator, b. (–378).

456 Aeschylus d. (69).

454 Inaros of Egypt d.

450–441 B.C.   Pericles negotiates peace treaties with Persia and Sparta;
                Nehemiah goes to Jerusalem

450 The Athenian expedition to help Cyprus against the Persians is a failure, Cimon
    meeting his death there and the Cypriots remaining under Phoenician (i.e. basically
    Persian) control.

449 The Greek city-states finally make peace with Persia, the so-called Peace of Callias,
    named after the chief ambassador to the Persian court, a rich Athenian and brother-
    in-law of Cimon.

448 Pericles tries to obtain agreement from the other members of the Delian Confederacy
    for the funds collected for combatting Persia to be used to repair the damage done
    to Athens by those same Persians. He fails but perseveres with his project so to use
    the funds. The statesman (not the historian) Thucydides objects.

447 Athens loses control of Megara and Boeotia, her general Tolmides suffering defeat at
    the battle of Coronea.
    Pericles starts, in the Cheronese, a policy of *kleruchos* or "out-settlements", in fact
    a new form of colonization, poor and unemployed people being helped to emigrate.

446 Pericles, for whom things have not been going too well in foreign affairs, negotiates a
    somewhat humiliating peace treaty with Sparta and her Peloponnesian allies, ex-
    tending the 5 years truce for another 30 years. Achaea regains her independence.
    Euboea revolts from Athens.

445 Nehemiah, the Jewish cup-bearer to Artaxerxes at Susa, is given permission to return
    to Jerusalem as governor. He inspires the people of Jerusalem to enthusiasm and the
    city's walls are rebuilt in spite of active gentile opposition (and see C).

443 The attempt to build a new (and Athenian) Sybaris (see 510) having failed, Pericles
    founds the nearby colony of Thurii.

442 Thucydides, continuing his opposition to the Periclean use of the Delian funds (see
    448), is ostracized, Pericles is now unopposed and governs Athens for a further
    15 years.

By the beginning of this half century the practice of democracy in many of the Greek
city-states, especially in Athens, has created a demand for education, particularly in
the art of rhetoric. This is reflected in the names compounded of *agoras* (i.e. those
who talk or teach in the market place) and in the rise of the Sophists (see C).
Babylon, in this decade (the time of Herodotus' visit) has to bear a considerable
burden as a part of the Persian Empire. An annual levy of about 30 tons of silver is
enforced and Babylon has to provide supplies for the Persian army and court for
4 months of each year; the local satrap makes a daily collection towards his expenses
and expects to be provided with fodder for his 800 stallions and 16,000 mares,
whilst the sole taxation of four large villages goes to the upkeep of his dogs. Babylon
has also to supply 500 boys each year to be made eunuchs.

A. Politics, Law and Economics

450   The Roman *decemviri* (see 451 C) refuse to disband themselves and threaten to assume dictatorial powers. Appius Claudius, their leader, wishing to seduce Virginia, is discredited by the spectacular killing of the girl by her father to save her from a fate which he considers worse than death. The plebeian element in the Army once more goes on strike (see 494 A). Claudius commits suicide, and the attempt at dictatorship collapses.

The Athenians reduce the tribute due from their subject city-states (i.e. members of the Delian Confederacy), and each city is allowed to issue its own coinage.

449   Under the consulship of Valerius and Horatius, the Twelve Tables of the Law (see 451 A) are officially adopted.

In the Peace of Callias (see opposite) the Persian king does not stoop to make a formal treaty acknowledging the existence of the individual Greek city-states. He makes concessions however: for a century the Graeco-Persian enmity is virtually ended.

Pericles begins a great building plan and the refortification of the Piraeus and its long walls extending to Athens. This port of Athens has been growing enormously, an indication of the increasing trade and wealth of Athens; the total population of Attica has reached to possibly a quarter of a million, a very large city-state. The manufacturing industries (e.g. pottery) increase the demand for slaves, which may have comprised nearly half the total population. Increased silver coinage has helped towards a considerable inflation in the last hundred years, the price of wheat and barley having more than doubled.

Trade and industry has to a large extent migrated westwards across the Aegean, from the Ionian cities. Athenian pottery has reached Etruria and the Po valley.

445   In Rome the Lex Canuleia removes the ban on inter-marriage of the Orders, i.e. plebeian with patrician.

443   The Roman consul's task is lightened by the creation of two Censors; one of their jobs is to keep a moral eye on the rôle of Senator.

441   Sophocles' *Antigone* is significant in the development of political thought: the problem of divided loyalties, to state or to conscience.

B. Science and Discovery

445   Empedocles (see C) distinguishes the "four elements" and explains the development of the universe by the forces of attraction and repulsion.

C. Religion and Philosophy

450   Protagoras begins his career in Athens as a Sophist, commanding large fees.

448   The temple and statues that Pericles has made for the adornment of Athens (see D) have a religious intent second only to their patriotic.

448   Zeno, pupil of Parmenides, "father of didactics" *fl.* in Athens.

445   Empedocles *fl.*, philosopher, scientist (see B), physician and poet.

450 At La Tène the lake of Neuchatel becomes a site for Celtic votive offerings. These (well preserved in water) mark definite progress in Celtic art and have given their name to the iron-age culture of N.W. Europe which lasts until the time, some three and a half centuries later, of Germanic interference and then Roman conquest. (And see D).

C. Religion and Philosophy (continued)

445 Nehemiah after having the wall of Jerusalem rebuilt (see opposite) institutes a religious revival (and see 433).

D. The Arts

450 The La Tène votive offerings (see opposite), mostly weapons, show not only imports from the classical world (including Etruscan) but also a development of the distinctive Celtic art, with its accent on pattern and the love of curves rather than pictures.

The Athenian sculptor Myron makes the *discobolos*, the original of which has been lost.

448 Under Pericles, the building of the great temple of Athena on some ancient foundations on the acropolis is begun, to be dedicated 10 years later and to become known as the Parthenon. Ictinus designs it (in the Doric style), assisted by Callicrates. All work on the acropolis is supervised by Phidias. Also on the acropolis are the Propylaea and (later) the temple of Athena Nike and the Erechtheion.

E. Literature

450/45 Herodotus visits Babylon and Egypt, collecting facts and stories for his *Histories*.

448 Cratinus, one of the famous writers of Athenian comedies, *fl.* He wages literary war against Pericles, calling him "the squill-headed God Almighty".

443 Cratinus makes fun of Pericles' Sybaris venture.

441 Euripides wins his first prize for a play. Sophocles' *Antigone* is written.

F. Births and Deaths

450 Cimon d.

450 Alcibiades b. (-404). Aristophanes b. (-385c).

449 Themistocles d. (65).

448 Pindar d. (74).

447 Camillus of Rome b. (-365).

446 Timotheus (musician of Miletus) b. (-357).

444 Xenophon b. (-345c).

441 Agesilaus of Sparta b. (-360).

440–431 B.C. **The golden age of Athens continues; the Peloponnesian War begins**

440/39   Samos, an autonomous member of the Delian Confederacy, quarrels with Miletus and appeals to Athens. Pericles, having decided in favour of Miletus, sails to Samos with a fleet, overthrows its oligarchic government and instals a democratic one. Help however comes to Samos from Persia and it takes a nine-month siege to make the Samians surrender. Sparta threatens to interfere.

437   Pericles, concerned for his eastern trade, and in order to counteract a new and possibly threatening Thracian-Scythian alliance, pays an impressive visit into the Black Sea area.

436   To follow up this showing of the flag, an Athenian colony is founded at Amphipolis.

435/4   The first incident that leads to the Peloponnesian War occurs: Corinth attacks her recalcitrant colony Corcyra in a dispute concerning the latter's colony Epidamnus.

433   Nehemiah leaves Jerusalem for a while and has to correct some backsliding on his return.
Corcyra, afraid of the further warlike preparations of Corinth, appeals to Athens, who responds. At the naval battle of Sybota Athenian ships participate and the Corinthians retire.
The quarrel spreads to the Chalcidian city of Potidaea, a member of the Athenian Empire but originally a Corinthian colony.

432   The Athenians invest the city of Potidaea; Corinth appeals to Sparta. At an inter-city assembly at Sparta Athens is accused of breaking the Thirty Year Peace treaty.

431   The war is precipitated by an incident at Plataea, the only pro-Athenian city in Boeotia. A Theban raid on the city is a failure and the Plataeans, taking 180 prisoners, put them to death. Athens supports Plataea and Sparta aligns herself on the other side. Sparta enlists the help of the Greek cities of Italy and Sicily, and both sides appeal (without result) to Persia.

431, (late May).   The Spartans invade Attica. Pericles does not seriously oppose them, withdrawing the population of the country districts within the city of Athens whilst he pursues an active *naval* warfare and insures himself against danger from the island of Aegina by supplanting its Doric population with Athenians. (And see E).

431   The Romans finally defeat the Volsci, and also the Aequi at the battle of the River Algidus.

A. Politics, Law and Economics

On the walls of the Cretan town of Gortyn is incised at about this time a code of law, one of the few evidences of Doric occupation of the island. It is mainly a civil code, with a mixture of premature and developed regulations.

440 During the Samian war (see opposite) Pericles puts some restraint on free speech, i.e. on the licence of the comic drama.

439 To alleviate famine in Rome the distribution of cheap corn is said to have been tried for the first time.

435/2 In the last years of his life Pericles has political pressure put on him by attacks on his friends: Anaxagoras (see C), and his mistress Aspasia, who is accused of being a procuress. She is exonerated.

432 Pericles punishes Megara for assisting Corinth, by depriving her of her maritime trade.

B. Science and Discovery

432 Meton, Athenian astronomer, calculates accurately the comparative chronology of the solar and lunar cycles.

C. Religion and Philosophy

435 Leucippus *fl.*, promulgator of the atomic theory developed by Democritus.

434 Anaxagoras is accused of impiety and only the oratory of Pericles saves him from the death penalty; he is fined and banished.

432 Socrates fights at Potidaea as a hoplite (and saves the life of Alcibiades).

D. The Arts

437 The chryselaphantine statue of Athena (36 ft high) by Phidias is set up and the Parthenon is dedicated.

431 Phidias moves to Olympia, and carves his Zeus statue.

E. Literature

440 One of the generals sent to subdue Samos is Sophocles.

439 In his funeral oration for the Athenian dead at Samos, Pericles uses his famous phrase: "the Spring has been taken out of the year".

438 Euripides' *Alcestis.*

432 Thucydides, the historian, in describing the Assemblies held to decide on the Athenian-Corinthian dispute, draws a contrast between the Athenian and Spartan, the Ionian and Dorian, character.

E   Literature (continued)
431   Euripides' *Medea*.
       (Winter) Pericles makes his famous speech at the customary oration for the fallen
       in the year's campaigns: a statement of Athenian values and aspirations.

F.   Births and Deaths
440   Ducetius of Sicily d.

436   Isocrates b. (–338).

Athens suffers plague and other misfortunes in the
Peloponnesian War

430 The Spartans make the second of their five invasions of Attica. The Athenians have
some successes in sea raids on their enemies, and Potidaea is taken. In Athens,
however, full to bursting point with refugees, (see 431), plague breaks out (see E).
Pericles is deposed from his position as General or Strategos and fined, but is re-
appointed. He loses his two sons in the Plague and is attacked by it himself but
temporarily recovers.

429 Pericles dies. Cleon, the tanner, his opponent and a popular demagogue, succeeds to
power.
The Spartans besiege Plataea.

428 Mytilene revolts against a weakened Athens.
The Greek colony of Cumae in Italy falls to the Samnites, who begin to take control
of the Campanian plain (and see 343).

427 Plataea surrenders to Sparta, and Mytilene to Athens. The Athenians are more merici-
ful in victory than the Spartans (see A & E).
A civil war in Corcyra, in which the Athenians and Spartans interfere ineffectually,
results in a victory of the democrats over the oligarchs and a massacre of the latter.
Attica is again invaded by Sparta.

426 Athens has some naval successes under her new general Demosthenes.

425 Demosthenes with an Athenian fleet lands at Pylos and fortifies it and the neighbouring island of Sphacteria. Sparta, breaking off her invasion of Attica, sends
troops to Pylos. Cleon, taking command, wins a victory for Athens. Sparta makes
peace overtures, which Cleon persuades Athens to reject.

424 Cleon captures the Peloponnesian island of Cythera, from which to harry the Spartans.
The Athenians spread the war into Boeotia, but are defeated at the battle of Delium.
Worse defeats are suffered by them in Thrace, the Spartans having found a great
general in Brasidas. Brasidas captures the city of Amphipolis (see 436), a reverse
for which Thucydides, the future historian and the general in command, is held
responsible and banished (see E).

424 In Persia a period of palace intrigue results in the assassination of Artaxerxes I.

423 A year's truce in the Peloponnesian war is agreed.
A son of Artaxerxes I and a Babylonian concubine comes to the Persian throne as
Darius II.

422 Cleon ends the truce and resolves on the rescue of Amphipolis. It a battle outside
the city both Cleon and Brasidas are killed, but the victory goes to the Spartans.
Alcibiades takes over leadership of the pro-war party in Athens.

421 Nicias, leader of the aristocratic and peace party in Athens, arranges a treaty of peace
with Sparta and her Peloponnesian allies. Some of the allies, the Corinthians
included, consider the terms unjust and break with Sparta, making an alliance
with Argos.

The Peloponnesian war, essentially between a land power and a sea power, goes first
in favour of the sea power, Athens, and, after 424, in favour of the land power,
Sparta.

Socrates begins to teach and Thucydides to write his history; 430–421 B.C. the Athenian Assembly reverses a harsh decision

A. Politics, Law and Economics

429 The son of Pericles and Aspasia (also called Pericles) is legitimized by the Athenian Assembly.

427 The Assembly, influenced by the demagogue Cleon, votes for the destruction of the population of Mytilene and sends a ship with this order to their army commander on the spot. However, in response to the pleading of one Diodotus, the harsh decision is reversed on the next day and the order of mercy arrives just in time, only the ringleaders of Mytilenean revolt being executed.

427 On the other hand there is no mercy shown by Thebes or Sparta to the Plataeans. Each prisoner is asked, "Have you in the present war done any service to the Lacedaemonians (Spartans) or their allies" and is executed if he cannot say yes, 200 being put to death.

In an effort to blockade Sparta, in need of Sicilian corn, Athens responds to a plea for help made by the city of Leontini (and see C). Little is effected however.

In Rome the Quaestorship is opened to the Plebs.

C. Religion and Philosophy

430 Socrates—having given up his trade as a sculptor, and between his bouts of military service—begins to establish himself as teacher and general instigator of thought. He teaches in the agora, the gymnasium, etc—and not for pay as the Sophists do.

427 The leader of the deputation from Leontini (see A) is Gorgias, the sophist and rhetorician.

426/3 On the instigation of Nicias (rival of Cleon) and to commemorate the end of the plague of Athens, the island of Delos is "purified" by the removal of its inhabitants: it shall be a shrine of worship solely, with no one dying or being born thereon.

424 At the battle of Delium Socrates is said to have saved the lives of both Alcibiades and Xenophon.

D. The Arts

430/21 Polycleitus of Argos *fl.*, sculptor and architect. He is said to have been unsurpassed in making images of men, as Phidias was of gods.

430 Alcibiades makes the flute unpopular in Athens: one looks, he says, ridiculous playing it and it is the favourite instrument of the crude Boeotians.

E. Literature

430 Prodicus, Sophist, *fl.*

Thucydides (in his History, see 424 below) tells of the terrible effects of the Plague upon the Athenians, mentally and morally as well as physically.

430 Herodotus, who has been living at Thurii, publishes the last part of his History.

429 Sophocles, *Oedipus Rex*.

E. Literature (continued)

428 Euripides' *Hippolytus*.

427 Euripides, in his *Andromache*, attacks Spartan cruelty and duplicity, probably because of her treatment of Plataea (see A).

425 The book of *Esther* is written (see 475 E).

424 Thucydides, on his banishment (see opposite), travels widely and begins to write his *History*.
Diagoras of Melos ("the Atheist") *fl.* in Athens.
Aristophanes' *The Knights*.

423 Aristophanes' *The Clouds*.

422 Aristophanes' *The Wasps*.

F. Births and Deaths

430 Dionysius the Elder of Syracuse b. (–367).

429 Pericles d. (61).

428 Plato b. (–347).
Anaxagoras d. (72).

424 Artaxerxes I d.

424 Herodotus d. (60: exact date not known).

422 Cratinus, comic playwright, d.
Cleon d.
Brasidas d.

420   Athens enters into alliance with Argos (see 421), and the young and popular Alcibiades is elected "Strategos" (one of a board of ten generals).

418   Sparta invades Argolis, and Athens, breaking the peace, comes to the aid of the Argives.
      At Mantinea, in the centre of the Peloponnese, a full scale battle is fought, with as many as 10,000 troops on each side. The Spartans are the victors. Argos, impressed and changing her democracy for an oligarchy, goes over from Athens to Sparta, as do her allies. Athens is becoming isolated.

416   With the encouragement of Alcibiades the Athenians take the island of Melos. Its inhabitants are treated with great cruelty by the Athenians, an action later to be bitterly regretted.
      In Sicily the Hellenized and rich city of Segesta asks for Athenian help from the Dorian city of Selinus (with powerful Syracuse in the background). The Athenians, again with Alcibiades' encouragement and following up their previous interference in Sicily (see 427 A), prepare a large expedition.

415   The Athenian expedition to Sicily sets sail, under Nicias and Alcibiades. On arrival Alcibiades is recalled to meet charges of impiety (see C). He flees to the court of the Spartan King, Agis II.

414   Nicias lays siege to Syracuse and has an initial success outside its walls. This is not followed up however and Nicias finds himself the besieged rather than the besieger.

413   The Spartans, with strategical advice from the traitor Alcibiades, advance almost to the gates of Athens. The Athenians send a second fleet to Sicily, under the command of their general Demosthenes.
      (Sept.) At a sea and land battle outside Syracuse the Athenians are defeated. Nicias and Demosthenes are captured and put to death; most of the surviving soldiers are sent to die in the Sicilian quarries.

412   The Persians see their opportunity to play off one Greek city-state against another and to recover control of the Greek cities of Asia Minor. The Spartans sign a treaty of mutual help with the Persian satrap of Lower Asia, Tissaphernes. Alcibiades deserts the Spartans in turn, and goes to the court of Tissaphernes — whom he dissuades from helping Sparta.
      Athens' allies desert her, Chios however is besieged and punished.

411   In Athens, after an unsuccessful oligarchic revolution (see A), Thrasybulus takes control and wins a naval battle over the Spartans at Cynossema in the Hellespont. Alcibiades is taken back into favour by the Athenians.

Rome, continuing to increase her dominance in Italy, defeats the Aequi and clears the coastal plain of the Volscians.
In India a new dynasty, the Shishunaga, reigns successfully at Magadha for about half a century.

A. Politics, Law and Economics

418/7 Political intrigue in Athens results in the unexpected alliance of Alcibiades and Nicias and the ostracism of the demagogue Hyperbolus. This is the last use of ostracism.

411 In Athens a temporary oligarchic revolution takes place in an effort to exert more efficient control in the conduct of the war. The Assembly is to be reduced to 5,000, elected by a commission of a hundred men, ten from each tribe, while pay for all public offices is to be abolished. A Council of Four Hundred is set up, with some intimidation on the part of the conspirators. Its rule however is high-handed and only lasts for 3 months. Euboea revolts, and Athens is in grave danger—an opportunity which Sparta fails to take. In September the Council of 400 is deposed and the old Council of Five Hundred is re-established: the Assembly resumes its old form of a committee of all citizens.

B. Science and Discovery

420 The Gauls (see 390) invent for themselves the claymore or "great sword", double-edged and double-handled.

413 (Aug. 27th) At Syracuse the Athenian soldiers demand a fatal delay because of a lunar eclipse on the night of their attack.

C. Religion and Philosophy

In Athens the cult of Aesculapius flourishes.

420 Thrasymachus of Chalcedon, sophist and rhetorician, *fl.*

Democritus of Abdera, disciple of Leucippus, *fl.* Establishing a reputation as the cheerful philosopher, he has travelled much in pursuit of knowledge. He is a materialist and develops the Greek atomic theory—the Universe is the result of an undesigned combination of atoms falling in space.

415 On the eve of the Sicilian expedition, all the protective statues of Hermes outside the house of Athens, the *Hermae*, are mutilated. Alcibiades is suspected of the sacrilege and is ordered to return from Sicily (see opposite).

415 Protagoras (see 450 C) is accused of impiety, and flees from Athens to Sicily, but is lost at sea.

D. The Arts

420 The Corinthian column in Greek architecture is introduced about now.

There is a development in the treatment of drapery in Greek sculpture and an interest in feminine subjects in painting.

The temple of Athene Nike is built on Athens' acropolis.

412 Coins are struck at Syracuse to commemorate its deliverance, the artists being Cimon and Evaenetus, celebrated for coin-engraving.

E. Literature

416 The prize for tragedy at Athens goes to Agathon. (It is the banquet he gave in celebration of his victory which is the occasion of Plato's *Symposium*).

415 The *Troades* of Euripides.

414 *The Birds* of Aristophanes.

413 The *Electra* of Euripides.

411 The *Lysistrata* of Aristophanes (in which women seek to force their menfolk to make peace, thus voicing the war-weariness of Athens).
Thucydides' history ends in this year; Xenophon's begins. (See 353 E).
Antiphon, orator, is one of the chief instigators of Athens' oligarchic revolution, and one of the two who are executed.

F Births and Deaths

418 Epaminondas b. (-362).

415 Nehemiah d.
Protagoras d. (69).

413 (Sept.) Nicias and Demosthenes d.

412 Diogenes b. (-323).

411 Antiphon d. (69).

410/7 Alcibiades, careful not to appear in Athens itself, wins naval victories for the Athenians, gaining control of the Hellespont area. Athens is however ill led at home and these are her last successes.

409 Taking the opportunity of the quarrels of the Greek cities in Sicily and of the mutual exhaustion of Athens and Syracuse, Carthage seeks to reimpose her influence over the island. Hannibal, grandson of Hamilcar (see 480), invades Sicily with a strong force. At a second battle of Himera he defeats the Sicilian Greeks and avenges his grandfather by the torture and immolation of 3000 prisoners.

407 King Darius II of Persia sends his second son Cyrus as his Satrap to Sardis with instructions to increase Persian support of Sparta (see 408 C); Tissaphernes is set to watch him. Cyrus begins to collect an army of mercenaries (including Greeks) for his own ends.
Alcibiades returns to Athens and is acclaimed and appointed commander-in-chief. Almost immediately however he is blamed for a defeat of one of his lieutenants by the Spartan general Lysander and is relieved of his command. He retires into voluntary exile in Bithynia.

406 Athens wins her last naval battle at Arginusae, near Lesbos. For not saving their shattered vessels and their dead, the Athenian generals (including Pericles' son, see 429 A) are put to death.
The Carthaginians again invade Sicily. Plague breaks out in their camp, and Hannibal dies. Himilco assumes command, and invests Acragas. Plague is carried back by her soldiers to Carthage.
The Roman siege of Veii (and see 396) is said to have begun.

405 In Sicily the tyrant Dionysius the Elder rises to power. He makes peace with Carthage, and fortifies Syracuse. (and see A).
At the battle of Aegospotami in the Sea of Marmara the Athenian fleet is defeated by Lysander and the Spartans; her naval supremacy is finally shattered. Alcibiades, in nearby exile, comes to warn the Athenian commander of his unsound strategical position, but is mistrusted. News of Aegospotami reaches the Athenians, who remember Melos (see 416) and are afraid.
The siege of Athens begins.

404 Alcibiades flees to the Persians, and is assassinated.
Athens, over-full of refugees herded into the city by Lysander, falls to the Spartans. (And see A) Her long walls are pulled down and a puppet government, the Council of Thirty, is set up—to exert a bloody tyranny. The Peloponnesian War is over.
Lysander sails to Samos, conquers it, and becomes its ruler (and see C).

403 Artaxerxes II ascends the Persian throne.
In Sicily Dionysius the Elder extends his power over the native, Sicel, cities.
Thrasybulus (see 411) leads a revolt in Athens and the Council of Thirty is dissolved, its leader Critias being killed. Democracy is once more restored in Athens.

A. Politics, Law and Economics

409 The city of Rhodes is founded.

407 The gold and silver of the statues of the Acropolis are melted down to help pay for a new Athenian fleet.

405 Dionysius the Elder (who gains power and a bodyguard by a trick similar to Pisistratus's) shows great political acumen as a tyrant: he is cruel and oppressive but never commits outrages to gratify purely personal aims.

404 The Spartan peace terms are not vindictive: Athens loses all her foreign possessions and what is left of her fleet; she has to become the ally of Sparta but retains her independence.

403 The Spartan governors, "Harmosts", who are appointed over the Athenians and her late dependencies and allies, prove generally highly unpopular, the very insular Spartans seeming to lose their morality as well as their political sense once they have left their homeland.

B. Science and Discovery

401 Xenophon and his men (see next page) find a local ointment of use against frostbite: it is made of hog's lard, sesame, bitter almonds and turpentine.

C. Religion and Philosophy

410 The Jewish temple of Jehovah at Elephantine is destroyed by the Egyptian priests, an apparently isolated and exceptional occurrence, the many Greeks and Jews being generally tolerated by the Egyptians.

408 At the Panhellenic gathering at Olympia the philosopher Gorgias raises up his voice against the shame of Greek (i.e. Spartan) alliance with Persia.

404 Socrates defies, with impunity, an order of the Council of Thirty (see opposite) to make what he considers a wrongful arrest.
Lysander holds royal court at Samos and is accorded divine honours by the Samites, who rename a feast of Hera after him.

D. The Arts

409 The Athenian Erechtheion is completed.

406 Timotheus of Miletus *fl.*, musician and dithyrambic poet. He is an innovator and is discouraged by Euripides. He increases the strings of the cithara to eleven; he writes the "nome" (sung to the cithara), called the *Persae*.

404 The Long Walls of Athens are pulled down (see opposite) to the playing of flutes.

E. Literature

409 Sophocles' *Philoctetes*.

401   Cyrus sets out from Sardis with his army (see 407) in an attempt to win the Persian throne. He is defeated at the battle of Cunaxa (N. of Babylon). The Greek mercenaries are left stranded but make their way back home under Xenophon, who becomes their leader when Tissaphernes traitorously murders Clearchus and the other senior Greek captains. (See 394 E)

       The defeat of Cyrus at Cunaxa has a repercussion in Egypt. The Persian governor of Ionia, Tamos an Egyptian, flees home, where he is said to have been put to death by Amyrteos (who is shown by Manetho as the sole Pharaoh of the 28th Dynasty, ruling probably from 404 to 399 B.C.).

---

410   The Celts (soon to be known to the Romans as the Gauls—see 390) migrate south across the Alps.

E. **Literature** (continued)

408 Euripides' *Orestes* is produced. He goes for the last two years of his life to the court of the king of Macedon.

405 Aristophanes' *Frogs*.

403 Lysias, Athenian orator, writes speeches and otherwise helps Thrasybulus oust the Thirty (see opposite).
Thucydides returns to Athens (see 424 E).
Thucydides' *History* is published, soon after his death.

F. **Births and Deaths**

406 Sophocles d. (89).
Euripides d. (74).
Hannibal (I) d.

404 Alcibiades d. (46c).
Darius II of Persia d.

403 Critias d.

401 Cyrus, son of Darius II d.

401 Thucydides d. (70).

400   (Jan.) Xenophon's Ten Thousand, retreating from Cunaxa, reach the Black Sea,
whence they make their way home—mostly to enlist under the Spartans. (And see
394 E).

After the defeat and death of the rebellious Cyrus at Cunaxa, Artaxerxes II, the
Persian king, appoints Tissaphernes to take over all the districts in Asia Minor over
which Cyrus has been governor.

The Greeks are encouraged in their natural enmity of the Persians by Xenophon's
bold and successful march through the Persian empire. One result is that Sparta
turns on Persia and wars against her in Asia Minor.

399   Agesilaus becomes king of Sparta.

398   Dionysius of Syracuse, striking at Carthage while she is still weakened by plague,
attacks her cities in the western corner of Sicily; there is a massacre of Carthaginians
in many cities and Motya with its fine harbour is attacked and taken.

397   Himilco (see 406) crosses to Sicily from Carthage with a fresh army, puts Dionysius
on the defensive and besieges Syracuse. His army again suffers from plague and he
is defeated and escapes back to Carthage (see A & C). The Carthaginian, however,
established the town of Lilybaeum, to replace Motya.

396   Camillus is made Dictator by the Romans and finally destroys the Etruscan town of
Veii.

396/5   Agesilaus, King of Sparta, campaigns with some success in Asia Minor against the
Persian satraps Pharnabazus and Tissaphernes. In a personal meeting with the former he strikes up an honourable friendship (though it is agreed that the war must
go on). Tissaphernes is assassinated by the order of the Persian queen, Parysatis,
who cannot forgive the rough treatment handed out to her favourite son, the dead
Cyrus.

395   Sparta is now in trouble at home. The "Corinthian War" begins, with Corinth,
Thebes and Argos, soon joined by Athens, all allied against Sparta. Lysander dies
fighting the Thebans.

Conon, the Athenian general, having escaped from Lysander's victory at Aegospotami,
is appointed admiral, of a *Persian* fleet.

394   Conon and Pharnabazus win a naval victory over the Spartans at Cnidus (near Rhodes).
The Athenians are avenged, at the expense of receiving help from Persia, and the
Spartan bid for empire begins to crumble. Persia is virtually arbiter of Greece.

393   The Long Walls of Athens are rebuilt, with Persian aid.

392   Abortive peace conference at Sparta.

Dionysius of Syracuse, having increased his power over the native Sicilians (Sicels), is
now attacked by a second Carthaginian expedition, and allies himself with the Sicels.
The Carthaginian army, under Mago, is defeated, makes peace, and returns to
Carthage.

391   Dionysius begins an attempt to extend his rule to the Greek cities of southern Italy:
he unsuccessfully besieges Rhegium.

A. Politics, Law and Economics

By this decade war and plague have drastically reduced the population of Athens. She does not lose her commerce however, and the Piraeus increases in size and importance. There, commercial banks grow up, taking over from the temples and priests the depositing and lending of money.

The restoration of democracy in Athens after the end of the tyranny of the Thirty is accomplished with remarkable restraint and success. A small change is effected by making members of the Council preside in the Assembly.

400   In the Troad a certain widow named Mania strikes an early blow for women's rights, demanding to know of Pharnabazus why she should not be appointed satrap in place of her deceased husband. She gains her point, rules well and has a body of Greek mercenaries at her disposal. She is however assassinated by her son-in-law, and the ensuing unrest enables the invading Spartans to gain some successes here.

399/8 Lysander tries to effect a political revolution in Sparta, whereby the kingship shall be separated from leadership of the army and shall also be elective. He is unsuccessful and earns the disfavour of Agesilaus who becomes king in the usual way. (And see C).

397   Dionysius, on defeating Himilco, purposely allows him to escape, being aware of the political truth that a dictator is safer if he has an enemy from whom he can save his people.

396   During the siege of Veii (see opposite) the Roman citizen-soldier for the first time receives pay.

395   Agesilaus treats his prisoners with remarkable humanity, though he is not above showing them off to his soldiers as a warning against leading an unathletic life (cf Hannibal, 218 B).

393   Isocrates sets up a school of rhetoric in Chios and writes speeches for the island's very efficient law courts.

391   In Rome Camillus (see 396) is accused of making an unfair distribution of the spoils of Veii. He goes into voluntary exile. (But see 390.)

B. Science and Discovery

Probably in the century on each side of 400 B.C., there is laid down the corpus of the Hippocratic medical treatises. Hippocrates, of Cos, is said to have lived to the age of 104.

396   The siege of Veii (see opposite) is said to have finally succeeded by means of the Romans tunnelling a sap under the city's wall.

C. Religion and Philosophy

399   Socrates is accused by Anytus, a democratic politician, as follows: "Socrates is guilty of crime, because he does not believe in the gods recognized by the city, but introduces strange supernatural beings; he is also guilty because he corrupts the youth." Socrates is tried and found guilty by a majority of 60 out of 501. He refuses to go into exile and is therefore condemned to drink the hemlock (and see E).

---

399   Egypt, probably in this year, begins her 29th Dynasty, and is virtually free from the domination of a Persia too occupied to attend to her. She gives some help to Sparta.

     The Romans, who have for long been struggling (with other members of the Latin League) against Etruscan Veii (see 406) seem to have been overbearing and to have demanded too much of their allies—hence the latter are not helpful in the forthcoming sharp struggle (see 390) with the Gauls.

     The Greek city states in this decade (and those that follow, up to the times of Philip and Alexander of Macedon) pursue their enmities, signally failing to unite against the common threat from the north. For the next 30 years Sparta pursues a policy of aggrandisement, until she collapses before Thebes.

C. **Religion and Philosophy** (continued)

399/8   Lysander in his effort to change the laws of kingship in Sparta (see A) tries to bring religious influence to bear and persuades some of the priests at Olympia to enter with him into a plot to reveal some alleged hidden documents that tell a tale in his favour. This fails.

397   Himilco, on returning from Carthage, abases himself because of his defeat, confesses his sins in every temple of his city, and starves himself to death.

D. **The Arts**

A Scythian king is buried with treasure of Greek craftsmanship (the "Tolstoi" burial north of the Crimea).

396   The Romans, having defeated Veii, take away the effigy of its goddess, Juno.

E. **Literature**

400/399   Andocides' extant speech, de Mysteriis, is made.

399   The death of Socrates is described in Plato's *Phaedo*. According to this Socrates' last discourse is largely taken up with his attempt to prove that there is a life after death.

394   Xenophon, in retirement, begins to write his *Anabasis*, the story of the Persian Expedition and the retreat of the 10,000 Greek mercenaries.

F. **Births and Deaths**

399   Socrates d. (70); King Agis of Sparta d.

397   Himilco d.

395   Tissaphernes d.
Lysander d.

392   Conon d.

390–381 B.C.   Rome is sacked by the Gauls; the Ionian cities return to Persian rule

390 (July) A wandering tribe of Celts (whom the Romans call Gauls), under Brennus, advance down the Tiber and defeat the Romans (unsupported by any allies) at the battle of Allia. Rome is besieged for 6 months until only the Capitol is unconquered. The Gauls are probably bought off with gold, though the legend grows that Camillus is recalled from exile (see 391 A) and defeats them. They retire without trace.

390 King Evagoras of Cyprus is assisted against Persia by the Athenians.

388 Sparta seeks and gets help from Dionysius of Syracuse.

387 Dionysius captures Rhegium in Italy, and turns his attention to the Adriatic (see 386 A).

387/6 Sparta, less successful in her war against Persia and her attempt at empire, concludes "the King's Peace" (sometimes known as the Peace of Antalcidas, after the Spartan envoy). This is in spite of Athens' efforts to prevent it. The peace hands over the Greek Asia Minor cities (once saved by Marathon and Thermopylae) to Persian rule.

386/1 Persia, freed from Spartan attacks, turns to the quietening of Cyprus and Egypt. Owing to the skill of Evagoras of Cyprus (who for a time captures Tyre) and of Egypt's Greek mercenary general Chabrias, these wars drag on through the rest of the decade.

383 War breaks out again between Dionysius of Syracuse and Carthage.
Sparta, whose policy it is to keep Greeks disunited, sends an expedition northwards to disrupt the Chalcidian League of petty kings (with whom King Amyntas, grandfather of Alexander of Macedon, has formed temporary alliance).
On their way the Spartans are helped to gain control of the Theban citadel by a pro-Spartan party of Thebans.

382/1 Sparta increases her hold of central Greece still further by refounding the city of Plataea (which she has previously destroyed—see 427).

381 Persia makes peace with Evagoras of Cyprus, accepting his submission on honourable terms.

The Romans, after the sack of their city, realize that they must secure the country to the north; they proceed to do so, largely by annexation. They also build a wall—the "Servian" wall is round Rome.

A. Politics, Law and Economics

390   When the citizens of Rome flee to the Capitol, the senators, according to the legend, stay seated majestically in their robes, while the barbarian Gauls wonder at them. When one of them, Papirius, has his beard stroked, he strikes the offending Gaul, and he and all the senators are killed.

387/6   Athens is deprived of her Bosphorus trade and tolls by Spartan military action on the spot, in spite of initial successes by Iphicrates (see B).

386/3   Dionysius, in his continual efforts at expansion, extends the influence and trade of Syracuse to the Adriatic, planting a colony as far north as Hadria.

384   Lysias the Athenian orator, on the occasion of the Olympiad, rebukes the Greeks for allowing themselves to be dominated by the Syracusan tyrant and the barbarian Persians.

B. Science and Discovery

388   Plato's visit to Syracuse (see C) is partly because of an interest in volcanoes and a desire to see Etna.

387   Iphicrates (see A) introduces into the Athenian army the *peltastae* or targeteers, equipped with a lighter target or shield, lighter armour, and longer sword and spear.

C. Religion and Philosophy

390   On the Roman capitol the sacred geese of the temple of Juno are reputed to have given warning of the Gauls' approach.
Antisthenes, pupil of Socrates and founder of the Cynics, *fl.*

388/7   Plato, having left Athens on Socrates' death to visit Megara and possibly Egypt, now travels to Syracuse at the invitation of the Tyrant's brother-in-law Dion. Having exercized the right of free speech too freely he is deported by Dionysius.

385   Plato, back in Athens, writes his *Symposium*, a disquisition on love, that is to say homosexual love.
Plato forms his *Academy*, teaching mathematics, astronomy and other sciences as well as philosophy. It is open to women; and it remains open until A.D. 529.

D. The Arts

390   The temple of Aesculapius is built at Epidaurus.

E. Literature

Aristophanes' *Plutus*, his last extant play.

383   Xenophon writes his *Hellenica*, a history of his own times, beginning in the year 411, when Thucydides' history ends.

F. **Births and Deaths**

389 Aeschines (orator) b.

388 Thrasybulus d.

385 Aristophanes d. (65).

384 Aristotle b. (–322).

384 Demosthenes b. (–322).

382 Philip of Macedon b. (–336).

380   Persia forces the Athenians to withdraw their successful general Chabrias (see 386) from Egypt.

Egypt's 30th Dynasty (the last according to Manetho) begins with the pharaoh called Nectanebes (or sometimes Nectabeno).

379   Sparta suppresses the Chalcidian League (see 383) and imposes terms favourable to King Amyntas of Macedonia.

379/8   Athens becomes involved with Thebes in a dramatic anti-Spartan incident. Thebans in Athens, refugees from the Spartan occupation (see 383), devise and execute a plot, whereby seven conspirators, dressed as women, gain access to the Spartan rulers at Thebes and murder them. The Spartans retire from Thebes, the conspirators are crowned with wreaths, and Epaminondas (whose great friend Pelopidas has led the conspiracy) takes command.

A Spartan attempt to seize the Piraeus sends Athens further into the arms of Thebes.

In Sicily, Dionysius, after initial successes and the death of the Carthaginian general Mago, suffers a severe defeat and has to make a disadvantageous peace, surrendering some western towns to the Carthaginians.

378/7   Athens allies herself with Thebes and also forms a second Athenian Confederacy (the first being the so-called Delian—see 478 A). To this belong most of the other Boeotian cities besides Thebes and some of the Ionian islands.

The Thebans form their Sacred Band of dedicated and highly trained warriors, 150 pairs of friends and lovers.

377/3   Sparta and Thebes make war in Boeotia, with little success for Sparta.

376   The admiral Chabrias, returned from Egypt, wins a naval victory for Athens over the Spartan fleet, off the island of Naxos.

374   Athens wishes to retire from the Theban–Spartan war and makes peace with Sparta—which is at once broken.

374/2   Sparta attacks Corcyra, enlisting Syracusan help; Athens comes to the island's aid. Sparta is discouraged by a series of earthquakes.

Jason, ruler of Pherae in Thessaly, allies himself first with Athens and then with Macedon.

373   Artaxerxes II at last achieves an invasion of Egypt to bring her back under Persian rule. It is led by Pharnabazus (see 396). After initial successes the Greek mercenaries push on towards Memphis too boldly, and—with the help of the Nile inundations—the Persians are forced to retreat.

371   Sparta and Athens make peace, another "Peace of Callias", (cf 448), again named after one of the Athenian envoys.

At the battle of Leuctra (July) the Theban general Epaminondas wins a decisive victory over the Spartans (and see B). Athens does not welcome the victory, rightly fearing the rising aggressiveness of Thebes.

The Arcadians—shocked like the rest of Greece to find that Spartan soldiers are not invincible—decide to re-assert their independence. They rebuild Mantinea, form an Arcadian League, and build a new federal city, Megalopolis.

A. Politics, Laws and Economics

380 The orator Isocrates publishes a speech at the Olympian festival (cf Lysias, 384 A) advocating a grand expedition to free again the Greek cities of Asia Minor. It is called the *Panegyric*—and it is not a practical proposition.

377 Athens, in preparing herself for participation in the Spartan–Theban struggle, reorganizes her finances and her taxation, inaugurating a system whereby the richer citizens are responsible for collection of the taxes from those less rich.

376 The naval battle of Naxos (see opposite) is fought by the Athenians to break the Spartans' blockade of her corn-ships from the Black Sea.
In Rome Licinius is Tribune and for nine years, he is said to have done much to end the enmity between patricians and *plebs* with liberalizing laws.

B. Science and Discovery

371 At the battle of Leuctra the accepted science of hoplite warfare is changed by Epaminondas, who does not draw out a long even line of soldiers but forms a heavy wedge, fifty men deep, on one wing. (This includes the Theban "sacred band".)

C. Religion and Philosophy

380 The Pharaoh of the 30th Dynasty, Nectanebes, taxes his Greek city of Naucratis—so that his Saite goddess Neith may be served.

375 Plato publishes his *Phaedrus* and is working on his *Republic*.

D. The Arts

380 Pharaoh Nectanebes builds many monuments and restores many temples, including one of Thoth's at Hermopolis.

375 A princess of the early Celtic La Tène culture is buried at Rainheim near Saarbrucken. She leaves behind magnificent gold torques (but not imported treasures as at Vix—see 520 D).

E. Literature

374 Evagoras' son Nicocles continues his father's liberal Hellenizing policy in Cyprus, encouraged by Isocrates, who writes his *Exhortation to Nicocles*.

F. Births and Deaths

378 Lysias d. (80).

378 Theopompus of Chios b. (–305).

374 Evagoras of Cyprus d.

372 Mencius of China b. (–289).

370   The Spartans under Agesilaus invade a dangerously resuscitated Arcadia (see 371). Arcadia, appealing in vain to the Athenians, turns to the Thebans. Epaminondas arrives with an army, finds the Spartans gone home, and follows them, ravaging in his turn.

369   Epaminondas advances into Messenia and frees the country from Spartan rule. In a search for balance of power, Athens responds to an appeal for help from Sparta and allies herself with her traditional enemy.

368   Dionysius of Syracuse renews his war against Carthaginian Sicily, but with little success.

368/7   Dionysius gives help to Sparta. The Thebans again invade Sparta.

367   Dionysius (sometimes known as the Elder) dies.

366   Thebes makes peace with Sparta and turns her attention to her other rival, Athens, who is trying to revive her maritime empire and is interfering in Macedonian dynastic quarrels.

365   The Arcadian League is splitting apart.

364   On the advice of Epaminondas, Thebes builds a fleet of 100 triremes, as the only way of combatting Athens. It wins no battles but influences the ever-changing kaleidoscope of Greek city alliances. Thebes, however, shocks the Greek world by destroying her Boeotian rival Orchomenus.
Philip of Macedon, brother of the reigning king, returns to his native land after having spent a few years as a hostage in Thebes.

363/1   The Pharaoh Teos or Tachos, succeeding to the throne, plans a great attack on Persia and invites the ageing Spartan king Agesilaus to help him. Agesilaus arrives with 1000 hoplites.

362   Arcadia is drifting into an alliance with Sparta, and Epaminondas makes his final advance into that country. At another battle of Mantinea (see also 418), Epaminondas is victorious but is killed. His dying command, "Make peace with the enemy!" is obeyed: *Koine Eirene*, general peace, is established in Greece. The brief supremacy of Thebes is at an end.

361   (winter) The Egyptians and Spartans, with some Athenian mercenaries under Chabrias, set out for an attack on the Persian king's Phoenician cities, but have to return almost at once to meet revolt at home.
The Persian empire is weakening, with revolts on the part of many satraps, including that of Sidon, which city at this time is rich and prosperous again (see D).

---

370   The short-lived (low-caste) Nanda dynasty is founded in the Magadha kingdom of India.

Plato attempts to create a philosopher-king; in Rome, the Lician laws

A. Politics, Law and Economics

Dionysius has taken the initiative against Carthage and is acting as champion of Europe against Asia and the Semite. Towards the end of his reign Syracuse is the most powerful of Greek cities.

370   The new Arcadian capital city of Megalopolis is completed and a democratic system is set up with an Assembly "of Ten Thousand" and a Council of 50.
The Nanda dynasty of Magadha taxes efficiently, creates a large army, and builds canals.

369   The town of Messene is founded as capital of a new Messenia (see opposite).

367   The Persian king, the aged Artaxerxes, issues one of his edicts in the shape of peace terms for the Greeks to observe. He is not obeyed.
In Rome, after a bitter struggle, the Licinian laws are promulgated, an important change being that the Plebs win the concession that one of the two consuls must be of their order. The aged Camillus is largely responsible for this achievement. At this time there are enlarged in scope the offices of Praetor (magesterial) and of Aediles, equivalent of Mayors of Rome. The number of Aediles is doubled from two to four.

C. Religion and Philosophy

370   Aristippus of Cyrene *fl.* He has been a pupil of Socrates and founds the Cyrenaic school of Hedonistic philosophy.

368   Plato's *Republic* is completed. It lays down the rules for an ideal "righteous" society, warns that poetry is "an utter delusion" and suggests that kings ought to be philosophers or at least taught by philosophers.

367   Dionysius I by the time of his death has had statues raised showing himself as the god after whom he is named.
Dion, brother-in-law of the young and pliable Dionysius II who has succeeded his father, sends for Plato, whose teaching he admires. Plato arrives for a second time in Syracuse, hopeful of putting his precepts into practice. For a while the Syracusan king and court are eager to learn. But reaction sets in and intrigue enters: Dion is exiled and Plato returns once more to Athens.
Aristotle arrives in Athens from his native Chalcidice to become the pupil of Plato.

364   (13th July) Pelopidas, friend of Epaminondas (see 379) is killed in battle after setting out under the bad auspices of a solar eclipse.

361   Plato returns once more to Syracuse to teach Dionysius II. He fails to reconcile the king to Dion, (who has been banished) and has to flee for his life.

D. The Arts

364   Praxiteles of Athens *fl.* At about this time he makes his Hermes, (a copy found at Olympia), and his Aphrodite of Cnidus (not extant but referred to and praised in current literature). He illustrates the fact that Greek sculpture is growing less subservient to architecture and more individualistic; it is also being more talked about.

D.   The Arts (continued)

362   The sarcophagi of the Satrap of Sidon, Straton I, and of his predecessors, show evidence of increased Greek influence in the Phoenician towns.

E.   Literature

367   Dionysius I, often competing for the tragedy prize at Athens, receives news of winning first place with his *Ransom of Hector*. His ensuing carouse leads to his death.

365   Antiphanes, writer of Athenian comedies, *fl.*

364   Demosthenes, aged twenty, succeeds in a lawsuit against one of his guardians and is encouraged to come forward as a speaker in the Athenian Assembly.

F.   Births and Deaths

370   Jason of Pherae d.

370   Theophrastus b. (–285*c*).

367   Dionysius the Elder d. (63).

365   Camillus d. (82).

364   Pelopidas, Theban general, d.

362   Epaminondas d. (56).

361   Democritus d. (99*c*).
       Agathocles b. (–289).

360   Agesilaus (see 363/1), unpleased with his reception in Egypt, supports a revolt against the Pharaoh Teos, who flees to Susa and makes peace with the Persians. The new pharaoh, Nectanebos, pays the Spartans 230 talents for their help. Agesilaus dies on setting out for home, his body being enbalmed in honey and sent to Sparta for burial. Nectanebos reigns for about 17 years and follows his predecessor and near-namesake Nectanebes in considerable building activity. With him there ends Egypt's 30th and last dynasty (see 343). These two pharaohs are sometimes known as Nectanebo I and II).
Gauls again reach the gates of Rome; they are beaten back.

359   The Macedonian king Perdiccas, being killed in defending his country against an Illyrian attack, dies and leaves an infant son, Amyntas. The child's uncle, Philip, assumes the regency.

358   Artaxerxes III ("Ochus") succeeds Artaxerxes II and restores central authority over the Persian empire's satraps.
The Gauls are again beaten off from Rome.

357   Dion, exiled from Syracuse (see 361 C), makes a spectacular return and for a while wrests power from the weak Dionysius II.
Philip of Macedon, having disposed of an Illyrian threat, occupies the Athenian city of Amphipolis, which would otherwise bar his way south.

356   Philip takes Potidaea and other Athenian strongholds in Thessaly and Chalcidice. At home he assumes the full title of king.
In this year the internecine quarrels of the Greek world continue and the troubles of the Athenians in particular increase by reason of two events. The first is the action of Mausolus, tyrant of Caria, who instigates a rebellion against the Athenian alliance on the part of Chios, Cos and Rhodes. The second is another "Sacred War", arising out of the seizure of Delphi by the people of Phocis, in whose territory the famous temple and oracle stand.

355   Timotheus, son of Conon (see 395), who has been one of Athens' successful generals for 20 years, fails in an attempt to re-establish Athenian control of Chios and is indicted and heavily fined; he leaves Athens a broken man.

354   In Sicily Dion is murdered and Syracuse suffers from a number of short-lived tyrants, while Dionysius II, in exile in Italy, bides his time.
Athens recognizes the independence of Chios, Cos and Rhodes and makes peace with Mausolus of Caria.
The Phocians suffer a defeat in the Sacred War, but revive under a new leader.
Rome allies herself with the Samnites (see 343). She also defeats the Etruscans of the city of Caere, who have helped him against the Gauls.

353   The Phocians threaten Thessaly to their north—and Philip of Macedon sees his opportunity to penetrate south.

A. Politics, Law and Economics

359 Philip of Macedon, coming to power and ambitious to command the Greek world, has three things to help him, ample man-power, a recently discovered gold mine in his country, and his political acumen.

356 From out of his subjects, who are a miscellany of warring tribesmen, Philip creates a professional army with a national spirit.

The Phocians (see opposite) come into temporary power in Greece, supported by their control of Delphi (and see C) and their great use of mercenary soldiers.

351 Demosthenes (see E) tries to get the Athenians to cease depending on paid mercenaries and to return to their old conception of a citizen army.

B. Science and Discovery

359 Philip of Macedon, having noted the military tactics of the Thebans (see 337B), improves on the strength-in-depths principle of Epaminondos and invents the more open and freer-moving *phalanx*.

C. Religion and Philosophy

Plato in this decade probably writes the *Timaeus* and the *Critias*, which contain his descriptions of Atlantis and its destruction (a destruction that may embody memories of the eruption of Thera and its effects upon Minoan Crete, see 1450). Plato also probably finishes his *Laws* (in which he is still advocating a philosopher-led king).

356 The Phocians scandalize the Greek world by regarding Delphi as a private possession rather than a pan-hellenic asset. Tales are told of dedicatory offerings being given to the Phocian general's favourites, a golden wreath to a dancing girl, a silver beaker to a flute-player.

D. The Arts

353 A royal tomb with a colossal statue at Halicarnassus is made for the dead king of Caria, Mausolus—the first "mausoleum." Scopas is the chief architect and sculptor, and his frieze is still intact (and in the British Museum).

E. Literature

355 Demosthenes, having cured his physical defects, begins to come to the fore as a public orator and critic of those in power in Athens.

354 Alexis, Athenian comedy writer, *fl.*

353 Demosthenes speaks in favour of the Rhodians (see 356).

351 Demosthenes, who has been trying for some time to get his countrymen to realize the Macedonian danger, delivers his first *Philippic*, warning his countrymen in particular of the folly of persuading themselves that the danger will disappear merely because Philip is ill (see 352).

352 After two initial defeats, Philip drives the Phocians south. Help is given however by Athens and Sparta, and Philip is checked at Thermopylae. He then moves against Thrace. Athens, in panic at the prospect of losing control of the Chersonese and beginning to take some notice of the warnings of Demosthenes (see 351E) votes for increased armaments. She is saved by Philip falling ill.

351 Encouraged apparently by an abortive effort at invasion of Egypt by Artaxerxes III, Phoenicia and Cyprus revolt against Persia.

F. **Births and Deaths**

360 Agesilaus of Sparta d. (84).

359 Perdiccas d.

358 Artaxerxes II d.

357 Seleucus I (Nicator) b. (–280).
Hippocrates d. (104*c*).

356 Alexander the Great b. (–323).

354 Dion d. Xenophon d. (90).

353 Mausolus of Caria d.

351 Timotheus, Athenian general, d.

350–341 B.C.   Egypt's last native pharaoh dies; the threat of Philip of Macedon grows

350 The Gauls, once more threatening Rome, are decisively beaten.

350/48 Sidon, the centre of the revolt against Persia (see 351) seeks help from her sister city Tyre but fails to get it; she seeks help from Egypt but gets only very little. She is besieged, taken, and punished with great cruelty by Artaxerxes III.

349/8 Philip, recovered from illness, turns his attention to the remaining Greek cities in Macedonia and to the city of Olynthus in particular. The Athenians at last send help, but it is diverted by a revolt in Euboea which Philip has fomented. Euboea is declared independent and Olynthus falls to Philip.

347/6 Athens sends embassies to Philip, which include both Demosthenes and his political opponent, Eubulus. Philip delays ratification for his own ends, but the peace of Philocrates is finally signed. It agrees to a *status-quo ante* but Philip refuses to forego the right to punish the Phocians for their "sacrilege" in the Sacred War.

346 The Phocians are punished; the pass of Thermopylae is opened to Philip; Philip is elected president of the Pythian games and a member of the Greek religious league, the Amphictyonic (see 595 A).
Dionysius II returns as tyrant to Syracuse, leaving his family behind in Italy to be murdered.

346/1 In Greece and Macedonia there is an interval of uneasy peace and a preparation for war.

344 The Corinthians, on being asked by the Syracusans for help against tyranny, send Timoleon. Timoleon has already destroyed a would-be tyrant in Corinth—his own brother.

343 Sparta similarly responds to Hellenic calls for help. In southern Italy the native tribes, no longer awed by the might of Syracuse, are attacking the Magna Graecia cities, in particular Tarentum. King Archidamus of Sparta, emulating his father Agesilaus, sets sail with a band of mercenaries, unemployed since the end of the Sacred War.
The Samnites appeal to Rome to settle their internal quarrels and to save their city, Capua, from destruction. The Romans respond.
Dionysius II surrenders to Timoleon, who takes over the rule of Syracuse (see A) whilst Dionysius is allowed to retire to Corinth, there to end his days in obscurity.
(autumn) Artaxerxes III personally leads his invading force into Egypt. The frontier town of Pelusium (biblical Sin) puts up a resistance; but Pharaoh Nectanebos is forced to retreat to Memphis. Pelusium and other strongholds then capitulate on promise of good treatment, and the last native pharaoh leaves Egypt for Ethiopia. Artaxerxes and his favourite general Bagoas retire loaded with spoil.

343/1 Timoleon spreads his rule over Sicily, destroying other tyrannies and preparing against another threatened Carthaginian invasion.

A. Politics, Law and Economics

350 In Rome for the first time a plebeian is elected as Censor.

350 In China the use of coinage is introduced, as is also the horse as a cavalry charger rather than a drawer of the chariot. Protective earthwork walls are beginning to be made at various places along the northern and western frontiers against the surrounding nomads (later used as a basis for the Great Wall, see 225). In central China, the Han state begins to be formed, though it is the Ch'in state that is the most powerful.

348 Rome and Carthage make a second trade agreement (see 496 A): Carthage will not attack such Latin states as are faithful to Rome.

347 In Rome a coinage is introduced for the first time, leading to much borrowing and a financial crisis. The first "coin" is the *as*, a pound-weight of copper—merchants use a Greek silver drachma.

346/5 Demosthenes in the long Athenian dispute as to whether Philip of Macedon should be treated as friend or foe procures an impeachment of his opponent the orator Aeschines, but has to let it drop when Aeschines drags up the unsavoury past of one of Demosthenes' associates.

343 Persia in sending a full-scale force to re-subdue Egypt is attracted by Egypt's gold and in very great need of her corn.

Syracuse, rescued by Timoleon (see opposite) from years of tyranny and warfare, is repopulated and set on a new democratic course, the constitution that had existed before the Carthaginian defeat of 409 being restored and remodelled.

In Rome there is another mutiny in the citizen army and an attempt is made to make usury illegal.

341 The Latin League proposes to Rome a political amalgamation which would restrict the latter's freedom of action. Rome refuses and declares war (see 340).

C. Religion and Philosophy

347 Aristotle, after Plato's death, goes to Assos in Mysia where he marries the young Pythias.

343 Artaxerxes III is credited by the Egyptians with being nearly as destructive of their religious monuments as Cambyses (see 522 C). He has the sacred bull of Apis destroyed.

Aristotle goes as tutor to Alexander (his father having been physician to the Macedonian court).

D. The Arts

350 Now, or 20 years later, the bronze "Apollo Belvedere" is sculpted: only extant in Roman copies.

The terracotta figures of Tanagra begin to appear and continue for about 150 years.

Greek sculpture begins to show facial expression, so leading to individual portraiture, one of the first examples being that of Mausolus (353 D).

343 The freeing of Syracuse, and also the attempt to free Tarentum, are commemorated by the issue of beautiful gold coins.

342/1   Philip conquers Thrace (governed by native princes since Persia's expulsion from Europe by the Greeks). This is regarded by Athens as a further threat to her safety. (Philip suffers great personal hardship in this winter campaign).

341   Rome renews her alliance with the Samnites but retains a garrison at Capua.

By the beginning of this decade the Romans have finally recovered from the set-back caused by the sack of their city in 390 and have re-asserted their ascendancy in Italy.

E. Literature
The so-called Middle Comedy, more naturalistic than previously, flourishes in Athens, Antiphanes and Alexis being the exponents best known.

344 Demosthenes' second *Philippic*. Isocates' *Letter to Philip*.

341 Demosthenes' third *Phillippic*, a reaction to Philip's conquest of Thrace and a strong appeal for a Hellenic league against "the Macedonian wretch".

F. Births and Deaths
350 Iphicrates, Athenian general, d.

347 Plato d. (81).

346 Chandragupta Maurya b. (–297c).

345 Demetrius of Phalerum b. (–283).

342 Menander b. (–291).
Epicurus b. (–270).

340   The Romans defeat the Latin League at a battle or battles on the Campanian coast—
       Livy says near Mt. Vesuvius. (See also A & E.)

       Philip of Macedon starts a war against Athens in the Bosphorus area. He is not at
       first successful, and Demosthenes receives from the Athenians a public vote of
       thanks. Philip has to attend to trouble from the Scythians near the mouth of the
       Danube; he is wounded but soon recovers.

339   Timoleon (see 344/3) meets a large force of Carthaginians at the battle of Crimisus
       (in the W. of Sicily) and wins a brilliant victory against superior odds.

338   Timoleon makes advantageous peace terms with Carthage, deposes two more tyrants
       in Sicily and gives the island a peace that lasts for 20 years. He retires into private
       life but dies soon afterwards.

       Archidamus of Sparta (see 343), after five years of campaigning in S. Italy, fails of
       any decisive results and is killed in battle.

       The Persian general Bagoas murders Artaxerxes III; the king's younger son, Arses,
       is put in his place.

       Philip advances through the pass of Thermopylae. Athens and Macedon compete for
       the alliance of Thebes, and Thebes elects to join with Athens.

       At Chaeronea, W. of Thebes, the battle for the supremacy of the Greek world is
       fought. There are no great generals on the Greek side (Demosthenes fighting as a
       mere hoplite), and Philip is victorious. Philip is harsh on Thebes but merciful to
       Athens. He advances into the Peloponnese, subdues Sparta, and summons a pan-
       Hellenic congress at Corinth. Isocrates, in despair, commits suicide.

337   At a second congress at Corinth Philip announces that the Greeks will set about re-
       liberating from Persian rule the Greek cities of Asia Minor.

336   Philip, while sending an advance force to begin the invasion of Asia Minor, attends
       to personal affairs. He puts away his wife Olympias, sister of Alexander, King of
       Epirus—see 334 below—and marries a nobleman's daughter called Cleopatra.
       Then, to appease Alexander of Epirus, he gives the latter his own daughter in
       marriage and attends the wedding feast. At the feast he is murdered. Olympias is
       believed the murderer.

       Prince Alexander, aged 20, becomes King of Macedonia. He puts down rebellion at
       home; he appears at the gates of Thebes and receives that city's submission; he
       advances to the Corinthian isthmus; and he is elected by the assembled Greeks as
       their commander against Persia.

       Court intrigues and weakness of rule continue in Persia: General Bagoas murders the
       king, Arses, and is himself murdered.

       Darius III comes to the Persian throne.

335   While Alexander is campaigning against the barbarians across the Danube, a report
       of his death causes the Thebans to take up arms again. Alexander defeats them and
       punishes them mercilessly (Oct.).

A. Politics Law and Economics

340   Rome in making peace with the cities of the defeated Latin League (see opposite) gives remarkably liberal terms; the men of many cities are granted citizenship, and Rome finds herself surrounded by friends rather than enemies.

Demosthenes alters and makes more equitable an archaic law whereby groups of richer citizens are responsible for financing the building of ships for the Athenian navy, this bearing unfairly on the less rich members of the group. He also persuades the citizens to devote the Athenian festival funds to military purposes.

338   The shops in the Roman Forum make way for bankers' establishments.

336   In Athens there is introduced a form of conscription of the young men—the *Ephebi*—whose duties are part military, part civic.

331   Alexander takes the first major step in his hellenizing process by founding in the Nile Delta the greatest of the cities he names after himself, Alexandria. Many Greeks will emigrate to these new cities.

B. Science and Discovery

340   In his Bosphorus campaign (see opposite) Philip introduces new siege machinery in the way of towers and rams.

334   Alexander, in his first defeat of the Persians at the battle of the Granicus, shows the superiority of his military inventions, having added a considerable force of cavalry on his wings to his father's *phalanx*. The Persian generals show little awareness of the use of either strategy or tactics.

331   An eclipse of the moon occurs as Alexander is approaching Nineveh (probably Sept. 20th); it is regarded as an omen of his conquest of Asia.

C. Religion and Philosophy

339   Carthage, having, like Thebes, built up a Sacred Band of dedicated warriors, sees them defeated at the battle of Crimisus. On the way to this battle Timoleon defeats a superstitious fear on the part of his soldiers: meeting mules laden with wild celery used to decorate graves he makes a wreath of it for his own head, and his soldiers follow suit.

335   Aristotle returns to Athens, where he founds his "peripatetic" school in the old gymnasium called the Lyceum. In the following years, until his death, he writes his treatises on logic and philosophy, on biology and physics etc (see 330 C) which however are not published books but rather notes and memoranda.

334/3   Alexander proves to the priests and people of Gordium that he is the destined conqueror of Asia by cutting their famous knot.

332   The Chinese philosopher Mencius begins his travels from court to court as Confucius had done: his is also an ethical rather than a religious teaching.

332/1   Alexander pleases the Egyptians by *not* killing the sacred bull of Apis (see 343 C) and by generally respecting their religion. He travels 300 miles into the desert to visit the temple of Zeus Ammon, where the priests salute him as son of the god.

334 Alexander of Epirus (see 336 above) responds to an appeal for help from the citizens of Tarentum (who have failed of any benefit from Spartan intervention—see 343). He wins victories over the Italian tribes and enters into an agreement with the Romans, who fear he may have designs on Sicily. (And see 330.)

Alexander of Macedon (with no help, other than some mercenaries from the subdued mainland Greeks), sets out on his conquest of the Persian Empire. He crosses the Hellespont, with some 35,000 men, and visits Troy (see E). He marches eastwards to the River Granicus, where he wins his first victory over a Persian army commanded by the Greek mercenary, Memnon. His life is saved by one of his friends and generals, Clitus. Of the Ionian cities, Miletus and Halicarnassus defy him and have to be subdued.

334/3 Alexander winters in Gordium, the ancient capital of Phrygia and in one-time Hittite territory. (And see C.)

333 Alexander marches southwards and, on the River Issus, meets King Darius III in battle for the first time (Oct.). Darius is beaten and escapes without his family— which is well treated by Alexander. Alexander has become master of Syria. The Greeks send congratulations and a golden crown.

333/2 Alexander has to pay attention to the Phoenician sea-coast towns in his rear. Tyre takes 7 months to subdue.

332 (Nov.) Alexander enters Egypt, meeting no Persian resistance. (And see C.)

331 Alexander leaves Egypt early in the year and advances against Darius who has collected another and a vast army. He crosses the upper reaches of the Tigris and Euphrates and in October meets the Persians near ancient Nineveh. There, at the battle of Gaugamela (sometimes called the battle of Arbela, Darius' H.Q.) Darius is finally defeated and Alexander becomes master of Persia's empire. Alexander advances to Babylon, which surrenders to him, then into Persia, where at Susa he takes over vast treasure.

Sparta makes a last attempt to fight against Macedonian control of Greece, but she is beaten at a battle near Megalopolis.

D. The Arts

338 The Magna Graecia town of Tarentum shows its thanks to the Spartans' efforts on her behalf (see 343 and 338) by the issue of golden coins.

337 The Syracusans erect a group of public buildings, the Timoleonteion, to the memory of their deliverer.

336 Philip of Macedon is buried at Aegae (modern Vergina), where his tomb was discovered in 1977. The burial was intact and contained grave goods of a splendour unparalleled in the Greek world.

332 A funerary sarcophagus of a Sidonian king shows Alexander at the battle of Issus.

E. Literature

340 A legend concerning the Roman defeat of the Latin League tells how a consul's son is killed by his father for disobeying the order *not* to indulge in personal combats.

336 Diogenes, the Cynic, is said to have met Alexander at Corinth and, on being offered any favour, to have asked him to "stand out of the sun".

336 Theopompus of Chios, pupil of Isocrates, begins to write his *Philippica* (not extant, except for later quotations) wherein he considers the ills of Greece to be attributable to her "three heads", Athens, Sparta and Thebes.

335 In Alexander's destruction of Thebes only the house where Pindar lived is saved.

334 At Troy Alexander indulges in a number of actions which show how imbued he is with the Homeric legend and how it inspires him. He crowns the grave of "his ancestor" Achilles whilst his friend Hephaistion does the same to that of Patroclus.

F. Births and Deaths

338 Artaxerxes III d.
Archidamus of Sparta d.
Isocrates (98).

336 Philip of Macedon d. (46).

336 Timoleon d.
King Arses and General Bagoas of Persia d.

333 Zeno b. (-263).

331 King Agis III of Sparta d.

330   Alexander of Epirus (see 334) finds the Tarentines turning against him, thus giving
the native Italians the same opportunity. He is defeated and killed in battle, and
the possibility of an Epirot kingdom in Magna Graecia ends. Tarentum however is
able to hold her own against the Italian tribes.

Alexander the Great, after the first four months of the year at Persepolis (see D),
moves East in pursuit of Darius. Darius is made prisoner by his general and satrap
of Bactria, Bessus, and is assassinated (July) just as Alexander catches up with the
Persians. Their resistance ends.

329/8   Alexander penetrates eastwards into Bactria and northwards into Sogdiana, crossing
the R. Jaxartes to subdue the Scythians. In Sogdiana he meets resistance and is
wounded. Bessus is captured, and crucified.

327   The Romans, who have been pushing southwards while the Samnites have been
occupied with Tarentum (see 330 above), are invited to interfere in a dispute over
the city of Neapolis (Naples). They take the opportunity and after a long siege
evict the Samnites from Naples.

Alexander at Samarkand in the early months of the year, kills his foster-brother
Clitus who dares to criticize him.

He marries Roxana, the captured princess of a Bactrian chief. A plot against him is
discovered. He crosses the Hindu-Kush and invades India. On one of the
tributaries of the River Indus, the Hydaspes, he defeats the Indian king Porus in a
well-contested battle. Porus asks for "treatment like a king", and gets it.

On the death of his horse, Alexander founds a city in its memory, Bucephala.

326   The Samnites declare war on Rome—the Second Samnite War.

Having crossed two more tributaries of the Indus, Alexander reaches his farthest
point east, the River Hyphasis—where his Macedonian troops refuse to go any
farther. He retraces his steps to the R. Hydaspes, and, by water and by land,
retreats down that river and then down the Indus to the sea.

At the siege of the capital of a local tribe, the Malli, Alexander receives another, and
serious, wound.

325   Alexander reaches the Indian Ocean (see C). He, with his army of perhaps 30,000,
makes a very difficult retreat westwards along the coast and through the desert of
Gedrosia, (modern Makran) losing, it is said, more men than he has in all his
campaigns. His army reaches Persepolis in December, whilst his navy, under
Nearchus, reaches Susa in the same month.

325   In Sicily Agathocles, a rich and ambitious citizen of Syracuse, is exiled.

324   Alexander at Susa punishes those who have failed in their duties in his absence,
particularly those who have plundered tombs and temples. His treasurer, Harpalus,
flees to Athens.

Alexander spends the summer and autumn at the Median capital, Ecbatana, where
his greatest friend Hephaistion dies. He sets out for Babylon, destroying a tribe
of brigands on the way, as an offering to the spirit of his friend.

A. Politics, Law and Economics

330/28   Alexander, regarding himself as the successor to, as well as conqueror of, the king of Persia, begins to wear Persian dress and to have regard for Persian customs and court ritual. His oriental treatment of Bessus (see opposite) is part of this policy. Alexander also has his general Parmenio assassinated, on unproven suspicion of treason.

327   Alexander, in subduing the Punjab, intends to secure trade routes to India; he has Phoenician merchants accompanying his army.

325   Similarly in sending Nearchus (see opposite) on his voyage back to Persia Alexander envisages maritime trade, the Indian Ocean to be another Mediterranean.

324   In another effort to bring East and West together, Alexander has established military schools in conquered territory: by this date he is said to have 30,000 hellenized barbarians at his military disposition.
In Rhodes the first-known system of insurance is inaugurated—against runaway slaves.

322   On Macedonian orders Athens ceases to be a true democracy, the poorer of her citizens, and more than half, being disenfranchised.

B. Science and Discovery

327   One reason for Alexander's advance into India is his interest in geography and the extent of the all-surrounding "Ocean".
At the battle of the River Hydaspes, King Porus' elephants, the oriental contribution to the history of arms, first cause some confusion amongst Alexander's crack guards, the Hypaspitae, but finally they cause equal confusion on their own side.

325   Having sailed down the Indus, Alexander's ships, under Nearchus, make a pioneering voyage, with much hardship, along the N. Indian coast and up the Persian Gulf.

325   Aristotle refers to the Greek water clock (much improved from the Egyptians' and now approaching the limit of its perfection, see 250 B).

323   Before his death Alexander puts in hand preparations for voyages around the shores of the Caspian as well as round Arabia. He also experiments with the Macedonian *phalanx*, inserting Persian light-armed troops between the Macedonians at front and rear.

C. Religion and Philosophy

330/23   Aristotle in this period and in the previous five years (see 335 C) composes his *History of Animals*, *Rhetoric*, *Physics*, *Metaphysics*, *Ethics*, *Logic*, *Poetics*, and *Politics*. As with his predecessors his ideal is the small city-state, and he has no sympathy with his one-time pupil, Alexander. Nor has he any great love for the Athenians.

326   On the banks of the R. Hyphasis (see opposite) Alexander erects, as a thank offering for his victories, twelve towering altars to the Olympian gods.

325   Alexander before sending Nearchus on his voyage makes sacrifices to Poseidon from a ship in the Indian Ocean and hurls the cup into the waves.

323   On reaching Babylon Alexander is met by deputations from most of the western Mediterranean peoples, fearful that the great King now plans the conquest of Europe. Alexander makes plans for developing Babylon as the capital of his empire, and also for the conquest of Arabia.

The magnificent funeral of Hephaistion takes place.

Alexander develops a fever, and—probably on June 13th, and in the palace of Nebuchadnezzar—he dies.

In Athens Demosthenes is accused of misappropriating some of the funds that Harpalus (see 324 above) has brought with him. Demosthenes is convicted and imprisoned, but escapes.

323/2   Ptolemy, one of Alexander's generals and possibly his half-brother, has Alexander's body brought to Memphis and there buried in a gold sarcophagus. He marries Alexander's mistress, Thaïs.

Some of the northern Greek cities, Athens included, revolt against the Macedonian Regent, Antipater. After some brief successes around Thermopylae (including one at Lamia, after which the war is named) the Greeks are defeated and their resistance peters out for want of unity.

322   Demosthenes, who has returned to favour in Athens, flees from the Macedonians who demand his surrender. Upon arrest he takes poison.

Agathocles returns to Syracuse.

In Babylon the struggle for the Alexandrian succession develops. Roxana has given birth to Alexander Aegus; and a compromise is reached wherein he and the dead king's young and dim-witted half-brother Arrhidaeus, are to be considered rulers. Perdiccas—C. in C. at Babylon and to whom Alexander has given his signet ring— tries to keep effective control.

321   Perdiccas invades Egypt; but, failing to cross the Nile, is murdered by his own mutinous army, prominent among the mutineers being Seleucus. A truce is arranged, leaving Ptolemy in power in Egypt and Seleucus in Babylon.

In India the young adventurer Chandragupta Maurya, guided by the Brahman Kautalya, defeats the Nandas and begins to create the Mauryan empire by gaining control of the Ganges valley.

A Roman army is caught by the Samnites in a pass in their mountains, the Caudine Forks, and forced to capitulate. It suffers the indignity of "passing under the yoke".

Athens, accepting Macedonian overlordship, experiences a prosperous and peaceful decade under the leadership of Phocion and Lycurgus.

C. Religion and Philosophy (continued)

322 Aristotle is accused of impiety by the Athenians, but escapes to Chalcis in Euboea, where, in the same year he dies.

D. The Arts

330 At the instigation of his Greek mistress Thaïs, Alexander sets alight the palace of Xerxes, but regrets his barbarism and has the flames put out.

330 The Athenian architect Philo *fl.*; he is responsible for the portico of the temple of Demeter at Eleusis and the marble storehouse at Zea, one of the harbours of the Piraeus.
Lycurgus (see opposite) renovates the theatre of Dionysus below Athens' acropolis. (Or possibly in previous decade.)
Lysippus of Sicyon, sculptor, *fl.* He is said to have been the favourite of Alexander; his athletic figures are famous, e.g. the copy known as the Farnese Hercules.

324 3000 "Dionysiac artists", i.e. professional players, arrive from Greece at Ecbatana, to entertain Alexander and his court.

322 Theophrastus of Lesbos, Aristotles's pupil, takes over the Peripatetic school at Athens on his master's death. Two of his works on botany and his *Characters* are extant.

E. Literature

330 Demosthenes, in *On the Crown*, defends himself accusation of egotism.

325 One of the results of Alexander's penetration into India is the knowledge of that land acquired by the Greeks. Some of this is fabulous; but the description by Nearchus of Indian dress and the use of cotton "produced on trees" appears accurate.

323 There is a legend that Alexander on his deathbed bequeaths his kingdom "to the strongest".

F. Births and Deaths

330 Darius II d.
Alexander of Epirus d.

328 Bessus d.

327 Clitus d.

324 Hephaistion d.

323 Diogenes d. (89).

323 Alexander d. (32).
Alexander Aegus b. (–311).

322 Lycurgus d.

322 Demosthenes d. (62).
Aristotle d. (62).

320–311 B.C.   Alexander's generals struggle for power; Carthaginian army in Sicily

320/19 Judaea and Syria are annexed by Ptolemy (see below), to remain as part of the Egyptian domains of the Ptolemies until the beginning of the 2nd century B.C.

319 Antipater, Regent of Macedonia, dies. His son, Cassander (one of the "Diadochi" or contenders for Alexander's empire) is not appointed his successor and begins to fight for his rights.
Eumenes and Antigonus (see list below) fight for control of Asia.

318 Eumenes captures Babylon.

317 Seleucus (see below) joins Antigonus against Eumenes and recaptures Babylon. Antigonus turns him out.

316 In Sicily Agathocles (see 325) becomes tyrant of Syracuse, whence he extends his rule over most of the island.
Thebes, destroyed by Alexander, is rebuilt by Cassander with the help of Athens.
Eumenes is defeated by Antigonus and is executed.
Cassander has Philip's widow, Olympias, murdered and Alexander's widow and son imprisoned (and see 311 below).
The Romans, reviving from their Caudine defeat (see 321) and with an eye on Apulia (towards the heel of Italy) send an army to seize the town of Luceria. Again they are badly beaten and the Samnites reach to within 20 miles of Rome.

315 Among the Diadochi Antigonus begins to be recognized as the common enemy by the others. They combine against him and Cassander is joined by his brother-in-law Lysimachus (see B).

314 The Romans rally and inflict at the battle of Tarracina, a crushing defeat on the Samnites, whose losses are said to be over 10,000.
Antigonus captures Tyre.

313 In fighting over central Greece Cassander largely loses his grip of that country. Antigonus declares the "freedom" of Greek cities.
Ptolemy, whose Egyptian hegemony includes Cyprus, puts down a revolt there.

312/11 The Syracusans ask for help against their tyrant Agathocles from the Carthaginians—who respond. Another General Hamilcar crosses over with an army, wins a battle on the Himeras River, in which many of the soldiers die of thirst as well as wounds, the river being salt. Agathocles is then besieged in Syracuse.

311 Antigonus makes a truce with his rivals, except with Seleucus, who now holds Babylon.
Cassander (see 316 above) has Roxana and Alexander Aegus put to death.

The central, but confused, situation after the death of Alexander is a struggle for power amongst his generals which lasts for two decades. The protagonists, the "Diadochi", are:—

Ptolemy (Egypt)
Seleucus (Babylon and Syria)
Antipater and his son *Cassander* (Macedon and Greece)
Antigonus (Phrygia and other parts of Asia Minor)
Lysimachus (Thrace and Pergamum)
Eumenes (the Pontus area).

A. **Politics, Law and Economics**

The spread of hellenism (see C) is helped by the founding by the Diadochi of many new cities (mostly named after themselves).

Egyptian agriculture is encouraged by Ptolemy I (and his successors), so that she becomes eventually the granary of Rome.

Judaea is given a large measure of self-government by Ptolemy I.

312   Appius Claudius, Roman Censor, asserts the right of freed slaves to hold office. There is begun the great southern road named after him, the Via Appia.

B. **Science and Discovery**

320   Pytheas, the navigator of Marseilles, *fl.* (or possibly a little earlier). In his *Ocean* and *Periplus* (only fragments of which remains) he tells of tin-mining in Cornwall, of the Goths who collect amber on the shores of the Baltic, and of "Thule", 6 days sail north of Britain. He makes astronomical observations for determining latitude.

Euclid begins his work in Alexandria.

Theophrastus writes his "herbal", *On Plants.*

317   Seleucus is helped in his capture of Babylon by his effecting an alteration in the course of the Euphrates (as Cyrus had done – see 539).

315   Learning from their defeats, the Romans revise their adherence to the phalanx as the best tactical weapon in favour of a formation less cumbersome and better suited to a more mountainous type of warfare. This is the *maniple* or "handful" of men, 120 strong, armed with javelin and short sword.

312   Appius Claudius builds an aqueduct for Rome's most populous quarter.

C. **Religion and Philosophy**

The Diadochi, ruling in hellenic courts by the aid of Greek soldiers and ministers, deliberately diffuse hellenic culture, a fact more significant than their wars against one another. Conversely the religions of the East begin to affect Greek thought. The rulers themselves deified, and do not object.

317   Cassander entrusts the government of Athens to the philosopher and orator Demetrius Phalereus (but see 307 C).

D. **The Arts**

318   Aristoxenus of Tarsas, a pupil of Aristotle, writes a treatise on music, *Harmonics.*

E. **Literature**

Athens' so-called New Comedy flourishes at this time, the chief writers being Philemon and, a younger man and nephew of Alexis (354 E), Menander.

316   Menander's *Dyscolus* wins first prize at the Lenaea. (This is the only complete play of Menander to survive, though fragments of other plays have been found on papyri from Egypt).

F.   **Births and Deaths**

319   Antipater d.

318   Pyrrhus of Epirus b. (–272).

316   Eumenes of Pontus d.
Olympias d.

315   Theocritus, poet of Syracuse, b.

311   Roxana and Alexander Aegus (12) d.

310   Rome has to deal with renewed trouble from the Etruscans.

310/8   Antigonus resumes his attacks on Seleucus in Babylon, but without success.

310/7   Agathocles (see 312) escapes from Syracuse and carries the war into his enemy's territory. In the next three years he nearly succeeds in conquering Carthage, the city being in the throes of a civil war against its would-be tyrant Bomilcar. In spite of the fact however that Hamilcar fails to take Syracuse and is killed, Agathocles has at length to return to attend to trouble at home. Peace is made with Carthage, the Syracusans being bought off with 300 talents.

308/5   The tribes of the central Apennines rise against the Romans, who, with the Samnite war on their hands, have a very difficult time. Their command of the coastal strip and their growing military efficiency save them.

307   Antigonus makes peace with Seleucus, who is left free to consolidate his kingdom.

306   Antigonus gives himself the title of king, and the other Diadochi follow suit.

305/4   Demetrius, son of Antigonus, tries to invest Rhodes (see B & D) but fails; help is given to the Rhodians by Ptolemy (who has built himself a fleet), thereby earning the title of *Soter*, Saviour.

305/3   Seleucus consolidates his Asian empire as far as India—where however, meeting opposition from Chandragupta, he relinquishes all claims, receiving as a gift 500 war-trained elephants (see 301). Chandragupta gains control of the Indus valley as well as the Ganges valley.

304   Agathocles, ruling with cruelty in Syracuse, follows the Diadochi's example and calls himself king.
The Second Samnite war ends with a peace wherein Rome gains no territory but the Samnites renounce their hegemony over Campania.

303   Cassander and Lysimachus persuade Seleucus and Ptolemy to join them in trying to destroy Antigonus.

302   Antigonus' son Demetrius makes a main attack on Cassander in Thessaly. This however has to be abandoned when Antigonus finds his enemies closing in on him and a truce is made. Demetrius reaches Ephesus in his father's support.

301   Lysimachus effects a junction with Seleucus and there ensues at Ipsus in Phrygia the "battle of the kings" wherein is decided the fate of Alexander's empire. The numbers involved are about equal, some 70 to 80 thousand on each side; but Lysimachus and Seleucus have 120 chariots and also some 480 elephants to Antigonus' 75 chariots. The mass of elephants helps to cut off Demetrius and his cavalry, who fail to save Antigonus from death. The Phrygians, now to be subjected to a harsher rule, mourn Antigonus.
Pyrrhus, the young king of Epirus, is turned out of his kingdom at the instigation of Cassander and is present at the battle of Ipsus.

----

303   The treaty between Seleucus and Chandragupta leaves the latter in a strong position with the foundations of the Mauryan empire well laid.

A. **Politics, Law and Economics**
   During the fourth century prices rise in the hellenic world disproportionately to wages, the drachma losing half its value.

310 Agathocles has a ruthless method of raising funds for his invasion of Carthage: he helps rich citizens of Syracuse to escape the siege and then has them murdered and relieved of their riches.

305 Under Chandragupta the city of Taxila becomes a centre of learning and law.
   Though Lysimachus and Antigonus both found cities to which they give their own names, it is only the one founded by Seleucus at this time, Seleucia on the Tigris, that grows to historical and economic importance. Its prosperity spells the final end of the dominance of Babylon.

B. **Science and Discovery**
307 Wu Ling, king of the northern chinese state of Chao, having experienced much fighting with the Huns, makes his army change over from horse chariots to cavalry, and to adopt a form of dress more suitable to riding.

306 In physics Epicurus (see C) supports the atomic theory of Democritus.

305 Demetrius, son of Antigonus, earns the title, *Poliorcetes* or Besieger of Cities, by the construction of the great engines with which he fails to subdue Rhodes (and see 304 D).

C. **Religion and Philosophy**
310 Euhemerus, at the court of Cassander, writes his *Sacred History*, ascirbing to all myths an historical basis (hence "euhemerism": a book with an atheistical slant).

307 Demetrius Phalereus (see 317 C) is obliged to flee from Athens on the approach of his namesake the son of Antigonus. He settles in Alexandria.

306 Epicurus of Samos takes up permanent residence in Athens, purchases a garden and there establishes his philosophic school, the Epicurean. He allows women pupils.

D. **The Arts**
304 Demetrius Poliorcetes in admiration of the valour of the Rhodians, bequeaths to them his siege engines—which they sell and so provide themselves with means to build their "Colossus" (see 280 D).

E. **Literature**
307 With the help of Demetrius Phalereus (see C) Ptolemy I begins the foundation of Alexandria's famous library and museum.

303 Seleucus leaves behind his ambassador Megasthenes at the court of Chandragupta. Megasthenes writes most informative reports.

F. **Births and Deaths**

308 Hamilcar (II) d.

305 Theopompus, Greek historian, d. (73).

301 Antigonus d. (81c).

The Romans defeat the Samnites; the Mauryan empire is
                  extended

299   The Samnites, seizing their chance when Rome is engaged on the Lombard plain,
      start the Third Samnite War with a collection of Gaulish marauders and Etruscan
      allies to help them.

298   The Romans penetrate into the heart of the Samnite country.

297   Cassander, secure as King of Macedon after the battle of Ipsus, dies a natural death.

297/1 In India Chandragupta abdicates in favour of his son Bindusara (known to the
      Greeks as Amitrochates, perhaps from the Sanskrit for "The Destroyer of Foes").
      Bindusara extends the Mauryan empire as far south as Mysore. He continues cul-
      tural contact with the Seleucids, asking, it is said, for a Sophist to be sent to his
      court.

296   A Samnite force slips north and, with the Gauls, prepares to advance on Rome. It is
      held and defeated at the battle of Sentinum.

295   Pyrrhus, with forces supplied by Ptolemy, regains his Epirot throne.

294   Demetrius Poliorcetes is acknowledged king of Macedonia, and manages to keep his
      throne for 7 years.

293   Seleucus I hands over the government of his lands W. of the Euphrates to his son
      Antiochus; he also hands over his young wife Stratonice.
      Rome suffers from the Plague (see C).

291   The Third Samnite War ends, with the Samnites subdued but recognized by the
      Romans as autonomous allies.

———————————

Greece, in her trade and culture and emigration, is concerned henceforward much
more with the lands to the east of her than to the west; the western Mediterranean
becomes the scene of the Roman–Carthaginian struggle—introduced however by
the last adventure of Greek blood in these parts, Pyrrhus.

A. Politics, Law and Economics

300 Athens and Corinth remain the most important of the Greek cities; but even these are suffering from the self-seeking of the rich and a decline in economic prosperity: the only openings for the people seem to be emigration or service as mercenary soldiers abroad.

Pyrrhus (see 301) goes as a hostage to Egypt after the battle of Ipsus and makes a diplomatic marriage with the princess Antigone, daughter of Ptolemy I and Berenice.

300 Seleucus I founds the city of Antioch, some 20 miles up the river Orontes, naming it after his father. At his capital city of Seleucia (see 305 A) he perpetuates an absolute monarchy that is, in spite of hellenism, essentially oriental.

The early Ptolemies set up in Egypt an efficient bureaucracy, run mostly by Greeks; trade increases, and is mostly in the hands of Jews.

B. Science and Discovery

Greek science, as opposed to Greek literature, reaches its height in this hellenistic age, and chiefly at Alexandria.

300 Ptolemy I for the last fifteen years of his reign (to 285 B.C.) devotes himself to the patronage of science and literature, surrounding himself with such men as Demetrius Phalereus and Euclid.

C. Religion and Philosophy

300 Zeno of Cyprus, at the age of about 40 and having lived and learnt in Athens for some dozen years, opens his school of philosophy at the Stoa Poikile; his disciples become known as the Stoics. The date of his death are not known but he is reputed to have lived to the age of 98. Antigonus II (see 277 C) becomes his great admirer.

The Jews of Jerusalem, surrounded and threatened by a sophisticated hellenism, found a puritan sect called Chasidim.

Generally in the Seleucid empire, as a counterpart to hellenism, oriental religions and mysticism permeate the Greeks: Artemis (Diana) of Ephesus becomes many-breasted.

297 Chandragupta, after abdicating in favour of his son Bindusara, is said to have gently starved himself to death in the method of Jainism, which religion he has adopted.

293 The worship of Aesculapius is introduced from Epidaurus to Rome, in the hope of averting the Plague.

D. The Arts

Antioch—like many of the new hellenistic cities—is *planned* in its building and is magnificent in an ornate Corinthian style.

E. Literature

300 Ptolemy I, in the last 15 years of his reign, writes a history of the wars of Alexander the Great.

E.   Literature (continued)

296   Even so late in the history of the disintegrating Chou dynasty, the literary output is still immense in China: the books found buried in a king's tomb of this date are said to have filled ten waggons.

300   Manetho, the Egyptian priest, historian and chronologist, *fl.* (See 3200 E).

F.   **Births and Deaths**

300   Cleanthes, Stoic, b. (–220).

297   Cassander d.
      Chandragupta d.

291   Menander d. (51).

290–281 B.C.   **The city of Pergamum begins its rise to greatness, as does King Pyrrhus**

289 Agathocles of Syracuse ends his life amidst dynastic turmoil.
Some of Agathocles' disbanded mercenaries seize Messana in N.E. Sicily and set up a society, calling themselves Mamertines or Children of Mars (and see 265).

287 Demetrius Poliorcetes (see 294) is deserted by his troops, who proclaim Pyrrhus king of Macedonia.

286 Pyrrhus is driven out by Lysimachus, who becomes for a while king of Macedon.
Demetrius flees to Seleucus, and dies three years later —it is said, of drink.

285 Ptolemy I (Soter) abdicates in favour of his youngest son Ptolemy II (Philadelphus).

283 Antigonus II (Gonates) assumes the title of King of Macedon, on the death of his father Demetrius.
Ptolemy I dies.
At a battle near Lake Vadimo Rome finally quells the allied Etruscans and Gauls (see 299). Rome is at last undisputed master of northern and central Italy.

282 The Asia Minor city of Pergamum gets rid of Lysimachus (see 320) and begins its years of greatness.
The Magna Graecia city of Thurii appeals to Rome for help against the pressure of native tribes. Though the Senate hesitates, the plebean Assembly decides to respond. Thurii is saved; but Tarentum, jealous of Rome's interference, attacks and sinks some Roman ships entering her harbour. Roman envoys, sent to protest, are maltreated, and Rome declares war on Tarentum. Tarentum finds a new champion in King Pyrrhus of Epirus, always willing to fight for anything Greek and to assume the mantle of Alexander, (from whom, though only by marriage, he is descended).

281 Seleucus I invades Macedonia and meets Lysimachus in battle. Lysimachus is killed, leaving Seleucus the surviving "Diadochus" (heir to Alexander).

A. Politics, Law and Economics
290 Berenice, wife of Ptolemy I, has the city of Berenice built on the Red Sea; it becomes a great emporium for Egyptian trade with the East.

289 The death of Agathocles of Syracuse, whose power and prestige has spread to southern Italy, leaves the somewhat effete cities of Magna Graecia at the mercy again of the native Italians (see 382).
In Rome the *Lex Hortensia* gives much greater power to the plebeian Assembly *vis-à-vis* the Senate.

283 The canal from the Nile to the Red Sea, built by Necho and repaired by Dairus I, is again repaired by Ptolemy II.

B. Science and Discovery
285 Herophilus, anatomist working at Alexandria, dissects the human eye and brain and establishes the latter as the seat of thought.

283 The great Alexandrine lighthouse on the island of Pharos is built. Sostratus of Cnidus is said to have been the architect.
Ptolemy II enlarges his father's museum at Alexandria.

C. Religion and Philosophy
289 After the death of Mencius his disciples publish his teachings, the *Book of Meng-tzu*.

D. The Arts
A school of sculpture develops in Rhodes (and see 378 D).

E. Literature
283 Ptolemy II enlarges the library at Alexandria and appoints the grammarian Zenodotus to collect and edit all the Greek poets.

F. Births and Deaths
289 Mencius d. (83*c*).
Agathocles d. (72).

288 Theophrastus d. (82).

287 Archimedes b. (–212).

283 Demetrius Phalereus d.
Demetrius Poliorcetes d. (56).
Ptolemy I d.
Euclid d. (40).

281 Lysimachus d.

280   Seleucus I, having defeated Lysimachus in Macedonia, is assassinated by one of the sons of Ptolemy I. Antiochus I (see 293) succeeds fully to the throne of the Seleucid or Syrian empire.

Pyrrhus, responding with enthusiasm to the appeal of Tarentum (see 282) lands in Italy with an army of 20,000. Near Heraclea the armies meet, and the Romans are beaten; Pyrrhus' losses however are nearly as great as theirs.

279   Pyrrhus, approaching Rome, realizes he cannot take the city, and suggests peace terms. These are refused, largely at the instigation of the ex-censor, Appius Claudius (see 312 A). Pyrrhus' efforts to impress the Romans in parley include the sudden confrontation of one of the Consuls with an elephant hidden behind a screen. The consul is not impressed; nor can he be bribed.

In renewed fighting, the Epirot king wins another "Pyrrhic" victory, at Asculum; disheartened, he retires on Tarentum; and—despising the effete Tarentines—makes renewed peace overtures to Rome.

A horde of Gauls, under another Brennus (see 390), sweep down through Macedonia into Greece, killing and plundering. They are halted only just before reaching Delphi (see C).

278   These Gauls cross to Asia Minor where they eventually settle down to become the "Galatians".

278/6   The Carthaginians, seizing an opportunity to interfere in a quarrel between Syracuse and Agrigentum (Greek Acragas), besiege the Syracusans—who send for help to Pyrrhus. Pyrrhus abandons the Tarentines and moves on to Sicily. He again wins battles and thinks even of attacking Carthage. After two years the Greeks of Sicily ask him to go away, which he does—leaving, as he says, a "fair wrestling ring" for Carthage and Rome.

277   Antigonus II gains possession of his Macedonian throne.

275   Pyrrhus, having lost some of his fleet to the Carthaginians on crossing to Italy, continues the fight against Rome with diminishing success and after a defeat at Malventum (soon to be called Beneventum, see 268 C), returns home with only about a third of his original army. His captured elephants appear in the Roman "triumph", the first to be seen.

274/1   Antiochus I (see 280) is defending his Seleucid possessions in the so-called 1st Syrian War.

273   Pyrrhus invades Macedonia and turns out Antigonus II.

272   Antigonus II regains his throne, and settles down to rule with moderation for 33 years (and see C). Pyrrhus turns his arms against Sparta and Argos and in the latter city he is killed by a tile hurled by a woman from an upper window.

Rome makes peace with Tarentum and the other Greek cities of S. Italy: they are left as free allies, and have to supply a quota of ships rather than of soldiers.

272   Asoka succeeds Bindusara on the Mauryan throne and continues the policy of war and expansion.

A. Politics, Law and Economics

280   Ptolemy II introduces the camel and a camel-post into Egypt.

Rhodes, rising to prosperity after her defiance of Demetrius (see 305), becomes head of an "Island League" and helps to keep the peace and freedom of the Aegean Sea.

Under the Seleucids the Asia Minor cities regain commercial prosperity and even achieve some specialisation, Miletus becoming a textile centre. There is some slave-manned mass production.

279   Two further efforts at co-operation are made by the mainland cities of Greece: the Aetolian League north of the Corinthian Gulf and the Achaean League to the south are refounded. Both achieve a common coinage and foreign policy, and they pool their armed forces. (And see 251 and 220).

278   The Gauls in Asia Minor are subsidized by the Seleucids to keep the peace: 2000 talents a year are paid out, and for about 50 years.

273   Ptolemy II, impressed by Rome's defeat of Pyrrhus, sends a friendly embassy, and the visit is reciprocated: Rome has begun to be recognized as a power in the international scene and hellenic world.

B. Science and Discovery

280   Aristarchus of Samos, astronomer, *fl.*, now and for the next 20 years. He writes *On the Size and Distances of the Sun and the Moon.*

At the battle of Heraclea (see opposite) the Romans meet for the first time a professional army on the Macedonian plan, together with Pyrrhus' 20 elephants — which defeat their cavalry (never a very strong Roman arm).

C. Religion and Philosophy

280   Ptolemy II makes Alexandria, even more than his father has done, the centre of art, science, philosophy and literature. He himself favours the philosophy of hedonism.

279   Brennus, the Gaul, is said to have been prevented from desecrating the shrine of Apollo at Delphi by a miraculous storm, and, when so defeated, to have killed himself in shame.

275   Timon of Phlius *fl.*, sophist and sceptic. As a sophist he has amassed a fortune.

272   Antigonus II of Macedon, a liberal and artistic ruler, endeavours — without success — to persuade Zeno (see 300 C) to reside at his court and teach him to be a Platonic philosopher-king.

D. The Arts

280   The Colossus of Rhodes is finally set up (see 304 D), the greatest of many new statues in this now flourishing city. It is made in bronze by Chares (who is said to have committed suicide when the cost exceeded his estimate), and then by Laches. It is 105 ft high and holds a torch aloft.

E. Literature

275   Theocritus, Syracusan poet, writes in praise of Ptolemy II.

275   Celts from the River Marne district settle in England, occupying particularly the Yorkshire wolds. These Celts are of the La Tène culture (see 450 D), known so far as Britain is concerned as the Iron Age B culture. They spread (see 100)—and where they meet Iron Age A forts they tend to re-fortify them in a most elaborate way, with triple fortifications.

E. **Literature** (continued)
272 Livius Andronicus (see 240 E) is brought to Rome as a captive slave.

F. **Births and Deaths**
280 Seleucus I (77).
     Chrysippus b. (–207).

276 Eratosthenes b. (–196).

272 Bindusara d.
     Pyrrhus d. (46).

271 Aratus of Sicyon b. (–213).

270   The town of Rhegium in S. Italy, having been seized by the Romans in their Pyrrhic war, is restored to its Greek inhabitants.

270/61   Asoka consolidates his Mauryan empire but fails to conquer Kalinga (modern Orissa).

267   The Athenians, under a young disciple of Zeno called Chremonides, make a last bid for freedom from Macedonian overlordship. They secure some help from Egypt and turn out the Macedonian garrison.

267   Hieron, the young King of Syracuse (descendant of the tyrant Hieron, see 474) beats back the Mamertines (see 289) from his territory.

265   On Hieron threatening to renew his attack on the Mamertines, the latter appeal to Carthage and receive a Carthaginian garrison: they then appeal to the Romans, who also respond. The Mamertines get rid of their Carthaginian garrison and welcome Appius Claudius (a relative of the Censor) and his two legions. The Carthaginians, affronted, send a force to Sicily, and they are supported by Hieron. Appius Claudius beats them off. The first Punic war has begun.

263   The Romans attack Syracuse and force Hieron into alliance with them. Hieron continues a beneficent rule of Syracuse.

262   Antiochus I is succeeded by Antiochus II on the Seleucid throne.
The Carthaginians are defeated by the Romans at Agrigentum. They retire to organize their fleet; the Romans sack Agrigentum and enslave its Greek inhabitants.

261   The Romans, determined now to win Sicily from Carthage and realizing the need for a navy, rapidly make a hundred copies of a captured Carthaginian quinquireme and train the necessary oarsmen.
Antigonus II recaptures Athens (see 267), re-garrisons her and forbids her to make war, but otherwise leaves her to herself as the seat, still, of philosophy and learning.

A. Politics, Law and Economics

270   Rome, having successfully concluded her long-drawn Italian wars, continues with a determined economic policy of colony-planting (in Italy—see e.g. 268 C) and road making: the Via Appia is extended southwards.

Carthage, already in control of Sardinia as well as of southern Spain and of her own Numidian neighbours, is ruled by an oligarchy of merchants under two Suffetes or Chief Magistrates, the stability of her government having been admired by Aristotle. She throws up good and dedicated military commanders but inclines to rely on mercenaries (e.g. from Spain) for her soldiers; she has naval control of the western Mediterranean. In Sicily, since Pyrrhus' departure, she has re-occupied most of the island, excluding however Syracuse.

269   First silver coinage in Rome.

B. Science and Discovery

270   Aratus, poet of Soli in Cilicia, writes on astronomy.

266   Eudoxus of Cnidus, *fl.* Having studied in Athens and Egypt, he builds an observatory and is said to be the first to teach the Greeks the motions of the planets.

262   The Carthaginians send elephants to Sicily, but at the battle of Agrigentum these cause rather more confusion in their own ranks than in those of the Romans.

C. Religion and Philosophy

268   The Romans, founding a colony at Malventum (see 275), change the name, for superstitious reasons, to Beneventum.

263   Cleanthes succeeds Zeno in his Stoic school at Athens. The story goes that he has been previously brought before the Areopagus for having no visible means of support; on showing however that he works at night (at gardening) so that his teaching should not be interfered with, he is awarded 10 minae—which Zeno will not let him accept.

D. The Arts

270   Ptolemy II erects on Samothrace the Rotunda, dedicated to his wife and sister Arsinoe, after whom he has named several cities.

E. Literature

270   Aratus of Soli, didactic poet, *fl.* and is patronized by Antigonus II. (And see B).

F. Births and Deaths

270   Epicurus d. (72).
        Arsinoe d.

263   Zeno d. (70).

262   Antiochus I d.

260–251 B.C.   Regulus is defeated outside Carthage; the Chou Dynasty of
China ends

260   The Mauryan emperor Asoka completes the conquest of virtually the whole of the
Indian sub-continent by the bloody defeat of Kalinga—but see 258 C.

The Romans with their new fleet (see 261) win a resounding naval victory over the
Carthaginians off Mylae, near the Straits of Messina. (And see B). (This victory
may have occurred 2 years earlier).

260/53   The Seleucids and Ptolemies are at war again—2nd Syrian War.

259   In China the state of Ch'in, climbing rapidly to power, defeats the state of Chao at the
battle of Ch'ang P'ing (in the great bend of the Yellow River).

258   The Romans take Corsica from the Carthaginians.

256   The state of Ch'in makes war upon the last of the Chou emperors, who abdicates.
(And see 246).

The Romans repeat their naval success at the battle of Ecnomus. They send a force
under Regulus to Africa, which begins very well and settles down for the winter in
hope of capturing the city of Carthage in the Spring.

255   The Carthaginians, revitalized by the Spartan mercenary Xanthippus, defeat and
capture Regulus. A Roman fleet, sent to the rescue, is wrecked.

254   In Sicily the Romans capture the Carthaginian naval base of Panormus but find it
difficult to make further progress without command of the sea.

253   A second Roman fleet is wrecked.

252   A census gives the number of Roman citizens as 297,797. The trustworthiness of the
figures however must be doubtful.

251   The Achaean League (see 279 A) is revivified by the accession of the young Aratus of
Sicyon, who frees his city from its tyrants.

A. Politics, Law and Economics

256   Asoka (following the Persian practice of erecting rock-inscriptions) mentions that he has exchanged diplomatic missions during his reign with kings who have been identified as Antiochus II, Ptolemy III and Antigonus II. For the next hundred years there is considerable Indian contact with the West, with the Seleucid empire in particular.

     Asoka also makes diplomatic contacts with Nepal and Ceylon (and see C).

B. Science and Discovery

260   The Romans owe their naval victory of Mylae largely to their invention of the corvus or crow's bill, a hinged and hooked boarding plank.

258   Erasistratus of Ceos founds a medical school at Alexandria.

256   Asoka founds hospitals and herb gardens, and encourages the education of women.

C. Religion and Philosophy

258   Asoka (see 260) experiences a revulsion of feeling after his conquests and becomes a Buddhist and a pacifist. He then helps to spread abroad the original teachings of Gautama Buddha, and his missionaries carry to Ceylon a cutting of the original Bo tree under which Gautama sat (see 524 C).

D. The Arts

258   The great Buddhist *stupa* at Sanchi (in Madhya Pradesh) is probably begun now, under the direction of Asoka.

E. Literature

260   Callimachus of Cyrene, learned poet and grammarian, catalogues the library at Alexandria; some of his poems, on the *Origins* of local rituals, are extant. Other works of his that survive include hymns and epigrams.

F. Births and Deaths

254   Plautus b. (-184).

250–241 B.C. **China's Ch'in Dynasty is founded; the Romans win the first Punic war**

250 The Romans begin the siege of the Carthaginian city of Lilybaeum in Sicily.

249 Berenice, daughter of Ptolemy II, is married to the Seleucid Antiochus II, he divorcing his wife Laodice for the occasion. (This may have been 3 years earlier.)
The Romans meet further naval reverses outside Lilybaeum and fail to take the city. The captive Regulus (see 255) goes home on parole with Carthaginian peace terms. These are refused—on Regulus' advice (and see E).

247 The Carthaginians, suffering from divided counsels and failing to take the opportunity of Rome's weakness, at length find a new general, Hamilcar Barca, and send him to Sicily.
Arsaces, chief of an Iranian nomad tribe, the Parsii, murders the Seleucid governor of Persia and sets up the kingdom of the Parthians.

246 The short-lived Ch'in Dynasty is set up in China with the accession of Shih-Huang-ti (or "First August Emperor," a title remarkably similar to that later adopted by Octavian).
Ptolemy II dies and is succeeded by Ptolemy III, more interested in military conquest than his predecessor.
Laodice murders Antiochus II and Berenice (see 249). Ptolemy III sets out to avenge his sister and also on a career of conquest in the Seleucid empire (now under Seleucus II). This is the 3rd Syrian War.

246/2 With Hamilcar Barca wearing them down in Sicily, the Romans determine on an effort to regain command of the sea; they build yet another fleet.

245 Aratus of Sicyon (see 251) is elected general of the Achaean League and frees Corinth from its Macedonian garrison.

245/1 Ptolemy III temporarily defeats and permanently weakens most of the Seleucid empire, reaching as far as Bactria and the borders of India. He is forced however to return to Egypt to meet internal trouble, and the Seleucid rulers resume control. (And see C).

241 The Romans with their new fleet win a resounding victory off Lilybaeum and the Carthaginians accept severe terms of peace (see A).
Attulus I succeeds to throne of Pergamum.

A. Politics, Law and Economics

247   The Carthaginian oligarchy show more interest in carving out large estates in the African interior than prosecuting the Roman war.

Rome contracts a treaty, on equal terms, with Hieron of Syracuse, stated to be "for ever".

242   A second praetor is appointed in Rome with the special function of dispensing justice in suits where non-citizens are involved. This official's yearly edict becomes the basis of Rome's code of law for foreigners, the *Jus Gentium*.

241   By the peace terms at the end of the First Punic War Carthage agrees to abandon all claim to Sicily, to refrain from sailing her warships in Italian waters, and to pay an indemnity of 3,200 talents. Her army however is allowed to return home with its arms.

B. Science and Discovery

250   Hero of Alexandria *fl.* In geometry he invents the formula for the area of a triangle in the terms of its sides; in pneumatics he invents many ingenious machines, including the automatic opening of doors (e.g. temple doors by apparent magic) and a steam engine working on the jet-reaction principle. No practical use is made of these inventions—with the exception of the water clock. (And see 175 B. The Greek name for the water clock is clepsydra; the mechanical clock with its train of gears is a medieval invention).

C. Religion and Philosophy

250   Ptolemy II encourages the Jews in Alexandria to have their Bible translated into Greek. By tradition there were seventy translators: hence the name of their product, the Septuagint.

245/1 Ptolemy III returns from his conquests of the Seleucids with much booty, including many statues of Egyptian gods carried off by Cambyses. These he restores to their temples, earning the title of Euergetes, the Benefactor.

D. The Arts

In Greece and Egypt the art of mosaic, with cube tesserae, is established.

E. Literature

250   Iambulus, a follower of Zeno the Stoic, writes a kind of Utopia of a "blessed Isle in the Indian Ocean".

249   Regulus, on parole (see opposite), faithfully returns to captivity, and the Roman legend arises that he was tortured to death. His widow tortures two Carthaginian prisoners in reprisal.

241   Ptolemy III's wife Berenice enthuses the poets by dedicating a lock of her hair to the gods in thanks for her husband's military successes; a constellation is called "Berenice's Hair".

F. **Births and Deaths**

249 Regulus d.

247 Hannibal the Great b. (–183*c*).

246 Ptolemy II d.
Antiochus II and his wife Berenice d.

240   Rome takes over full control of Sicily and stations a legion there.
China's emperor Shih Huang-ti, beats back the Huns before building his Great Wall (see 225).

240/37   Carthage's returned troops, mostly mercenaries, are deprived of their arrears of pay and badly treated by the city's rulers; a ruthless and terrible civil war ensues (called by Polybius "the truceless war") in which the proletariat join the mercenaries under two leaders, Spendius and Matho. Hamilcar Barca finally puts down the rebellion and the two leaders are killed.

239   Sardinia revolts against Carthage, and Rome takes the opportunity to annex the island.

237   Carthage having in the last three decades lost her hold upon Spain, Hamilcar Barca is sent to re-establish it. Hamilcar sees in this command the chance to build up a base from which war can be renewed against Rome.

235   Rome closes the gates of the Temple of Janus, as a signal that she is at peace.

235/1   Attalus I, Pergamum's greatest king, begins to build up the city's power and importance.

231   Seleucus II, following the example of Ptolemy III (see 246) campaigns in Bactria, and also in the newly formed Parthia, where King Tiridates, brother of Arsaces (see 247) defeats him.

231   In Illyria the Queen Mother, Teuta, comes into power as regent.

A. Politics, Law and Economics

240   The emperor Shih Huang-ti (see 246) does his best to change China's feudal system into a totalitarian one, with communal land-holding and a standardization of all weights, measures and tools throughout the land.

240   Rome treats Sicily more like a defeated country than she has ever treated any part of Italy. She taxes the Sicilian peasant and imports from her an increasing amount of corn, the Roman farmer turning more to the olive and the vine.

232   The land just north of Rome, the Ager Gallicus, is parcelled out in small holdings to poor citizens; it proves an attraction to the Gauls further north (see 226).

B. Science and Discovery

240   Eratosthenes (see E) writes on most current branches of knowledge; his systematic treatise on geography is to be made great use of by Strabo.

C. Religion and Philosophy

240   Rome in annexing Sicily makes its first really close contact with hellenism and a rather decadent hellenism at that, with considerable influence on the staid puritanical morality of the Republican Romans.

240   Chryspippus *fl.* He teaches Stoic philosophy at Athens and combats scepticism: a prolific writer.

D. The Arts

The Emperor Shih Huang-ti, at his new capital of Hsien-yan, builds a vast number of palaces, a new one for each prince he defeats; the plan of the city is said to imitate the milky way, each house representing a star.
At Alexandria an organ with bronze pipes is made.

E. Literature

240   Livius Andronicus has his first tragedy produced in Rome. He is the first known Roman poet and playwright, and a Greek slave. He translates the Odyssey into Latin.
Eratosthenes of Cyrene succeeds Callimachus as librarian at Alexandria (and see B).

237   There is a Roman legend that Hamilcar Barca, on setting out for his campaign in Spain, makes his young son Hannibal vow eternal hostility to Rome.

F. Births and Deaths

240   Callimachus, poet, d.

239   Antigonus II d.
Ennius (Roman poet) b. (–169).

238   Masinissa of Numidia b. (–148).

F.   **Births and Deaths** (continued)
237   Philip V of Macedon (–179).

234   P. Cornelius Scipio (Africanus Major) b. (–183c).
        Cato the Censor b. (–169).

232   Asoka d.

230   The city of Pergamum, under its king Attalus I, beats off a fresh wave of invading
       Gauls (and see D).
       Italian merchants, and then Roman envoys, are murdered by the Illyrians (see 231).
       The Romans occupy the island of Corcyra, where they stay; they humble Queen
       Teuta.

229   Antigonus III ("Doson", so-called because he had the probably unjustified reputation
       of making promises he does not keep) comes to the Macedonian throne as regent for
       the future King Philip V of Macedon, now only 8 years old.
       Hamilcar Barca, in his successful campaign to re-subdue Spain, is drowned; his son-
       in-law Hasdrubal succeeds him. Hasdrubal founds New Carthage as a Spanish
       naval base, and penetrates further inland.

227   Rome makes Sardinia and Corsica a combined province (see 258 & 239); she appoints,
       and in future annually elects, two ner Praetors (with autocratic consular powers) for
       this province and for Sicily.

226   A formidable host of Gauls, some of them from across the Alps, threaten Rome.

225   Rhodes is ruined by an earthquake, and the whole hellenic world—Seleucid, Ptole-
       maic and Macedonian—comes to her aid with magnificent and practical gifts.
       The Romans decisively defeat the Gauls, led by the Boii, at the battle of Telamon.

225   The Emperor Shih Huang-ti begins building China's Great Wall against the en-
       croachment of the Huns, incorporating some early fortifications, and stretching in
       all over 2000 miles. It is said to have taken 12 years to build (and see C).

223   Seleucus III after a reign of only 3 years is assassinated and is succeeded by his
       brother Antiochus III, called the Great.

222   Mediolanum (Milan), stronghold of the Gallic tribe of the Insubres, is taken by the
       Romans, the consul, Marcellus, personally slaying the chief Britomartus. The
       threat of the year 226 subsides.
       Cleomenes III of Sparta becomes involved in war with Antigonus III and the
       Achaean League; on being defeated he flees to Egypt but commits suicide. (And see
       230 A).

221   Ptolemy IV comes to the Egyptian throne, murders his mother (the Berenice of the
       lock of hair, see 241 E) and begins a reign of personal luxury and the deterioration
       of his kingdom.
       Hasdrubal, still campaigning to increase Carthaginian hold over Spain, is murdered.
       Hamilcar Bara's young son, Hannibal, succeeds to the command.
       Shih Huang-ti, having defeated all his enemies, is now undisputed Emperor of China.

The Mauryan Empire, after the death of Asoka in 232, declines rapidly, to disappear
completely in the next fifty years.

A. Politics, Law and Economics

230 King Cleomenes III of Sparta, having come to the throne in 236, endeavours to restore his country's ancient constitution and becomes in the process something of a proletarian champion in the Peloponnese (but see 222).

230/228 By the defence of her nationals and her interference in Illyria, Rome becomes embroiled for the first time with the affairs of Greece. The Greeks congratulate Rome on quelling the Illyrian pirates and Corinth offers to let her take part in the Ismithian games. Antigonus III, the new king of Macedonia, is not so pleased however and pursues a policy of befriending the Illyrians—a policy which his successor Philip V is to continue.

226 The Greek merchants of Massilia, frightened by Carthaginian successes in Spain (including their exploitation of the silver-mines) appeal to Rome. Hasdrubal has to confine his activities to south of the R. Ebro. Rome makes an alliance with the independent city S. of the Ebro, Saguntum.

B. Science and Discovery

230 Archimedes constructs an enormous pleasure-boat for Hieron, with sports-deck, garden-deck and a marble swimming bath. It is said to have been a stadium (407 ft) in length and to have weighed 1000 tons. Proving too expensive to run, it is sent, filled with corn, to Egypt which is experiencing a famine.
Apollonius Pergaeus, geometer and pupil of Euclid, *fl.*

C. Religion and Philosophy

228 After their success over the Illyrians, (see A & opposite), the Romans are offered by Athens initiation into the Eleusinian mysteries.

225 The Emperor Shih Huang-ti, on being warned by a sooth-sayer that the success of the Great Wall depends on 10,000 men being buried beneath it, is said to have buried one man whose name embodies the word for "ten thousand".

D. The Arts

The defeat of the Gauls by the city of Pergamum is celebrated by statuary, some of which is extant, including the "Dying Gaul", (Byron's Dying Gladiator).

E. Literature

223 The Emperor of China, Shih Huang-ti, and his premier Li Ssu, order "the burning of the books" and generally discourage the ancient learning as being too conservative and reactionary. A copy of Confucius' works is officially kept however.

F. Births and Deaths

226 Seleucus II d.

223 Seleucus III d.

221 Ptolemy III d.
Hasdrubal, brother-in-law of Hannibal, d.
Berenice (III) d.

220 Antigonus Doson is succeeded by the young Philip V as King of Macedon. Philip immediately comes in collision with Rome over the Illyrian pirates. Rome strikes at these again and their chief seeks refuge with Philip—who is very resentful of Roman interference.

220/17 Internal war in Greece (the Social War).

219 The two ex-Alexandrian empires, of the Ptolemies and the Seleucids, go to war over the ownership of Phoenicia and Palestine. The 4th Syrian War.
Hannibal begins the Second Punic War by attacking Rome's Spanish city, Saguntum.

218 (Spring) Hannibal sets out from New Carthage (Cartagena) to march round the Mediterranean coast, over the Rhone and the Alps, to invade Italy. He is said to have started with nearly 100,000 men and 50 elephants.
The Romans send an army to Spain, which arrives too late to stop the Carthaginians. Hannibal crosses the Alps and after meeting great hardships and dangers (see B) reaches to Po valley in the late autumn.
(Dec.) The Roman consuls, Publius Scipio the Elder and Sempronius hasten to meet the Carthaginians with what troops can be mustered. At a skirmish on the River Ticinus Scipio is wounded and saved from death by his son (aged 17 and later to be the famous Scipio Africanus). The less skilful general, Sempronius, is left to fight the battle of the River Trebia and to be defeated by Hannibal's superior tactics.

217 Hannibal, on the way south, entraps the Romans and wins another victory at Trasimene. Quintus Fabius is elected Dictator and begins his strategy of "delay", avoiding a set battle and creating a "scorched earth" area around Hannibal's army.
Antiochus the Great is defeated in his war with the Ptolemies (see 219 above) at the battle of Raphia.

216 Quintus Fabius is relieved of his command by an impatient Senate. The Roman and Carthaginian armies meet at Cannae (east of Naples), and the Romans suffer a devastating defeat—according to Polybius their losses are 70,000 dead. Q. Fabius takes control again. The city of Capua takes sides with Hannibal, and the Carthaginian army winters there. Hannibal fails however to obtain much-needed reinforcements from Carthage.
Philip V of Macedon, still resenting Rome's interference, and seizing his opportunity, invades Illyria. (See also 215 A.) There begins, and continues in a desultory way for eleven years, Rome's First Macedonian War.
A revolt of the Egyptian peasants is put down by Ptolemy IV.

215/2 The Carthaginians fail to recapture Sardinia. Hannibal captures Tarentum but makes no further progress and hesitates to march on Rome. He is denied any reinforcements from Spain by the activities of Publius Scipio senior and his brother Gnaeus. Carthage has a success in persuading Syracuse, after the death of Hieron, to revolt against Rome.

214 The building of the Great Wall of China is completed.

212 Antiochus III, the Great, begins an effort to emulate Alexander in his eastern conquests (and see 205).

Archimedes helps Syracuse to withstand its siege, but dies with its fall

A. Politics, Law and Economics

220 The Via Flaminia is built.

219 Quintus Fabius, sent to Carthage to negotiate peace or war, makes a symbolic gesture with the folds of his toga: shall it be peace or war? The decision is left by the Carthaginians to him. He chooses war.

218 The Greek trading town of Ampurias, below the Pyranees and on the Spanish coast, allows Hannibal to pass unmolested.

215 Philip V of Macedon and Hannibal enter into a treaty of promised mutual help. It leads to no immediate action however.

212 The Romans have 25 legions and, it is said, a quarter of Italian manhood under arms. Their corn supplies are failing.
Scipio the younger (see 218) later to be "Africanus", is elected aedile though legally too young for the post.

211 Hannibal is discouraged outside Rome when he hears that the land on which he is encamped is up for auction in the city and that no less than the normal price is being offered.

B. Science and Discovery

218 Hannibal uses both science and psychology in crossing the Alps. When his elephants become stuck in a pass he uses fire and the soldiers' ration of vinegar with which to crack the rocks that are in the way. When his men become discouraged he puts on a show of prisoners who, it is demonstrated, jump at the chance to fight each other when told that the winner shall be set free: the Carthaginian army, Hannibal points out, is in a like situation.
At the battle on the river Trebia Hannibal's elephants help to win him victory; but in the ensuing winter they succumb to cold and damp.

213 Some of Archimedes' inventions help Syracuse to withstand its siege.

211 Archimedes dies when Syracuse falls—killed, it is said, by a Roman soldier while intent upon a mathematical problem.

C. Religion and Philosophy

220 Contacts with Carthage introduce to a small extent into Rome a practice of the Carthaginian religion, Dagon or Baal becoming Saturn.

213 The prophetic verses of the Italian seer, Marcius, are discovered and placed in the Capitol with the Sybilline books.

D. The Arts

216 At the funeral of one of the Lepidus family a spectacle of 22 combats is staged—the Greek funeral games are turning into the Roman gladiatorial combats.

212/11 The Numidian chiefs Syphax and Masinissa (senior) declare war on Carthage with Roman encouragement; Hannibal's brother Hasdrubal dashes across to Africa from Spain and stamps out this rebellion. Hasdrubal then returns to Spain, taking one of the chief's sons, Masinissa junior, with him. Then he manages to turn the tide against the Romans, and the two senior Scipios are killed in battle.

211 Syracuse falls to the siege of the Roman commander Marcellus (see 222).

In Italy the Romans besiege Capua (which has sided with Hannibal) and Hannibal, as a diversion, marches northwards on Rome, thus making a belated and unsuccessful effort to capture the city. Capua falls, and is punished.

E. **Literature**

220 Apollonius Rhodius *fl.* He worked as chief librarian at Alexandria. His *Argonautica* is extant.

F. **Births and Deaths**

220 Antigonus III d.
Cleomenes III of Sparta d.
Cleanthes, d. (80).

216 Hieron II d. (92).

213 Aratus of Sicyon d. (58).

213 Carneades b. (-129).

211 Archimedes d. (78).
Publius Scipio the Elder and his brother Gnaeus d.

210 The young Scipio (see 212 A), after the death of his father and uncle in Spain, is chosen to take over command in that country.

Shih Huang-ti dies and leaves a weak successor, Er Shi Huang-ti.

209 Scipio besieges and captures New Carthage. He recruits the young Numidian chief, Masinissa junior (see 212) onto his side, glad to have him as a dashing cavalry leader.

208 Marcellus (see 222), fighting under Scipio, is killed in battle.

207 Hasdrubal escapes from defeat in Spain and, crossing the Alps, tries to come to his brother Hannibal's rescue. On the River Metaurus (at the northern end of the Via Flaminia) Hasdrubal is defeated and his head is thrown into Hannibal's camp. Hannibal realizes that he has virtually lost the war in Italy and is powerless in the country he has invaded.

206 Er Shih Huang-ti is deposed after a reign of only four years, and China's Han dynasty is formed by Liu Pang, a man of the people.

206/5 Scipio, having successfully driven the Carthaginians out of Spain, returns in triumph to Rome and is elected Consul. He prepares to carry the war into the enemy's country but meets some difficulty with a jealous Senate (see A).

205 Antiochus III returns from his eastern campaigns, having failed to subjugate either the Bactrians or the Parthians.

Philip V of Macedon makes a temporary peace with Rome.

204 Ptolemy IV ends his life in dissipation and is succeeded by Ptolemy V, aged 5. Philip and Antiochus plan to divide the Ptolemaic kingdom between them.

Scipio invades Carthaginia; he besieges the city of Utica but fails to take it.

203 The Numidian chief Syphax, natural enemy of Masinissa (see 212 & 209), has now changed sides, and his army is encamped with that of the Carthaginian general, Gisco. Scipio, while pretending to prolong peace negotiations, makes a surprise attack on this camp and destroys it. Syphax and Gisco escape, and the latter prevails on the Carthaginians to raise new forces and to send for Hannibal to return home from Italy.

Hannibal finally leaves Italy and returns home.

202 Scipio, with Masinissa, advances on Carthage. Masinissa captures Syphax but becomes ensnared by the latter's wife Sophonisba. Scipio extricates him (see E).

Hannibal, returned, musters a considerable army; Scipio strikes into the interior to harry the country.

(Oct.) At Zama, 80 miles S.W. of Carthage, the two armies meet. The victory goes to Scipio (and see A & B).

201 A peace treaty (see A) ends the Second Punic War.

The Romans oust the Carthaginians from Malta (see 500).

A. Politics, Law and Economics

207 Nabis, a Syrian sold into slavery, rises to power in Sparta and succeeds (but see 193) in a social revolution, freeing all helots, and destroying the ruling oligarchy, redistributing land and cancelling debts.

205/4 The Roman senators are cautious and jealous of Scipio, and allot him no legions; they however appoint him to the command of Sicily—whence he may attack Carthage if he judges the action to the advantage of the State! Scipio recruits his own army; and in Sicily he finds survivors from Cannae sent there in disgrace. He boosts their morale by arming 300 of them as cavalry: this at the expense of the young Syracusan nobility who have also been recruited as cavalry but then allowed to resign if they will hand over their accoutrements and horses.

202 Before the battle of Zama the two leaders, Scipio and Hannibal, meet in front of their armies: the latter makes peace proposals, which are refused.

201 By the peace terms, Carthage loses all but 10 ships of her great fleet; pays an indemnity of 10,000 talents; allows Masinissa independence as King of Numidia; renounces all claims to foreign possessions; subordinates her foreign policy to Rome.

B. Science and Discovery

202 At Zama the Romans find ways of combating the East's favourite tactical weapon, the elephant. The beasts are first frightened by a blare of trumpets which creates chaos amongst their owners; then lanes are left between the Roman ranks, through which the elephants pass harmlessly.

C. Religion and Philosophy

209 In capturing New Carthage Scipio makes skilful use of the tide—and encourages his soldiers by telling them that Neptune is on their side.

204 An image of Cybele is brought to Rome from Pessinus.

D. The Arts

210 A magnificent tomb is built for the dead Chinese emperor Shih Huang-ti. To avoid any treachery, the workmen are said to have been buried alive in it.

E. Literature

202 The tragic story of Masinissa and Sophonisba, and of Sophonisbas' suicide, is later told by Livy, who probably had it from Polybius.

F. Births and Deaths

210 Shih Huang-ti, Chinese Emperor, d.

208 Marcellus d.

207 Chrysippus d. (73).
Hasdrubal (Hannibal's brother) d.

204 Polybius, historian, b. (–122c). Livius Andronicus d.

203 Ptolemy IV d.

**Rome meets her increased responsibilities in the West;
China enters upon her great Han period**

200   The Romans warn Philip V of Macedon that he must keep the peace; then, on appeals from the Aetolian League and many Greek cities, declares war on him, the Second Macedonian War.

200/198   In accordance with his agreement with Philip V (see 204) Antiochus the Great goes to war with the Ptolemies and wrests Judaea from them. The Jews at first welcome a change of master.

198   The Roman consul Flamininus crosses to Macedonia with an army and pushes Philip's forces to disaster in the vale or gorge of Tempe (see E). Abortive peace negotiations take place.

197   Flamininus defeats the Macedonians at Cynoscephalae in Thessaly and dictates peace (see 196 A).
Eumenes II becomes king of Pergamum.

196   The Gaulish Insubres of the Po valley, believed by the Romans to have been incited to revolt by Carthage, are finally defeated.

195   Rome demands from Carthage the surrender of Hannibal (see 196 A); Hannibal voluntarily goes into exile.
A Spanish revolt against Roman consolidation of the ex-Carthaginian colonies is put down by Cato ("Major" or "the Censor"). Aemilius Paullus succeeds him, and Spain continues to be a thorn in the Roman flesh and a most unpopular assignment for the legionaries.

194   Antiochus the Great, patching up his quarrel with Egypt by marrying his daughter to the now adolescent Ptolemy V, turns his warlike attentions to the West. He is encouraged to challenge Rome's protection of the Greeks by Hannibal, who, on being exiled, has come to the Seleucid court.

193/2   Unrest is smouldering among the Greeks, who take unkindly to Roman interference on their behalf. First the Spartan revolutionary, Nabis, moves to recover lost territory. He is defeated by the general of the Achaean League, Philopoemen, and is later assassinated. The Aetolian League decides to revolt against Rome and asks for help from Antiochus. Antiochus, hopeful of creating the grand alliance against Rome that Hannibal envisaged, lands with an army in Thessaly and moves south.

192   At another battle of Thermopylae Antiochus is defeated and only just manages to escape. His flank is turned, as had been the Greeks' by the Persians, by a Roman contingent under Cato (see 195).

191   Scipio "Africanus", having been given that title after the battle of Zama and now a man of great authority in Rome, persuades the Senate to continue the war against Antiochus and to complete his defeat by following him into Asia Minor.

The Han Dynasty (see 206), which is to last for four centuries, begins its consolidation of China, gradually increasing its trade with the West, instituting a settled bureaucracy (with recruitment on an examination basis), and expanding its population, even beyond the Great Wall (and see 150).

A. Politics, Law and Economics

200 The Second Punic war has changed the Romans, as it has changed the whole political situation in the Mediterranean. They proceed to treat their Italian allies more harshly, demanding man-power but not conceding citizenship (but see 90 A). The power of the aristocracy and of the Senate is supreme. The yeoman farmer is giving place to the great land proprietor.

Education in the simple Roman virtues is giving way to education in Greek given by Greek slaves.

In mainland and Ionian Greece the population declines: abortion and infanticide are practised.

196 Hannibal, who has been struggling to rehabilitate Carthage, is elected Magistrate. He restores democratic election and reorganizes public finance and taxation.

196 (July) Flamininus becomes the hero of the Greek world, an idolatry to which he is not adverse. At the Isthmian Games (at Corinth) he proclaims the "Freedom" of Hellas. However, the Greeks soon show dissatisfaction with his peace terms.

191 The Carthaginians have managed to collect their indemnity due to Rome, only stipulated to be paid in 50 years. The Romans, in order to keep their hold on Carthage, refuse to accept it in advance.

B. Science and Discovery

197 At Cynoscephalae the Roman maniple defeats the Macedonian phalanx.

196 The foundation of a library at Pergamum leads to the invention of parchment helped by an embargo on papyrus by Ptolemy V.

C. Religion and Philosophy

200 The biblical book of Ecclesiastes may have been written about this time. But see 931 E).

193 Carneades of Cyrene comes to Athens, to found the third or new Academy, and, as an extreme sceptic, to become the antagonist of Chrysippus.

D. The Arts

Some time during this century the Venus de Milo (discovered on the island of Melos) is sculptured.

E. Literature

198 The Vale of Tempe, scene of the victory of Flamininus (see opposite) is known to Greek poetry as the scene of Apollo's chase of Daphne.

196 The young Ptolemy V is crowned in traditional Egyptian style. The Rosetta stone (written in both Greek and ancient Coptic and hence helping greatly the decipherment of Egyptian hieroglyphics) describes the coronation.

A library is founded at Pergamum (and see B).

E. **Literature** (continued)
195 Aristophanes of Byzantium, grammarian, becomes librarian at Alexandria; he introduces the use of accents into the writing of Greek and of punctuation into the ancient writings generally.

F. **Births and Deaths**
196 Eratosthenes d. (80).

195 Terence b. (–159).

192 Nabis of Sparta d.

190–181 B.C.　　Scipio Africanus and his brother defeat Antiochus the Great; Hannibal commits suicide

190　Scipio Africanus and his brother Lucius, with King Eumenes of Pergamum and other allies, inflict a final defeat upon Antiochus III at the set battle of Magnesia in Caria. Eumenes is rewarded with a great increase of territory. Hannibal is forced to flee from Carthage and seeks refuge first in Crete and then with the king of Bithynia.

189　The Romans finish off their campaign in Asia Minor by chastising the Galatians (see 278) and forcing them into subjection to Pergamum (and see D). In mainland Greece the Aetolian League is punished and made a subject-ally. Rome then retires—with much booty (see A).

188　Philopoemen, general of the Achaean League (see 193), marches into Sparta, restores its oligarchic rulers and ends the revolution started by Nabis by selling his remaining followers into slavery.

188/1　The Greek cities and leagues continue to quarrel amongst themselves and the conviction grows in Rome that there will be no peace in that land until she takes full control.

187　Antiochus the Great is succeeded by the feeble Seleuchus IV (and see C).
Tiberius Gracchus senior is rewarded by Scipio Africanus (for services rendered as Tribune of the Plebs) with the hand of his younger daughter Cornelia (mother of "the Gracchi").

185　Scipio Africanus and his brother Lucius are accused of having received bribes from Antiochus III. Africanus defies the law (see A), reminds the Romans of their debt to him, and retires to his country house—where he dies, probably two years later.

182　Hannibal, on the Romans demanding his extradition from Bithynia, commits suicide.

181　Ptolemy V is poisoned after a reign of 24 years in which the Egyptian monarchy declines and little is left of its empire but Cyprus and Cyrenaica. Ptolemy VI, a child, becomes king.

190　In a little more than a decade after the 2nd Punic War Rome has become master of the eastern Mediterranean.

A. Politics, Law and Economics

189   Booty and indemnity bring much wealth to Rome, encouraging extravagance and financial speculation. At Flamininus' triumph are paraded, besides marble and bronze statues, 18,000 lbs. of silver and 3,714 lbs. of gold.

187   Via Aemilia is built from Ariminum to Placentia.

185   Scipio Africanus, having publicly torn up the evidence against his brother, defies the tribune who is accusing him, leaving him to talk to an empty forum while he takes everyone to the Capitol to give thanks for the victory of Zama (the day being its anniversary).

184   Cato becomes Censor. He has already become champion of the ancient, austere, Roman way of life, and he now inaugurates a campaign of puritanical tyranny.

181   Rome plants a colony at Aquileia at the head of the Adriatic, to control the Veneti and bar the passage of the eastern Alps.

C. Religion and Philosophy

187   In order to help pay his indemnity to Rome, Antiochus III plunders the temple a Jerusalem and a lso raises a temple in Elymais (the ancient Elam), and is murdered for his pains.

D. The Arts

Under King Eumenes II Pergamum reaches its cultural and artistic heights (see 180 D).

183   A lifelike bust is made of Scipio Africanus, possibly from his death-mask, one of the earliest examples of Roman skill in this form of sculpture.

E. Literature

At this time "the father of Roman poetry", Ennius, and also the writer of comedies, Plautus, introduce the Roman citizen to the art of the drama. Ennius writes his *Annals*, a history of Rome, and is accorded Roman citizenship.

F. Births and Deaths

188   Tiberius Gracchus (–133).

187   Antiochus III d.

185   Scipio Aemilianus b. (–129).

184   Plautus d. (70).

183   Scipio Africanus d. (51).
     Philopoemen, d.

182   Hannibal d. (65).

181   Ptolemy V d.

179   Tiberius Gracchus senior (see 187) goes to Roman Spain as governor and bequeathes a quarter of a century of tranquility.
Philip V dies, remorseful for having put his son Demetrius to death at the instigation of his other son Perseus—who becomes the last king of Macedon.

179/2   Perseus is as anti-Roman as his father, and has killed his brother for not being so. He builds up his army and puts out feelers for alliance with the Greek leagues, with his northern barbarian neighbours, and also with Seleucus IV, whose daughter he marries (a Rhodian navy escorting the bride).

177/6   T. Gracchus senior subdues Sardinia, enslaving some of the population.

175   Seleucus IV is assassinated and succeeded by his brother Antiochus IV ("Epiphanes"). Antiochus regards Judaea as a source of revenue and also a fit theatre for forcible hellenization (see C).

172   Eumenes of Pergamum travels to Rome to warn the Senate of danger from Perseus of Macedon. On his return, at Delphi, rocks fall upon him and nearly kill him; Perseus is suspected as the instigator.
Rome declares war on Perseus—the short Third Macedonian War—and sends troops to Thessaly.

171   The young Ptolemy VI, assuming the reigns of government, makes war on Antiochus IV (and see 170).
At the start of the third Macedonian War the Romans, badly led, suffer defeats. Epirus joins Macedonia, but not the Greek leagues.

---

180   The descendants of Arsaces (see 247) are making a strong kingdom—partly hellenized but wholly belligerent—out of Parthia. In the Ganges area the warlike Shungas follow the Mauryan kings and exist as a dynasty for about 100 years. Brahmanism returns and Buddhism decays.
The western part of the Mauryan empire is largely taken over by the line of kings known as the Indo-Greeks. On the retirement of Antiochus the Great from Bactria (see 205), where Greeks have settled in the 5th century, a king called Demetrius I pushes southwards through Afghanistan; he is followed by Demetrius II, who at this time rules as far as the Indus delta (and see 155).

A. Politics, Law and Economics

180 Rome rounds off her subjugation of all Italy by the defeat of the Ligurians (in the area of modern Genoa) and a deportation of 40,000 of them.

175 Private minting of copper coins is allowed in China: the result, serious inflation.

173 There are for the first time in Rome two plebeian consuls together.

171 Under the beneficent government of Tiberius Gracchus (see opposite), Spanish claims for redress against official extortion are heard in Rome. The first Roman colony outside Italy is founded at Carteia near the Pillars of Hercules.

B. Science and Discovery

175 Another ingenious inventor of pneumatic devices flourishes in Alexandria (see 250 B): Ctesibius. (He may have been somewhat earlier than this date.) His chief claim to fame is an improved organ (see 240 D) and he also makes water-clocks.

C. Religion and Philosophy

180 The *Wisdom* of Joshua ben-Sira (known as the Apocryphal book of *Ecclesiasticus*) is written at about this time.

175 Antiochus IV, with the aid of the high priests Jason and Menelaus, imposes the worship of Zeus on the Jews. Swine are sacrificed in the temple; a Greek gymnasium is opened in Jerusalem.

D. The Arts

The altar to Zeus at Pergamum is probably erected in this decade; it shows in outstanding relief a battle between the gods and the giants.

179 The Roman censors for this year have basilicae or halls of justice built in the Forum, in the Greek open, pillared style. They also improve the look of the city along the banks of the Tiber.

E. Literature

180 Aristarchus of Samothrace becomes librarian at Alexandria. He publishes an edition of Homer, which is the basis of the modern text, dividing the *Iliad* and *Odyssey* each into 24 "books".

F. Births and Deaths

180 Aristophanes of Byzantium d.

179 Philip V of Macedon d. (58).

175 Seleucus IV d.

170/68 The Ptolemies and Seleucids continue to make war upon one another—until the Roman ambassador to the latter tells them to stop.

169 Perseus of Macedon has the Roman army trapped near Tempe but fails to take advantage of the tactical position.

168 Aemilius Paullus, a connection of the Scipio family, and another ardent Hellenist, comes out to Thessaly to save the Roman army. This he does, defeating and capturing Perseus at the battle of Pydna. Perseus adorns his triumph.

167 Before leaving, Aemilius is goaded into brutal revenge on the Epirots (see 171); he destroys 70 of their towns and sells 100,000 citizens into slavery. The Greek mainland remains in discontented tranquility for 20 years.
The private papers of Perseus having incriminated political leaders of the Achaean League, a thousand distinguished Greeks are deported to Rome. The future historian Polybius is among them.
Mattathias, of the family of Hasmonai, in the little Judaian town of Modin, refuses to sacrifice to Zeus and slays the official and the Jew who attempt to obey. He and his five sons raise the banner of rebellion.

166 Mattathias dies and his son Judas, called Maccabee or the Hammer, takes the leadership.

164 Ptolemy VI, who has been deposed by his brother, travels to Rome, and is reinstated on the Egyptian throne—not the only time in these decades that Roman influence is decisive in the affairs of both the Ptolemies and the Seleucids.
Judas Maccabaeus, by guerilla tactics, defeats the Seleucid forces in December of this year and gains control of Jerusalem. He cleanses and rededicates the Temple.
Antiochus IV goes mad; his madness is taken as a judgment on his sacrileges and he is given the nickname Epimanes instead of Epiphanes.

163 Antiochus IV dies and his 9 year old son reigns for a year as Antiochus V.
On news of Antiochus' death the Syrian general in Judaea offers the Jews full religious freedom if they will lay down their arms. Even though the Chasidim consent, Judas Maccabaeus declares for full political as well as religious freedom.

162 The Maccabaeus brothers continue the struggle with fanaticism and persecute the hellenizing faction in Judaea.
The child king, Antiochus V, is assassinated by his uncle Demetrius—who becomes the next Seleucid king. Demetrius has spent his youth as a hostage in Rome.

161 Judas Maccabaeus strengthens himself by an alliance with Rome, but is slain in battle. His brother Jonathan continues the struggle.

Carthage is rebuilding her prosperity; but so too is Masinissa building up his in his kingdom of Numidia, and he is encroaching on Carthaginian territory.

A. Politics, Law and Economics

167 Aemilius Paullus imposes peace on Macedon whereby the monarchy is suppressed; the country is divided into four administrative areas (the citizens of each being forbidden to intermarry) and an elaborate democratic constitution is invented which lasts for no more than 20 years. Aemilius brings back to Rome so much looted treasure that for over 100 years no war-tax upon property has to be levied in Italy.

B. Science and Discovery

168 At the battle of Pydna the Macedonian phalanx is shown to disadvantage on rough ground and the Roman maniple to be more flexible.

C. Religion and Philosophy

167 Mattathias (see opposite) makes his famous appeal, "Whoever is zealous for Torah and maintains the Covenant, let him come forth after me!" He leads a religious revolt; but it is of the people rather than of the priests.

165 The book of Daniel, the hero of the time of the Jewish captivity in Babylon, is written, in an effort to boost the morale of the Jews (cf the *Aenid* and the Romans).

D. The Arts

170 A temple on the Oxus river buries its treasure, mostly dating from Achaemenid times. It includes a beautiful model in gold of a chariot and horses.

E. Literature

Probably in this decade Cato writes his book on agriculture, *De Re Rustica*.

168/6 Terence, a freed slave from Carthage, reads his play *Andria* to an established playwright in Rome and is afforded recognition and the production of his play—not without some opposition and jealousy however.

167 Polybius forms in Rome a friendship with the adopted son of the great Scipio (known as Scipio Aemilianus and later as Africanus minor—see 148. A literary set is formed.

F. Births and Deaths

169 Ennius, Roman poet, d. (70).

167 Tiberius Gracchus junior b. (–133).

166 Mattathias, father of the Maccabees, d.

163 Antiochus IV d.

162 Antiochus V d.

161 Judas Maccabaeus d.

160–151 B.C.   The Indo-Greek kingdom flourishes; Rome meets trouble in Spain and Carthage

159 The number of Roman citizens has grown in about 100 years (see 252) by about an eighth, to 338,314.

157 Jonathan Maccabaeus is recognized by the Seleucids as a minor king within the Syrian dominions.

155 Menander (or Milinda) the most famous of the Indo-Greek kings (see 180), rules for about 25 years and extends his kingdom north and east.

154 The last of the hellenizing high priests dies in Jerusalem.
The Lusitanians (of modern Portugal) harry the Roman provinces in Spain.

153 The Carthaginians, prevented by treaty from armed resistance but equally guaranteed against loss of territory, appeal to Rome against the depradations of Masinissa of Numidia (see 170). Rome sends out a commission, of which Cato is a member, and Cato is impressed with the prosperity that he witnesses and begins his campaign for the final destruction of Rome's old enemy. (And see E).
Rome supports a pretender to the Syrian throne, Alexander Balas.

152 Jonathan Maccabaeus continues in his religious-cum-political rise to power by becoming High Priest and being given Samarian territory.

151 The people of Carthage expel the supporters of Masinissa from their city and then defend themselves when the Numidian attacks.
The Greek exiles, including Polybisu (see 167) are allowed to return home.

In this decade the Seleucid Demetrius I (see 162) is struggling to protect his weakened and reduced kingdom of Syria against the enemies that surround it, Pergamum, Parthia, Egypt and Rome, none of whom are above fomenting internal faction and civil war.

A. **Politics, Law and Economics**
In Rome the increase in personal wealth, and the desire to make more, continues: Rome is afraid of Carthage economically as well as militarily.

151   The Romans, treating the thriving Greek commercial port of Massilia with remarkable friendliness, help her to combat raids from the Cisalpine Gauls.

B. **Science and Discovery**
Hipparchus of Bithynia, astronomer, *fl.* He comes to Alexandria; and his catalogue of the stars is later used by Ptolemy.

C. **Religion and Philosophy**
155   The Greek sceptic Carneades, coming to Rome, confuses the Senate by praising Justice on one day and on the next dismissing it as an impractical dream. He disgusts Polybius as a talker of paradoxical nonsense, and so annoys Cato that on the third day he is sent home.
The Indo-Greek king Menander or Milinda becomes the hero of a Buddhist text, *Milinda-panho*, wherein the king is converted to Buddhism. On his death 25 years later many cities vie for his ashes.

E. **Literature**
153   On his return from Carthage (see opposite). Cato begins his practice of winding up all his speeches to the Senate with the phrase, "*Delenda est Carthago!*"

F. **Births and Deaths**
160   Aemilius Paullus d.

159   Terence d. (64).
Eumenes II d.

157   Marius, C. b. (–86).

Carthage and Corinth are destroyed; Macedon becomes a Roman province

150 Demetrius I of Syria dies fighting the pretender Alexander Balas whom Rome is supporting—see 153. Alexander reigns for 5 years, a puppet of Rome and of his mistress.

The Roman praetor Galba, breaking his promise to the defeated Lusitanian rebels (see 154), institutes a massacre. Prosecuted by Cato, he is however acquitted.

149 In the Peloponnese one of the returned exiles (see 151) now head of the Achaean League, quarrels with the Spartans, who appeal to Rome.

The Third Punic War begins. Rome regards the action of Carthage in defending herself (see 151) as a *casus belli* and sends out an invading army. The oligarchic government of Carthage capitulates unconditionally. However, on the announcement of the Roman terms—see A—the people put their leaders to death and new ones take command—two Hasdrubals and a Himilco.

148 In Spain a survivor of the Lusitanian massacre, Viriathus, defeats and kills a Roman governor.

Masinissa, king of Numidia, dies, and Rome supervises the division of his kingdom between his three sons.

148/6 Carthage endures a prolonged and terrible siege and is finally invicted by Scipio Aemilianus, son of Aemillius Paullus and adopted heir of Scipio Africanus (whose name he takes, being known as Scipio Africanus minor). (And see B & E.)

In Macedonia popular discontent breaks out and men enlist under the banner of an adventurer, Andriscus, who claims to be an illegitimate son of the dead king Perseus. A Roman force is annihilated, but the Macedonian revolt is then crushed by the praetor Metellus, and Macedonian self-government under the Romans ends. Macedonia becomes a Roman province.

147 A Roman delegation, arriving at Corinth to compose the Spartan-Achaean League dispute (see 149), is insulted. The League declares war on Sparta. Metellus hurries south from his success in Macedon. He defeats a Greek force but is recalled at the expiration of his term of office.

146 The Roman province of "Africa" is established.

Metellus is replaced by Mummius, by no means a Hellenophile. Corinth is destroyed, its treasures shipped to Rome and its population sold into slavery—see A and D.

Alexander Balas is defeated by Ptolemy VI (see 164), the last act of one of the mildest and best of the Ptolemies—who dies soon after from a fall from his horse. Ptolemy VII has to marry his predecessor's widow (and his own sister) to win the throne.

143 Revolt grows in Spain, encouraged by the success of Viriathus (see 148).

Jonathan Maccabaeusis murdered; he is succeeded by his brother Simon.

142 Scipio Aemilianus is censor.

141 In northern Spain the Roman siege of Numantia begins.

———————

The Huns, faced with a strong and expanding China under the Han Dynasty, find themselves pushed inwards from the east rather than themselves pushing into China. They press on a kindred people, the Yüeh-Chi, who infiltrate westwards into Turkestan and around the Sea of Aral. This affects the Scythians, soon to be known by the Indians as the Shakas.

A fresh wave of Celts, partly Germanic, begins to arrive in Britain, the Belgae (and see 80). These are known as the Iron Age C people.

A. Politics, Law and Economics

149 The Roman terms which the Carthaginians reject (see opposite) are that the city shall be destroyed and that its 700,000 inhabitants shall rebuild their homes elsewhere, *but not within 10 miles of the sea.*

146 Carthage is literally levelled to the ground. Much of the surrounding land is sold or leased to Roman capitalists.

After Corinth has suffered similar treatment all semblance of Greek liberty finally vanishes; the country, though not yet made a province, is placed under the close surveillance of the Roman governor of Macedonia.

The commerce of the island of Delos benefits from the fall of Corinth, particularly in the sale of slaves.

B. Science and Discovery

147 Scipio Aemilianus builds an enormous mole nearly 100 ft wide, in an endeavour to cut Carthage off from its supplies by sea.

C. Religion and Philosophy

146 The final stand of the Carthaginians is made in their temple of Eshmoun (equivalent of Aesculapius). They are said to have set fire to the building and died in the flames, the wife of the remaining Hasdrubal showing herself in splendour with her two children before immolating herself and them.

141 Simon Maccabee gets the high priesthood made hereditary in his family.

D. The Arts

150 About this time, in the Kansu province of China, is fashioned the bronze "flying horse" with his feet upon a swallow. The introduction of the "celestial" breed (see 122) has led to the horse being a favourite subject for Chinese art — as well as a status symbol.

146 Mummius is reputed to have told the contractors who are shipping away Corinth's priceless treasures that if any are lost they must be replaced by others "of similar value".

142 The first stone bridge over the Tiber is built.

E. Literature

148/6 Polybius returns from Greece to campaign under his friend Scipio Aemilianus and witnesses the destruction of Carthage. He hurries back to Greece and helps to alleviate the sufferings of Corinth. He then begins to accumulate information for his great *History* of Rome (from 221 to 144 B.C., of which only part is extant).

F. Births and Deaths

150 Demetrius I (Seleucid) d.

F. **Births and Deaths** (continued)

149   Cato d.

148   Masinissa of Numidia d. (90).

146   Ptolemy VI d.

145   Alexander Balas d.

143   Jonathan Maccabaeus d.

140–131 B.C.   **Rome inherits the Pergamene empire; Wu Ti comes to the Han throne**

140   China's greatest Han emperor, Wu Ti, comes to the throne and accelerates the expansion of China (see 150 and 140 A).
In Spain Viriathus (see 143) is murdered and his rebellion peters out.

138   The Chinese send an embassy under Chang Ch'ien to seek alliance with the Yüeh-Chi (see 150) against the Huns—without success.

137   Antiochus VII comes to the Seleucid throne after his predecessor has been defeated and taken prisoner by the Parthians; the fight with the Parthians goes on.
In Spain at the siege of Numantia a Roman force of 20,000 is cut off and total disaster is only averted by the arrival of Tiberius Gracchus, son of the former governor (see 179).

134   Simon Maccabee and his two elder sons are murdered; he is succeeded by a younger son, John Hyrcanus, who becomes known as Hyrcanus I (see C).
In Sicily there is an uprising of the slaves in the "First Servile War"—which takes 3 years to suppress.

133   Tiberius, the elder of the two Gracchi brothers, is elected Tribune of the Plebs. He institutes drastic land reforms but is killed before his term of office is ended—see A.
The king of Pergamum (Attalus III) dies and bequeaths his treasure and his kingdom to the Romans. Tiberius Gracchus wishes to take the disposition of the treasure away from the Senate.
In Spain the siege of Numantia is finally brought to a successful conclusion by Scipio Aemilianus (who adds "Numantinus" to his other title of Africanus). He has Marius serving under him, as also Jugurtha.

132   Scipio Aemilianus, on returning from Spain, finds himself in opposition to the policy of Tiberius Gracchus his brother-in-law; he champions Rome's Italian allies (many of whom he has led in battle) against the intended re-distribution of land, which, he fears, will be to their disadvantage.

A. Politics, Law and Economics

140   The Chinese emperor Wu Ti begins his reign of over 50 years in which he makes great social reforms, curbing the speculator and middleman, creating state monopolies and socialized industries and regulating prices and incomes (according to the near-contemporary historian, Szuma Ch'ien). He enlarges the currency, issuing coins of silver alloyed with tin.

133   Tiberius Gracchus, in an effort to create a middle class of agriculturalists, procures the enforcement of part of the Licinian laws (see 367 A), restricting the amount of land any individual may own, and also the appointment of a Land Commission to direct the redistribution. He demonstrates the latent power of the tribuniciate against both the Senate and the *imperium* of the magistracy (i.e. the consuls and praetors). Faced with a veto of his purposes by a fellow tribune, Tiberius retaliates by vetoing all government business. Then, with his term of office running out, he takes the unprecedented course of seeking immediate re-election, an action that smacks of a wish for dictatorship. The result is the clash on the Capitol hill of his democratic followers and the senatorial aristocracy, in which Tiberius Gracchus is killed.

131   As a result of Tiberius Gracchus' legislation upwards of 80,000 Roman citizens are resettled on the land.

B. Science and Discovery

140   Wu Ti has bridges, canals and irrigation channels built in China.

C. Religion and Philosophy

134   The Maccabee ruler of Judaea, John Hyrcanus or Hyrcanus I, is virtually a king and acts like one, extending his kingdom. In his reign there comes to a head the Jewish conflict over the interpretation of the Law, the Pentateuchal texts. There are formed the rival sects of the Pharisees and the Sadducees.

E. Literature

The great impression made by the actions and character of the [Tiberius] Gracchi brothers and of their mother Cornelia, is shown by the extensive legend they leave behind.

F. Births and Deaths

140   Viriathus (Spain) d.

138   Sulla b. (–78).

136   Szuma Ch'ien b. (–85c).

134   Simon Maccabee d.

134   Mithridates of Pontus b. (–63).

133   Tiberius Gracchus d. (35c).

130 Ptolemy VII (see 146), having divorced his wife and sister to marry his niece and step-daughter (both Cleopatra by name), flees to Cyprus from an insurrection in Alexandria.

129 Scipio Aemilianus (see 132) is found dead, believed to have been murdered by the followers of the Gracchi.

128 In the Deccan area of the Indian peninsula there arises the Satavahana Dynasty, also called the Andhra. Its first king, Satakarni, extends his kingdom by conquest; he is an orthodox Brahman.
The Pergamene territory is made into a Roman province, to be called "Asia".
Antiochus VII is defeated and slain in battle by the Parthian king, Phraates II—who however is himself shortly defeated and killed by the Scythians (see below).

127 Ptolemy VII regains his throne.

126 Unrest in Sardinia under Roman rule.

125 The Romans again assist the people of Massilia against the Gauls; but it is agreed that they also shall plant a colony—see 122 below.
Fulvius Flaccus, follower of the Gracchi, tries to obtain Roman enfranchisement for the Italians but fails; the town of Fregellae consequently revolts and is destroyed.

123 Gaius, the younger Gracchi brother, having served a term as Quaestor, in Sardinia, is elected Tribune. His popularity is at first immense; his interests are wide and his command of business most efficient—see A.

122 The Province of Narbonese Gaul is formed out of the coastal strip between the Alps and the Pyrenees—hence France's "Provence". (And see B). Rome also absorbs the Balearic Is.

122 Gaius Gracchus gets himself re-elected Tribune. Wishing to supervise the planting of one of his commercial colonies at Carthage, he leaves Rome to visit the place. In his absence his popularity wanes, more especially since the Senate support a colleague of his, Livius Drusus, who develops into a more effective demagogue.
Chang Ch'ien is sent on a mission to the far west and reports upon the fine horses that exist in Sogdiana; before the end of the century the Chinese have acquired some of the breed and are tremendously impressed, calling it the "celestial" or the "blood-sweating" horse. (And see 150 D).

121 Gaius Gracchus fails to get elected Tribune for a third time. He appears in the Forum to protest against the repeal of some of his enactments. A riot ensues; Gaius is induced to flee, but, on the point of capture, prevails on his slave to kill him. About 3000 of the Gracchi's followers are killed.

At about this time the Iron Age forts on the continent, e.g. in Gaul and Bohemia, are at their most elaborate. (These are the *oppida* or "towns" which Caesar will later talk of having captured.)

A. Politics, Law and Economics

123/122   Gaius Gracchus, having got his brother's land laws reinstated, attacks the power of the Senate by seeking to enhance the powers of the "Equites" (the commercial magnates who receive this title on a property basis, a relic of the army reforms of the Servius Tullius—see 578 A). He manages to get the jury panels examining cases of praetorial extortion manned by Equites. He also regularizes and extends the "corn dole" to the Roman populace, whereby they receive bread at a cheap rate. This act helps later to decrease his popularity when, unlike his brother, he tries to obtain Roman citizenship for the Italians: an increase in citizenship may mean less corn to go round. In his wider aim of increasing the power of the popular Assembly vis-à-vis the Senate, he fails.

B. Science and Discovery

125   Parts of Roman Africa are laid waste by locusts.

122   Aquae Sextiae is founded by the Romans in Narbonese Gaul; its medicinal waters are used.

C. Religion and Philosophy

122   Superstitious objections are raised to Gaius Gracchus' Carthaginian colonizing project (see opposite): Scipio Africanus has cursed the site!

F. Literature

130   Dionysius Thrax (of Thrace), pupil of Aristarchus, produces a Greek grammar.

F. Births and Deaths

129   Scipio Aemilianus d. (54c).
      Carneades d. (84c).

128   Antiochus VII d.

122   Polybius d. (82c).

121   Gaius Gracchus d.

128   The Shakas (Scythians), ousted by the Yüeh-Chi (see 150) infiltrate into Bactria and Parthia: a Chinese traveller of this date finds the Sea of Aral area (see 150) already clear of the Shakas.

120   The kingdom of Pontus (on the eastern half of the southern shores of the Black Sea) receives its most forceful king upon the accession of Mithridates VI, the Great. Opportunity for expansion is open to him with the steep decline of the Seleucid empire; he is as yet however only about 14 years old.

119   Marius is elected a Tribune of the Plebs.

118   Marius marries Julia, aunt of the Julius Caesar to be.

118/7 The two grandsons of Masinissa are bequeathed the Numidian throne but to be shared with their cousin Jugurtha. Jugurtha —who has noted the worse side of the Roman character in the way of corruption and intrigue, see 133—kills one grandson, causes the second to abdicate, and appeals to Rome to judge him true king.

117   Ptolemy VII is succeeded by his son Ptolemy VIII, who reigns jointly with his mother.

116/12 While a Senatorial commission is lengthily examining his claim, Jugurtha defeats his surviving rival, at Cirta, but also massacres some of the Italian merchants there.

115   The Census figure for the number of Roman citizens has gone up to 394,336. (See 252 & 159—extent of dependability unknown)

114   Celtic tribes, called by Rome the Cimbri, having migrated south, probably from the Baltic, and having reached the Meuse, sets out on another trek in their covered waggons into Noricum (modern Austria) and threatens northern Italy.
      The Greek cities of the Crimea seek help from Mithridates of Pontus against Scythian marauders. They get it, and Mithridates becomes their ruler (and see A).

113   A Roman army, meeting the Cimbri, suffers a defeat; the Cimbri however, continuing their wanderings in another direction, cease for a while to be a threat to Rome.

111   The Roman Senate, at last acting against Jugurtha, sends one of the consuls, Bestia, to subjugate him; Bestia achieves little, and makes peace.
      The Chinese Emperor Wu Ti conquers and annexes the kingdom of Nan Yüeh (modern S. China and N. Vietnam).

A. Politics, Law and Economics

118   The Gracchi's Land Commission is dissolved. However, a commercial colony such as Gaius Gracchus favours is planted at Narbo, near to, and in rivalry to, Massilia.

114   Mithridates, in obtaining control of the Crimea, gains control too of the corn and timber trade around the Black Sea and up the Danube.

113   In China (see 175 A) all existing coins are declared of no value, and all minting is placed under central control.

C. Religion and Philosophy

120   The Temple of Apollo at Pompeii is built.

E. Literature

120   The Roman poet Lucilius *fl*. His scenes and commentaries of social life—a medley or *satura*—give birth to the literary form known as satire, later developed by Horace.

114   The Celtic *league* or "Cumrhi" of tribes is mistakenly called by Rome the Cimbri.

F. Births and Deaths

117   Ptolemy VII d.

116   Varro, Roman author, b. (–28).

114   Hortensius, Roman orator, b. (–50).

Sulla kidnaps Jugurtha; Marius reforms the army and saves Rome from the barbarians

110   The Romans are indignant that Bestia has made peace (see 111 A); an enquiry is held and Jugurtha is sent for. While in Rome Jugurtha murders a rival—and is sent home in disgrace. War is reopened agaisnt him.

     Under the consul Albinus the Roman army, following Jugurtha into the desert, is trapped and made to pass under the yoke. Both Bestia and Albinus are exiled.

109   The consul Metellus, incorruptible and a good soldier, comes out to conduct the Jugurthian war. On his staff is Gaius Marius, who has made his name as a solider in Spain.

     The wandering Cimbri (see 113) inflict another defeat on the Romans.

108   With the Jugurthian war threatening to relapse into stalemate, Marius sees his opportunity. He presses his commander to let him return to Rome to seek election as consul, receives a reluctant permission just in time, and at the end of a whirlwind demagogic campaign gets himself elected to both the consulship and the African command.

     The Chinese Emperor, Wu Ti, founds a military colony, Lak Lang, in N. Korea.

107   Marius provides himself with a new army (see A), and appoints the aristocratic Lucius Cornelius Sulla to his Staff.

     Back in Numidia, Marius penetrates deep and reduces the oasis-fortress of Capsa (see 6000 D). Jugurtha however eludes him and is strengthened by support from his father-in-law, King Bocchus of Mauretania.

     The Cimbri inflict yet another defeat on the Romans.

     Ptolemy VIII is expelled from Alexandria, as has been his father (see 130). He leaves his brother (Ptolemy IX) and his forceful mother Cleopatra ruling in Egypt. (She is the great-grand-mother of Caesar's Cleopatra.)

106/5   Sulla is entrusted with the mission of subduing King Bocchus. Not only does he do this but he persuades Bocchus to turn traitor to Jugurtha. Jugurtha is lured to a conference, and kidnapped. Sulla has the scene of capture carved on his signet ring; and makes no secret of his jealousy of Marius.

105   The Cimbri inflict one more defeat on the Romans, at Arausio (modern Orange) on the Rhone: the Province of Transalpine Gaul seems at their mercy and Rome itself threatened.

104   The year begins with Jugurtha gracing the Triumph of Marius and Sulla (and later dying in prison). It continues with the second election to the consulship of Marius and with his reform of the army (see B) to meet the threat of the Cimbri.

104/1   Other difficulties face the Roman Senate. The first is piracy in the eastern Mediterranean, increased since the decline of Rhodes and Pergamum; this is for a while mastered. The second is a renewed revolt of the mass of imported slaves in Sicily, a further "Servile War"; this is only subdued at the cost, it is said, of 100,000 lives.

102   The Cimbri, with Teutonic allies, return to a determined and concerted attack on Rome. Marius defeats the Teutons utterly at Aquae Sextiae. Sulla, conscious of Marius' jealousy, gets himself transferred to another command before the battle.

101   Marius turns to meet the Cimbri, and at the battle of Vercellae in the Po Valley, with a reputed slaughter of 120,000, utterly defeats them, thus saving Rome from the Celtic and Germanic barbarians for another 5 centuries. He returns to Rome a hero and to face his great political opportunity.

A. Politics, Law and Economics

110   The Equites press for the continuance of the Jugurthan war, seeing in Numidia a new
sphere for money-making.

107   Marius, in recruiting for his army, finds the old method, dating back to Servius
Tullius (see 578 A), contrary both to his own taste and to efficiency. He recruits
from all classes, including even slaves, and he recruits too on a personal basis—
loyalty to himself. (And see 104 B.)

105/4   The Equites, in their struggle with the Senate, nearly lose their control of the Law
Court panels of jurors and in retaliation interfere with the College of Augurs (see C).

102   Marius, preparing to meet the Cimbri, trains his army with great strictness. Homo-
sexuality is punished, in the case of one of Marius' own nephews with death. His
soldiers, practising route-marches, call themselves "Marius' Mules".

B. Science and Discovery

104   Marius makes his contribution to military science and history by his sweeping reforms
of the Roman army. He increases the Legion from about 5,000 to 6,000. He creates
a closer and more flexible formation by changing the 120-strong maniple to the
600-strong cohort. He changes the heavy *hasta* for the lighter *pilum*, which he
makes bendable on impact so that it cannot be hurled back again; he lightens the
soldier's pack. He does away with the Tullian dependence of type of soldier upon
civilian wealth or class, and the cavalry is scrapped, to be recruited wholly from
Rome's allies. He gives the legions names and numbers and the possession of a
standard, the Eagle. In fact he both democratizes and professionalizes the Roman
army.

C. Religion and Philosophy

104   The interpretation of the auguries being now more an instrument of political obstruc-
tion than a religious observance, the Equites seek to take away the right of appointment to the College of Augurs from the Senate. They succeed in imposing election
for the office.

102   Marius' wife sends him a Syrian prophetess, of whom he makes much, telling the
troops that he is waiting for her to announce the propitious moment to attack and
thus curbing their impatience. After the battle of Aquae Sextiae he burns a great
sacrifice of captured arms to Mars: news comes to him of his re-election as Consul
as he watches.

D. The Arts

109   The Milvian bridge into Rome is re-built in stone.

F. Births and Deaths

109   Atticus (friend of Cicero) b. (−32).

106   Cicero b. (−43).
Pompey b. (−48).

F.   **Births and Deaths** (continued)
104   Jugurtha d.
       Hyrcanus I of Judaea d.

102   (July 12th) Julius Caesar b. (–44).

102   Lucilius d.

100/98   Marius, a better soldier than politician, in obtaining election as consul for the sixth
time, becomes involved with two unscrupulous demagogues (see A) and leaves
Rome in disgust. This is however not before he has forced his one-time commander
Metellus, into temporary exile.

97   Sulla is made Praetor.

96   The city of Cyrene is bequeathed to the Romans.

95   Italians, anxious to obtain the benefits of Roman citizenship (see 125 A) have been
seeping into the city and achieving enfranchisement; an enquiry is now set on foot
and many are struck off the rolls. In many towns secret Italian societies begin to be
formed.

92   Mithridates of Pontus (see 120) has forced the king of Cappadocia off the throne, and
Sulla is sent to restore the *status quo*—which he successfully does.
(A King Mithridates is also on the Parthian throne at this time; he remains at peace
with Rome.)

91   M. Livius Drusus (probably son of the earlier Drusus, see 122) becomes Tribune of
the Plebs and a successful orator and politician. Amongst his proposed reforms is
the enfranchisement of the Italians (sometimes known as Confederates or *Socii*).
The Senate vote against him (see C); he forms a conspiracy—and is murdered. The
hopes of the Italians are dashed, and they revolt. The War of the Socii or Social War
begins.
Nicomedes Philopator becomes King of Bithynia; he is a friend of Rome but in great
danger from the ambitious Mithridates of Pontus.

————————

The two main lines of Alexandrine succession, the Ptolemic and the Seleucid, continue their downward path in a welter of petty and complicated intrigue, both to
end in Roman absorption (the former by Augustus, the latter by Pompey). Parthia,
Pontus and Armenia are all gaining in strength.
Celts, probably of the Iron Age B culture of England (see 275), build at this time in
Scotland their most remarkable stone forts, as strong and elaborate in their way as
are their hill forts of Wessex such as Maiden Castle and North Cadbury. These,
known as *broches*, are dry-stone towers surrounding a circular internal area of about
28 ft diameter with walls as thick as 13 ft, in which are sometimes inset rooms and
staircases. They abound in the Hebrides; some have been in existence for a century or two already; and they will continue to be occupied until at least A.D. 100.

A. Politics, Law and Economics

100   Marius at this date represents a new phenomenon in Rome, the successful general with an army at his back. He is encumbered however by the backing of the two unscrupulous demagogues Saturninus and Glaucia, who finally resort to violence and seize the Capitol. Marius has the unenviable task of ousting them, which he does with his usual military efficiency. He then fails to prevent their massacre.

100   Q. Mucius Scaevola becomes Pontifex Maximus, and institutes a scientific study of the Law. He is considered the founder of Roman jurisprudence.

91   Drusus, in search of popularity, so increases the corn dole as to cause inflation. He debases the currency, issuing copper coins merely coated with silver.

C. Religion and Philosophy

100   The popularity of Marius is such that libations are poured out to him linking his name with the gods.

91   The method of the Senate to defeat Drusus (see opposite) is to declare his laws to have been carried against the direction of the auspices and so null and void.

D. The Arts

The Celts are bringing their distinctive curvilinear type of decorative art of the so-called La Tène culture into Britain, as they are also bringing their practice of throwing votive offerings into the water. This is shown at Llyn Cerrid in Anglesey (which site is probably used as a holy place, until the Roman destruction of A.D. 61) and in the bronze shield found in the Thames at Battersea, which probably dates to this time.

E. Literature

F. Births and Deaths

100   Saturninus and Glaucia, demagogues, d.

97   Nepos (historian) b. (-26).

95   Cato Uticensis b. (-49).
Lucretius b. (51*c*).

91   Drusus the younger d.

90 Cleopatra, wife, sister and mother of Ptolemies, is assassinated by her son Ptolemy IX.

90/89 Rome, in the Social War, is seriously threatened by the Italians, who have combined effectively and are beginning to form a federal capital at Corfinium, east of Rome; the Samnites threaten Campania, but the Etruscans and Umbrians in the north do not join in so effectively. After a bad start for the Romans, Marius takes command, but even he cannot obtain outright victory. The Senate, with an apprehensive eye on the threat of Mithridates, compromises. While giving command in Campania to Sulla—who achieves a resounding victory—it offers the Italians, with only few provisos, what they are fighting for: Roman citizenship.

89 Ptolemy VIII (see 107) on the death of his mother and brother, Ptolemy IX, returns to his throne.

88 On Roman advice the King of Bithynia tries to invade Pontus. Mithridates, aware of Rome's home troubles, sets out on a conquest of her province of Asia. He captures the city of Pergamum, and there he is welcomed, whilst a vast number of unpopular Roman and Italian merchants and officials are massacred.
Sulla is elected Consul and given the command against Mithridates. Marius, however, gets a law pushed through giving himself the command. Sulla with his army advances on and enters Rome. There is street fighting, and Marius flees and is declared an outlaw (and see E).

88/7 Meanwhile the Mithridatic army under its general Archelaus sweeps westwards. An Athenian teacher of philosophy turned tyrant, Aristion, persuades his city to throw in its lot with Mithridates and openly rebels against Rome.

87/6 Sulla sails with five legions and lands in Epirus. He presses Archelaus back onto Athens and besieges the city. In the spring of 86 Athens falls and is sacked, though once again her great reputation saves her from total destruction. Aristion is captured and killed.
Archelaus receives reinforcements and meets the Romans in battle near Chaeronea in Boeotia. Sulla achieves a brilliant victory—and publishes his losses as only 15 men. In Rome Cinna, the consul left behind by Sulla, a patrician turned democrat, stirs up trouble and after a riot is forced to leave Rome. He joins forces with an ageing and vindictive Marius. The two return to Rome, name themselves consuls and institute a massacre of patricians, a five-day reign of terror. After only 18 days of his last consulship Marius dies of pleurisy.

86 Egyptian Thebes, having revolted against Ptolemy VIII, is reduced to a permanent ruin.

85 Sulla wins another victory in his war with Mithridates in Greece, at Orchomenus; he then chases Mithridates across the Hellespont.

84 At a meeting near Troy Sulla and Mithridates agree peace terms (see A). Sulla hurries back to Rome. There Cinna is ruling as a tyrant, packing the Senate with his followers; he has declared Sulla an outlaw.

A. Politics, Law and Economics

90   In the Social War the Italians, once enemies of Rome, fight for the privilege of becoming Roman citizens: it gives them prestige, redress against injustice, the privilege of fighting in the regular legions, and taxation relief.

87   Sulla adds 300 new (conservative) members to the Senate and makes the popular Assembly wholly subservient to it.

84   Sulla, in according easy terms to Mithridates, leaves an unhappy state of affairs in Greece and Asia Minor, making forced loans and leaving behind once more the tax-farmer and money-lender. In Rome there is a financial crisis, which Cinna tries to allay by the remission of debts. Cinna is killed by his own troops.

82   One aim of Sulla's proscription is to accumulate wealth. The young Cicero boldly defends a victim in the law courts.

81   Cicero as pleader in the Forum makes his first extant speech, *Pro Quinctio*.

B. Science and Discovery

87   The Chinese record a comet, probably Halley's, which appears about every 75 years— see 12 B.

C. Religion and Philosophy

88   Mithridates, in capturing Delos, makes off with the temple treasure.

86   Marius gives his nephew Julius Caesar his first appointment, at the age of 14—that of *Flamen diales*, Priest of Jupiter. It carries membership of the Sacred College, and an appreciable income.

84   Sulla, in returning home via Athens, shows his love of learning by making off with the library of Apellicon of Teos, containing most of the works of Aristotle and Theophrastus.

D. The Arts

86   At Chaeronea, according to Plutarch, the Mithridatic army presents "a flaming and terrible sight" owing to the brightness of its armour "embellished magnificently with gold and silver".

85   At Lak Lang in N. Korea (see 108) the earliest known Chinese lacquer has been found. Dates thereon range from this year to A.D. 52.

E. Literature

88/7   Tales arise from the strange adventures that Marius (now nearly 70) experiences after his flight from Rome. Sailing down the coast he is shipwrecked and imprisoned. On his executioner entering his cell, he roars "Wouldst thou dare slay Caius Marius!" and the man flees in terror.

83 King Tigranes of Armenia, son-in-law of Mithdridates, takes over the Seleucid throne, by invitation.

Julius Caesar, at the age of 17, marries Cornelia, the daughter of Cinna.

Sulla lands at Brundisium, recruits many Marian soldiers to his side, and advances victoriously northwards. The young Pompey helps him.

Sertorius, a Marian general, is sent out to Spain, to secure that country against Sulla.

82 Sulla enters Rome as victor, and institutes a worse terror than has Marius. He writes down lists of those he wishes to be murdered—his "Proscription" (see A). He includes Julius Caesar's name in this list, on the latter refusing to put away his wife (see 83 above); but he is induced to delete it.

81 Sulla continues his absolute rule, having a bodyguard of slaves left over from the victims of his proscription.

F. Births and Deaths

90 Clepoatra the elder d.

87 Catullus, Roman poet, b. (–47*c*).

87 Wu Ti, Chinese emperor, d.

86 Marius d. (71). Sallust b. (–34).
Aristion d.

85 Szuma Ch'ien d. (51*c*).

84 Cinna d.

81 Ptolemy VIII d.

80   The young Julius Caesar, feeling himself unsafe in Sullan Rome and seeking military experience, campaigns in Asia Minor, where mopping-up operations are being taken against Mithridatrs. He is entrusted with a political mission to the court of the King of Bithynia—at which he is later accused, without evidence, of acting as a catamite. He then takes part in the siege of Mytilene and is rewarded with the civic crown for saving the life of a fellow soldier.

      Sertorius (see 83) having been driven out of Spain into Africa by Sulla's troops, returns on the invitation of the Lusitanians and sets up an anti-Sullan regime with the enthusiastic support of the natives.

      Ptolemy XI ("Auletes" or the Piper, father of Caesar's Cleopatra) comes to the Egyptian throne after a reign of a few months by Ptolemy X.

79   Sulla, having put through reactionary reforms (see 80 A), retires to a private life of dissolute ease.

      Cicero goes to Athens to study for 2 years.

78   In witnessing the strangulation of a man on his orders, Sulla breaks a blood vessel and dies.

      The consul Lepidus quarrels with his co-consul to the point of bloodshed. He collects a scratchy army, advances on Rome, is beaten and flees the country. The task of rounding up the rebels is entrusted to Pompey.

77   Pompey, having accomplished this task, carefully does not disband his troops. In Spain, Sertorius is reinforced with the remnants of Lepidus' army, under Perpenna.

76   Pompey obtains the Spanish command. He finds it difficult however to come to grips with Sertorius and his men.

74   Mithridates of Pontus invades Bithynia, which country has been bequeathed to Rome.

      Sertorius does a deal with Mithridates, exchanging Roman officers for money and ships. He is however in process of losing his struggle against Pompey and his popularity is waning.

73   Mithridates is driven from his kingdom by the Romans under Luccullus and takes refuge with King Tigranes of Armenia.

      Spartacus, who has been a shepherd and is now a trainer of gladiators, takes up the cause of the badly treated agricultural slaves, with his bandit headquarters on the slopes of Vesuvius. His followers increase rapidly and he tries to curb their worst excesses, hoping to march north and found a new home across the Alps.

72   Crassus, (like Pompey, another of Sulla's officers) is given the task, with six legions, of suppressing the Spartacus revolt.

      Sertorius is murdered by his lieutenant Perpenna, and his regime crumbles.

A. **Politics, Law and Economics**

80   Sulla, in an effort to restore the Senate's authority, curbs the power of the tribunes and restricts the Assembly to the discussion only of what the Senate passes down to it. He improves the method of bestowing overseas commands by the Lex Annalis, whereby such commands become a *post*-magisterial privilege.

77   Julius Caesar gains some renown as an orator in the Law Courts.

76   Julius Caesar journeys to Rhodes to study philosophy and to improve his oratory. He is captured by pirates but ransomed.

75   Sertorius sets out on a deliberate policy to Romanize the provincials: he encourages his Spanish officials to wear the toga and starts a school where Latin and Greek are taught.

72   Crassus, a notoriously rich man, has made his money by clever speculation in the Roman property market, buying up the slum tenements or *insulae* at opportune moments. He makes loans to promising young men, Julius Caesar included.

71   As a result of Sertorius's efforts, Roman citizenship is afforded to some Spaniards (including Balbus, who returns to Rome with Pompey, to become an engineering expert and friend of Julius Caesar).

C. **Religion and Philosophy**

75   Sertorius, almost worshipped by the Spaniards, puts it about that his pet fawn is an intermediary between himself and the goddess Diana, who instils him with prophetic vision.

D. **The Arts**

75   The Laocoon group is sculptured in Rhodes (later to reach Nero's Palace).

F. **Births and Deaths**

80   Diodorus Siculus b. (–29).

79   Brutus b. (–42).

78   Sulla d. (60).

74   Herod the Great b. (–4).

72   Sertorius d.

71   Spartacus d.

71 Crassus drives the Sparticists into the tip of the peninsula, defeats them, and has 6000 of them crucified along the Appian Way.

Pompey returns from Spain and on the way home meets a forlorn hope of the Spartacists, which he destroys. He then seeks to take from Crassus the kudos for the stamping out of the rebellion. The two, now recognized as the champions of the aristocracy and the people respectively, are persuaded to compose their differences and to stand for the consulate.

The second and larger wave of the Belgae (see 150) arrives in Britain. These settle mostly in the S.E.; and for the first time in Britain the less well drained and still forested land is tackled and farmed—with a plough that can turn the sod. The Belgae are probably responsible for the white horse on the Downs at Uffington.

The Shakas (see 128), having streamed through Parthia, enter the Indus valley through the Bolan Pass and found a dynasty in Gandhara.

70–61 B.C.   Pompey is victorious over Mithridates in the East but fails in Rome

70   Pompey and Crassus become Consuls.

69   Lucullus is forced to extend his military campaign eastwards by the belligerence of Tigranes of Armenia (see 73). He restores the king's new capital city of Tigranocerta. He restores Syria to the Seleucid line in the person of Antiochus XIII.

68   Lucullus, pushing enthusiastically ever eastwards, is met by mutiny on the part of his troops, many of whom have been away from home for nearly 20 years.
Julius Caesar, seeking both popularity and high office, gains his first considerable step, in being appointed Quaestor (roughly, Army Paymaster). He serves in Spain for a while.

67   Lucullus is recalled. He retires into private life, to make a name for himself as a man of luxury.
Pompey is given the task of clearing the Mediterranean of pirates, who have again become a menace. He does the job rapidly and efficiently. He is comparatively lenient and settles many of the defeated pirates in various parts of the empire. Crete is taken over by Rome (and see E).
Caesar marries Pompeia (cousin of Pompey) on the death of Cornelia.

66   A bill is passed, with the support of Cicero and Caesar, giving Pompey command in the East, with powers of declaring war. Pompey sets out on a 4-year career of conquest and settlement in the East.
Catilina, earlier a supporter of Sulla, is prevented from becoming consul by being convicted of bribery.

65   Tigranes and Mithridates are defeated by Pompey. The former is allowed to retain his kingdom of Armenia as a vassal prince and a bulwark against Parthia. The latter flees to the Crimea, where he is left to struggle ineffectually and fade out. Parthia puts forward the Euphrates as the frontier between herself and Rome, but Pompey fails to agree.
In Rome the situation is deteriorating into a struggle for power between individual men, with the support of the common people felt to be a necessary asset. Caesar becomes Aedile. Public Games become one of his responsibilities, and he spends vast sums on pleasing the public.
Catilina conspires to gain power by force.

64   Pompey, ambitious to make a Roman province out of the remains of the Seleucid empire, arrives at Antioch and dictates terms: Antiochus XIII is deposed and the Seleucid dynasty ends. The rival claimants for the Hasmonian throne arrive to put their claims.

64/3   Silicia and Syria are made Roman provinces.

A. Politics, Law and Economics

70   Pompey and Crassus repeal Sulla's reactionary legislation.

Cicero makes his name in his prosecution of Caius Verres for his misgovernment of Sicily.

68   Lucullus, before leaving Asia, does much for the country financially, curbing the Roman magnates and money-lenders.

64/3 Pompey in his settlement of his Asian conquests, follows the usual Roman practice of creating client kingdoms and of allowing self-government under Roman tutelage wherever possible. In Palestine he appoints Hyracanus as High Priest of the Jews but the Idumean Antipater as Governor of Judaea (see 69 C).

63   Cicero, by his denunciation of Catilina, rises to the height of his fame as orator and statesman. He outshines the more florid orator Hortensius.

B. Science and Discovery

63   A discovery in homeopathy in reverse is made on the suicide of Mithridates. The king is said to have customarily taken small doses of poison as an antidote against assassination, and to have found it to work only too well when he tries to poison himself: he has to get a Gaulish servant to kill him.

C. Religion and Philosophy

69   Maccabean rule has degenerated, and the dispute is now between Hyracanus II the legitimate holder of the office of High Priest, supported by the Pharasaic priests, and his brother Aristobulus, who is backed by the more hellenized Sadducees and has called in an Idumean prince, Antipater, to help him.

63   On the collapse of Aristobulus, Pompey (see opposite) enters the Holy of Holies, (though he does not seize its treasure). The Jews later see in this the reason for his ensuing turn in fortune.

Julius Caesar, having put up against two aristocrats for the post of Pontifex Maximus or High Priest of Rome, tells his mother that he will surely succeed—which he does. The post carries little political benefit, but some financial benefit and, certainly with the people, some religious.

62   Clodius (or Claudius) Pulcher, a profligate nobleman, profanes the mystic and female rites of Bona Dea by penetrating into them dressed as a woman. This religious scandal has political repercussions: it makes Caesar divorce his second wife Pompeia (for love of whom Clodius had committed the sacrilege, and who, as Caesar's wife, must be "above suspicion"); and it makes Clodius the lifelong enemy of Cicero, who tries to convict him.

D. The Arts

70   Verres (see A) is convicted of, amongst other things, thefts of works of art, both publicly and privately owned.

69   Tigranes builds his new capital city (see opposite) in hellenistic style, and in imitation of all the eponymous city-founders of the post-Alexandrian period.

63 Pompey marches on Jerusalem. The Hasmonian King Hyrcanus II admits him to the city but his brother Aristobulus resists him on the Temple hill and is besieged; after a 3 month siege he capitulates. (And see A.)

Mithridates the Great of Pontus commits suicide.

In Rome Cicero is consul for the year (the other consul being Mark Anthony's uncle). The Catiline conspiracy (see 65) to obtain power by a coup d'état is brought to light by Cicero. Cato (the great-grandson of the Censor) is Tribune of the Plebs and supports Cicero.

Caesar becomes Pontifex Maximus.

62 (Jan) Catilina is discredited by Cicero, and, his supporters executed, he dies in battle.

(Dec) Pompey makes a triumphal return to Italy after his successful campaigns and administrative activities in the East. With his army behind him he has his great opportunity to seize absolute power. He however disbands his army.

Caesar is made Praetor.

61 Pompey, though his Triumph is magnificent, is used slightingly by the Senate, who refuse to ratify his political settlements in the East (but see 59) or his land settlements in favour of his disbanded soldiers.

Caesar is made Pro-praetor for Spain. He conducts small successful campaigns against the Lusitanians and improves the commercial position of Gades.

E. **Literature**
68   The extant correspondence of Cicero begins.

67   L. Cornelius Sisenna, historian and legate of Pompey, dies in Crete.

F.   **Births and Deaths**
70   Virgil b. (–20).

68   Cleopatra the Great b. (–30).

67   Cornelia, Caesar's first wife, d.; Sisenna d.

65   Horace b. (–8).

64   Strabo, geographer, b. (A.D. –24).

63   Mithridates the Great of Pontus d. (71c).
     Octavian (later Augustus) b. (A.D. –14).
     Agrippa, Vipsanianus b. (A.D. –12)

62   Catilina d.

60 Caesar, back from Spain, is refused a Triumph by the Senate. Caesar, Pompey, and Crassus form the first "Triumvirate" (see 43).

59 Caesar's year as Consul. Having subdued the Senate and improved the laws (see A), he turns to wider fields. In return for forcing the Senate to sanction Pompey's activities on the eastern frontiers, he receives from Pompey help in getting his coveted command in Gaul. He gives his daughter Julia in marriage to Pompey, and himself marries Calpurnia, his third wife, who outlives him.

58 The Helvetii decide to migrate south-eastwards under their leader Orgetorix, but are prevented by Caesar, in alliance with the Gaulish Aedui, at the battle of Bibracte.

Ariovistus, with a Teutonic army said to be 120,000 strong and stationed between the Vosges and the Rhine, defies Caesar. Caesar defeats the Teutons near modern Colmar.

Cato (see 63) goes on a commission to annexe Cyprus to the Roman Empire.

Clodius forces Cicero into banishment, from which however he returns in the following year.

57 Caesar advances to the Aisne and defeats the Belgae, and to the Sambre and defeats the Nervii, fighting in person. All resistance from Gaulish and Belgian tribes is for the moment ended. Some of the Belgae, having received help from Britain, retire thither.

(Aug.) Cicero returns from Greece and, after venting his spleen on the Senate, goes into semi-retirement.

Ptolemy XI, Auletes, (see 80), is turned out of his throne by the Egyptian people and appeals to Rome to reinstate him.

Pompey's influence in Rome is waning.

Civil war in Parthia.

56 The Breton tribe of the Veneti revolt, and Caesar imposes a naval defeat on them (see B).

The Teutons, at Belgian invitation, again sweep southwards across the Rhine. A conference between Caesar and Pompey.

55 Caesar defeats the Teutons on the Meuse and with a terrific massacre, for which he is criticized in the Senate. He follows up his success by crossing the Rhine (see B) and making a punitive raid into Germany.

Commius, king of the Gaulish tribe, the Atrebates, is sent by Caesar to Britain as an ambassador, but on arrival is put in chains.

(Sept.) Caesar, with two legions, sails for Britain. He achieves an opposed landing, probably near modern Walmer. The Britons return Commius to Caesar but sue for peace. However, a high tide having destroyed some of Caesar's ships, they renew the fighting. Caesar, content to do no more than show his superiority in arms, recrosses the Channel—to be received with popular acclaim in Rome.

Ptolemy XI is restored to his Egyptian throne by Rome and institutes a proscription of his enemies.

Pompey and Crassus are Consuls for the year.

A. Politics, Law and Economics

59 Caesar, in his year as Consul, introduces his *Agrarian Laws* (to settle Pompey's veterans at the expense of aristocratic land-owners) and has them ratified by the popular Assembly in a riotous scene in the Forum. This is followed by his *Leges Juliae*, protecting the people from bribery and corruption and immorality generally.

B. Science and Discovery

56 Caesar wins his naval battle over the Veneti by supplying his sailors with the simple device of a sickle wherewith to cut down the enemy rigging as the ships pass. Many of these Veneti flee to England, and it may have been they, showing their own war-like ingenuity, who elaborate the defences of Maiden Castle and other West Country Iron Age forts so that their slingers may command a better line of fire. It is also probably these Celts who built the "Lake Villages" at Meare and Glastonbury (see 50).

55 Caesar's legionaries build a bridge over the Rhine (near modern Bonn) in 10 days, and greatly impress the Germans.

C. Religion and Philosophy

Druidism is flourishing in Britain and Gaul; and Mithraism is beginning to permeate the Roman legions, spreading from Persia via Asia Minor.
P. Nigidius Figulus, Pythagorean philosopher, *fl.*

58 Lucretius publishes *De Rerum Natura* (on the doctrines of Epicurus).

52 Caesar, in *De Belle Gallico*, gives the earliest extant description of the Druids, attributing to them barbaric customs but also much wisdom and much power, their headquarters, he says, being in Britain.

51 Posidonius, Stoic philosopher and teacher of Cicero, moves from Rhodes to Rome (but probably dies in the next year).
Cleopatra, on accession, makes a point of going in person to upper Egypt and of escorting the sacred bull, manifestation of Apis, to its home.
The sect of the Essenes probably begins to flourish in this decade.

D. The Arts

55 Pompey builds a theatre in Rome.

E. Literature

60 Catullus' *Love Poems to Lesbia*.

55/52 Cicero retires from public life and to literary pursuits; in 52 however he is forced to go to Cilicia as Governor.

52 Caesar's *De Bella Gallico* is probably written, or, if partially written during the campaigns, completed.

54 The Aeduan chief, Dumnorix, attempts treachery and is destroyed. (July) Caesar returns to Britain with a large fleet and 5 legions. He lands near Deal, unopposed.

Cassivellaunus, Chieftain of the Catuvellauni, crosses the Thames to meet Caesar, and is repulsed. At Sunbury the Legions cross northwards and defeat Cassivellaunus in his stronghold near modern Wheathampstead in Hertfordshire. He sues for peace; and Caesar, having shown his strength, returns. In Caesar's absence the Gauls revolt and the Roman army suffers a reverse.

Julia dies in childbirth; and the ties between Pompey and Caesar loosen.

Crassus plunders the Temple at Jerusalem before proceeding on his spectacular bid to make his military name in the East.

Mark Antony comes to serve under Caesar in Gaul.

53 (June) Crassus rashly penetrates into the Mesopotamian desert; he is killed and his army utterly defeated, at the battle of Carrhae, by the Parthians under their Arsacian king Orodes. Caesar prepares for renewed trouble in Gaul.

52 The Gauls unite in revolt under Vercingetorix. The Romans suffer a reverse at Gergovia; but finally they win the difficult battle and siege of Alesia, Caesar's greatest military success against great odds. Commius, now turns against Caesar, fails to relieve the fortress.

In a rapidly deteriorating situation in Rome, Clodius is killed at the head of his band of gladiators by the tribune Milo and Pompey is made sole Consul in an effort to restore order, having become reconciled with the Senate.

Mark Antony is elected Quaestor. He conducts mopping-up operations in Gaul; Commius makes peace with him on condition that he shall never have to look upon the face of a Roman again.

51 The Parthians are defeated in Syria by Cassius (the future murderer of Caesar) who has taken over command from Crassus. Caesar remains in Gaul to pacify and restore a defeated country. Cleopatra and her brother Ptolemy XII succeed to the Egyptian throne.

F. **Births and Deaths**

  59 Livy b. (–17 A.D.).

  55 Tigranes, King of Armenia, d.

  54 Julia, Caesar's daughter d.

  54 Tibullus (Roman poet) b. (–18c).

  54 Dumnorix d.

  53 Crassus. d.

  52 Clodius. d.

  51 (or 52) Lucretius d. (44).

  51 Ptolemy XI. d.

  51 Propertius (Roman poet) b.

50   Caesar is in dispute with the Senate over his promised consulship at the end of his Gallic command and over the demand that he shall disband his army. He is declared by the Senate an enemy of the people. Cicero returns to Italy (see 55 E).

50   The Kalingas (see 260) throw up a militant king Kharavela, who claims to conquer as widely as in the Deccau and Burma. Indian culture also penetrates into Cambodia about this time.

49   (Jan.) Caesar returns to Roman soil by crossing the little River Rubicon. Mark Antony accompanies him. This is civil war.
Pompey flees to Greece, with Cicero and Cato.
Caesar pacifies Italy with clemency, gains control of Sicily, and defeats Pompey's forces in Spain. In Numidia, King Juba I gains a victory over Caesar's forces on Pompey's behalf. Caesar's general, Labienus, defects to Pompey.

48   Caesar is elected Consul again. He follows Pompey to Greece, loses the battle of Dyrrhacium but defeats Pompey at Pharsalus (August). Brutus and Cassius, having fought on Pompey's side, are pardoned, as is also Cicero.
Pompey flees to Egypt and is assassinated on landing by Ptolemy's troops. Caesar, following, becomes involved in that country's dynastic quarrel, and espouses Cleopatra's cause. Herod (the Gt., son of Antipater, see 64 A) is made ruler of Galilee: the power of the Maccabees, the Hasmonean dynasty, is ended.

47   Caesar settles affairs in Egypt, restoring Cleopatra to her throne, defeating her brother, Ptolemy XII; he then marches rapidly through Syria and Asia Minor. He defeats Pharnaces, King of Pontus and son of Mithridates the Gt., at the battle of Zela. ('Veni, vidi, vici!') He returns to Rome, but passes on into Africa to meet the Pompeian threat there.
Antipater (see 48) is appointed by Caesar Procurator of Judaea.

46   Caesar achieves an overwhelming defeat of the Pompeian party at the battle of Thapsus in Carthaginia. Cato and Juba I, retiring to Utica, commit suicide. Numidia becomes a Roman province.
Caesar returns to Rome and, after a 4-day Triumph, is made Dictator and Consul for 10 years, also Inspector of Public Morals. He declares an amnesty for those who have borne arms against him. Vercingetourix graces Caesar's triumph and is then put to death. Lepidus (see 43) is Consul with Caesar.

45   Caesar is forced to return to Spain, where he finally defeats Pompey's sons (and Labienus) at the battle of Munda. He returns to Rome and continues his conciliatory policy, promoting Caius Cassius and Marcus Brutus.

44   (Feb.) At the carnival of the Lupercalia Caesar refuses the kingly crown offered by Mark Antony.
(March 15th) The conspiracy of 60 senators, led by Cassius and Marcus Brutus, achieves its purpose and Julius Caesar is assassinated.
Octavian, Caesar's grand-nephew, (born in 63) returns to Rome from Illyria, learns of his adoption into the *Gens Julia*, and claims the succession.

A. Politics, Law and Economics

47   Caesar protects the rights of property but reduces the rate of interest.

46   Caesar purifies the Law Courts and reduces bribery: the *Leges Juliae* (see 59 A) become a practical reality.

The Roman colony at Carthage begins to be developed, a process continued by Augustus.

45   Caesar increases the Senate to 900 and widens its recruitment. He reduced the free corn ration but encourages men to colonize. He begins the rebuilding and repopulation of both Carthage and Corinth. He issues sumptuary laws against luxury, and executes his favourite freedman for adultery. He appoints a commission to simplify the laws and begins the task of putting Rome's finances in order.

B. Science and Discovery

50   The water mill (i.e. mill-wheel driven by water-power) seems to have been invented about this time: first appearing in Greece but to be also used in the Roman world (see 20 B).

46   Caesar introduces the Julian Calendar, the previously used "lunar" year of 12 lunar months having in the recent decades of civil war etc. become as much as 65 days in advance of the sun. Sosigenes, Alexandrian astronomer, helps him. The year is made into one of 365 days with an extra day every fourth year and the months lengthened to fit. (This is still our present system except for a non-leap-year every century.)

45   Caesar encourages physicians and men of science to settle in Rome, and starts large engineering projects, including the draining of the Pontine Marshes and the cutting of a Corinth Canal. Aclepiades of Bithynia *fl.*; he founds a medical school in Rome.

C. Religion and Philosophy

48/44   Cicero, *De Natura Deorum* and *De Divinatione* (including unfavourable criticism of astrology).

44   (July) A comet appears at the time of the games held in Caesar's honour; it is taken as proof of his godhead.

43   During a time of great religious and superstitious emotion amongst the *plebs*, the building of a civic temple to Isis is ordered (but probably not carried out). (But see A.D. 19.)

D. The Arts

In the half century now beginning there arrives in the Roman world the art of "carpet mosaics', i.e. with a continuous pattern.

There is sculpted a seated figure of Buddha at Gandhara, showing Hellenistic influence.

50   In the 'Villa of Mysteries', Pompeii, there is painted a frieze showing the Dionysiac Mysteries.

48   Varro (see E) writes a book, *De Musica*.

43 Mark Antony having been given command in Gaul, is besieged in Mutina and is defeated by Octavius. Lepidus, holding the largest army, is welcomed into alliance by Octavian; with Mark Antony there is formed the second Triumvirate (see 60).
Cleopatra kills her younger brother, who has been reigning with her as Ptolemy XIII.
(Dec.) Cicero, who has long played a double game but who after Caesar's death has acted nobly and efficiently as Head of State, is assassinated at the order of the Triumvirate, one victim of a large proscription.
Octavian becomes Consul.

42 At the battle of Philippi, Octavian and Mark Antony defeat Cassius and Brutus, who both kill themselves.
Tiberius is born to Livia (see 38).

41 The Triumvirate divide the Roman world between them, Africa to Lepidus, the East to Mark Antony and the West (including the vital home front) to Octavian.
At Tarsus Mark Antony meets Cleopatra and succumbs to her carefully staged charms.
War occurs in Italy between Octavian and forces supporting the absent Mark Antony and his wife Fulvia.

After Caesar's departure, Gaul begins its upward path to become in a many ways Rome's most prosperous colony.
In Britain at about this time there are built lake villages, as at Meare and Glastonbury in Somerset. They are made with elaborate sunken foundations, and the risk of fire—cf. 4000 B.C.—is diminished by the use of clay fireplaces. (These lake dwellings are sometimes called Crannochs, after their Irish equivalents—which are occupied into medieval times.)

45   Caesar re-dedicates the fallen statue of Pompey in Rome.

E. Literature

50/44   Caesar's only other extant publication, *The Civil War*, is written.

48   Varro, the encyclopaedist, is pardoned by Caesar for having fought against him at Pharsala, and is employed as librarian.

47   The library at Alexandria is partially destroyed (finally in A.D. 642).

46   Sallust, the historian, is left by Caesar as Governor of Numidia, where he enriches himself and whence he retires into private life.
Cicero makes literary fun of the Julian calendar.

45   Caesar begins to form libraries in large towns.

44   8th and last book of *De Bella Gallico* is written by Aulus Hirtius.
Cicero delivers his 'Philippics' against Mark Antony.

42   Sallust writes *The Jugurthan War and the Catalinarian War*. Cicero leaves behind much famous writings, including *De Oratore, De Republica, De Legibus, De Officiis, De Senectute, De Amicitia, De Finibus* (enquiry into the chief good) and *Tusculan Disputations*; also his *Orations* and his *Letters*, covering 26 years, to Atticus, his family, and others.

F. Births and Deaths

50   Hortensius, orator, d.

47   Ptolemy XII d.
Catullus d. (40).
Caesarion b. (–30).
Pharnaces of Pontus d.

46   Cato II d. (49). Juba I d.

45   Tullia (Cicero's daughter) d.
Labienus d.

44   (March 15th) Julius Caesar d. (57).

43   Cicero d. (63).
Ptolemy XIII d.
Antipater d.
Marcellus b. (–23).
Ovid b. (A.D. –18).

42   Emperor Tiberius b. (A.D. –37).
Cassius d.
Brutus d. (37).

40 Octavian captures Perusia, Fulvia dies, and the forces of Mark Antony in Italy
    collapse. Mark Antony returns to Italy.
    (Oct.) The Pact of Brundisium is arranged by Octavian's friend Maecenas, recon-
    ciling the Triumvirate and slightly rearranging their territories and command of
    troops. Octavian gives his sister Octavia in marriage to Mark Antony.
    Herod the Gt. is made King of Judaea, and Hyrcanus II ceases to be High Priest.

39 Mark Antony goes back to the East.
    The Parthians harry Syria.
    Treaty of Misenum, between Mark Antony, Octavian and Sextus Pompeius (see
    36 below).

38 Ventidius, Mark Antony's lieutenant, defeats the Parthians in Syria under both
    Pacorus, son of King Orodes I, and the Roman Labienus, son of Caesar's general.
    Orodes surrenders the Parthian crown to Phraates IV.
    Octavian marries Livia, forcing her husband, T. Claudius Nero (by whom she has
    had two sons Tiberius and Drusus) to divorce her.

37 Mark Antony returns Octavia to her brother and marries Cleopatra. Herod captures
    Jerusalem.

36 Mark Antony unsuccessfully invades Parthia.
    Sextus Pompeius, Pompey's surviving son, who has held possession of Sicily with a
    powerful fleet since Caesar's death and has constantly interrupted Rome's vital
    corn supply, is defeated by Octavian's friend, the general Agrippa, at the naval
    battle of Naulochus.
    Lepidus, the third man of the Triumvirate, is forced into retirement by Octavian.

35 Sextus Pompeius, escaping, returns to Asia Minor, thinks of joining the Parthians,
    but is executed by Octavian's orders.

34 Mark Antony invades Armenia and carries its king Artavasdes captive to Alexandria.

33 Mark Antony lapses into the life of an eastern potentate with Cleopatra. They claim
    that Cleopatra's son Caesarion is also Ceasar's and so the rightful heir to the Roman
    Empire.
    Mauretania falls to Rome.

32 The two consuls and some senators defect to Mark Antony, and Octavian declares
    war on him.
    Antony and Cleopatra winter in Greece.
    Cheng Ti becomes Emperor of China, but is in the hands of a Court clique, the fate
    of many of his successors: the slow decline of the Han dynasty is beginning.

31 (Oct.) The fleet of Octavian, under Agrippa, defeats Antony and Cleopatra at the
    battle of Actium; they flee back to Alexandria.

A. Politics, Law and Economics

36   The traditional Tribunes rights of sacrosanctity are conferred on Octavian.

32   Octavian institutes the oath of personal loyalty, a growing instrument of power for the Emperors of Rome.

31   Octavian is made Consul year by year (until 23).

B. Science and Discovery

36   At the naval defeat of Sextus Pompeius, Agrippa's invention the *harpax*, a grapnel shot by catapult, is used to advantage. The Via Flaminia is tunneled through the Furlo Pass.

33   Octavian expels astrologers and magicians from Rome.
Agrippa builds the Julian aqueduct for Rome.

C. Religion

35   Sextus Pompeius, as a final act of defiance, pillages the rich temple of Hera at Lake Lacinium.

34/33   Octavian, endeavouring to rekindle pride in the old Roman religion, repairs many of Rome's ancient temples and creates new patrician families to recruit to the priesthood.

D. The Arts

34/32   Octavian rebuilds in Rome, restoring at great expense the theatre of Pompey. The Basilica Aemila is restored.

31   At Snettisham in Norfolk are buried magnificent gold torques, the typical Celtish ornament. One contains a coin of the Atrabates—coins are increasing in use in Britain, many being copies of the Macedonian stater, with the figures deteriorating into an unintelligible pattern.

E. Literature

40   Virgil's *Eclogues*.

37   Varro, *de Re Rustica*.

31   Virgil's *Georgics* completed.

31   Diodorus Siculus' *Historical Library* (surviving books giving not very reliable Roman history in 4th and 5th Cent. B.C.).
C. Nepos, writes *Lives* of Cato the Censor, Atticus and others.

F. Births and Deaths

40   Fulvia d.

31   Violent earthquake, in the Jericho area, probably causes the temporary abandonment of Qumran.

Herod the Gt., patronized by Mark Antony, makes his murderous way to power, marrying a member of the Hasmonean royal family, but having her grandfather and brother put to death. He builds great fortresses around his kingdom, as at Masada.

In Britain, following the Veneti, there arrives a further wave of Belgae, who, coming into opposition with the Catuvellauni, extend through Hampshire into Dorset. This expedition is almost certainly led by Commius (see 52).

The last of the Indo-Greek kings (see 180) by name Hermaeus, is dethroned by the Yueh Chi, in spite of support from China.

F. **Births and Deaths** (continued)
39 Julia, daughter of Octavian, b. (A.D. –14).
Drusus senior b. (–9 B.C.).
Pacorus, King of Parthia, d.

35 Sextus Pompeius d.

34 Sallust d. (52).

32 P. Atticus (correspondent of Cicero) d. (77).

31 Artavasdes, king of Armenia.

30–21 B.C.   Death of Antony and Cleopatra, Octavian becomes Augustus and the Roman Empire is born

30   Mark Antony commits suicide. Cleopatra, failing to influence Octavian, does likewise: the end of the Ptolemaic dynasty in Egypt, which becomes a Roman dependancy.

Caesarion (see 33) is executed.

Cornelius Gallus, (poet but with no poems extant) is made governor of Egypt.

Juba II, son of Juba I, having been brought up in Rome and become by reputation most learned, is made king of Numidia by Octavian and married to Salome, daughter of Antony and Cleopatra.

29   Octavian returns to Rome and begins his political reformation (see A). He receives a triple triumph and is hailed by the Senate and people as their saviour.

C. Gallus puts down a revolt in Egypt and boasts of it in a trilingual inscription.

28   A census in held by Octavian.

27   Octavian becomes Augustus (see A). He visits Gaul, leaving his right hand man Agrippa in charge.

26   Augustus moves on to Spain and begins its difficult pacification.

C. Gallus, setting up statues to himself rather than to Augustus, is removed from the Prefecture of Egypt. He commits suicide.

25   Augustus, continuing a firm policy against Parthia without becoming involved, holds on to Armenia and annexes Galatia.

The doors of the temple of Janus are closed, signifying that peace reigns—it is the first time since 235 B.C.

King Juba II is transferred to the throne of Mauretania and Numidia becomes a Roman province.

Augustus marries his daughter Julia, aged 14, to his nephew and adopted son Marcellus.

25/24   A. Gallus, succeeding to C. Gallus in Egypt, is sent by Augustus on a military expedition into Arabia Felix, an exception to Augustus' usual policy of consolidation rather than expansion. The expedition is forced to return through lack of water.

23   Augustus is ill. He meets incipient rebellion by making concessions to republican sentiment but ends with enhanced powers.

Herod sends his two sons Alexander and Aristobulus to the Roman court.

22   Augustus refuses dictatorships and consulship for life. He travels the provinces, in Greece and Asia Minor.

21   Marcellus having died, Julia is married to Agrippa.

From 26 to 19 B.C. Spain suffers bitter warfare, the Cantabrians proving brave and fierce enemies of Rome.

Trade and contact between Rome and N.W. India (see 25 A) is growing.

A. Politics, Law and Economics

28 Octavian purges the Senate, brings its numbers back to 600, and in theory though not in practice restores it to its republican power.

27 (1st Jan.) The Senate, in gratitude, bestow on Octavian the name of *Augustus*. Augustus remains *Imperator* or Emperor, that is to say head of the Army, and invents for himself the new title of *Princeps*. He prefers to use his *auctoritas* as an elder statesman and ex-consul, this authority however gradually hardening into imperial power. The Senate give him also tribunical powers, probably by a *Lex de Imperio*, and provincial *imperium* for 10 years.

Augustus begins to create a Home and Foreign Civil Service and to regularize the taxation of the Provinces, each new province being subjected to a census to assess its tax potential.

He reduces the Army to not more than 28 legions, disbanding over 100,000 veterans, settling them in new colonies in Italy or such ancient and dilapidated cities as Carthage. He also resumes control of the issue of coinage, lost by the Senate to successful generals. He contributes large sums from his private fortune (including the spoils of Egypt) to the public treasury.

25 Herod provides corn for his people during a famine.

25/21 An embassy sails to Rome from Broach in N.W. India, starting in 25 but not arriving until about 21. Presents include snakes, tortoises, pheasants, tigers, and a monk and an armless boy who can shoot arrows with his toes.

22 Herod makes Caesarea into a great seaport.

B. Science and Discovery

27 Augustus improves the roads in Italy.

24 Strabo, the geographer, travels in Egypt with A. Gallus.

23 Augustus is cured of illness by the cold water treatment of the Greek physician, A. Musa—the treatment however failing when applied to Augustus' intended heir, Marcellus.

With the help of Agrippa, Augustus collects geographical and economic information of his Empire. Agrippa produces a map of the world, which after his death is engraved on marble and displayed to the citizens of Rome by Augustus.

C. Religion and Philosophy

30 Nicolaus of Damascus removes himself from the court of Cleopatra to that of Herod. (He writes a life of Augustus).

23 An epidemic in Rome is attributed by the people to the displeasure of the gods at Octavian's resignation of his consulship.

The later deification of emperors is foreshadowed by the cult permitted reluctantly by Augustus of "Augustus et Roma". The Eastern Hellenistic world begin to regard Rome as "the City of the Great Ruler", in fact of God Manifest.

D. The Arts

29   Dedication of the Temple of Divus Julius in Rome. Octavian builds a mausoleum for his family.

28   Dedication of the Temple of Apollo.

27   Agrippa builds the first Pantheon in Rome.
    With the securing of peace by Augustus, the beautification of Rome, by the building of temples, theatres, public baths, monuments, etc. gathers pace.

E. Literature

Maecenas is patron of the Roman writers, in particular Horace and Virgil, and the elegaic poet Propertius. Livy is writing his *History of Rome*. What has been regarded as the Golden Age of Latin literature has arrived.

Dionysius of Halicarnassus resides in Rome and begins his *Roman Antiquities*, a history of Rome from mythical times, of which only the first eleven books have survived. He also writes literary criticism.

Tibullus' *Elegies*.

27   At the instigation of Augustus, who wishes the Romans to become more conscious of their noble heritage, Virgil begins his *Aeneid*.

23   The death of Marcellus is mourned in the *Aeneid*.
    First three books of Horace's *Odes* are published.

F. Births and Deaths

30   Mark Antony d. (*c*53).
    Hyrcanus II of Judaea d.
    Caesarion d. (17).
    Cleopatra d. (38).

29   Diodorus Siculus (historian) d. (51).

28   Varro (Roman polymath) d. (89).

26   C. Gallus (Roman poet) d.

26   C. Nepos (Roman historian) d. (71).

23   Marcellus d. (20).

20–11 B.C. The successes, in frontier wars, of Augustus' step-sons, Tiberius and Drusus

20 Augustus puts pressure on the Parthians and threatens them with an army under Tiberius; he thereby recovers the Roman standards lost at the battle of Carrhae (53 B.C.) and any prisoners remaining alive—a diplomatic triumph.
A first son, Gaius, is born to Julia (Augustus' daughter) and Agrippa.

19 Augustus returns to Rome and the day is made an annual holiday. Agrippa ends his war of pacification in Spain.

18 Herod, styling himself Friend of the Romans, pays a state visit to Augustus. Augustus's imperium is extended. Agrippa becomes co-regent.

17 A second son, Lucius, is born to Julia and Agrippa; Augustus, with an eye on the succession, adopts his two grandsons, giving them the title Caesar.
The Secular Games are celebrated in Rome to mark the inception of a new and better age (see C. and E.).
Herod's sons, Alexander and Aristobulus, return from Rome to their father's court.

16 Tiberius is made Praetor and Drusus Quaestor, and their period of responsible and successful military command begins. Augustus leaves Rome again to quell trouble on the northern frontiers.

16/14 Agrippa is sent East with powers to prevent Parthian domination on the Bosporan shores of the Euxine. He settles affairs there to Roman advantage, receiving some slight help from Herod.

15 Agrippa shows appreciation of Herod's pro-Roman policy by visiting Jerusalem and sacrificing in the temple.

14 Agrippa sets up a colony of veterans in Syria.

13 Augustus returns to Rome. Agrippa conducts war on the Balkan and Danubian boundaries, in Dalmatia and Panonia. Augustus accepts from the Senate on his return to Rome no other honour than the building of an Altar of Peace. His *imperium* is again extended.

12 The Danubian war is continued successfully by Tiberius after Agrippa's death in this year, whilst Drusus, warring against the German tribes, advances to the Elbe.

11 Julia, on Agrippa's death, is married to an unwilling Tiberius.

––––––––––––

Augustus effects the reorganization of the Roman Army: it virtually becomes a standing army, of 25 legions (or roughly 125,000 men).
In Britain Tasciovanus, King of the Catuvellauni, moves his capital from the fortress at Wheathampstead of Cassivellaunus (probably his grandfather) to unfortified Verulamium. His people are thriving.

A. Politics, Law and Economics

19   After the pacification of Spain her tin mines are opened up thus decreasing the Cornish tin trade, which has been in the hands of the Veneti.

18   *Lex Julia* encourages procreation (within the family).
Agrippa has roads built radiating from Lugdunum, and in general roads are beginning to be built in all the newly acquired provinces; the system of *cursus publicu*, using posting stations for official couriers, is begun.

15   Augustus, instituting a strict control of coinage-issue, establishes a mint at Lugdunum (Lyons).

B. Science and Discovery

20   Vitruvius (see D) mentions a water mill, showing that the use of water power for grinding corn has begun to come into use.

12   The comet later to be called Halley's probably appears. (And see 87 B).

C. Religion and Philosophy

19   Herod begins the restoration of the temple in Jerusalem (the temple that Jesus knew). He allows such scholars as Hiller and Shammai to teach and respects such sects as the Essenes (see 51 C).

17   At the Secular Games, ordered by Augustus, the Sibylline books are re-copied and all the old religious customs are observed.

14   Nicolaus of Damascus pleads with Agrippa for the rights of the Jews.

12   Augustus is made Pontifex Maximus, i.e. head of the state religion, an office held by the Emperors until Theodosius.

E. The Arts

The magnificent statue from Prima Porta shows a handsome Augustus; the scene engraved on his cuirass, of Parthian surrender, dates the statue at 20 B.C. or a little after.

20   Temple of Mars Ultor is erected on the Capitol, to house the recovered standards (see opposite).

20   Vitruvius, once an engineer under Caesar, writes *De Architectura.*

15   The friend of Augustus, V. Pollio, leaves him most of his property; he has had built a fine villa at Pausilypum, near Naples, and achieves fame by feeding his lampreys (for the table) on human flesh.

13   The building of the Altar of Peace on the Campus Martius is begun. Its surrounding walls are covered with reliefs instituting a new era in representational art, including female portraiture.

D. **The Arts** (continued)

12 A temple is dedicated to Vesta on the Palatine Hill.

11 Dedication of the Theatre of Marcellus.

E. **Literature**

20 Virgil and Augustus meet in Athens. No more of the *Aeneid* is written.

17 Horace's *Carmen Saeculare* is sung at the Secular Games by a choir of traditional size, 27 boys and 27 girls.

13 Horace, *Odes*, Bk. IV (celebrating the military fame of Tiberius and Drusus).

F. **Births and Deaths**

20 Gaius Caesar b. (A.D. −4).

19 (Sept.) Virgil d. (51).

19 Juba II d.

19 Arminius ("Hermann", of the Teutonic Cherusci) b. (A.D. −19).

18 Tibullus (Roman poet) d. (36).
Agrippina I b. (A.D. −33).

17 Lucius Caesar b. (A.D. −2).

15 V. Pollio d. (see F).
Germanicus Caesar b. (A.D. −19).

15 Drusus junior, son of Tiberius b. (A.D. −23).

13 M. Lepidus (triumvir) d.

12 Agrippa d. (51).

11 Octavia, sister of Augustus d.

10   Herod's building of Caesarea is completed (see A).

10 or 9   Phraates IV of Parthia, at peace with Rome, hands over his four legitimate sons as hostages to be brought up in Rome .

9   Drusus successfully draws his German campaigns towards completion but in the same year dies from a fall from his horse. He and his brother Tiberius are at last allowed the military title of Imperator by Augustus.

Maroboduus rises to power over the Germanic Marcomanni in the valley of the Main and persuades his people to migrate to Bohemia, involving the Romans in fighting again on the Danube.

8   Augustus' *imperium* is again renewed by the Senate. Tiberius is sent to finish off Drusus' German conquests.

7   Tiberius is made Consul.

Herod's sons, Alexander and Aristobulus are murdered at the command of their father.

6   Possible date for the birth of Jesus Christ. (It must be before the death of Herod in 4 B.C.).

Tiberius is made a colleague of the ageing Augustus by being granted Tribunician powers. Finding however that the two grandsons of Augustus, Gaius and Lucius Caesar, are beginning to be favoured (or for other unknown reasons), he retires for seven years to Rhodes, to study.

5   Gaius Caesar is introduced to public life and reserved for the consulship in 5 years' time.

4   Most probable date for the birth of Jesus Christ.

Execution of Antipater, Herod's eldest son, and, shortly thereafter, in March, the death of Herod. Before his death he institutes a massacre of Pharisees who have attempted to pull down the Roman eagle from the Temple and may also have instituted the Biblical "massacre of the innocents".

A Roman legion keeps order in Jerusalem, and Augustus' policy of weakening the kingdom of Herod the Great is continued. Herod Antipas, son of Herod the great, succeeds to the Tetrarchy of Galilee.

3   Phraates IV of Parthia is murdered and succeeded by Phraates V. ("Phraataces", an usurper).

2   Augustus is made *Pater Patriae*.

Augustus' daughter Julia, left behind by Tiberius soon after his enforced marriage to her and his retirement to Rhodes, is accused of misconduct with many men including a son of Mark Antony, and is banished.

Julia's younger son Lucius Caesar follows his brother Gaius in being introduced into man's estate and public responsibility.

Augustus forms the Praetorian Guard, the imperial boydguard within the city of Rome: minimum service, 12 years.

A. Politics, Law and Economics

10 *Portus Augustus* is built at Syrian Caesarea to mark Herod's completion of it as a great seaport; Augustus responds with a donation of 500 talents.

8 Augustus' *imperium* is renewed and another census taken.

7 Rome's local administration is put on a sound basis by its division into 14 regions.

2 By the *Lex Fufia Caninia*, Augustus limits the too rapid liberation of slaves by restricting the number that can be freed at a master's death.

B. Science and Discovery

9 Augustus has the Julian calendar adjusted (see 46 B.C. B) because leap years had been erroneously inserted every 3 years.

6 Tiberius, at Rhodes, studies astrology, under Thracyllus. First draft of Strabo's *Geography* completed.

C. Religion and Philosophy

6 Theodorus of Gadara, rhetorician, teaches Tiberius in Rhodes.

5 The settlement at Qumran (where the "Dead Sea Scrolls" are produced) is re-occupied and rebuilt.

D. The Arts

9 In Rome the Altar of Peace is dedicated.
Petra becomes the "rose-red city" by reason of its crude rock-face sculptures.

8 The aqueduct at Nemausus (Nîmes) built.

2 The temple of Mars Ultor, in the Forum Augusti, is dedicated.
A *quadriga* statue—a popular form at this time—is erected to Augustus in his forum.

E. Literature

7 Dionysius of Halicarnassus finishes his *Roman Antiquities*.

1 Ovid, *Art of love* and *Remedies of Love*.

F. Births and Deaths

10 Claudius (Emperor) b. (A.D. –54).

9 Drusus senior d. (29).

8 Horace d. (56).
Maecenas d.

7 Dionysius of Halicanessus, Greek historian, d.

1 Augustus refuses to let Tiberius return to Rome. He sends his grandson Gaius Caesar to combat the influence of the Parthian king Phraataces in Armenia, this country being in revolt.

---

9 Under King Aretas IV of the Nabatean Arabs, the kingdom known to the Romans as Arabia Petraea reaches its height and prospers until the time of Trajan. Its capital, Petra, on the caravan route from Aqaba to Gaza, is a hellenistic city though its language is a form of Aramaic.

F. **Births and Deaths** (continued)
 4 Most probable date of the birth of Christ.
    Herod the Gt. d. (70).

 3 Galba b. (A.D. –69).
    Phraates IV d.

 3 Seneca b. (A.D. –65).

Note : cross-references to dates referring to the era other than that of the page concerned are given the necessary suffix, B.C. on an A.D. page and vice versa. Otherwise no suffix is given and it may be taken that the figure quoted refers to the same era as that of the page. *In the index B.C. dates are given in italics.*

A.D. 1–10   A Romano-Parthian treaty; the crucial defeat of a Roman army by the German Arminius

1   Beginning of the Christian Era (a system first used by Dionysius Exigius, see 527 C.)
Phraatces V, king of Parthia, decides to come to terms with Rome over Armenia.

2   A meeting takes place between the Parthian king and the young Gaius Caesar on an
island in the Euphrates. Amidst reciprocal courtesies Rome recognizes Parthia as a
power of some standing and Parthia renounces the right to interfere in Armenia.
Rome puts a Median king on the Armenian throne; and Gaius, in quelling a revolt, is
treacherously wounded. Gaius' brother Lucius dies on the way to an appointment
in Spain.

3   Tiberius, out of favour for absenting himself to Rhodes, is allowed to return to Rome.

4   (Feb.) Gaius Caesar dies of his wounds. Augustus, with all his hoped-for successors
dead except Tiberius, officially adopts Tiberius as his heir, and makes Tiberius do
the same for Germanicus, son of his dead brother Drusus.
Tiberius resumes his military career, beginning with success in Germany.

5   Tiberius reaches the Elbe and prepares to surround and subdue the Germanic
chieftain, Maroboduus in Bohemia.

6   The subjugation of Maroboduus is prevented by a revolt in Pannonia and Dalmatia;
instead he is recognized as King and Friend of Rome. Three years are needed for
Tiberius to put down this revolt. Germanicus campaigns with his uncle Tiberius.
Judaea is made a Roman province (on the misrule of one of Herod the Great's sons
under S. Quirinius, Governor of Syria. (This is the Cyrenius of St Luke, ch. 2,
referring to the Roman census during which Christ was born. Quirinius does hold
a census, in A.D. 6; there may have been an earlier census).

6–9   Dynastic troubles in Parthia.

8   Claudius (aged 18) made Augur.

9   A deceptive peace having reigned in Roman-occupied Germany, with the ex-consul
Q. Varus as governor and exercizing a conciliatory policy, the German petty leader
Arminius (Hermann) entices the three Roman legions (17th, 18th and 19th) out of
their summer camp and ambushes them, gaining a resounding victory. Augustus is
stunned by the defeat, which has lasting consequences, the Romanization of
Germany thereby virtually coming to an end.
Augustus banishes his grand-daughter, Julia, for immorality.

10   Germanicus is sent against Arminius: inconclusive battles.

----

5   In Britain Cunobelinus (Shakespeare's Cymbeline) comes to the throne of the
Catuvellauni; he completely absorbs the Trinovantes and moves his capital to
Camulodonum (Colchester) in their area; he makes it the largest and richest centre
in Britain.

A. Politics, Law and Economics

2   The treaty between Gaius Caesar and Phraataces on the Euphrates at last settles that river as the dividing line between Rome and Parthia but leaves Rome dominant in Armenia, an important area in regard to East-West trade.

4   There is passed the *Lex Aelia Sentia* further restricting the manumission of slaves (see 2 B.C. A) and the infusion of too much alien blood into Roman citizenship.

5   The pay and service of the Roman Army is reorganized. The legionary's length of service is lengthened from 16 to 20 years and that of a Praetorian guardsman from 12 to 16. The former receives 10 *asses* (5/8ths of a denarius) a day and a gratuity of 3000 denarii; the latter receives 2 denarii a day and a gratuity of 5000 denarii. (The denarius is the "penny" of the New Testament and was supposed to represent a day's pay for a labourer, though it decreasingly did so.)
Famine and floods in Rome.

9   *Lex Papia Poppaea* continues the *Lex Julia* (see 18 B.C. C.) in encouraging strictly moral procreation.

B. Science and Discovery

8   The Julian calendar (see 46 B.C. B) settles down to accuracy.

C. Religion and Philosophy

8   Probable date of the visit of Mary and Joseph to Jerusalem, and of the young Jesus to the temple.

D. The Arts

10   A beginning is made, with the Temple of Jupiter, to the magnificent Roman buildings at Heliopolis (Baalbek).
The painters of landscapes on house walls, whose work at Pompeii (and elsewhere) dates from the 1st Cent. B.C. to the 1st Cent. A.D., were flourishing at this time.

E. Literature

Trogus Pompeius, historian of Rome and the East, *fl.* He writes *Historiae Philippicae*, now lost but partly saved by the historian of the 2nd Century A.D., Justinius).

1   Ovid, *Metamorphoses*.

2   Velleius Paterculus, a young tribune, describes the meeting on the Euphrates (see A).

8   Ovid banished, possibly for immorality with Julia (see A A.D. 9): the pretext, his *Art of Love*.

F. Births and Deaths

2   Lucius Caesar d. (19).
Phraates V (King of Parthia) d.

F. **Births and Deaths** (continued)
   3   St. Paul (–65c).

   4   Gaius Caesar d. (24).
       A. Pollio d. (80).

   9   Vespasian b. (–79).

11   The Bosporan rule (see 16 B.C.) is taken over by a Samartian king, who (in 14) receives the title of Friend of Rome and remains a loyal vassal. Dynastic changes and unrest in Parthia.

12   Tiberius returns to a Triumph in Rome, leaving his young and popular nephew Germanicus to continue the long war against Germany and the avenging of Varus (see 9).

13   Tiberius is granted equal powers with Augustus.

14   Augustus (75) dies and Tiberius (55) succeeds.
     Herod Antipas, Tetrarch of Galilee, marries his half-brother's wife, Herodias.
     Sejanus is made head of the Praetorian Guard.
     The Legions on the Rhine revolt on hearing of Augustus' death; they are pacified by Germanicus. Those in Pannonia do likewise and are pacified more efficiently by Drusus junior, Tiberius' son.

14/16   Germanicus campaigns in Germany, with only doubtful success.
     His wife Agrippina I accompanies his campaign and his son Caius Caesar becomes a pet of the soldiers, who call him Caligula ("Little Boots"). He visits the scene of Varus' disaster but fails to subdue Arminius.

15   A consulship is given to Tiberius' son Drusus junior.

17   Tiberius, uneasy at Germanicus' popularity, and believing that Germany were better dealt with by diplomacy than war, recalls his nephew, but grants him a Triumph. (There is no serious trouble from Germany for fifty years).
     In Numidia, a native auxiliary named Tacfarinas, deserts and leads a band of brigands.

18   With special powers over all the governors of the eastern provinces, Germanicus makes a triumphant way through Asia Minor towards Armenia, where a popular king, Artaxias, is put on the throne. (Peace reigns there until his death in A.D. 34).
     As a counterbalance to Germanicus, Tiberius appoints Cn. Piso Governor of Syria.
     Cappadocia and Commagene are annexed to the Roman Empire.

19   Germanicus goes for a holiday in Egypt and on his return to duty falls foul of Piso, whom he apparently orders home. At Antioch he dies of some kind of fever, convinced that Piso has had him poisoned.
     The German heroes, Arminius and Maroboduus, both come to the end of their success: the former is killed by his people and the latter expelled, receiving asylum in Italy.

20   The question of Piso's guilt, on his return to Rome, is investigated by the Senate; Piso commits suicide. Germanicus' widow, Agrippina, suspects Tiberius of having engineered her husband's death; and, generally, the popularity of Tiberius is further lowered.

A. Politics, Law and Economics
Tiberius continues his predecessor's policy of gracious cooperation with the Senate.

14 Tiberius puts through a scheme of Augustus' whereby the Senate becomes the sole electoral body, leaving the People without any direct voice.

18 Herod Antipas builds the city of Tiberias on the Sea of Galilee.

19 On a Jew obtaining some money under false pretences, Tiberius expels all Jews from Italy. 4000 of the strongest are sent to Sardinia as a police force.

B. Science and Discovery
Strabo augments his *Geography* with further economic information of the Empire compiled in the early years of Tiberius' reign. He enumerates the exports from Britain: wheat, cattle, gold, silver, iron, brides, slaves and hunting dogs.

17 Earthquake in Asia Minor; Ephesus suffers.

The physicians of Rome found a meeting place in Rome, a *Schola medicorum*.

C. Religion and Philosophy
14 Godhead is accorded to Augustus at death, with a temple and priests.

17 Caiaphas is appointed High Priest at Jerusalem.

19 In support of orthodox religion, Tiberius has an image of Isis thrown into the Tiber and its priests crucified.

D. The Arts
13 (or 10) Tiberius dedicates the Temple of Concordia Augusta in Rome.
The Portland vase (probably made in Greece for a Roman) dates at about this decade. The cup, and historic frieze scenes, from the house at Boscoreale, date probably from Tiberius' reign.

E. Literature
With the death of Augustus the "golden age" of Latin literature ends and the silver age begins.

18 The *Universal History* of Nicolaus of Damascus (secretary of Herod the Gt.) probably completed—it is used by Josephus.

F. Births and Deaths
12 Caius Caesar (Caligula) b. (−41).

14 Julia, Octavian's daughter. Augustus d. (75).

17 Livy d. (76).

F.   **Births and Deaths** (continued)
   18   Ovid d. (59).

      19   Germanicus d. (34).
            Arminius d. (38).

      19   Juba II d.

21   Tiberius begins to groom his son Drusus junior for office, making him consul for the
     year in partnership with himself.
     A revolt in Gaul is suppressed; but Gaul is developing into one of the most successful
     Roman provinces.

22   Drusus junior is given tribunicate powers.

23   Drusus junior is poisoned—almost certainly by Sejanus, commander of the Praetorian
     guard. Tiberius is increasingly putting his trust in Sejanus, who is steadily plotting
     for power.

24   China under the Han Dynasty suffers a recession. A usurper, Wang Mang, having
     occupied the throne, is assassinated. There is drought and famine and invasion of
     mongolian barbarians from the north. The capital city is shifted eastwards and the
     second or eastern Han Dynasty is begun, a less successful affair than its predecessor.

25   Sejanus urges Tiberius to retire.

26   Pontius Pilate is appointed Procurator of Judaea.

27   John the Baptist conducts his mission. He is imprisoned and executed by Herod
     Antipas, Tetrarch of Galilee (son of Herod the Great). Jesus Christ begins his
     mission.

27   Tiberius retires to Capri. Sejanus saves his life from a fall of rock. More popular
     than ever with the Emperor, but less so with the people, Sejanus governs tyran-
     nously in Rome.

29   Tiberius loses his aged mother, Livia, to whom however he has been careful to grant
     no powers.

30   At the instigation of Sejanus, Tiberius banishes his sister-in-law Agrippina (widow of
     Germanicus) with her sons (potential emperors). They are all soon dead.

30   Death of Jesus Christ (most probable year: in April).

A. Politics, Law and Economics

21   Sejanus begins to increase the power of the Praetorian Guard which is concentrated in one large barracks just outside Rome.

Tiberius exercises restraint in interpreting that part of Caesar's *Lex Juliae* whereby informers are able to enrich themselves in bringing to light treasonable accusations against the Emperor. Tiberius rules that accusations against him as a private person (i.e. concerning the Piso affair, see 20) shall not count as treasonable.

B. Science and Discovery

30   The Roman aristocrat and encyclopaedist, Aurelius Celsus, *fl.* Of his *De Artibus*, which covers agriculture, war, oratory, law, philosophy and medicine, only the treatise on medicine is extant. This ranks second only to Hippocrates and shows very considerable medical and surgical knowledge.

C. Religion and Philosophy

27   The execution of John the Baptist is attributed by Josephus to Herod's fear of a political rebellion and by the Gospels to John's criticism of Herod for marrying his half-brother's wife, Herodias.

30   On the 14th day of the Jewish month of Nisan (April 3rd), and almost certainly in this year, Christ eats the Passover supper with his disciples in Jerusalem, and is betrayed by Judas Iscariot and taken to the house of Caiaphas, the High Priest, the Sanhedrin having ordered his arrest. The next day he is taken before Pontius Pilate and is crucified.

D. The Arts

In Rome the art of glass blowing, said to have come from Sidon or Alexandria, flourishes from about this time and reaches great artistic heights. The Romans also import Murrhine glass vases, both Augustus and Nero much prizing them.

E. Literature

In this decade Apollonius of Tyana *fl.*—philosopher and quack. Also: Phaedrus, fabulist, and Valerius Maximus, compiler of historical anecdotes.

F. Births and Deaths

23   Drusus junior d.
Pliny the elder b. (–79).

24   Strabo, geographer, d. (88*c*).
Tacfarnias, brigand, d.

27   John the Baptist d.

29   Livia d.

30   Jesus Christ d. (33*c*).
Judas Iscariot d.
Nerva b. (–98).

31   Tiberius, at last convinced of the treasonable intentions of Sejanus, has both him and his wife and children executed.

32/37   Tiberius spends the rest of his days as a morose and cruel recluse in his palace at Capri.

35   Cunobelinus, most powerful British chief, (see 5) is growing old, and there appear at his court two factions, the pro-Roman under his son Amminius and the anti-Roman under his sons Togodumnus and Caractacus. (And see below.)

36   The Samaritans having complained of his severity, Pontius Pilate is superseded and ordered to return to Rome. He is believed to have been banished and to have ended his days at Vienne on the Rhone.

37   Tiberius is succeeded as emperor by Caius Caesar, son of Germanicus and Agrippina and known as Caligula or Little Boots, his pet name with the soldiers as a child. He is 25.

39   Caligula advances with an army to the Rhine, but diverts it to the coast with the intention of invading Britain. At the last moment however he cancels his orders (and see E).
Caligula deprives Herod Antipas of his tetrarchy of Galilee and appoints in his place Herod Agrippa, grandson of Herod the Great and a companion of Caligula's youth. This Herod proves a popular ruler.

40   Caligula brings the son of Juba II of Mauretania to Rome and starves him to death. (This is one of the many deeds of extravagant and maniacal cruelty with which Caligula is credited towards the end of his life—see E.)

Britain, while Caligula is playing with the idea of her invasion, is prospering, with four main kingdoms: that of Cunobelinus in the S.E., the Brigantes around the Humber, the Iceni in E. Anglia and the Dobuni in the W. as far as Devonshire. At this time a place that the Romans call Londinium comes into existence; a wooden bridge over the Thames may have been built before the Roman invasion. Several kings are issuing their own coinage.

Spain, besides developing Roman centres of learning (see 39 E) is being used by Rome as a source of mineral wealth.

A.   Politics, Law and Economics

32   Tiberius reverses his earlier liberal interpretation of treason and has many executed under this charge, thus encouraging informers.

40   Caligula exhausts the Roman treasury by his extravagance.

B.   Science and Discovery

33   Pontius Pilate builds an aqueduct at Jerusalem, in spite of opposition on the grounds that he is using sacred funds.

C.   Religion and Philosophy

33   Saul of Tarsus, on his way to Damascus to persecute the followers of Christ, is converted to Christianity.
In Jerusalem Stephen is brought before the Sanhedrin, convicted of blasphemy and subversive teaching and stoned to death, the first Christian martyr.

36   Paul meets Peter in Jerusalem and becomes his friend, as he does also of a new convert, Barnabas. In danger of his life, Paul returns to his native city, Tarsus.

39   Caligula sets himself up as a god, and various absurd excesses are attributed to him.

40   Philo Judaeus of Alexandria *fl.* He comes on an embassy to Rome in this year. His writings, seeking to reconcile the Jewish Scriptures and Platonic philosophy, revelation with reason, has a great influence on the Christian Church. To him mostly is owed the conception of the *Logos*, the "word" or the wisdom of the power of God, sometimes thought of, poetically, as a person, "the first-begotten of God".

E.   Literature

The personal conduct of the Roman emperors from the time of the deterioration of Tiberius to the death of Nero, appears almost as that of power-drunk madmen; yet their rule over the Roman Empire continues to be efficient: the main authority for the emperors' excesses is that of Suetonius and Tacitus, and both are undoubtedly biased against the emperors.

39   The story is told of Caligula that on cancelling his invasion of Britain he draws his army up on the beach and commands them to collect shells, "the spoils of conquered Ocean".
Corduba (Cordova), birthplace of Lucan, is achieving a reputation as a school of rhetoric.

F.   Births and Deaths

31   Sejanus d.

33   Agrippina, wife of Germanicus, d.

33   St. Stephen d.

F. **Births and Deaths** (continued)
  37 (March) Tiberius d. (78).
        Agricola b. (–93).
        Nero b. (–68).
        Josephus b. (–100c).

  39 Lucan, poet, b. (–65).

  40 Quintilian, rhetorician, b. (–118c).
        Titus, Emperor, b. (–81).

  40 Martial, poet, b. (–104c).

41 (Jan) Caligula is murdered by soldiers of the Praetorian Guard and Claudius is made emperor in his place. He is nephew of Tiberius, brother of Germanicus and uncle of Caligula.

42 A son, Britannicus, is born to Claudius.
Mauretania is made a Roman province.

43 The Romans invade Britain with 4 legions, under Aulus Plautius. They land unopposed and defeat Caractacus and his army, first in East Kent and then decisively on the Medway. Claudius follows in person, with reinforcements which include an elephant corps; he crosses the Thames with his army, receives the submission of many tribes at Colchester, and returns to Rome. (See A below and 75 C and D).)

43/7 Aulus Plautius, basing himself strategically on London, sends two of his legions into the Midlands, one to the north, and one, the Second Augusta, under the future emperor Vespasian, westwards, where the Isle of Wight and the Wessex *oppida* or hill forts, including Maiden Castle, are taken. The conquest of the South and East is consolidated.

44 Caractacus, escaping from the battle of the Medway, makes his way into Wales and begins to collect a new force of Britons of the Silures tribe around him.

46 There is famine in Judaea (and see below).

47 The new commander in Britain, Ostorius Scapula, establishes a frontier (see A) and orders the tribes on his side of the line to disarm. The Iceni revolt, and are subdued, though allowed to remain nominally independent.
Aulus Plautius is afforded a Triumph in Rome.

47/50 Caractacus makes raids across the Welsh border upon the Romans.

48 Claudius has his third wife, the nymphomaniac Messalina, put to death and marries the forceful sister of Caligula, the second Agrippina. Agrippina persuades Claudius to adopt her son Nero and to set aside his own son Britannicus.

After the death of Herod Agrippa (and see 44 C) the Jews suffer a series of venal procurators; there is a revolt when a Roman soldier tears up a scroll of the Bible, and discontent and religious fervour increase.

A. Politics, Law and Economics

Probably in this mid-century the Romans begin to make glass for windows. (It is known from Pompeii).

43 Claudius has a new Colchester (Camulodonum) built for his officials but grants to Verulamium the status of self-governing *municipium*. He confers on Cogidubnus, King of the W. Sussex Regni, the title of "Rex et Legatus Augusti in Britannia".

47 A Roman frontier is drawn across Britain from the Trent to the Severn; within are the corn-growing lands—and the Roman soldier's ration is largely corn.

49 The Romans begin to exploit the Mendip lead mines.

50 The town of Colonia Agrippinensis is so called after Nero's mother who was born there; it helps to control the Rhine frontier and becomes Cologne.

B. Science and Discovery

43 Pomponius Mela writes an extant work on geography, *De Situ Orbis*, dividing the world into torrid and temperate zones. (Only the more practical sciences are flourishing in Rome, e.g. agriculture, geography and medicine (see 30 and 77 B).

C. Religion and Philosophy

41 The philosopher and rhetorician Seneca, now in his forties and already famous in the law courts, is banished to Corsica, for alleged misconduct with one of the emperor's nieces. He remains there 8 years, writing tragedies.
Claudius has a temple built to himself at Colchester.

43 Paul and Barnabus begin their mission in Antioch, and their followers are called "Christians".

44 Herod Agrippa has James the Apostle killed and Peter put in prison. Peter escapes; Herod in the same year dies, the Bible says (Acts 12) "eaten by worms".

45/7 Paul goes on his first missionary journey, with Barnabas and Mark, leaving Peter the home field. At Lystra in Asia Minor, on Paul curing a man, he and Barnabas are taken for gods, to their consternation. Paul is unpopular with the Jews for preaching to the Gentiles.

49 Seneca is pardoned, through Agrippina's influence, and returns to Rome, to become the tutor of the young Nero.

50 Paul, having succeeded in his contention that the Christian mission should minister to Gentile as well as Jew, sets out on his second journey through Asia Minor into Thrace. He finds his disciple Timothy and meets Luke.

50 There is a tradition that at about this time the disciple Thomas travels to the court at Gandhara of the Shaka king, Gondophernes, and is there martyred.

D. **The Arts**

41 A burial mound is raised at Lexden, near Colchester, either that of one of Cunobelinus' nobles or of the king himself. The dead man is buried with his war chariot
and many other grave goods; the type of art however has by now become more
Roman than Celtic.

F. **Births and Deaths**

41 Caligula d. (29).

41 Cunobelinus d.

42 Britannicus b. (–55).

44 James the Apostle d.
Herod Agrippa d.

46 Plutarch b. (–120c).

48 Messalina d.

51   In N.W. Wales Caractacus is finally defeated by the Romans. He escapes to Queen
     Cartimandua of the Brigantes. She however is committed to Rome, and hands
     Caractacus over to them. He graces a Roman triumph but is allowed his life and
     to end his days in exile.
     Rome has to protect herself once more against the Parthians, who gain control of
     Armenia (but see 63).

53   Nero, aged 16, is married to Claudius' daughter Octavia.

54   Agrippina has her husband Claudius poisoned and her son Nero made emperor in his
     stead. Nero is under the tutelage of the philosopher Seneca and of Burrus, Prefect
     of the Praetorian Guard.

55   Agrippina begins to favour her stepson Britannicus in the place of Nero. Britannicus
     is accordingly assassinated.

57   The efficiency of Rome's central administration, whilst Nero commits his excesses, is
     illustrated by the fact that the governors of both Cilicia and Asia are recalled on the
     grounds of misgovernment.
     A Japanese chieftain sends an envoy to the Chinese court.

58/9 The Roman general Corbulo wages war against Parthia and Armenia.
      Armenia's southern capital falls.

59   Nero has his mother Agrippina assassinated; he is tired and afraid of her domination
     but is also anxious to please his mistress Poppaea Sabina (whom he intends, against
     his mother's wishes, to make his wife). Agrippina, having saved herself from
     drowning in a specially constructed sinkable boat, is bludgeoned to death.
     Britain is given a new governor, Suetonius Paulinus. There are four legions stationed
     in England; and Colchester had become a town of veterans, i.e. retired Roman
     soldiers. Paulinus begins training for a conquest of Wales.

60   The king of the Iceni (of East Anglia) dies, leaving his kingdom jointly to his widow
     Boudicca (Boadicea) and Rome. The Romans interpret this will very much in
     their own favour; according to Tacitus Boudicca is flogged and her two daughters
     raped. Suetonius Paulinus has begun his campaign in Wales.

A. Politics, Law and Economics

Roman trade with both N. and S. India is considerable at this mid-century, the Romans importing not only native goods such as muslin but also goods from farther East that the rising class of Indian merchants collect for them, turquoise from Afghanistan, silk along the Silk Route, spices from the East Indies, etc. Rome's wars with Parthia divert trade through N. India.

59 The Senate illustrates its own servility by submitting an address congratulating Nero on the death of his mother.

C. Religion and Philosophy

During this decade Seneca writes his books *De Beneficiis* (On Clemency, On Anger, etc).

51/2 Paul reaches Athens, where he tries to reconcile the pagan and Christian theology; he moves on to the community of Jewish merchants at Corinth, where he stays 18 months, preaching also to the Greeks.

53/7 Paul goes on his third journey, from Jerusalem. He spends two years at Ephesus, until the consequent slackening in the trade in the images of "Diana of the Ephesians", makes him unpopular. He revisits the Corinthians, after chiding them by letters for backsliding. He writes to the Galatians, breaking completely with the Judaizing Christians who wish to tie Christianity to the Mosaic Law. He returns to Jerusalem.

58 Paul in Jerusalem is saved from irate Jews by Roman arrest and sent on to the Roman procurator at Caesarea, Felix. There again he is accused by Jews of preaching against the Law. Felix keeps him under house arrest for two years. Felix is then succeeded by Festus.

60 Paul is interviewed by Festus and by King Agrippa (son of Herod Agrippa) who is passing through Caesarea. Having appealed to be tried in Rome, Paul is sent there. (And see E.)

D. The Arts

55 Nero is said to have been jealous of Britannicus for having a better singing voice.

59 Nero, turning from chariot racing, in which pastime his advisors encourage him, insists on a stage appearance — which according to Tacitus, is achieved before a compulsory audience of a battalion of the Guard.

Nero's skill on the lyre — probably quite genuine — illustrates the fact that by now the Romans have quite overcome their earlier rugged disapproval of Greek music and dancing.

E. Literature

F.   Births and Deaths

52   Trajan b. (–117).

54   Claudius d. (64).

55   Britannicus, son of Claudius, d. (14).

55   Epictetus b. (–135c).
     Tacitus b. (–120c).

59   Agrippina d.

60   Juvenal b. (–140c).

A.D. 61–70   Queen Boudicca and the Jews both revolt; a year of many emperors

61 Suetonius Paulinus reaches the Menai Straits, crosses them, and massacres the hordes on the shores of Anglesey (see C). Meanwhile Boudicca and the Iceni revolt against the Roman ill-treatment, and they are joined by the Trinovantes (annoyed particularly at having had laid on them the upkeep of Claudius' temple at Colchester). Massacres of Romans and Romano-Britons occur at Colchester and Verulamium and London, 70,000 being said to have died. Paulinus returns and defeats the rebels at a battle somewhere in the Midlands; Boudicca commits suicide; Paulinus is recalled, and his replacement is instructed to be more pacific.

62 Nero gets rid of his advisers Seneca and Burrus, divorces his wife Octavia and marries the licentious Poppaea, under whose influence he increasingly falls. Burrus dies shortly afterwards and Nero is suspected of hastening his end. Seneca retires and survives for three years (see E). Octavia is put to death.

63/6 The Parthians make peace with Rome, whereby the pro-Parthian Tiridates shall be king of Armenia. Tiridates comes to Rome and is bequeathed the kingdom by Nero.

64 Rome suffers a great fire, which Nero is said to have watched, reciting lines on the destruction of Troy. There is no evidence that he caused it; but he is suspected, and he finds a scapegoat (see C). However, he does much to relieve the suffering.

65 Poppaea dies in pregnancy, allegedly from a kick in the stomach by Nero. Nero uncovers a plot against himself and takes vengeance (and see E).

66 Revolt breaks out in Judaea against Florus, probably the worst of the procurators since Pontius Pilate. There follows internecine war between Jew and Gentile, the latter massacring the former in Caesarea. The Jews seize Masada, the strongest of Herod the Great's fortresses.
The Janus temple is opened for peace.

66/7 Nero tours Greece (see D).

67 The experienced soldier Vespasian (who has been touring Greece with Nero) is sent to bring order to Judaea. There follows the siege and fall of Jotopata (in Galilee) which Josephus the historian (see E) describes and at which he is taken prisoner by the Romans.

68 Vespasian spends the year forcibly restoring order in Judaea.
(June) Nero, having returned to Rome and to further misdeeds, has sickened his subjects. A revolt by the legions in Gaul and Spain is followed by one on the part of the Praetorian Guard in the city itself. Nero flees from Rome, but on being surrounded commits suicide.

68/9 There follows in Rome a year of anarchy, no less than four emperors occupying the throne during a period of 13 months—see A. Vespasian, when he is declared emperor, leaves the Jewish war to his son Titus. He reaches Rome, defeats Vitellius (see A) in battle, and proceeds to restore order in Rome. (Vespasian is the first emperor of the Flavian family or *Flavia Gens*).

70 Jerusalem suffers a siege of 139 days, being heroically defended. It is largely destroyed, the temple having already caught fire, in spite of Titus' efforts to save it. (And see C.)

A. Politics, Law and Economics

61 An added reason for the wrath of the Iceni (see opposite) is that the large loans made to the British nobles to help romanize themselves are called in—Seneca being the chief creditor.

66 Cassius, a celebrated jurist, is banished from Rome by Nero, for possessing an ancestral image of Caesars' murderer. He writes 10 books on civil law.

68 Quintilian, a Spaniard, comes to Rome with Galba and makes his name as a rhetorician in the Law Courts.

68/9 The politics of Rome during the "year of four emperors" illustrate the power not only of army leaders but also, temporarily, of the Praetorian Guard. First Galba, backed by the legions in Spain and Gaul, wins the throne; but, instituting decrees of economy and anti-bribery, he is assassinated by the Praetorian Guards. These then set up their easygoing puppet Otho, once the husband of Poppaea. The armies of the frontiers then again come to the rescue, and the race for power is between Vitellius of the armies of the Rhine and Vespasian of the armies of the East. Vitellius makes a spectacular crossing of the Alps and helps himself for a few months to the fruits of office. In July 69 Vespasian is declared Emperor at Alexandria.

B. Science and Discovery

64/7 Nero has a canal built from Ostia to Lake Avernus and makes another abortive attempt at a Corinth canal.

67 At the siege of Jotopata the Romans use not only the catapult and ballista but also the ram. Josephus tells how the Jews use bags of chaff to deaden its effect and the Romans use long scythes to cut down the bags of chaff.

C. Religion and Philosophy

61 The Roman conquest of Anglesey brings an end to Druidism in Britain. On crossing the Menai Straits the legionaries are faced with women in ceremonial dress mingled with the warriors and druid priests standing by the fires of human sacrifice.

61 Paul, after shipwreck on the coast of Malta, reaches Rome. Awaiting trial he is allowed much freedom; he offends however the Jewish Christians by insisting that his mission is also to the Gentiles.

62 St Mark, who has been in Rome with St Peter, is by tradition martyred in this year in Venice.
James, brother (or cousin) of Jesus and leader of his early followers, is assassinated.

64 Nero lays the blame for Rome's fire on the Christians and has many tortured and killed. By tradition Peter, now in Rome, is one of the victims, condemned to crucifixion and humbly electing to die in a position reversed from that of Christ. (As first Bishop of Rome he founds the hierarchy of Popes).

C. **Religion and Philosophy** (continued)

65   This is the most probable year for the trial and execution of Paul in Rome.

    The Phrygian city of Laodicea (whose Christian community was lukewarm) is destroyed by earthquake.

65/7   Envoys are sent to India by the Chinese emperor to study Buddhism. Buddhist missionaries begin to visit China.

70   The Romans' destruction of Jerusalem may be said to begin the Jewish dispersal or *diaspora* (and see 132). In future it will be the Law, the *Torah*, which will hold the Jews together and the rabbis will be the instrument of that binding power. From this time there dates the addition of the oral laws of Moses to the Pentateuch to form the Torah.

D. **The Arts**

65   After the great fire, Nero does much to build a less congested, nobler and handsomer Rome. He also starts to build his vast and extravagant "Golden House".

66/7   Nero's tour of Greece is made into an artistic but somewhat farcical triumph. All the Greek games are held in the same year and he is allowed to win no less than 1808 prizes. Seutonius says that no one is allowed to leave during his performances, not even women to have their babies!

67   The entrance of Buddhist missionaries into Chian has its effect upon her art.

E. **Literature**

61   Paul in Rome continues to dictate his letters to his converts around the Middle East. These epistles become rapidly and widely known and have a profound influence on the early Christian faith. (The authenticity of Paul as author of all those that appear in the Bible is a matter of dispute.)

64   The poet Martial, a Spaniard, comes to Rome, to secure later the patronage of Titus.

65   The young poet Lucan is implicated in the plot against Nero and is forced to commit suicide. So also is Seneca (who is Lucan's uncle). Seneca dies nobly and his wife elects to die beside him. Lucan has written a heroic poem on the struggle between Caesar and Pompey *De Bello Civili*, sometimes known as the *Pharsalia*. Seneca leaves his *Letters*, ten tragedies, and many works on philosophy and ethics (see 51 C).

67/70   Josephus in his *Jewish War* tells of the horrors and degredations, on both sides, of the sieges of Jotapata and Jerusalem.

70   Probable date for the writing of *The Revelations of St. John the Divine* (almost certainly not John the Apostle).

F. **Births and Deaths**

61   Pliny the Younger b. (–113*c*).

    P.P. Statius (poet) b. (96*c*).

    Boudicca d.

F.   **Births and Deaths** (continued)
  62   Burrus d.
        James, brother of Jesus, d.
        Octavia, wife of Nero, d.

  64   (St.) Peter d.

  65   Seneca d. (68*c*).
        Lucan, poet, d. (26).
        Poppaea d.

  65   (St.) Paul d. (62*c*).

  68   Nero d. (31).

  69   Galba, Otho and Vitellius d.

  70   Suetonius, Roman historian, b.

71 Titus returns to Rome from the Jewish War and is accorded a Triumph with his father. The Janus temple is closed.

72 Helvidius Priscus, an outspoken critic of dictatorial rule, having been exiled by Nero but pardoned, demands in the Senate the restoration of the Republic. Vespasian, unable to suppress him, forces him into suicide—the one official murder of his reign and one which he afterwards regrets.

73 (April) The Herodian fortress of Masada, occupied by the Jewish Zealots, is at last invested by the Romans under Titus after a two year siege, the last of the garrison committing suicide. (The Roman earthworks needed to take this wellnigh impregnable stronghold are still visible.)

74 Agricola is made governor of Aquitania.

74/8 Britain is governed by Frontinus, who continues the subjugation of Wales.

77 In N.W. India Kanishka (either of Yueh-Chi or Shaka origin) founds the Kushan kingdom of Kashmir. He favours Buddhist missionary efforts.

77/8 Agricola (who has earlier served there under Paulinus) is made governor of Britain. He completes the conquest of Wales and consolidates the subjugation of the Brigantes. (He also becomes the father-in-law of Tacitus.)

79 Vespasian dies and is succeeded as Emperor by his son Titus.

79 (Aug.) Vesuvius erupts, and Herculaneum and Pompeii and Stabiae are overwhelmed. There is also a fire in Rome. Titus does what he can to repair the damage. (And see B and D.)

79/80 Agricola conquers the lowlands of Scotland and reaches the Forth-Clyde line. He builds a naval base for a projected invasion of Ireland, which never materializes.

80 Plague follows the fire in Rome.

The Colosseum is completed; destruction at Qumran; a villa at   A.D. 71–80
  Fishbourne; St. Luke's gospel

A. Politics, Law and Economics

71 Vespasian, the first commoner to come to the imperial throne, sets an example of simplicity and frugality. He re-imposes taxes; he brings new, provincial, blood into the Senate.

71/3 Vespasian sells many Jews into slavery. (Often these manage to buy their freedom and to found a Jewish community—one, it is thought, being that at Cologne, brought by a legion being transferred there after the Jewish War.)

74/8 Frontinus, being engineer and lawyer besides soldier, builds roads and forts and helps the Britons to become Romanized and to learn to govern themselves.

B. Science and Discovery

77 The *Historia Naturalis* of Pliny the Elder appears. It is the only extant literary product of the vast output of a hard-working and dedicated man. It is a conglomeration of keen observation, absurd hearsay, and philosophic comment. He regrets the discovery of iron, since it has made war more terrible.

79 Pliny the elder is overwhelmed by the Vesuvius eruption; in command of the Roman fleet, he lands in order to observe the phenomenon.

80 An epigram of Martial (see E) shows that false teeth are used in Rome.

80 Dioscorides, Greek physician, *fl.* He writes *Materia Medica*, a description of herbs.

C. Religion and Philosophy

The Gospel according to St Luke is probably written in this decade, i.e. after the fall of Jerusalem. It is thought that both Luke and Matthew draw on Mark, and that all four gospels are written between A.D. 65 and 100.

71/3 Vespasian forbids the Jews to proseletyze.

73 At about the same time as the destruction of Masada the Romans also destroy the community at Qumran near the Dead Sea; these are either the Essenes or a similar ascetic sect. They leave behind, hidden in nearby caves, the so-called Dead Sea Scrolls. Generally, this Roman destruction sees the end of all the Jewish ascetic sects which have flourished since the time of the Macabees.

75 King Cogidubnus, of the British Regni, publicly demonstrates his Romanization by building a temple to Neptune and Minerva (and see D below).

D. The Arts

75 The vast and magnificent Romano-British palace at Fishbourne near Chichester is being built at about this time: it can hardly have been anybody's but King Cogidubnus's (see C above and 43 A). There are at least sixty rooms with tesselated floors, and artists from Italy—perhaps out of work from the destruction of Pompeii —must have been imported.

D. **The Arts** (continued)

77 A statue of Kanishka (see opposite) is made (and survives, showing his typical Tartar quilted boots). In this Kushan monarch's reign Graeco-Buddhist sculpture develops and fine buildings are erected in Taxila and elsewhere.

79 A wealth of Hellenistic art is lavished on the walls and columns of the rich men's villas at Pompeii, Herculanium and Stabiae that are overwhelmed by the eruption of Vesuvius. The girl gathering flowers, and the head of a faun, are well-known examples; and there are innumerable paintings of idyllic scenery.
The Mime or *Pantomime*, besides the chariot race and the gladiatorial show, has supplanted the drama in Rome. On the day of Vespasian's funeral, Suetonius reports, a mime is put on making fun of his parsimony.

80 The Colosseum, begun by Vespasian, is finished under Titus in this year. It seats 87,000 spectators.
The baths of Titus in Rome are dedicated.

E. **Literature**

71 Quintilian is appointed by Vespasian as the first state-salaried teacher (of rhetoric).

79 Pliny the younger writes a letter describing the Vesuvius eruption.

80 Martial grows to fame under Titus and continues so under Domitian. He is read, he says, even by the Goths.

F. **Births and Deaths**

75 Helvitius Priscus d.

76 Hadrian b. (–138).

79 Vespasian d. (69).
Pliny the Elder d. (56).

81   Emperor Titus dies (and see A); his brother Domitian, who succeeds him, is suspected of hastening his end.

82   Further fires in Rome.
Agricola advances into central Scotland, encamping on navigable rivers and using his fleet for supplies.

83   Agricola wins the set battle of Mons Graupius and considers that he has conquered Scotland.
Domitian crosses the Rhine to subdue a German tribe, the Chatti, and then retires to begin the road-and-rampart *limes* along the river's southern bank.

84   Agricola is recalled. The occupation of Scotland, at least as far north as Perthshire, appears to continue for another 20 years.

86   The Dacians, a people possibly Aryan and from Thrace and living between the Danube and the Carpathians, cross the Danube under their king Decebalus (and see below).

87   The Romans drive the Dacians across the Danube and follow them into their own country. They are however pushed back over the Danube again.

88   The Roman governor of Upper Germany, A. Saturninus, persuades two legions at Mainz to declare him emperor. His revolt is suppressed; but the strategy of Domitian, who has come in person to save Rome from the Dacians, is disconcerted and he patches up a peace with Decebalus, which includes in its terms the payment of an annual bribe to the latter.

89   Domitian, profoundly affected by the revolt of Saturninus, becomes increasingly reactionary and suspicious (see A and C). He is accorded a Triumph however.

90   The foundation of Lindum Colonia (Lincoln) begins.

In China the Han Dynasty is struggling increasingly against pressure from the "Hsuing-Ny", i.e. the Huns. The Silk Route to the west is threatened, as is the Tarim basin (north of Tibet) as a whole. In this decade and the next however, the Chinese general Pan Chao takes the offensive. He reaches the Caspian, whence incidentally he sends men to report on the power of Rome. He goes no further; but his push has accelerated the Hunnish drift westwards rather than eastwards.

87   The crossing of the Danube by the Dacians (see 86) marks the beginning of pressure upon the Roman Empire from that region, the Dacians being themselves pressed southwards by the Sarmatians of the Russian steppes. Similarly (see 83) pressure from beyond the Rhine, quiet since the time of Tiberius, shows sign of resumption in Domitian's reign.

A. Politics, Law and Economics

Frontinus, after his return from Britain, reorganizes Rome's water-supply (and see E).

In Londinium a basilica is built about this time—on modern Cornhill.

81   Titus in his short reign shows himself merciful and generous—so generous that the Treasury sinks almost as low as his father had found it.

81/88   Domitian in the first part of his reign is puritanical and competent. He enforces the Julian moral laws, ends the creation of eunuchs, stops speculation, issues fine coinage, and cancels tax arrears over 5 years old.

84   In Britain Agricola has encouraged the building of towns and the living of a town life by the Britons, a process that continues, with some opposition, during the rest of the century.

89   Those suspected of implication in the revolt of Saturninus are hunted down, and Domitian, like Tiberius before him, encourages the use of informers.

B. Science and Discovery

84   Agricola's fleet, which has been supporting his land campaign, circumnavigates Britain.

87   Once more the Romans build a bridge over the Danube.

C. Religion and Philosophy

89   Domitian, ruling more and more dictatorially, announces the divinity of himself and family. Afraid both of prophecy and criticism, he has astrologers and philosophers expelled from Rome.

E. The Arts

81   The triumphal arch of Titus is raised at the eastern end of the Forum. Its reliefs show the taking away from the temple at Jerusalem of the Jews' sacred seven-branched candlestick.

82/90   After its fires Rome has its temple of Jupiter, Juno and Minerva restored at great expense, also the Pantheon and the public libraries. Domitian also builds a palace for himself, the Domus Flavia, nearly as overwhelming as Nero's Golden House.

E. Literature

The young poet, P. Papinius Statius, flourishes. He is patronized by Domitian and his court and becomes famous for his extemporary effusions. Martial, jealous of him, and referring no doubt to the latter's *Thebais*, observes that a live epigram is worth more than a dead epic.

Frontinus (see 74) writes two treatises, one on war and one on surveying and water-supply.

The Emperor Domitian, according to Suetonius, writes a book *On the Care of the Hair*, but goes bald.

E. **Literature** (continued)
  86 Domitian, in imitation of Greece, institutes the Capitoline "Games", for contests in literature and music.

  90 At about this time Plutarch, a native of Chaeronea, is lecturing on philosophy in Rome.

F. **Births and Deaths**
  81 Titus d. (40).

  86 Antoninus Pius b. (–161).

  89 A. Saturninus d.

A.D. 91–100 The Senate makes Nerva emperor, and Nerva nominates Trajan; Britain grows more Roman

91 Trajan, born in Spain and a professional soldier, having served with distinction in Germany and the East, is made one of the consuls for the year.

92 Domitian again campaigns in the Danube area.

93 Agricola dies, having been in retirement since recalled from Britain.

96 On Domitian ordering the execution of his secretary (for having helped Nero to commit suicide), the other freedmen of the royal household rise and murder their master, Domitian's wife being privy to the plot.

The Senate, in relief, have all statues of Domitian destroyed. They then have the courage—see 71 A *re* new blood—to appoint one of their own members as Emperor, M. Cocceius Nerva. Nerva, aged 66, has been a jurist and a minor poet. He restores tranquility, suppresses the mass of informers that have been raised again in Domitian's last years, and promises never to put a senator to death—a promise which he keeps.

The foundation of a settlement for retired legionaries is begun at Gloucester, and the consolidation of Roman Britain continues.

97 Nerva survives a revolt of the Praetorian Guard (who are angered that emperor-making has ceased to be one of their functions), and adopts the soldier Trajan as his son and successor.

98 Nerva dies and is succeeded as Emperor by Trajan. Trajan is campaigning on the Rhine frontier at the time and continues there for the best part of two years. The young Hadrian, also campaigning in the area, sets out on horseback, with the diplomatic intention of personally congratulating Trajan; he is waylaid by a rival and his horse is killed, but he still manages to be the first to arrive with congratulations.

100 Trajan arrives in Rome to take up his emperorship, entering unostentatiously on foot.

A. Politics, Law and Economics

96/8   Nerva in his short reign institutes several reforms, in taxation and in land tenure. He enconomizes on the public spectacles.

97   Tacitus is appointed consul, in replacement of one who has died during the year.

98   Nerva, in reviving the custom of adopting a son and a successor, creates thereby a precedent that is followed by Trajan, Hadrian and Antoninus Pius.

B. Science and Discovery

At about this time the Chinese are inventing a rudimentary compass; it is however derived from a divining board (where objects are scattered on a platter and the direction of their pointing is found significant) and it is not likely to have been used by mariners.

C. Religion and Philosophy

91   The Epistles of the apostle John are written about this time, John having by tradition become bishop of Ephesus, and dying soon after this date and at a great age.

92   Domitian has Christians executed for refusing to offer sacrifice before his image.

95   Domitian (see 89 C) now has philosophers banished from the whole of Italy. One of them is the Greek freed slave and Stoic philosopher Epictetus, who retires to Epirus, there to teach rather as Socrates had done and to have his teaching later put down in writing by a disciple.

Hadrian, having already served in the Army, completes his education in Athens, studying philosophy, mathematics and medicine. He acquires an admiration for all things Greek, and becomes known as "the Greekling".

98   Dion Chrysostomus ("the golden mouthed") *fl.* He is among the most eminent of Rome's Greek sophists and is highly regarded by Nerva and Trajan. Some 80 of his *Orations* are extant.

D. The Arts

96   Nerva's forum in Rome is opened.

100   Trajan founds Thamugadi in Numidia (see 117 A).

E. Literature

Juvenal annoys Domitian by his uncomplimentary reference in one of his satires to Paris the pantomime dancer and court minion.

In about this decade Plutarch returns to his native Chaeronea, to hold various magisterial offices, and to write (see 90 and 120 E).

96   Statius, having retired from Rome, where his popularity has waned, dies in his native Naples. (His earlier *Thebais* regains popularity in the Middle Ages).

E. **Literature** (continued)

98 Tacitus' *Germania* and his *Life of Agricola* are written about this time. (For his other works, see at date of his death, 120 E.)

100 Pliny the younger is chosen to write a *Panegyric* on Trajan.
Martial, with the financial help of Pliny the younger, retires to his native Spain.

F. **Births and Deaths**

93 Agricola d. (56).

96 Domitian d. (45).

96 P. P. Statius, poet, d. (35c).

98 Nerva d. (68).

101/2 King Decebalus has grown back into power and is proving himself implacably anti-Roman. Trajan therefore invades Dacia and, after a difficult campaign, forces Decebalus to surrender. The defeated chieftain is however allowed to continue on the throne, as a client king. Hadrian, who is serving under Trajan, swims his horse and himself across the icy Danube, not to be outdone by the Dacians.

104/6 Decebalus revolts, and Trajan leads a second invading force, of ten legions, into Dacia. Again it is a difficult and hard fought campaign but Trajan wins the confidence of his legionaries: the story is told that in one battle he tears up his own cloak to help bandage the wounded. Decebalus, his position finally made hopeless, summons his chiefs to a final feast, after which they all commit suicide. It is Hadrian who discovers the gruesome aftermath of this act.

106 Trajan returns to a Triumph; he gives the populace a great show of games, said to last for 123 days; Dacian prisoners are used as gladiators.

Dacia—the later Roumania—is colonized and developed by the Romans, though after Trajan has carried off much booty. Trajan recognizes the strategic value of Dacia in any further clash with Germany.

107 Trajan is said to have sent ambassadors to India, presumably to the Kushana dynasty (see 77).

108 Arabia Petraea is subjected to the Roman Empire in a campaign under A. Cornelius Palma.

Trajan—though only death may have prevented him from over-reaching himself in the East—is preparing the way for the Roman Empire's most peaceful and successful century.

The northern African coast is about to take the place of Sicily, which has altogether declined, as the area of expansion and city-making.

Britain is peaceful; but stone-built Roman forts are replacing temporary wooden ones.

A. Politics, Law and Economics

Trajan proves himself a careful and hardworking administrator and realizes, like Augustus, that he can rule personally so long as he gives the Senate the appearance of power. He is credited with the dictum: "It is better that the guilty should remain unpunished than that the innocent should be condemned." Agriculture is encouraged throughout Italy, 5% state mortgages being given. Family allowances are instituted and in Rome poor children as well as their parents receive the corn dole. Trajan's wife Plotina and sister Marciana set an example to women and endeavour to improve court morals.

106   In Dacia the Romans work the gold mines.

107/10   The Pontine marshes are drained, and Trajan has roads and harbours built.

B. Science and Discovery

105   Trajan builds a stone bridge over the Danube with the help of the architect Apollodorus of Damascus.

105   Ts'ai Lun informs the Chinese emperor that he has invented a better and lighter material than silk and bamboo on which to write. It is made of rags and fish-net, bark and hemp—i.e. paper. Ts'ai Lun is rewarded with high office, but intrigues with the Empress and has to take poison. (And see 150 B.)

C. Religion and Philosophy

108   Ignatius, bishop of Antioch since 69, polemic Christian and one of the early post-apostolic "Fathers" of the church, is summoned to Rome and martyred for refusing to abjure his faith. He is not the only Christian in Rome at this time to be persecuted for not worshipping in the orthodox manner—people are complaining that the spread of the new religion is causing unemployment among the pagan temple-servers!

D. The Arts

101   At about this date the Christians of Rome begin to bury their dead in the catacombs outside their city, and so continue until the end of the 4th century: the frescoes on the walls mark the beginning of distinctive Christian art.

109   A monument to Mars Ultor is raised in Dacia.

E. Literature

Juvenal flourishes in this decade and on into Hadrian's reign, having learnt not to annoy emperors (see 91 E). His satires however are a devastating indictment of the worse side of Roman society.

In this century is probably written the *Library* of Greek mythology, attributed to Apollodorus of Athens of the 2nd Cent. B.C.

F. Births and Deaths

104   Martial d. (64).

106   Decebalus d.

111 Pliny the younger is sent to govern Bithynia (and see C).

112 Trajan, happier with his legionaries than at his desk, decides that the Parthian power should be broken for all time. (The Parthians, under King Chosroes, or Osroes, though not threatening Rome, have invaded Armenia.) Trajan prepares for his campaign.

114/16 Trajan carries through a campaign of spectacular conquest. He takes Ctesiphon, the city on the Tigris opposite Seleucia which the Parthians have made their capital. He victoriously reaches the Persian Gulf, and, looking towards India, regrets that he is too old to emulate Alexander. He returns to Ctesiphon and crowns a Parthian puppet king. He falls ill.

117 Revolt breaks out behind Trajan in many parts of the Empire, begun often by the Jews of the Dispersion. King Chrosroes himself revolts. There is trouble along the African coast, and in N. Britain.
Trajan suffers a stroke and begins the journey of a sick man back to Rome, a journey which he never finishes. The rebellions are put down. Hadrian, uncertain whether Trajan has nominated him his successor, finds an ally in Trajan's widow, Plotina, and achieves the throne.

118 Hadrian reaches Rome. He halts his predecessor's expansionist policy, withdrawing the legions from Armenia, Assyria, Mesopotamia and Parthia and making Armenia a client kingdom instead of a province: like Augustus he accepts the Euphrates as the Roman frontier. His policy is not popular with his generals; nor does he achieve popularity at home, in spite of liberal gestures (see A).
Hadrian has returned to Rome bearded; he thus sets a new fashion for Roman Emperors.

118/20 There are serious revolts in Britain, with the 9th (Hispana) Legion, stationed at Lincoln, totally disappearing from the records.

120 The young Antoninus Pius is made one of the consuls for the year.

120 Tacitus (see E) refers to the Goths, and as having moved south from their original home on the Baltic.

A. Politics, Law and Economics

114/16 As a result of Trajan's campaign, Armenia, Assyria, Mesopotamia and Parthia are for a little while made Roman provinces.

117 Trajan, unable to advance into India, builds a Red Sea fleet to control the passage to, and commerce with, India.

117 In the Roman province of Africa (covering Carthaginia and Numidia) the city of Thamugadi is developed (remaining as the extensive ruins of Timgad).

118 Hadrian, besides spending money on games and gifts to the people, cancels tax arrears and has the tax records publicly burnt.

B. Science and Discovery

112 The transport and construction of Trajan's column is a major engineering feat, it being made of 18 cubes of Parian marble each weighing about 50 tons.

116 Soranus, physician of Ephesus practising at Alexandria, publishes his work on gynaecology; he suggests methods of contraception and recommends abortion where delivery would endanger the mother's life.

C. Religion and Philosophy

111 In reply to a letter from Pliny in Bithynia seeking advice, Trajan instructs him not to pay attention to anonymous denunciations of Christians "for that would be a very bad example, unworthy of our time".

117 In the revolts at the end of Trajan's reign there is much internecine strife between Jews and Gentiles, particularly in Cyrene and Cyprus.

117 Basilides, Christian Gnostic of Alexandria, *fl.*

D. The Arts

112/13 Trajan gives Rome another and larger and more magnificent forum; it is built to the design of Apollodorus who was responsible for the Danube bridge (see 105 B); it is named after Trajan; and in it is erected Trajan's column showing in high relief the Emperor's victorious campaigns.

118 Hadrian's Pantheon is started in Rome.

E. Literature

Suetonius is practising at the bar and writing letters to his friend Pliny.

114 On each side of Trajan's column two libraries are built, for Latin and Greek works respectively.

118 Suetonius becomes private secretary to Hadrian, but loses his job through the disfavour of Hadrian's wife Sabina, and retires, to write his *Histories of the Caesars*.

118 Quintilian dies; his chief work is a system of rhetoric, *Institutiones Oratoriae*.

E.   **Literature** (continued)

120   Tacitus dies, leaving behind his chief works, the *Historiae*, covering the period A.D. 68 to 96 and his *Annales*, covering the period from the death of Augustus to the death of Nero.

This is also the most likely date for the death of Plutarch, who has returned to Chaeronea for the latter part of his life (see 90 and 91 E) and has written his parallel *Lives* of Greeks and Romans.

At this date Classical literature is considered to have ended.

F.   **Births and Deaths**

117   Trajan d. (65).

117   Aelius Aristides b. (–187c).

118   Quintilian d. (78c).

120   Tacitus d. (59c).
      Plutarch d. (80).

121 Hadrian, having improved government administration at home (see A), sets out on the first of his businesslike and beneficial tours of the Roman Empire. In this year he visits Gaul and also the Rhine and Danube frontiers—which he orders to be strengthened. He improves the lot, and the discipline, of the legionaries.

122 Hadrian crosses to Britain and orders a wall to be built "to divide the barbarians from the Romans", running from the Solway Firth to the mouth of the Tyne. He returns via Provence, where he founds Avignon and builds a temple at Nîmes.

123/4 After leading a small punitive expedition in Mauretania, Hadrian visits Asia Minor where he affords relief after recent earthquake and generally boosts morale (and see A and D). He recruits to his staff the handsome Bithynian boy, Antinous, who becomes his favourite.

125 The Chinese general Pan Yong, son of Pan Chao (see 81) temporarily reconquers the Tarim basin from the Huns.

125/6 Hadrian arrives at Athens and winters there, returning to Rome in the spring, visiting Sicily and climbing Mt. Etna on the way home.

127 Probable date for the virtual completion of Hadrian's Wall in Britain. It is 73 miles long and interspersed with forts: if well manned it will be almost impregnable.

128 Hadrian begins his second tour in N. Africa, visiting Carthage and reviewing his troops at the new base at Lambaesis (see C and E).

128/9 Hadrian pays his second visit to Athens, and allows full play to his admiration for all things Greek and his passion to improve them (see D).

129 Hadrian tours Asia Minor again, fostering building and public works. He then visits Palmyra, which city is now prospering at the expense of Petra.

130 Hadrian reaches Jerusalem, and proceeds to impose his usual beneficence (but see C). Hadrian visits Alexandria, enriching the museum and rebuilding Pompey's tomb. He goes for a holiday trip up the Nile and asks questions of the Sphinx. His favourite Antinous is drowned, an event which affects the childless emperor profoundly. A shrine and temple and city, Antinoöpolis, are built on the banks of the Nile.

A. Politics, Law and Economics

121 Before setting out on his travels Hadrian builds a more efficient governing machine, with a *concilium* of business men, jurists and senators, to consider policy and a better bureaucracy to put policy into practice.

122 Hadrian, who in his own words "sets everything right in Britain", revives the town-building programme. In Wroxeter he scraps the half-finished baths and has a new forum built; Verulamium receives its magnificent gateway.

123 Hadrian increases the self-respect of the Asis Minor cities and their feeling of belonging to the Empire by allowing them to issue their own coinage.

128/9 Hadrian orders a codification of the laws of Athens.

B. Science and Discovery

128 Theon of Smyrna, mathematician, observes the transit of Venus.

C. Religion and Philosophy

128 Hadrian's visit to Carthage coincides with the end of a 5-year drought—the Carthaginians are grateful to him as a god.

130 Hadrian is distressed by the ruin of Jerusalem and, with no conception of Jewish feeling, orders the city to be rebuilt with the name Aelia (his *gens* name) Capitolina and with a temple to Jupiter.

D. The Arts

123 Hadrian, encouraging wherever he goes the erection of fine buildings, has a temple erected on the island of Cyzicus (in the Sea of Marmora); this, finished by Marcus Aurelius about 167, becomes one of the wonders of the world.

128/9 Hadrian leaves his mark upon Athens. He builds a library, a gymnasium, an aqueduct, and temples to Hera and to Zeus "the God of all the Greeks". He also completes the Olympieum, or temple to Zeus, started by Pisistratus.

E. Literature

122 Hadrian writes a simple but touching epitaph for his favourite horse.

124 Arrian of Bithynia, historian, receives Roman citizenship from Hadrian and assumes the name of Flavius.

128 There is left behind on a column at Lambaesis an account of the address Hadrian makes to his troops after reviewing them.

F. Births and Deaths

121 Marcus Aurelius b. (–180).

124 Apuleius b. (date of death unknown).

130 Antinous d. (18).

130 Galen b. (–200c).

131 Hadrian returns to Rome, to beautify the capital and to improve its laws (see A and D).

132/5 The Jews revolt under Simeon Bar-Cochba as a Messiah. They meet with initial success, but are forced into the fortress of Bethar, S.W. of Jerusalem, where they are destroyed after holding out for two years. This is the final destruction of the Jews as a nation in Judaea: to the Romans the land becomes Palestine and its capital (see 130 C) Aelia Capitolina—a city which no Jew may enter. It is the Jew of the "Dispersion", the *Diaspora*, who alone has significance in the future.

136 Hadrian, growing ill and old, contracts the occupational disease of the emperors, that of morose suspicion. He has some of his relatives killed.

136/7 Arrian (see 124 E) is made Prefect of Cappadocia; he defeats an invasion by the Alans, an Asiatic people allied in blood probably to the Scythians.

138 Hadrian moves into his villa at Tibur (see D). His first choice for the kingdom having died, he adopts as son and heir Titus Aurelius Antoninus (aged 52), and at the same time he instructs Antoninus to adopt two young men, Marcus Aurelius and Lucius Verus. Hadrian had his mausoleum, equally vast, built on the banks of the Tiber in Rome. He then retires to see the sea for the last time at Baiae, and dies (July). Antoninus succeeds him.

139 Antoninus, member of a rich family from Nîmes, proves himself possessor of all the Roman virtues and earns for himself the title of Pius. Unlike Hadrian he rules from Rome and does not travel his empire.

140 The two consuls for the year are the Emperor and the young Marcus Aurelius (see 138).

In Britain the governor, Q. Lollius Urbicus, is having trouble with the Lowland Scots, who have of recent years built themselves many hill forts. He advances towards the Forth-Clyde isthmus.

A. Politics, Law and Economics

131 Hadrian orders a codification of the Roman law, which has grown complicated, with a vast amount of judgement law added to the original Twelve Tables of the ancient city.

138 Antoninus Pius uses his personal fortune to augment the national exchequer and to promulgate charitable works. He is scrupulous to consult the Senate in all matters of legislation.

B. Science and Discovery

139 Claudius Ptolemaeus (Ptolemy), born in Egypt, is in this year making astronomical observations in Alexandria and does so at least for another 12 years. His greatest works are the *Syntaxis* (known to the medieval world as the *Almagest*) and his *Geographia*. In the former he works out a geocentric system for the Universe—which however does not prevent him from making accurate calculations of planetary movements—and invents the measurements, "minutes" and "seconds". In the latter work he describes the earth's surface with the greatest accuracy to date, though he underestimates the distance from Europe to the Indies; he is the first to use the terms "parallels" and "meridians". He also writes on the musical scale, on optics and on astrology. (The dates of his birth and death are unknown, but he is still alive in A.D. 161)

C. Religion and Philosophy

131 Hadrian adds to his unpopularity among the Jews by forbidding circumcision and instruction in the Law. This is the chief cause of the revolt of Simeon Bar-Cochba (see opposite). There is some persecution by Simeon of Christians in Judaea, for refusing to join his revolt.

133 Though the young Marcus Aurelius favours philosophy—and at this age of twelve years he is practising asceticism—his two chief tutors are rhetoricians, Cornelius Fronto and Herodes Atticus.

140 Marcion of Sinope comes to Rome, expounding a Christian heresy that the god of Jesus and the god of the Old Testament cannot be the same. The Christian church excommunicates him.

D. The Arts

Hadrian, with his own architectural ideas, builds his own villa at Tibur (Tivoli). He also has built Rome's largest temple, to "Venus and Rome", opposite the Colosseum.

135 A bust is made of the young Marcus Aurelius (and is extant).

E. Literature

138 Hadrian, dying, writes a poem of farewell to his soul.

140 Appian, Greek historian, of Alexandria, *fl.* He writes his *Histories* (of Rome and its wars).

F. **Births and Deaths**
138 Hadrian d. (62).

140 Juvenal d. (80*c*).
Suetonius d. (70*c*).

141/3   Urbicus, Governor of Britain, completes his campaign in the Lowlands and carries out a policy of depopulation, deporting tribesmen to new homes in the Wurtenburg forests. He then builds a second wall, north of Hadrian's and across the Forth–Clyde isthmus. It becomes known as the Antonine Wall; it is built cheaply and held lightly.

145   The Roman army is engaged for seven years from this date in suppressing uprisings by the Moors of Mauretania.

Antoninus has Marcus Aurelius married to the daughter of himself and his late wife Faustina. This daughter, another Faustina, is Aurelius' cousin.

146   Marcus Aurelius is named by Antoninus as a sharer with him in the government of the empire; Lucius Verus (see 138) is however not so named.

148   900th anniversary of the founding of Rome.

149   Vologeses III succeeds Vologeses II of Parthia (see below).

————————

With the reign of Antoninus Pius the Roman Empire enters upon what is generally recognized as its most prosperous, settled and peaceful period, this decade being particularly peaceful. Antonius' reputation is high: embassies arrive to see him from India and Bactria; he gives kings to the German Quadi and Armenians, and a letter from him stops Vologeses II of Parthia making war on the Armenians.

A. **Politics, Law and Economics**
143   The rhetoricians Fronto and Herodes Atticus (see 133 C) are made consuls. The latter acquires great wealth, much of which he spends on the embellishment of Athens—hence "Atticus".

B. **Science and Discovery**
140   Athens has an aqueduct built for her.

147   Galen, having had the profession of medicine chosen for him by his father as the result of a dream, receives his first education in his native Pergamum—to be continued at Smyrna, Corinth and Alexandria.

150   Chinese state documents, concerning events dating to about A.D. 137 and written on good rag paper (see 105 B) are stored in the Great Wall.

C. **Religion and Philosophy**
      Antoninus is tolerant towards Christians and more tolerant than Hadrian towards the Jews.

141   Probable date for the *Apologies* of Justin of Samaria, who, having come to Rome, addresses to the Emperor these tracts in defence of the Christians as good citizens.

145   A temple to "Hadrian the God" is built in Rome.

146   The worship of Serapis is permitted in Rome.

D. **The Arts**
147   A tomb is erected to a member of a certain Wu family of Shantung, inside which are incised typical Han bas reliefs. These are secular and not religious in content.

150   Extensions are made to the Romano–British palace at Fishbourne (see 75 D). The tesselation is by less expert, and probably native, craftsmen. This is also the time when Roman villas are being built widespread over the English countryside.
      A mummy-case at Havara of about this time shows that Egyptians honour their dead with a portrait in Hellenic style.
      A relief at Gandhara of about this time shows Gautama Buddha setting out on his journey from home.

E. **Literature**
146   Arrianus, back in Rome, is consul. He is writing his books of history, of which only the *Anabasis of Alexander* is extant.

147   Aelius Aristides *fl*; he teaches rhetoric in Smyrna.

E. **Literature** (continued)

149 Lucius Apuleius is believed to be in this year in Rome, lecturing on philosophy. He has travelled much, has studied in Carthage and Athens, and is to return shortly to his native Africa, where he will marry a rich Tripolitan lady and will counter a lawsuit against himself with his *Apologia*. His fame rests on his fantastic "novel", *The Golden Ass*.

F. **Births and Deaths**

146 Septimius Severus b. (–211).

152   There are floods in Rome and earthquake at Rhodes and a minor rising of the Jews. The campaign in Mauretania is successfully ended and peace imposed on the Moors.

152/3   The Egyptian peasants revolt, but are put down. As a result Rome's corn supply is cut and in a riot Antoninus is in danger of being stoned by the mob. He makes a distribution from his own funds—as he does on eight other occasions during his reign.

154/5   The Brigantes in the north of England (with most of the Roman troops busy manning the walls to their north) revolt. Reinforcements have to be brought from Germany to quell the uprising.

157/9   A minor disturbance in Dacia is put down, and the province is divided administratively into three parts.

160   A minor rising in Africa is put down.
Marcus Aurelius and Lucius Verus (see 138) are made consuls-designate. (There is no need for promulgation however, for Antoninus is approaching the end of his blameless life.)

In a peaceful empire the Christians, disappointed of a Second Coming, struggle for unity of belief and suffer from a multitude of heresies.

A. Politics, Law and Economics

Antoninus has established a rule outstandingly humanitarian, both at home and in the provinces. He punishes the harsh masters of slaves; he instructs his governors and client kings similarly to punish any resort to violence.

C. Religion and Philosophy

155 Eleven Christians are martyred in the amphitheatre of Smyrna.

155 Polycarp, apostolic father and native of Smyrna, visits Rome and contends with the heresies of Marcion (see 140 C).

156 In Phrygia Montanus denounces the worldliness of the Christian Church and pronounces himself to be the *Paraclete* bringing the promised Kingdom of Heaven upon Earth; he is encouraged by the trances of his two female disciples, Priscilla and Maximilla.

Most probable date for the martyrdom of Polycarp at Smyrna. Polycarp has failed to get agreement on the proper date on which to observe Easter.

E. Literature

158 Artemidorus, of Lydia, writes a book on the Interpretation of Dreams, which is extant.

F. Births and Deaths

155 Dio Cassius b. (–235c).

156 Polycarp d.

158 Gordian I b. (–238).

160 Tertullian b.

161   (March) Antoninus Pius calls Marcus Aurelius to his bedside, has his golden statue of
Fortune transferred to his adopted son's room, gives for the day's watchword
Aequanimitas, and dies.

Marcus Aurelius, remembering Hadrian's wish (see 138), has Lucius Verus made his
full colleague. A precedent is here set for later divisions of the imperial *majestas*.

Twin sons are born to Aurelius and Faustina; one, Commodus, survives.

162   As a first sign that Rome cannot easily remain at peace with the barbarians on her
borders, the Britons and the German Chatti revolt, whilst the Parthian king, Vologeses III, declares war and invades Armenia. Lucius Verus, Aurelius' handsome
but not very useful partner, is sent to fight the Parthians, but gets no farther than
Antioch where he succumbs to the charms of Panthea, among whose accomplish-
ments is skill on the lyre.

162/6   The Parthian war is carried through successfully by Avidius Cassius, a Syrian by
birth. Seleucia and Ctesiphon are taken and despoiled. Cassius is given a triumph,
which he shares with Aurelius, and is made governor of Rome's eastern provinces.

164   Aurelius marries his daughter Lucilla to Verus.

166   According to the Chinese, Marcus Aurelius sends an embassy to TongKing, possibly
more of a trading expedition.

167   Plague—probably bubonic—is brought back by the troops from the East. They infect
Rome as well as the cities through which they have passed, and others that they
are later to visit. Asia Minor, Greece, Gaul and Egypt are affected as well as Italy.

The second irruption of the northern barbarians takes place: the Marcomanni, the
Quadi and the Vandals. They cross the Danube, destroy a Roman garrison of 20,000
men, and pour southwards until they besiege Aquileia. Aurelius, realizing the
seriousness of the situation, recruits from all classes of a plague-depleted population,
trains his heterogeneous army, and takes command in person.

168/9   With help (duly paid for) from other German tribes and from Scythians, the Romans
beat back the invaders.

169   Lucius Verus dies on the way back from the campaign and Aurelius returns ill and
exhausted.

There now breaks out trouble on the northern frontiers again, the second Marco-
mannic War, whilst Eleusis in Greece is despoiled and Moors invade Spain. The
Lombards appear on the Rhine.

170   Aurelius unwillingly takes up the burden of military commander again.
Plague at last dies down.

––––––––––––––

The Empire's boundary in the north of England is unquiet and there are reports of
revolts in the years 161 and 169.

A. Politics, Law and Economics

161 Marcus Aurelius follows precedent in giving doles and games to the people—and 20,000 sesterces (about ten years' pay for a legionary) to each member of the Praetorian Guard. He insists however that foiled weapons be used in gladiatorial combats. He himself sits often as judge: severe against all forms of dishonesty.

E. Science and Discovery

162/4 Galen is at Rome during these years and attends both emperors as physician.

C. Religion and Philosophy

Though consciously a philosopher-king, Aurelius is a conservative one; he tells himself "never to hope to realize Plato's Republic".

The Christians (whose faith Aurelius considers "sheer obstinacy") develop their *agape* or Feast of Love, a forerunner of the Mass. At the same time the practice of the Mithraic mysteries increases: in Rome, as well as by the Legionaries (in London and on Hadrian's Wall included).

166 The Christian Justin of Samaria offends other philosophers in Rome, who get him put to death with six of his followers.

170 Campaigning in Pannonia, Aurelius appoints Alexander of Cotyaeum, Sophist, as his secretary.

D. The Arts

161 Marcus Aurelius completes the temple in the Forum that Antoninus has raised to his wife and re-dedicates it to Antoninus as well as Faustina.

162 Herodes Atticus has the Odeon at Athens built.

E. Literature

163 Hermogenes Tarsus, rhetorician, lectures, at the age of 15, before Aurelius.

164 Aurelius is still corresponding with his one-time tutor, Fronto.

165 Lucian, satirist and wit, Syrian by birth, settles in Athens and writes his *Dialgoues*.

F. Births and Deaths

161 Antoninus Pius d. (75).
Commodus b. (–192).

166 Justin of Samaria d.

169 Lucius Verus d.

Aurelius faces insurrection, resumes his fight against the barbarians, and dies

171/3 Aurelius continues the Marcomannian war.

173 Avidius Cassius is sent to quell a revolt in Egypt.

173 China suffers from Plague (as has Rome, see 167); it lasts for eleven years.

174 Aurelius comes back to Rome but then returns to the war front. He is successfully subduing the barbarians and extending the empire's boundaries to the Carpathians (and see C).

175 Commodus assumes the *toga virilis*.

In Egypt Cassius, having put down rebellion, declares himself emperor. Aurelius, asserting that he will gladly yield to Cassius if the soldiers wish it, advances eastwards to meet him; Cassius is however killed by one of his own centurions.

The chief result of this revolt is that Aurelius abandons all thoughts of extending the Empire to include the German tribes and makes peace, with only a ten-mile-wide strip across the Danube annexed.

During Aurelius' progress eastwards, his wife Faustina, who is with him, dies. A city, Faustinopolis, near Mount Taurus, is raised in her honour (and see D).

Aurelius returns to Rome via Smyrna and Athens (and see C).

Aurelius spares reinforcements of 5,400 auxiliary cavalry to Britain.

176 Aurelius is given a Triumph in Rome. Commodus is included in the honour, and is made partner with his father on the throne.

178 Smyrna suffers earthquake.

178/180 Aurelius, believing that Rome will only be safe with her frontiers extended to the Carpathians, renews the war, the Third Marcomannian War.

180 Having reached in his campaign as far as Vindobona (Vienna), Marcus Aurelius dies, enjoining upon his son the task of extending the Empire to the Elbe. Commodus, however, ends the war.

A. Politics, Law and Economics

Marcus Aurelius runs his war with remarkable economy and Rome is enjoying a degree of commercial prosperity. He settles captive Germans, known as *coloni* or cultivators, on imperial estates.

C. Religion and Philosophy

174 A legion of Christian soldiers are said to enlist storm and thunder to their aid in defeating the Marcomanni.

175 Aurelius attends lectures by Aelius Aristides at Smyrna and himself lectures in Athens (in Greek). In Athens he also endows professorships in the four doctrines, Platonic, Aristotelian, Stoic and Epicurean.

177 On Aurelius ordering the punishment of sects that "excite the ill-balanced minds of men", there are risings against Christians in and around Lyons: 47 Christians are tortured and killed, including the slave girl, Blandina.

D. The Arts

175 Aurelius, in memory of his wife, creates an endowment for the aid of young women: a bas relief is made showing a younger Faustina pouring coin into the laps of girls.

E. Literature

173 Pausanias, probably a Lydian, flourishes in the reigns of Antoninus and Aurelius and writes at about this time his famous guide book, *Periegesis*, of Greece. (Schliemann's intelligent interpretation of it helps him to make his discoveries at Mycenae).

173 The precocious Hermogenes (see 163 E) loses his reason.

174 While campaigning, Marcus Aurelius composes his philosophical and disillusioned *Meditations*.

180 The poet Oppian of Cilicia, author of *Halieutica* (on fishing) *fl.*

F. Births and Deaths

175 Avidius Cassius d.
Faustina, Aurelius' wife, d.

176 Pausanias d.

180 (March) Marcus Aurelius d. (59).

180 Hermogenes, rhetorician, d.
Herodes Atticus d. (76c).

181   Commodus returns to Rome and gives himself up to dissipation. A skilled huntsman, swordsman and bowman, he takes part in the gladiatorial shows. He is credited with a harem of 300 women and an equal number of boys.

In Britain, as elsewhere, the barbarians begin to take the initiative: the Highlanders of Scotland sweep over the Antonine wall and invade the lowlands.

183   Lucilla, sister of the Emperor, plots his assassination, She is executed, and most of the important men of the day are executed too. Informers re-appear in Rome.

Perennis is made head of the Praetorian Guard and given great powers, as Sejanus has been before him. Commodus continues with his sport and his gladiatorial prowess.

184   Ulpius Marcellus is sent to Britain to retrieve the situation. He re-instils discipline and achieves victory (and see D). He is however recalled by Commodus, possibly for his too harsh discipline.

185   Perennis is suspected (on evidence from legionaries from Illyria and Britain) and executed. He is followed as favourite by a one-time slave, Cleander, who spreads corruption.

Helvius Pertinax is sent to restore order amongst the legionaries in Britain, who are becoming mutinous. They cease to be mutinous but hardly become law-abiding: they intimate to Pertinax that they will serve whatever emperor he chooses, preferably himself. The Antonine wall is dismantled.

186   Crispina, wife of Commodus, is banished and put to death.

188   Revolt in Germany is suppressed.

190   The Roman mob rise up against Cleander, who is handed over to death by Commodus. Plague comes again to Rome, and famine.

Pertinax deals with trouble in Africa.

Hsien-Ti, the last of the Han emperors, a young boy, ascends the Chinese throne—as a puppet.

In this decade of Commodus' reign there is virtually no trouble from the barbarians of the north whom Aurelius had fought. Rome is at the apex of her power, but the marks of decay are obviously present, and in future the initiative will be largely with the barbarians.

184   The Han dynasty, continuously weakened by the misrule of eunuch ministers, suffers at this time from a popular rising known as the rebellion of the Yellow Turbans. China is sinking into division and anarchy.

Commodus poses as Hercules and assumes the title of Britannicus

A. Politics, Law and Economics
181 Commodus increases his extravagance and gifts to the people.

C. Religion and Philosophy
185 One of the concubines of Commodus, Marcia, is able to protect the Christians of Rome.

186 Irenaeus, Bishop of Lyons, strikes a blow for the unity of the christian church with his *Adversus Haereses*.

187 Septimius Severus, the future emperor, marries as his second wife the forceful Syrian Julia Domna, daughter of a priest to the god Elagabel of Emesa (on the Orontes).

189 Rabbi Jehuda writes down the old laws of Moses (see 70 C), to be known as the *Mishna*.

190 On Christians being persecuted in Asia Minor many of the Montanian sect clamour for martyrdom.

D. The Arts
184 An inscription at Carlisle appears to commemorate the Roman victories in the reign of Commodus—who is referred to as "Hercules". Commodus now also gives himself the title of Britannicus on the strength of Marcellus' successes (see opposite).

189 Commodus has a reproduction of his own head placed on a statue of Apollo.

E. Literature
190 Dio Cassius becomes a Senator.

F. Births and Deaths
183 Lucilla, sister of Commodus, d.

185 Perennis (Praetorian) d.

186 Crispina, empress, d.

186 Origen b. (–254c).

187 Aelius Aristides d. (70c).

188 Caracalla b. (–217).

190 Cleander (Praetorian) d.

Last ruler of the Han Dynasty; the Roman Imperial throne is up for sale; an empress in Japan

191 There is a serious fire in Rome.

192 In China a usurper assumes power, imprisoning the boy-emperor (see 190 A). The court eunuchs are destroyed; the four-hundred-year rule of the Han Dynasty is virtually at an end.

192 Commodus is becoming more suspicious and afraid and more murderous. To save their own lives Marcia (see 185 C) and the new head of the Praetorian Guard poison Commodus. Lingering, he is finished off by his late wrestling companion. This happens on the last day of the year.

193 (Jan. 1st) Pertinax, back in Rome from Britain, is chosen Emperor. Pertinax earns the displeasure of the soldiers for instituting needful economies and reforms and is murdered. The lowest degradation is reached by the Praetorian Guard putting the emperorship up to the highest bidder. The rich Didius Julianus wins. He lasts two months. The people of Rome appeal to the legions, in Britain, in Syria and in Pannonia.

Septimius Severus, in command in Pannonia, arrives in Rome and is declared Emperor. One of his first acts is to reorganize and tame the Praetorian Guard.

194 Of Severus's two rivals, one, Pescennius Niger, is defeated in Syria, whilst the other, Clodius Albinus, in Britain, is placated with the title of Caesar and promises of the succession.

195/6 Continuing his campaigning in the East, Severus lays siege to Byzantium and crosses the Euphrates, defeating the decaying kingdom of the Parthians and forming a Roman province called Arabia.

196 Severus returns to Rome. His son Caracalla (aged 8) is declared Caesar.

196/7 Albinus, on the discovery of treasonable correspondence, is named a public enemy. He declares himself emperor, leaves Britain with all the troops he can muster, and sets up court at Lyons. Outside the city he meets the army of Severus, is defeated, and commits suicide.

197 In Britain, denuded of troops and with the Antonine wall already abandoned, Hadrian's wall suffers great destruction from the Lowlanders, the Maeatae, who reach southwards as far as York. A new governor, Virius Lupus is sent to Britain, and restores order. He begins the very considerable task of rebuilding Hadrian's wall.

197/9 Severus renews his war against the Parthians. Ctesiphon is again captured and is destroyed.

198 Caracalla is made Augustus and Severus' other son Geta is made Caesar.

199 Severus visits Egypt by way of Palestine and the Roman province of Arabia; he relieves the Egyptians of burdensome taxation.

200 The Japanese warrior empress, Jingu, invades and subdues part of Korea.

A. Politics, Law and Economics

193 Septimius Severus punishes the Senate, with many executions, for having declared for Albinus and not himself. A Phoenician by birth, Severus has been well educated and has practised law as well as soldiering. Once more, all power is taken from the Senate. Ulpian, rising jurist, and the Emperor's chief adviser, obligingly argues in defence of absolute power (but see 206 A). The imperial throne is made virtually into an hereditary military monarchy. Military service is made compulsory but forbidden to citizens of Italy, power thus being given to the provincial legionaries.

B. Science and Discovery

191 The fire in Rome destroys libraries, recent works of Galen included.

C. Religion and Philosophy

195 Clement of Alexandria, Christian platonist, *fl.*

197 Tertullian, son of a centurion and lately converted to Christianity, writes his *Apology*, assuring the Romans, as Justin has done (see 141 C), that Christians are good citizens. He then however writes his *De Spectaculis*, an attack on the Roman theatre and the games. On his expressing the view that the end of the world is at hand a Syrian bishop leads his flock into the desert, to meet Christ in person.

200 Alexander of Aphrodisias *fl*: accepted as a great interpreter of Aristotle.

D. The Arts

200 Septimius Severus begins to build the last of the imperial palaces on the Palatine Hill, his Septizonium. Julia Domna provides funds for the Temple of Vesta in the Forum.

193 The Column of Marcus Aurelius is completed. (Sometimes called the Antonine column, it stands in Rome's Piazza Colonna and is now topped by a statue of St Paul.) Its reliefs are a source of knowledge of the appearance of the German tribesmen whom the Romans have been fighting.

E. Literature

193 Dio Cassius, the historian, is named a praetor by Pertinax in the latter's few months as emperor.

197 Tertullian (see C) marks the turning point at which christian literature becomes Latin rather than Greek. Minucius Felix, another christian apologist writing in Latin, also flourishes at this time.

F. Births and Deaths

192 Commodus d. (31).

193 Pertinax d.
Didius Julianus d.

193 Valerian, emperor, b.

F. **Births and Deaths** (continued)

194   Pescennius Niger d.

197   Clodius Albinus d.

200   Galen d. (70c).

201 Septimius Severus reaches Antioch; where he celebrates the bequeathment of the *toga virilis* upon his son Caracalla.

202 Severus returns in triumph to Rome (see 203 D).

203 Plautianus, head of the Praetorian Guard, is made one of the consuls for the year. He has great influence over the Emperor.
Severus visits his African provinces and strengthens their boundaries against the desert tribes.

205 Caracalla and Geta, Severus's sons, are made the two consuls for the year. Caracalla, jealous of the power of Plautianus, accuses him of a plot against the Emperor; Plautianus, while in the act of defending himself, is murdered by a court attendant. Plautilla, daughter of the dead man and wife of Caracalla, is banished.

206/8 A brigand by the name of Bulla Felix makes himself famous by waylaying travellers on the roads of Italy. Banditry is growing in the Empire, from Egypt to the Rhine.

208 In order to strengthen the northern boundaries of Britain and to prevent another Albinus episode (see 194/7), Severus decides to visit Britain with his two sons. He is now 62 years old.
Ardashir becomes king of Persis, a vassal kingdom of the Parthians with its capital near Persepolis.

208/10 Severus campaigns in northern Britain. Hadrian's wall having been repaired, his plan is to subdue once and for all the land to the north of it, and so to ravage it that anything such as a second, Antonine, wall will not be necessary. Road-building and forest-clearing as he goes, Severus reaches beyond modern Aberdeen. The Scottish tribes conduct skilful guerilla warfare against him.

The Goths, by the time of the reign of Septimius Severus, have founded an empire on the north shores of the Black Sea and around the Danube Delta.

A. Politics, Law and Economics

Severus raises the Roman Army to a position of paramount importance, at the expense of the Senate, the aristocracy and the civilians generally. For the first time he allows the legionaries to marry whilst on foreign service, their sons being entitled to become not only Roman soldiers but also Roman citizens. He considerably increases the legionaries' pay, thus causing an increasing taxation burden. There ensues from this time a decay of urban life throughout the empire—the centre of gravity has been transferred from the town to the camp. Severus extends the planting of *coloni* on imperial estates (see 171 A), a practice which is copied by many Roman landowners during the coming century, one reason for this being a scarcity of slaves. There is a general economic decline during this century, with a falling off of trade, high taxation, and a debasing of the currency, Septimius increasing the alloy in the denarius to 50%.

206/8   In these years Severus resides in Campania and away from the capital and its demoralizing influence on his sons. With the help of Ulpian and others of his Council he revises the law, making it more equitable and more humanitarian.

C. Religion and Philosophy

Severus' wife, Julia Domna, patronizes the arts and literature; she has a leaning towards orientalism in religion and philosophy.

203   Origen, aged 18, lectures at Alexandria.

D. The Arts

203   The arch of Septimius Severus, overlooking the Forum of Rome and commemorating his victories in the East, is dedicated.

E. Literature

203   Among Christian martyrs at Carthage is Perpetua, who in her *Passion* gives an account of her last days in prison.

206   Oppian II (see 180 E for Oppian I) writes his book on hunting, *Cynegetica*.

F. Births and Deaths

201   Postumus b. (–268).

203   Plotinus (Neoplatonist) b. (–270c).

204   Elagabalus b. (–222).

205   Plautianus d.

208   Alexander Severus b. (–235).

211 (Feb.) Septimius Severus, worn out by his campaigns, dies at York. His sons, bequeathed the Empire jointly, forthwith end the war and return to Rome. Though no decisive victory has been won, peace to the south of Hadrian's wall for nearly a century is achieved. The end of Severus—the last emperor for 80 years to die in bed—is said to have been hastened by Caracalla.

212 Caracalla, inheriting the oriental cruelty of his father but none of his statesmanship, has his brother Geta murdered, Geta dying in his mother's arms. Caracalla, like Commodus, prefers hunting and the company of gladiators to imperial business. He is reputed to have had 20,000 of the pro-Geta party put to death.

213/14 Caracalla expels some German marauders from Gaul, and gives himself the title of Germanicus. He then leads an army to the River Main, where he meets an increasingly powerful collection of German tribes calling themselves the Alemanni ("All Men") and claims a victory over them.

214 Edessa becomes a Roman colony.

215 Caracalla, fearing revolt in Egypt—and annoyed at the Alexandrians referring to himself and his mother as Oedipus and Jocasta—visits Alexandria and orders, it is said, the massacre of all its able-bodied citizens.

216 In emulation of Alexander conquering Persia (see B), Caracalla invades Parthia, entices its king Artabanus IV into his camp with offers of marriage to his daughter, and falls on him and his men. Artabanus escapes, and invades Syria.

217 Near to Edessa and not far from the ancient battlefield of Carrhea, Caracalla's legionaries, trained by example to prefer loot to fighting and discontented with lack of the former, stab him to death. Macrinus, head of the Praetorian Guard, declares himself Emperor; he has Caracalla made a god and Julia Domna banished to Antioch—where she starves herself to death. Peace is made with Parthia.

218 The fate of Rome continues to be decided in the East. Julia Maesa, sister of Julia Domna and equally forceful, declares her grandson Elagabalus emperor. This youth of about fourteen is so called because he is priest to the god of Emesa, Elagabal (i.e. Baal). The local legionaries, well bribed, support him. Macrinus advances westwards to meet Julia Maesa, who fights in person, defeats him, and has him executed.

219 Elagabalus enters Rome, rouged, bejewelled and dressed in gold and purple.

220 Elagabalus makes it clear that he wishes to enjoy the pleasures and not face the responsibilities of emperorship.

A. Politics, Law and Economics

211 Severus' final advice to his sons—"Enrich the Army!"—embodies his philosophy of rule, that the need for a strong army is paramount.

212 Papinian, one of the three famous jurists who flourish in Septimius' reign (the other two being Ulpian and Paulus) refuses to write a legal defence of Caracalla's murder of his brother, and is beheaded in Caracalla's presence.

212/16 Caracalla quietens the objections of the Army to Geta's murder by huge donations; to obtain more tax revenue he extends Roman citizenship to all free male adults throughout the Empire: the *Constitutio Antoniniana*.

219 A Jewish academy is set up at Sura in Persia. The Jews of the dispersion, who have spread all round the Mediterranean and the Middle East, thrive in Persia (in spite of sporadic persecution)—where they are allowed to practise polygamy.

B. Science and Discovery

216 Caracalla, in admiration of Alexander, forms a troop, 16,000 strong, which he calls "Alexander's Phalanx" and has it equipped with arms of ancient Macedonian type.

C. Religion and Philosophy

214 Under the patronage of Julia Domna, Philostratus of Lemnos writes his *Life of Apollonius* (the occultist of the time of Christ).

218 Calixtus, the sixteenth Pope (217/22) is declared unfit by a priest called Hippolytus, who sets up a rival Church (but see 235 C). (The dates of the previous Popes are not known exactly, nor are they of great historical significance.)
Elagabalus brings with him to Rome from Emesa the conical black stone which is the symbol of his god; he has a temple built for it.

218 Tertullian embraces Montanism and becomes more extreme and denunciatory.

220 Alexander Severus, cousin of Elagabalus and equally a protégé of Julia Maesa, is educated by the best philosophers in Rome.

D. The Arts

212/16 In Rome the magnificent baths of Caracalla are begun and dedicated.

219 Elagabalus, besides indulging in excessive and ridiculous extravagances like all the other young emperors before him, shows a love of jewellery and also some musical talent, playing the pipes, the organ and the horn.

E. Literature

218 The historian Dio Cassius, a senator, is at his time governor of Pergamum and Smyrna.

F. Births and Deaths

211 Septimius Severus d. (65).

F. **Births and Deaths** (continued)

212 Geta d.
Perpinian d.

213 Cassius Longinus, rhetorician, b. (–273).

215 Mani, founder of Manichaeism, b. (–276).

217 Caracalla d. (29).
Julia Domna d.

218 Macrinus d.

219 Gallienus, emperor, b. (–268).

221   Julia Maesa, unable to control Elagabalus' excesses, is training and building up her
other grandson Alexander Severus (see 220 C) for the emperorship. He is declared
Caesar; Elagabalus and his mother try to enlist the Praetorian Guard against
Alexander.
The puppet Chinese Emperor Hsien Ti is finally deposed: end of the Han Dynasty.

222   Elagabalus and his mother are themselves slain by the Praetorians. Alexander Severus
becomes Emperor, having responded to a philosophic and severe training as successfully as had Marcus Aurelius.

223   Mamaea, mother and guide of the Emperor, is made "Augusta".

224   The kingdom of Parthia comes to an end. Ardashir, King of Persis (see 208), having
made himself increasingly powerful, King Artabanus IV (sometimes known as V)
the last of the Parthian Arsacid Dynasty, advances against him. Artabanus is defeated
by Ardashir in three great battles.

225   Alexander Severus continues his good rule with the help of Ulpian.

226   Ardashir has himself crowned "King of Kings": he claims descent from Darius and
the Achaemenid kings of Persia, and founds a new Persian dynasty, the Sassanid
(after the name of his grandfather).

228   Ulpian, who tries to restrain the power and licentiousness of the Praetorian gurad, is
murdered by them; its ringleader is executed.

230   Rome hears that King Ardashir of Persia is advancing through Mesopotamia into
Syria and is claiming all the empire of the old Achaemenid Persia.
The Emperor's mild letter telling Ardashir that everyone ought to rest content with
his own domain, does not deter him.

With the accession of Ardashir, Rome exchanges one enemy for another, the long
declining Parthian for the rising Sassanid Persian.
In China the end of the Han Dynasty (see 221) is followed by a 45-year period of
treachery and violence known as the period of the Three Kingdoms.

A. Politics, Law and Economics

222 Alexander Severus curbs the power of the Army and endeavours to restore the power of the Senate and the aristocracy. He reduces taxes, lends money at 4%, encourages traders' and workers' associations, and censors public morals.

223 The jurist Ulpian becomes the emperor's adviser.

B. Science and Discovery

222 Alexander Severus encourages renewed building throughout the empire of roads and bridges and aqueducts.

C. Religion and Philosophy

222 During the reign of Alexander Severus all Christian persecution ceases.

226 An intense religious enthusiasm, and a belief that Zoroastrian teaching is returning in its original purity, help Ardashir to the new Persian throne. Ardashir forms a strong national Church and produces a new edition of the *Avesta*, the Holy Writ of the god Mazda.

D. The Arts

222/6 Alexander Severus shows artistic and musical ability. He restores the Colosseum and the baths of Nero, and completes the baths of Caracalla.

E. Literature

228 Ulpian leaves behind a famous library of historical archives.

229/30 Dio Cassius (now governor of Dalmatia and Pannonia) is supported by the Emperor against the legionaries' complaint of his strictness: he is made consul, and retires, to finish his great *History of Rome*. This, comprised in 80 books, takes the story from the arrival of Aeneas in Italy to the author's own times. Less than half the work is extant.

F. Births and Deaths

222 Elagabalus d. (18*c*).

224 Artabanus IV of Parthia d.

226 Gordian III b. (–244).

228 Ulpian d.

231/3 Alexander Severus, accompanied by his mother, campaigns against the Persian king, who retires. The Roman coinage depicts a Roman victory.

233/5 The German Alemanni and Marcomanni, noting Roman preoccupation in the East, break through the Rhine and Danube frontiers. Severus again leads his army and reaches Mainz. His army is undisciplined however and he can only achieve peace by buying off the barbarians. His troops condemn his weakness, and mutiny. They murder him and his mother, and declare their Thracian commander Maximinus as Emperor.

235/8 Maximinus, a good soldier but uneducated (and said to be 8 ft tall and to be able to wear comfortably his wife's bracelet on his thumb), campaigns on the Danube and Rhine and never visits Rome. He heavily taxes the rich aristocracy, who plot against him.

238 Gordian, proconsul of Africa and aged 80, accepts with his son the Emperorship. Both are defeated by Maximinus who then revenges himself by a brutal proscription in Rome. The Senate nominate two of their members to the throne, having outlawed Maximinus. Maximinus advances upon the Senate's nominees at Aquileia but is killed by his soldiers. The Senate's nominees return to be killed by the Praetorian Guard—who make a third Gordian their emperor. (Gordian III is son of Gordian II and grandson of Gordian I.)

239 The young Emperor, Gordian III, is helped to escape the power of the eunuchs of the court, and to rule, by a man who has had many posts, Timesithius (sometimes called Misetheus).

240 There begins to arrive the worst danger that Rome has so far experienced: enemies active on several fronts *at the same time*. Africa revolts, and tribes in N.W. Germany, under the name of the Franks, combine into a warlike federation. In Persia King Ardashir is assassinated.

235 With the assassination of Alexander Severus there follows an anarchic period in which the power rests with the legionaries and no less than 37 men are declared Emperor within 35 years.

A. Politics, Law and Economics

238 In spite of the immature age of Gordian III, administration of the Empire is for a while efficient and liberal. Informers are again suppressed; provincial governors are instructed to see that nothing happens which "is not in accordance with the spirit of the age".

C. Religion and Philosophy

231 Origen moves from Alexandria to Caesarea and attracts many pupils there.

235 Hippolytus (see 218 C) is excommunicated. (He is the first "Antipope".)

E. Literature

238 Herodianus, a Greek historian, brings his *History of Rome* (from the time of Marcus Aurelius) to a close, and dies.

239 Philostratus of Lemnos writes his *Lives of the Sophists*.

F. Births and Deaths

232 Probus b. (–282).

233 Porphyrius, neo-platonist, b. (–304c).

235 Alexander Severus d. (27).

235 Dio Cassius d. (80).

238 Gordian I d. (80).
Gordian II d.
Maximinus d.

240 Ardashir of Persia d.

241 Gordian III appoints Timesithius (see 239) head of the Praetorian Guard and marries his daughter.
Shapur I ascends the Persian throne and continues his father's policy of expansion.

242 In Rome the young Gordian III ceremoniously opens the doors of Janus and prepares an expedition, under Timesithius, against the Persians. He accompanies the expedition, as does Plotinus, who hopes to study the philosophy not only of Persia but also of India.

243 Timesithius (see 239) defeats the Persians and drives them back across the Tigris. He however falls ill and dies. His place is taken by Philip the Arab, who is ambitious.

244 Philip stirs up discontent amongst the legionaries against Gordian III, and Gordian is murdered (near Carchemish, where a mound is raised in his memory). Philip makes peace with Persia and returns to Rome, as Emperor.

245 Philip defeats a German tribe called the Carpi on the Danube. They are being pressed from behind by the Goths.

247 The Senate confirm Philip's appointment as Emperor, and also his seven year old son as Augustus, Philip hoping to found a dynasty.
Rome celebrates the thousandth year of its existence.

249 Discontented at having an Arab as Emperor, the legionaries revolt in several provinces. Philip, in Rome, offers to abdicate, and then sends his general, Decius, to pacify the legionaries in Pannonia (who seem particularly to consider themselves the guardian of true Roman virtues). Decius is compelled by these legionaries to assume the Purple himself and to lead them into Italy. At a battle at Verona Philip is defeated and slain. Decius becomes Emperor.
The Goths cross the Danube and ravage Thrace. Civil war in Gaul is suppressed.

250 Decius sends his son to encounter the Goths and then follows in person.

In this decade the southern state of China, Wu, sends envoys to Funan (modern Cambodia) and the northern state, Wei, receives envoys from Japan.

From the date of Rome's thousand-year commemoration to the death of the Emperor Gallienus in 269 there exists a time of confusion which historians have found difficult to record accurately: Gibbon makes this point, and also calls these times ones of shame and confusion: "During that calamitous time every instant was martial, every province of the Roman world was afflicted by barbarian invaders and military tyrants. . . ."

A. Politics, Law and Economics

247 Philip endeavours to rule well in Rome, declaring an amnesty for those suffering exile, building roads in the provinces (much needed for military purposes in these times of multiple danger), endeavouring to put down brigandage and receiving complaints.

250 Decius' persecution of the Christians (see C) has political motives behind it: a desire to achieve national unity in a time of danger.
Bishop Dionysius of Alexandria mourns to see the population of his city reduced to a half of its size in former times.

B. Science and Discovery

250 Diophantus of Alexandria *fl.* His *Arithmetica* is a treatise on Algebra, owing something to Chaldean mathematics.
Decius, continuing the practice of building huge public baths in Rome, has a dome placed on a ten-sided structure, an engineering feat.

C. Religion and Philosophy

241 At the coronation of Shapur I of Persia, a young mystic of Ctesiphon, Mani, proclaims himself a messiah. His teaching, borrowing from Zoroastianism, Judaism, Mithraism and Gnosticism, divides the world into the rival realms of Light and Darkness it is known as Manicheism.

244 Plotinus arrives in Rome and for the next 10 years teaches his neo-platonist philosophy (of hunger for reabsorption into the One). He leads a saintly and abstemious life.

247 The Emperor Philip is said by some to have embraced Christianity; he at least leaves the Christians alone.

248 Cyprian, recently converted, becomes bishop of Carthage and makes the Christian church there very influential.

250 Decius (from Illyria, where Christianjty has little hold) begins a persecution of the Christians, to whom are attributed by the people the ills they are suffering. Fabian, the 20th Pope, is martyred, and Cyprian at Carthage goes into hiding. Many Christians refuse to sacrifice to the pagan gods, and earn the admiration of the people.

D. The Arts

250 A statue of Buddha is made in Gandhara at about this time, in idealistic Greek style. (The head is extant.)
At a Roman garrison in Mesopotamia called Dura-Europos a mixture of religious painting is made: Christian, Jewish and Pagan.

E. Literature

248 Origen wages polemic war against the Roman anti-christian aristocrat, Celsus. He answers Celsus' *True Word* with his *Contra Celsum*.

E. **Literature** (continued)

250　This middle of the century may be taken as the most likely time in which Heliodorus of Emesa *fl.* He writes his *Aethiopica* or "Egyptian Tales", giving birth to the novel of romantic adventure.

F. **Births and Deaths**

243　Timesithius d.

244　Gordian III d. (18).

245　Diocletian b. (–313).

249　Philip, Emperor, d.

250　Fabian, Pope, d.

251   Decius receives a resounding defeat from the Goths in Moesia (north of Thrace), he and his son being killed in battle. Trebonianus Gallus is elected emperor by the troops.

252   Gallus buys off the Goths and returns to Rome. The Goths retire with much booty. The Persians take Armenia.

253   Gallus combats the Plague in Rome. In Moesia the general left behind by Gallus, Aemilianus, achieves some successes and is proclaimed emperor. He advances on Rome and is met by Gallus and his son; they however are in command of a body of troops so small and disloyal that it assassinates them rather than fight. Aemilianus, after four months, meets the same fate as Gallus, giving place to Valerian of the Rhine legions.

254   Valerian, aged 60, meets a very difficult situation, the empire being threatened at the same time by the Franks, Alemanni and Marcomanni, by the Persians, and also by the Goths. He makes his son Gallienus, aged 35, ruler of the West and himself of the East.

255   Gallienus seeks to protect Gaul from advancing Franks.

256   Franks penetrate (by sea) into Spain, the Goths ravage Macedonia, and the Persians invade Mesopotamia and Syria.

257/9 The Goths cross the Black Sea and sack the Greek cities on the southern shore.

258   In Gaul the Roman general Postumus, successful against the invaders, assumes the titles of ruler of Gaul and of Emperor, which latter title he retains for a decade—at least in the sight of his soldiers, who finally do away with him. Postumus declines a personal duel with Gallienus.

259   The Alemanni break into Italy but are repulsed by Gallienus at Milan. The Emperor Valerian advances eastwards to meet King Shapur of Persia.

260   Valerian decides to attack the Persians who have reached Edessa. He changes his mind however and offers to negotiate. Shapur demands a personal interview on the field; Valerian consents, and is treacherously captured. (Another source says that Valerian is captured in battle.) Valerian ends his days a captive of Shapur: he is said to have suffered the indignity of being used by the Persian king as his mounting block. (And see D.)
Gallienus (see 254) meets and overcomes rival claimants to the imperial throne in Illyria. He becomes Emperor.

Britain's prosperity has been checked; raids of Franks and Saxons around the S.E. coast are being made.

A. Politics, Law and Economics
258 Gallienus is given more power in the West by his father Valerian, in fact almost complete power. He reinforces both the Senate and the Army with new blood, having the ability to choose well.

B. Science and Discovery
In China in this half century mica begins to be used for windows.

254 An eruption of Mount Etna is recorded.

258 Gallienus makes the Roman army more flexible and mobile. In particular he improves and increases the cavalry arm, which has so far always been weak. The head of the Cavalry becomes almost as important a post as has been head of the Praetorian guard. Gallienus even creates a corps of *catafractarii* or heavily armoured horsemen, in imitation of the Persians. He improves the catapult and ballista.

C. Religion and Philosophy
252 Cyprian holds a council of bishops at Carthage, which urges stricter control and the universal acceptance of Rome as the head of the Church.

254/7 Pope Stephen I quarrels with Cyprian but dies before he has forced the powerful Church of Carthage to secede.

257 Valerian, for much the same reason as Decius (see 250 A), persecutes the Christians for non-conformity. Cyprian and Pope Sextus II are martyred.

D. The Arts
260 Shapur I imitates Darius in having a rock relief carved, showing the Emperor Valerian kneeling before his mounted captor.

E. Literature
252 Cyprian writes his best known work, pleading for Church unity: *De Catholicae Ecclesia Unitate*.

F. Births and Deaths
251 Decius d.

251 St. Antony b. (–356c).

253 Origen d.
Gallus d.
Aemilianus d.

256 Arius b. (–336c).

257 Cyprian d.

260 Lactantius, Christian Father, b. (–325c).

261/3   King Shapur of Persia advances ruthlessly westwards after his defeat of Valerian
        but is unexpectedly halted and driven back by Odenathus, Rome's vassal king of
        Palmyra. Odenathus defeats Shapur at Ctesiphon and declares himself king of the
        area west of the Euphrates.
        Revolts break out throughout the Empire, and Gallienus has difficulty in retaining his
        throne.

263   The Goths sail down the Ionian coast and sack Ephesus and its great Temple of
        Diana.

264   Odenathus is made by the Romans "Dux Orientalis".

265   Gallienus fails to oust Postumus (see 258) from Gaul.
        Rome and many other parts of the empire have suffered a five-year period of Plague.

266   Odenathus is assassinated; his young sons succeed to the throne but the real power is
        with his widow, Zenobia, a forceful and beautiful woman who claims descent from
        Cleopatra.

267   The Goths, with the Sarmatians, pour down into the Balkans and Greece and sail
        through the Hellespont into the Aegean. Athens, Argos, Sparta, Corinth, Thebes
        are all sacked.

268   Postumus ends his "emperorship" in Gaul by being killed by his soldiers.
        Gallienus wins a costly victory over the Goths in Thrace.
        Gallienus is killed by his soldiers. Claudius II, an Illyrian of obscure origin, becomes
        emperor.

269/70 Claudius II saves the Empire from the Goths, his great victory being at Naissus,
        modern Nish. This is a full scale battle in which 50,000 Goths are reputed to have
        been slain and in which Claudius shows great personal bravery: he earns the title
        Gothicus. He also thrusts back the Alemanni; but he then dies of the Plague.

270   Aurelian, another Illyrian, becomes Emperor. He wins a further battle over the
        Goths and then makes peace with them, relinquishing Dacia to them and transfer-
        ring the name to a province south of the Danube.

---

265   For half a century from this date China's northern kingdom of Wei exerts some
        suzerainty over the other kingdoms as the Tsin Dynasty.

A. **Politics, Law and Economics**
> The towns of Britain show, from archaeological evidence, to be suffering economic decline in the last half of the 3rd century: slum conditions in Silchester; Verulamium's theatre falling into ruin. The Cornish tin mines, however, seem to experience a revival, with decreased competition from Spain.

B. **Science and Discovery**
> 265   Pei Hsin, geographer, *fl*: he produces a large map of China in 18 sections.

C. **Religion and Philosophy**
> 261   Gallienus issues the first Roman edict of toleration in favour of the Christians, and restores their property.
>
> 263   Porphyrius comes to Rome from Athens and enrols as a pupil of Plotinus.
>
> 263   Longinus, who has taught Porphyrius at Athens, goes to Palmyra, where he becomes the adviser and teacher of Queen Zenobia.

D. **The Arts**
> 262   The arch of Gallienus is dedicated in Rome.
>
> 270   The Romano-British palace at Fishbourne suffers fire.

E. **Literature**
> 268   The miscellaneous accomplishments but doubtful character of Gallienus is summed up by Gibbon: "He was a master of several curious but useless sciences, a ready orator, an elegant poet, a skilful gardener, an excellent cook, and most contemptible prince."

F. **Births and Deaths**
> 264   Eusebius b. (−340c).
>
> 266   Odenathus d.
>
> 268   Postumus d. (66c); Gallienus d.
>
> 270   Plotinus d.
>   Claudius Gothicus d.

271   Aurelian, a soldier and a disciplinarian (with the nickname "*Manu-ad-Ferrum*"), pushes the Vandals back over the Danube and the Alemanni out of Italy.
Zenobia—it is said on the advice of Longinus—throws off all pretence of allegiance to Rome, calls herself Queen of the East and sends her eldest son to invade Egypt.

272/3 Aurelian, sending his commander, Probus, successfully to restore Roman rule in Egypt, advances on Queen Zenobia's capital, Palmyra. After two battles and a difficult campaign (see B) he invests the city. Zenobia, who has fled the city on a dromedary, reaches the Euphrates but is overtaken. Her life is spared, but Longinus is put to death. Having retraced his steps across the Bosphorus, Aurelian receives the news that Palmyra has revolted. He returns and deals more harshly with the city.

274   Aurelian turns to the other challenger of Roman sovereignty, the so-called Emperor of Gaul. Postumus has been succeeded by Tetricus, who is easily defeated. Rome greets Aurelian as "Restitutor Orbis" and accords him a magnificent Triumph, graced by both Tetricus and Zenobia, the latter loaded with golden chains. Zenobia is allowed to live out her life with her children at Hadrian's palace at Tivoli.

275   On his way to attack Persia Aurelian is murdered by a group of officers who imagine their lives in danger. The Army passes the next appointment of Emperor to the Senate, who choose the 75 year old Tacitus (who claims descent from the historian —see E).

276   Tacitus punishes the murderers of Aurelian, but dies after a 6 months reign, leading an expedition against the Goths. Probus (see 272) is proclaimed Emperor by the Army. He is another Illyrian, soldier and disciplinarian.

277/9 Probus continues Aurelian's forcible pacification of the Empire, expelling Franks and Goths and Vandals, and quelling trouble in Britain and Egypt and Illyria.

280   Probus faces unrest and rebellion.

A. Politics, Law and Economics

271/5 Aurelian persuades the Senate to finance the building of new walls round Rome. The building of fortification walls to cities is in fact being undertaken throughout the Empire, Britain included.

Aurelian moves towards a regimented State, beginning the regulation of the trade corporations and the direction of labour. He stabilizes the currency, which is suffering from inflation.

280 Probus, disciplining his armies, sets his troops to clear wasteland, drain marshes and plant vines; he promises Rome the rule of law again, when one day armies will not be necessary.

B. Science and Discovery

271 It is a sign of the changing accent in war that Aurelian, in ejecting the Alemanni from Italy makes good use of cavalry—composed in fact of loyal Vandals.

272 Aurelian, in complaining that Rome speaks with contempt of his warring against a woman (Zenobia) writes: "It is impossible to enumerate her warlike preparation. . . . Every part of the wall (of Palmyra) is provided with two or three *ballistae*, and artificial fires are thrown from her military engines."

C. Religion and Philosophy

273 Aurelian allows the defeated Palmyrians to retain their Temple of the Sun.

274 Aurelian in Rome does something to encourage the Oriental conception of monarchy by connecting himself with a new worship of the Sun God (owing something to Elagabalus of Emesa).

275 St Antony (born in upper Egypt) retires to a solitary life in the desert, being considered thereby to have inaugurated monasticism.
St Denis converts Paris to Christianity.

D. The Arts

274 Aurelian builds a magnificent temple to the Sun in Rome.

E. Literature

275 The Emperor Tacitus orders ten copies of the works of his progenitor, Tacitus the historian, to be deposited in the public libraries.

F. Births and Deaths

272 Constantine the Great b.
Shapur I d.

273 c. Longinus d. (60*c*).

275 Aurelian d.

276 Tacitus, emperor, d.

276 Mani d. (61*c*).

281   At the end of this year Probus returns to Rome from his campaigns and earns a Triumph remarkable for the variety of the prisoners displayed.

282   The Army is growing discontented with Probus (see 280 A); and at Sirmium, his birthplace, where he is superintending viticulture, the soldiers mutiny and kill him. Carus, said to be a scholar as well as a soldier, is elected emperor.

283   Carus actively pursues war against Persia, which his predecessor had intended. He crosses the Euphrates and takes Seleucia and then Ctesiphon.

283/4   Near Ctesiphon Carus dies in mysterious circumstances, it is said by a stroke of lightning. Of his two sons, who have been declared his heirs, one, Numerianus, is murdered in the East and the other, Carinus, fights for the throne with Diocletian (then called Diocles), who has been elected by the troops.

285   Carinus is defeated and killed.

286   Diocletian makes Maximian (who has been successfully campaigning in Gaul) his co-ruler, with responsibility for the West. (Thus the split of command between East and West—see 254 — is begun again.)

287   A soldier named Carausius is put in charge of the Roman fleet at Boulogne, the *Classis Britannica*. He catches many pirates, but keeps the spoils for himself. On Maximian ordering his execution he crosses to Britain, and sets up an independent empire on the model of Postumus in Gaul.

288   The Franks sue for peace in Gaul. In the East Diocletian makes a treaty with Persia; he nominates as King of Armenia another Tiridates. He then puts down a revolt in Egypt.

289   Diocletian campaigns against the Samartians.
In a naval battle, Maximian is beaten by Carausius.

290   Carausius is acknowledged by Maximian and Diocletian as one of themselves, a third Augustus. He rules in Britain for the next 3 years, efficiently keeping down the Saxon pirates.

A. Politics, Law and Economics

285/6   Diocletian transfers his capital from Rome to Nicomedia near Byzantium, as a more strategic base from which to defend the empire. Maximian similarly chooses Milan.

C. Religion and Philosophy

The orientalization of the Roman monarchy and the near-deification of the monarch during his lifetime is given considerable encouragement by Diocletian. He fosters the conception that he is the earthly embodiment of Jupiter and that Maximian is the same of Hercules. Court ritual becomes more elaborate.

288   The Christian brothers Crispin and Crispinian, shoemakers, are martyred at Soissons.

D. The Arts

Diocletian, to help surround himself with divinity and awe, wears robes of silk and cloth of gold, shoes studded with jewels and a pearl diadem.

E. Literature

283   Nemesianus, poet at the brief court of Carus, writes a poem (extant) on hunting, another book called *Cynegetica*.

F. Births and Deaths

282   Probus d. (50).

283   Carus d.

284   Numerianus d.

285   Carinus d.

288   Sts Crispin and Crispinian d.

291   Diocletian and Maximian meet in Milan.

293   A new quadruple system of government for the Empire is worked out, whereby rule is
      shared by two Augusti (for the East and West respectively), each of whom has a
      Caesar to help him and to succeed him after twenty years, being also married into
      the Augustus' family. All laws and edicts are to be issued in the names of all four
      rulers and are to be equally valid; no sanction from the Senate is required. The
      Caesar chosen by Diocletian is Galerius and by Maximian Constantius Chlorus
      (son of Claudius Gothicus and father of Constantine the Great).
      Constantius Chlorus besieges and captures Boulogne, preparatory to regaining Britain
      to the Empire. Carausius in Britain is murdered by his financial minister, Allectus.
      Persia suffers from dynastic troubles.

294/7 Galerius proves his worth in campaigning against the northern barbarians, ending
      however with the unspectacular job of land-reclamation and repopulation (the
      whole tribe of the Carpi being moved): Galerius is somewhat embittered thereby.

296   Constantius invades Britain, defeats and slays Allectus, and is greeted at the gates of
      London with the welcoming title, *Redditor Lucis Aeternae*. He rebuilds at York,
      London and Verulamium, fortifies the "Saxon Shore" (the Wash to the Isle of
      Wight) and does much to restore prosperity to Britain.
      In Persia the first strong king since Shapur I comes to the throne, by name Narses. He
      attacks Rome's puppet king, Tiridates of Armenia (see 288).

297   Rebellion again breaks out in Egypt and Diocletian goes there in person with the
      young Constantine on his staff). He invests Alexandria and deposes the city's
      "Emperor", Achilleus.
      At the same time Maximian has to quell a rising in Carthage.
      Galerius is given the job of combatting Narses of Persia. After an initial success he
      suffers a defeat: Diocletian deliberately inflames his pride by making him, as
      punishment, walk behind his, Diocletian's, chariot.

298   Galerius wins a complete victory over King Narses of Persia, who cedes Mesopotamia
      and five provinces beyond the Tigris to Rome.

299   The century ends in peace, with the Roman Empire recovered in power and prestige
      and Diocletian's innovations in government apparently vindicated.

A. Politics, Law and Economics

293 Diocletian, after the creation of his *Quattuor Principes Mundi* (see opposite) sets about his reforms, which help so much to save the Roman Empire but also to change it. A vast bureaucracy is formed and a system of state socialism and managed economy. The coinage is successfully tied to gold (and see 312 A). Most production is nationalized; the freedom of the individual to change his job is further restricted. The number of bureaucrats increases enormously—Lactantius says it is half the population! Taxes increase still further, tax evasion becomes rife, and a tax police comes into being and is accused of resorting to torture.

C. Religion and Philosophy

296 Marcellinus becomes the 29th Bishop of Rome or Pope. (And see 304 C.)

297 Diocletian issues a violent edict against the Manichaeans.

300 Methodius, Bishop of Olympus in Lycia, *fl.* He borrows from Plato in writing the philosophic dialogues, *Symposium of the Ten Virgins* and *Aglaophon*. The latter borrows from the *Phaedo* and combats Origen's views on the resurrection of the body.

D. The Arts

298 The baths of Diocletian are begun.

E. Literature

291 The *Historia Augusta* is probably begun about this time, and continues to be written until some time in the reign of Constantine. It covers the reigns of the emperors from Hadrian to Carus and is reputedly written by six different authors.

F. Births and Deaths

293 Carausius d.
      St Athanasius b. (–373).

296 Allectus d.

302 Diocletian visits Rome for the first time as emperor.
King Narses of Persia abdicates in favour of his son.

303 The greatest persecution of the Christians begins—see C.
Diocletian, celebrating the twentieth year of his reign, is disgusted with the manners of the Roman plebs.

304 Diocletian is ill.
In north China the Huns under the Chinese-educated Liu Yüan decide to connect themselves with China's past and form a "Hun Han" dynasty.

305 Diocletian abdicates and forces Maximian to do the same. They are succeeded as Augusti by Constantius and Galerius.

306 Constantius returns to Britain and undertakes a punitive expedition against the Picts beyond the repaired Hadrian's wall. He has his son Constantine with him, and together father and son win a brilliant victory. On his return to York however (July) Constantius dies. Constantine is declared Augustus by his troops, but assumes only, so far, the title of Caesar.

307 Constantine has to fight for his throne. His chief enemies are Galerius and Maximian, together with the latter's son Maxentius and a Dacian called Licinius. Constantine makes headway by taking possession of Gaul and marrying Maximian's daughter Fausta.

308 In a confused situation, there is a conference of Augusti and Caesars.

309 Constantine saves Gaul from a fresh attack of Franks and Allemanni.
Shapur II, sometimes called the Great and grandson of Shapur I, ascends the Sassanid throne as an infant and after internal wars.

310 Maximian is captured by Constantine and commits suicide. Galerius begins to suffer from a fatal illness.

———————

Constantius' work in Britain does much to ensure her renewed prosperity during the first part of the 4th century.

A. **Politics, Law and Economics**

Diocletian finances law schools and has post-Trajanic legislation codified—the *Codex Gregorianus*.

In southern China the habit of tea drinking begins, probably learnt from Tibet.

301   As an inevitable concommittant of the rest of his programme of state socialism, Diocletian issues his *Edictum de pretiis*, controlling prices and wages (and see E). It is not a success, and leads to riots as well as "black marketeering".

B. **Science and Discovery**

Under Diocletian, and further under Constantine, Roman military science is amended. The cavalry arm is given relatively much more importance. The general tendancy is to try to create a truly mobile field army, garrison armies being made as much as possible into a local militia.

C. **Religion and Philosophy**

301   Galerius tries to persuade Diocletian that religious conformity should be insisted upon for the safety of the State.

302   Christians are accused of destroying the efficacy of the Augurs by making the sign of the cross.

303   (Feb.) The four rulers meet and agree to a decree to the effect that the Christians' churches shall be destroyed, their books burnt, their property confiscated, their congregations dissolved. At the eastern capital, Nicomedia, soldiers burn down the Christian cathedral. Christians retaliate by setting fire to Diocletian's palace.

304   Pope Marcellinus dies—it is said after denying his faith under the persecution.

305/10   Galerius, becoming Augustus of the East, continues the Christian persecution with particular vigour. Constantius pursues the anti-christian policy rather more mildly in Gaul and Britain; the names of at least one martyr from Britain is however known for certain, Alban of Verulamium.

310   Pamphilus, Bishop of Caesarea and a great collector of books, is martyred.

D. **The Arts**

304   At Spalato is begun, in oriental style, the palace for Diocletian's retirement.

305   Tetrach statues are carved, e.g. the group built into the corner of San Marco, Venice.

306   Maxentius starts to build in Rome an immense *basilica*; it adapts the structure of Rome's previous great baths and marks the climax of classical architecture in the West. Constantine finishes it.

E. **Literature**

301   Diocletian in his *de Pretiis* edict (see A) allows himself to voice moral indignation against profiteering, particularly at the expense of the soldier.

E. **Literature** (continued)

301 The neo-platonist Iamblichus, a Semite, *fl.* He writes mystically of numbers, leaves behind a *Life of Pythagoras*, (and has been described as a nincompoop).

307 Lactantius expounds Christianity in his *Divinae Institutiones*.

F. **Births and Deaths**

303 Narses, king of Persia, d.

304 Marcellinus, Pope, d.

306 Constantius I (Chlorus) d.

310 Maximian d.
Pamphilus d.

310 Ausonius, poet, b. (–400c).

311   Galerius puts a stop to the persecution of the Christians and asks them to pray for the Roman Empire and himself. He dies however of his disease (see 310).
Constantine marches on Rome, to meet the army of Maxentius.

312   Constantine and Maxentius meet at the battle of the Milvian or Mulvian Bridge (over the Tiber some 9 miles above Rome—also called the battle of Saxa Rubra). Maxentius is manoeuvred into an unfavourable position, is pushed back onto the Tiber and is defeated and killed. This may be called Rome's first battle of the Christian religion (see C).
Constantine disbands the Praetorian guard.

313   Constantine meets in Milan his main rival, Licinius (who has been made an Augustus by Galerius, see 307). They issue an edict (see C) and agree to co-operate. Constantine moves to the defence of Gaul and Licinius to consolidate his eastern possessions. Licinius marries Constantine's sister.

314   Constantine and Licinius, neither being content with anything less than undivided rule, go to war. Constantine defeats Licinius in Pannonia and exacts surrender of all Roman Europe except Thrace. Licinius retires to his eastern capital Nicomedia (and see C).

316   The Tsin Dynasty (see 265) abandons all northern China competing nomad Hunnush kings.

317   Constantine's two sons Crispus and Constantine are made Caesars, as is also Licinius' son. Another son, Constantius, is born to Constantine. Crispus has Lactantius as tutor.
In north China the Han Hun Dynasty (see 304) is fully established.

319   Trouble breaks out again on the northern frontiers of the Empire. Constantine himself combats the barbarians on the Danube and his son Crispus does so on the Rhine.

320   Crispus wins a victory.

320   In the Magadha area of India (the Ganges plain) the first of the Gupta dynasty, Chandra Gupta, establishes a powerful kingdom. (He has no connection with his Mauryan predecessor, Chandragupta.)

A Hunnish or Tartar invasion of China through the Great Wall continues, as does a period of foreign rule and changing dynasties. Hunnish infiltration extends into Siberia.

A. Politics, Law and Economics

312   The Roman gold coinage is further stabilized (see 292 A) by the *Solidus* being set at a value of 72 to the lb. weight.

315   The Jewish population of Ethiopia is said to be as much as half the total.

317   Constantine's coins begin to lose their pagan effigies.

C. Religion and Philosophy

312   Before the battle of the Milvian Bridge Constantine is said to have seen a vision in the sky of the christian cross with the legend, "By this, conquer!" He accordingly has his soldiers mark on their shields the *labarum*, a cross above the initials of Christ, the Greek letters *Chi, Ro*.

313   The Edict of Milan (see opposite) confirms the christian toleration announced by the dying Galerius, and extends it to all religions; Christians' property is restored. Helena, widow of Constantius and mother of Constantine, becomes a Christian (or possibly earlier).

314   Licinius renews the persecution of Christians in his eastern empire, excluding them from his palace at Nicomedia and requiring his soldiers to worship the pagan gods.

314/16   Donatus, bishop of Carthage, having set up a rival administration in opposition to clergy who are considered to have surrendered to the persecution, is summoned by Constantine to a council at Arles. These "Donatists" are ordered to conform.

319   Constantine affords the Donatists toleration; they remain as a sect until the Saracens reach N. Africa.

E. Literature

The heroism of Christians under the great persecution is recounted in the *Acta Martyrum* and circulated.

314   In his *De Mortibus Persecutorum* Lactantius somewhat gloats over the final agonies of the anti-christian emperors, Galerius in particular.

315   Eusebius, historian born in Palestine, is made bishop of Caesarea. He has been brought up by his predecessor Pamphilus, with access to Origen's great library (which is part of Pamphilus' collection of books—see 310 E).

F. Births and Deaths

311   Galerius d.

312   Maxentius d.

314   Libanius, rhetorician, b. (–395c).

313   Diocletian d. (68).

316   St Martin b. (–397).

317   Constantius II b. (–361).

321/2   Constantine expels the barbarians from Roman Dacia, repairs Trajan's bridge over the Danube, penetrates the old province of Dacia and makes peace.

323   On the barbarians invading Thrace and Licinius taking no action, Constantine himself expels the barbarians. Licinius then declares war on him. In two battles, near Adrianople and Chrysopolis (Scutari), with more than 100,000 troops on each side, Licinius is defeated (and see C).

324   Licinius, though he has been pardoned on the supplication of his wife (who is Constantine's sister) and merely banished to Salonica, is executed on the charge of indulging in renewed intrigue.

325   Constantine, by convening and directing the Council of Nicea (see C) is now committed to a full support of Christianity.

326   Constantine at Byzantium (not recovered from the desolation by the Goths) dedicates a new city, Nova Roma (and see 330).

326/7   Constantine's son Crispus and wife Fausta are said to have been put to death, together with the son of Licinius, presumably for plotting against the throne. (The evidence for these assassinations is not considered conclusive.)

328   The severe laws against the Arians (see 325 C) are relaxed.
A Mayan stela at Uaxactun in Guatemala shows this date.

330   Constantine makes Nova Roma, or Constantinople, his new, Christian, capital setting up his court there with much impressive and Oriental pomp (and see D).

---

325   The culture of the Amer-Indian Mayas is considered to have ended its "Formative" and to have begun its "Classic" Period (see 500 B.C.), to last for six hundred years. At about this time stone begins to be used in place of wood for building, and hieroglyphic inscriptions appear on them.

330   With the setting up of Constantinople the long history of Rome as the centre of the world may be said to end (and see A).

A. Politics, Law and Economics

325 Constantine makes his settlement at Nicea (see C) not as a theologian but as a practical statesman seeking unity.

330 One reason for the decline of Rome and her empire has been the decrease in population. Family limitation and infanticide has been a practice for at least 200 years; the making of eunuchs has been a contributing factor.

B. Science and Discovery

325 The Mayas throughout their "Classic" period, now beginning, seem obsessed with the significance of *time* and its calculation. The arithmetic is based on a duodecimal system and involves the concept, *zero*.

C. Religion and Philosophy

In this decade, the last of her life, Constantine's mother Helena spends much of her time in Jerusalem. She levels to the ground a temple of Aphrodite thought to stand over the tomb of Christ and raises the Church of the Holy Sepulchre in its stead. She is said to have found there the wood of the true cross.

321 Arius, a Libyan, propounds in his old age his heresy; he is fearful that Christianity shall develop two gods and he denies that Christ is "consubstantial" with God the Father. He is unfrocked, but some bishops take his side and a great christian schism arises.

323 Constantine fights Licinius as a pagan enemy as well as a rival ruler.

325 St. Pachomius, feeling that solitude is selfishness, carries the monastic movement forward by collecting lone anchorites to him and founding an abbey at Tabenne in Egypt.

The Mayas (see B above) develop a fertility religion based on the cultivation of maize and the passage of the seasons.

Constantine, fearful for the unifying force of Christianity, summons a univeral or oecumenical council at Nicea in Bithynia to consider the Arian heresy. 318 bishops attend, their expenses paid; and Constantine is present at the debates.

Athanasius, secretary to the bishop of Alexandria, opposes the heresy, insisting on the consubstantiality of Christ with God. Finally the Nicean Creed is formulated stating that Christ is "of one substance" with the Father. Only Arius and two other bishops refuse to sign; they are anathematized and exiled by Constantine, whilst all Arian books are burnt.

326 Athanasius becomes Bishop of Alexandria. He favours the monastic system and patronizes St Antony.

329 Frumentius preaches Christianity to the Abyssinians.

330 St Nicholas, Bishop of Myra in Lycia (and patron saint of Russia) *fl.*

D. The Arts

330 In building the "New Rome" or Constantinople out of the old Byzantium the area of the city is trebled and a forum and column of Constantine are in due course erected. (See also 531 D.) A great cultural centre is being created.

E. Literature

325 Eusebius publishes his *Ecclesiastical History*. On the Arian controversy he comments that it "afforded a subject a profound merriment to the pagans, even in their theatres."

328 The stela at Uaxactun (see opposite) makes it seem likely that Mayan hieroglyphics have already at this date existed for some time (but have only been incised on perishable wood). The characters are ideograms rather than pictograms. Most can now be read.

F. Births and Deaths

321 Valentinian, emperor, b. (-375).

324 Licinius d.

325 Lactantius d.
Oribasius (physician) b.
Ammianus Marcellinus (historian) b. (-391*c*),

326 Crispus d.

327 Fausta d.

329 St Basil the Great b. (-379).

329 Gregory Nazienzen b. (-389).

330 Helena d.

331 Julian, the future emperor, and nephew of Constantine, is born in Constantinople.

332 The Sarmatians ask Rome for protection from the Goths. The Emperor's eldest son, Constantine II, defeats the Goths, the chieftain's son coming as a hostage to Rome.

333 There is pestilence and famine in Syria.

334 Vandal refugees from the Goths are allowed across the Danube to settle within the Empire.

335 Constantine, hoping to effect a peaceful transition of power at his death, apportions responsibilities to his sons and nephews: there are 6 young Caesars.

335 In India the second and greatest of his dynasty, Samudra Gupta, comes to the throne.

336 The Emperor's son Constantius marries his cousin and the sister of Julian.

337 (May) Having celebrated the thirtieth year of his reign, and having been at last baptized as a Christian, Constantine dies.

337/8 The Army rejects the authority of all except the dead emperor's sons, and all his nephews (except one who is ill and Julian who is not yet six) are done away with.

338 The three surviving sons of Constantine the Great, by name and in order of seniority Constantine, Constantius and Constans, meet in Pannonia and try to compose their differences.

339 Constantius wages not very successful war in Mesopotamia with a revivified Persia under King Shapur II.

340 Constantine II, dissatisfied with his share of the kingdom (chiefly Britain, Gaul and Spain) takes up arms against his brother, Constans (Italy and Illyria) and is defeated and killed at a battle near Aquileia. Constans is thus left master of the West, with Constantius master of the East.

A. **Politics, Law and Economics**
339   Constantius, dynastically minded, issues a decree making the marriage of uncle and niece a capital offence.

B. **Science and Discovery**
333   Medical and literary men are confirmed in their exemption from military service or public office.

C. **Religion and Philosophy**
The Christians suffer considerably from persecution in Persia under King Shapur II.

331   The young St Martin enlists as a soldier, but at the end of five years becomes a monk.

335   Constantine interviews Athanasius who has caused continued religious disagreement and tells him to retire to Treves.

336   Arius is re-admitted into the Church; he dies later in the same year. Arianism spreads in the East.

D. **The Arts**
Constantine in his last peaceful years patronizes the arts. He endows the schools of Athens, and encourages his governors to establish provincial schools of architecture. The art treasures of the empire are drawn upon to bedeck the new capital. In Rome an arch has been set up in Constantine's memory — showing him, among other things, distributing largesse. The first churches of *St. Peter* and of *St. Paul Without the Walls* are built. The *basilica* or public hall type of church architecture is established; however, *S. Maria Maggiore* in Rome is adapted from a pagan temple.

E. **Literature**
337   Eusebius writes a *Life* of Constantine.

F. **Births and Deaths**
331   Julian (emperor) b. (-363).

331   St. Jerome b. (-420).

335   Chandra Gupta I d.

336   Arius d. (80).

337   (May) Constantine d. (64).

340   Constantine II d.
St. Jerome b. (-420).

340   St. Ambrose b. (-397*c*).
Eusebius (historian) d.

Constans meets trouble in Britain, as does Constantius from Persia

341 The Franks invade Gaul.

342 Constans compels the Franks to sue for peace.

342/3 (winter) The Picts and Scots having for the first time combined, and being a threat to Wales and western England, Constans crosses the Channel and makes peace with them, probably allowing them to settle in Roman Britain.

345 The young Julian and his brother Gallus are being kept virtually prisoners, with only an aged slave to educate them.

346 Shapur II of Persia renews his pressure on the eastern Roman empire; he fails to take the town of Nisibis (near ancient Sumerian Akkad).

348 War is renewed between Constantius and Shapur and the latter wins a victory at Singara.

349/50 Constans having become extremely unpopular, a Gaulish leader from Amiens, Magnus Magnentius, usurps the throne and is welcomed in Britain and Spain and Italy as well as in Gaul. Constans flees to Spain and is assassinated.

Constantius, called to deal with these troubles in the West, has to leave the scene of the long-drawn trouble with Shapur II. Shapur however, having once more failed to take the heroically defended town of Nisibis, and himself threatened by pressure from the Huns, retires for a while from the Mesopotamian war.

During this decade Samudra Gupta extends his kingdom or his influence over most of India. A pillar found at Allahabad sings his praises.

B. Science and Discovery

341/5 There is a series of earthquakes in the Middle East. Syria, Pontus and Epirus suffer.

346 It is noted that during a total eclipse of the sun (probably June 6th) the stars are visible.

C. Religion and Philosophy

341 Ulfilas, a Goth, is made a bishop and sets up a community of Gothic Christians in Thrace. He translates the Bible into Gothic (and see E).
An imperial edict prohibits pagan sacrifice.
Athanasius, deposed from the bishopric of Alexandria, comes to Rome; he introduces the monastic system into Europe.

342 The edict of the previous year is redressed by an edict forbidding the destruction of pagan temples.

346 A meeting of bishops at Milan declares its adherence to the Nicean creed; the split between the eastern and western churches is beginning.

347 There is a defeat for Arianism at an ecclesiastical Council at Sardica (Sophia). British bishops attend.

349 Amid popular tumult, Athanasius (see 341 above) returns from Rome to Alexandria; Constans has put pressure on Constantius to let him come.

350 Julian, having arrived at Constantinople, is sent by a jealous Constantius to Nicomedia, where he studies under pagan philosophers.

D. The Arts

The Indian Guptan king Samudra is said to spend on the arts the treasure brought to him by vassal states.

E. Literature

341 Ulfilas, in order to translate the Bible into Gothic (which is not a literary language), composes an alphabet, based on the Greek, for the purpose. This is the only extant example of this Gothic language.

F. Births and Deaths

342 Eusebius d.
Tiridates (II) of Armenia d.

345 Symmachus b. (–410).

346 Theodosius the Gt. b. (–395).

347 St. Chrysostom b. (–407),

348 Prudentius (poet) b.

350 Constans d. (30).

351   Gallus (see 345) is made a Caesar and Governor at Antioch, whilst his younger brother
Julian is allowed to wander in search of teachers of philosophy.

352   There is a rebellion of Palestinian Jews, in which their city of Tiberius suffers.

352/3   Constantius, at the battle of Mursa, overthrows the usurping emperor of the West,
Magnentius, and becomes undisputed sole emperor. Magnentius's British follower
Martinus holds out; an official named Paulus is sent to control him and proves so
harsh in his rule that Martinus kills him and then kills himself. Savage vengeance is
taken on the followers of Martinus.

354   The brothers Gallus and Julian are summoned before Constantius. Gallus is tried on
a charge of despotic rule and executed; Julian is held prisoner for some months but
released on making it clear that his sole interest is philosophy and is banished to
Athens.

355   The Huns begin their great drive westwards by an advance into Russia. They overcome and absorb the Alans.

355   Julian is given Constantius' sister in marriage and made Caesar and governor of Gaul.

356/60   On the Germans again attacking Gaul, Julian is sent to combat them. He does well,
winning a battle at Strasbourg, and helps to restore Gaul's prosperity.

358   Constantius has to meet renewed attacks from Shapur II of Persia.

360   In Paris Julians' troops declare him Emperor, refusing to go East to the aid of Constantius.
Julian sends a mobile force to Britain to keep back the Picts and Scots, the first time
that an invasion of barbarians has necessitated such drastic action in Britain.

361   On the way to confront Julian, Constantius dies. Julian, with Constans and Constantius
both dead, takes over the combined emperorship of East and West. He rules from
Constantinople. He declares himself a pagan—see E.

362   Wishing to emulate and outdo Trajan, Julian sets up headquarters in Antioch and
prepares for a full scale invasion of the Persian empire.

363   Julian advances into Shapur's territory, but Shapur avoids battle and adopts a
scorched earth policy. The Romans reach Ctesiphon but are enticed into the desert
by a ruse. In a skirmish, Julian, leading his men, is mortally wounded. Jovian,
Captain of the Guard, succeeds him and makes peace, surrendering four of the five
provinces gained by Galerius in 298. He lives however for only 7 months.

364   The soldier Valentinian is elected Emperor; he retains the West and makes his younger
brother Valens emperor of the East.

365   Earthquake and tidal wave around the Aegaean.

367   Valentinian makes his son Gratian, aged 9, partner and Augustus.

A. Politics, Law and Economics

361/3   Julian in Constantinople follows the example of Augustus in showing great respect for his Senate and for the carriage of justice.

364/75   Valentinian rules wisely from Milan, checking political corruption and forbidding infanticide.

B. Science and Discovery

352   *Cataphracti* or mailed cavalry help Constantius to win the battle of Mursa.

356   Aetius, "the Atheist", *fl.*, combining medical with theological controversy.

362   Oribasius of Pergamum *fl.* and is physician to Julian. He writes a medical encyclopaedia.

C. Religion and Philosophy

351   Julian is taught by the anti-Christian philosopher Maximus of Ephesus.

355   On being banished to Athens (see 354), Julian studies with Gregory Nazienzen and Basil the Great.

359   The Patriarch of the Palestine Jews, Hillel II, issues a callendar of Jewish festivals.

361   St Jerome comes to Rome and studies the classics, loving them "to the point of sin".

361/3   Julian, known to the Christian world as the Apostate, changes the elaborate eastern court of Constantinople to one more fitting a Stoic philosopher. He lives with the austerity of a Marcus Aurelius. He orders that pagan temples be repaired and re-opened. He surrounds himself with hellenistic philosophers. including Libanius and his old friend Maximus (see 351 above) who grows rich.

361/3   The Christians are not so much persecuted as shorn of their privileges; though the pagan mob do murder the Bishop of Alexandria. At this, Athanasius comes out of hiding and resumes command of his old see; Julian forces him to retire, but Athanasius returns on Julian's death.
The Temple at Jerusalem begins to be rebuilt, with Julian's encouragement; but the rebuilding stops when Julian dies.

362   A Council at Gengra rules against the extreme view of some Christians, who, in reaction against pagan licence, denounce all marriage as sinful. Nevertheless, the idea that priests at least should be celibate is growing.
St Martin founds a monastery at Poitiers, the first in Gaul.

363   The Emperor Julian dies nobly, in a scene reminiscent—perhaps consciously so on the dying man's part—of Socrates' end. Jovian, the succeeding emperor, restores state support to the Christian church: the last effort to revive hellenism is ended.

370   St Basil becomes Bishop of Caesaraea.

371   St Martin becomes Bishop of Tours.

368/72 Britain suffers from a concerted attack by Picts, Scots, Saxons and Franks. The Roman soldier Count Theodosius is sent to restore order, which he does. His son, later to be Theodosius the Great, campaigns with him.

369 The Japanese invade Korea and establish a small colony and base.

372 The Huns, under Balamir, cross the Volga and attack the Ostrogoths in the Ukraine under their aged king, Ermanaric, who is defeated. Some Ostrogoths join in with the Huns; some penetrate into the land of the Visigoths, north of the Danube.

373 Count Theodosius puts down insurrection in Morocco.

374 Theodosius the younger (see 368 above) repels the Quadi in Illyria.

375 The Emperor of the West, Valentinian, dies suddenly, while negotiating with the Quadi. His son Gratian succeeds him.
Chandra Gupta II begins his reign in India.

In this quarter-century the Roman empire of the West is saved, by a series of efficient emperors, from repeated attacks of Germanic "barbarians" (but not now barbarous). However, pressure, as yet unfelt by the Romans themselves, is growing from the Huns.

The Irish "Scots" raid Wales, and even Gaul under their most famous king, reigning at Tara, Niall.

The Franks, spreading generally by peaceful penetration, have by now occupied north-western Gaul.

C. **Religion and Philosophy** (continued)

372 The pagan philosopher Maximus, teacher of Julian, is put to death.

374 St Jerome, leaving an ascetic brotherhood at Aquileia, enters a monastery in the desert near Antioch.

375 St Ambrose, after practising as a lawyer and becoming a local Governor in Milan, is elected bishop of that city.

D. **The Arts**

In the period in India, under the Gupta kings, Buddhist art reaches a high standard, as in the frescoes of the Ajanta caves of Hyderabad.

359 A sarcophagus placed in the crypt of St Peter's, Rome, shows an early representation of Christ, young and unbearded (and below him Zeus holding up the sky).

E. **Literature**

Julian, both as Caesar and as Emperor, collects books and also writes many books and pamphlets, some of which are extant. They range from a mystical *Hymn to Helios* to the witty *Hater of beards*.

375 Ausonius, poet and gentleman who has been tutor to Gratian, is showered with honours when his pupil comes to the throne.

F. **Births and Deaths**

353 Magnentius d.

354 St Augustine of Hippo b. (−430); Gallus d.

358 Gratian, emperor, b. (−383).

359 Stilicho b. (−408).

361 Constantius II d. (44).

363 Julian d. (32).

364 Jovian d. (34).

370 Hypatia, mathematician, b. (−415).

372 Maximus, philosopher, d.

373 St. Athanasius d. (80).

375 Valentinian I d. (54).
     Samudra Gupta d.

376/8   The Visigoths north of the Danube (see 372) are in turn defeated by the Huns. The survivors receive permission to cross south into Roman territory but are shamefully treated by the Romans. These Visigoths accordingly revolt and overrun Thrace. Valens, Emperor of the East, meets them near Hadrianople, and is defeated and killed, leaving Constantinople itself in danger from the Goths.

379   Gratian, Emperor of the West, calls upon Theodosius (see 374) to become Emperor of the East. Theodosius accepts.
Shapur II dies, leaving Persia at the height of her power and at peace with Rome.

382   After two victories over them Theodosius makes peace with the Goths (see A).

383   Magnus Maximus, Spaniard, left behind by Theodosius the elder in Britain, decides to claim the throne of the Western empire, Gratian having relapsed into a weak and inefficient ruler. He denudes Britain of troops, meets Gratian near Paris, and defeats him. Gratian flees and is killed by his own troops. Maximus becomes master of Gaul and Spain; in Britain Hadrian's wall is overrun and comes to its end. Valentinian II succeeds his half-brother Gratian as Emperor of the West.

384   Theodosius renews peace with Persia: Armenia, so long a cause of friction, is partitioned.

387   Magnus Maximus, in an effort to become fully Emperor of the West, invades Italy. Valentinian II flees with his mother and sister to Thessalonica—where Theodosius meets him and marries the sister.
South China is saved at the battle of Fei Shui from Hunnish invasion but the weakened north suffers another wave of Hunnish or Tartar tribes.

388   Maximus is defeated and killed by Theodosius.
Chandra Gupta II begins a war against the Shakas, which finally gives him control of N.W. India. He calls himself Vickramaditya or "Sun of Prowess".

390   Theodosius humbles himself before the power of the Church (see A and C).

392/4   Valentinian II, advancing into Gaul against a Frankish usurper Arbogast, is assassinated. Arbogast, the first of the barbarian king-makers of the Roman Empire, appoints a weakling, Eugenius, as Emperor of the West.
Theodosius comes over from Constantinople to restore order. Arbogast and Eugenius die after a defeat near Aquileia, at the battle of the river Frigidus. Theodosius for 3 years becomes Emperor of both East and West.

395   Theodosius appoints his 11 year old son Honorius Emperor of the West and his 18 year old son Arcadius Emperor of the East. He then dies.

396   Stilicho, son of a Vandal captain in the Roman army, gains control over the effete Honorius and becomes virtual ruler of the West. He ceases to employ or subsidise the Goths (see 382 A), who reply by responding to their leader Alaric's appeal to carve out a kingdom for themselves. Descending through the pass of Thermopylae, Alaric destroys the temple of Eleusis, robs but spares Athens, and harries the Peloponnese. Stilicho advances, makes peace with the Goths, and allows them to settle in Epirus. Alaric is quiet for 4 years.

A. Politics, Law and Economics

382   The policy of Theodosius in regard to the Goths is to keep them quiet with a subsidy but to let them release their energy by employing them as soldiers.

388   Chandra Gupta II's wars give him control of trade with the west, but also destroy any buffer state between him and the Huns.

390   An episode in Thessalonica demonstrates the continued intense popularity of the Games and chariot racing in the Roman Empire. A popular charioteer being imprisoned for gross immorality, the mob tear the governor to pieces. Theodosius takes his revenge (see C).

399   The Chinese traveller Fa-Hsien sets out to report on India.

400   Synesius of Cyrene, a pupil of Hypatia, tries in vain to sting the courts of Constantinople and Rome into action against the barbarians: he recommends military conscription and the end of luxury.

B. Science and Discovery

378   It is the cavalry of the Goths that dominates the battle of Hadrianople.

392   To add to his triumphal decoration of Constantinople, Theodosius I has the obelisk of Tuthmoses III brought from Karnak. Its erection is a major engineering feat.

400   Hypatia, philosopher and mathematician and famous too in her own right as a woman, flourishes in Alexandria. (And see 415 C.)

400   Zosymus of Panopolis *fl.* He describes semi-mystical experiments which foreshadow medieval alchemy but also show that some genuine chemical enquiry is being made. At about this time probably comes the first use of the still (Greek *ambix*, Arabic *alembic*), which the Arabs are to develop some 500 years later.

C. Religion and Philosophy

379   St Basil dies, having encouraged the growth of self-supporting monasteries in Cappadocia and elsewhere.

379   Gregory Nazienzen becomes bishop of Constantinople.
Jerome is ordained a priest at Antioch.
Buddhism is declared the state religion of China.

380   Pelagius (a Briton, possibly of Verulamium) leaves, with his Irish companion Caelestius, for Rome.

381   Gregory (see 379 above) becomes tired of disputation and retires to his native Nazienzen.

382   Jerome comes to Rome as secretary to the Pope, and begins his translation of the Old Testament into Latin, the *Vulgate*.

383   Augustine, so far a Manichaean and a man of carnal impulses, leaves his native N. Africa for Rome, and comes under the influence of Ambrose.

400   The danger for the Romans of employing barbarians in their armies is exemplified in Gainas the Goth who rebels in Asia Minor and, after negotiations with Arcadius, for a few months becomes virtual master of Constantinople. He is expelled from the city however and pursued over the Danube—and is murdered by a Hunnish Chieftain.

---

380   Easter Island has been occupied by neolithic seafarers and at about this time they begin to fortify the island and to build platforms of cut and polished stone on which they set statues (but not of giant size, these appearing later).

400   The Huns are spreading slowly but steadily to the west, reaching the Elbe by about the end of the century.

385 A Spanish bishop, Priscillian, accused of preaching Manichaeism, is burnt at the stake. St Ambrose and St Martin object.

386 Pope Siricius decrees that all married priests shall be unfrocked; St Ambrose, St Jerome and St Augustine all support him.

387 Augustine is baptized by Ambrose.

388 Augustine returns to Africa, to found his monastic order.

389 Theophilus, archbishop, of Alexandria, burns down the temple and library of Serapis —an unpopular act.

390 Theodosius the Great avenges the death of the Governor of Thessalonica (see A) by massacring the populace—7000 of them it is said—while watching the Games. Ambrose, now bishop of Milan, demonstrates the power of the Church by refusing to administer Mass to the Emperor until he enters the cathedral as a penitent. Theodosius, after hesitation, complies.

391 Symmachus, given office by Theodosius, upholds paganism.

392 At the seaport of Hippo Augustine wins a war of words with the local bishop, who is a Donatist (see 314 C); he takes the man's place—an office he holds, whilst he writes and teaches, until his death.

396 St Paulinus *fl.* With his wife he lives a gentle and abstemious life in what is virtually a private and personal monastery at Nola in Italy.

D. The Arts
380 Theodosius constructs on the western road into Constantinople its Golden Gate— through which he enters in triumph, drawn by elephants.

390 Ambrose inaugurates a custom of singing hymns and psalms "in the oriental manner" —i.e. antiphonal singing.

392 Theodosius, in imitation of Trajan, sets up his column in Constantinople to commemorate his victories over the Goths.

E. Literature
In this period, under King Chandra Gupta II, northern India rises to its cultural height. At his court the king entertains poets, playwrights, artists and philosophers, and among his "nine gems" is Kalidasa (whose plays have been translated into English).
Probably in this period is written, by a Sophist named Longus, the love story, *Daphnis and Chloe*.

378 Ammianus Marcellinus writes a History of Rome (describing Valens' defeat at Hadrianople as the worst since Cannae.)

388 Alypius writes his *Musical Introduction*, explaining Greek musical notations (which change about this time from letters of the alphabet to abstract signs, *neumes*).

E. **Literature** (continued)

395 Claudian, the last of the Latin classic poets, *fl.* He is patronized by Stilicho, to whom he writes a poem. The *Rape of Proserpine* is among his extant writings.

399 Claudian praises Stilicho for freeing Britain from depredations by Pict and Scot; "nor do Saxon ships come bearing down with every shift of the wind."

400 Under the Gupta kings the Brahmans are increasing their influence, at the expense of the Buddhists: Sanskrit is becoming the literary language and the Hindu epics are written down.
A rumic inscription is made on the Tune Stone at Ostfold in Norway (one of the oldest known, though the origin of the script may go back to the 1st Century B.C.).

F. **Births and Deaths**

377 Arcadius, emperor, b.

378 Valens, emperor, d.

379 St Basil the Great d. (50*c*).
Shapur II of Persia d.

383 Gratian, emperor, d. (25).

384 Honorius, emperor, b. (–423).

385 St Patrick b. (–461).

388 Maximus (pretender) d.

390 St Simeon Stylites b. (–459).

391 Ammianus Marcellinus d. (65).

392 Valentinian II d.

395 Ausonius d. (89).
Theodosius the Great d. (49*c*).

395 Libanius d. (81*c*).

397 St Martin d. (81*c*).

397 St Ambrose d. (57*c*).

401 Alaric invades Italy destroying as he comes and sending flights of refugees before him. Stilicho collects an army, denuding garrisons as far afield as Britain.

In Constantinople the Emperor Arcadius is presented with a son, whom he christens another Theodosius.

402 At Pollentia Alaric and Stilicho fight a drawn battle; Honorius is able to bribe Alaric to leave Italy.

403 Honorius deserts Milan for Ravenna, which he makes the western capital.

405 A barbarian called Radagaisus collects an army of Ostragoths, Vandals and others and invades Italy. Stilicho saves Florence from his horde and brings him in chains to Honorius.

406 The Romano-British, in despair at being deserted, elect their own emperors, first one, Marcus, and then another named Gratian. Neither survive.

Vandals (see 334) and other barbarians overrun much of Gaul, almost reaching the Channel.

407 A third usurper rises in Britain called Constantine. He crosses the Channel in an effort to create a realm for himself both in Gaul and Spain.

408 In Constantinople Arcadius dies, and his son, aged 7, becomes Emperor of the East as Theodosius II.

In Rome, the Chancellor Olympius, jealous of Stilicho and believing that he is at heart pro-German, persuades Honorius to have him assassinated, together with many of his Vandal soldiers.

Alaric, seizing his opportunity and complaining that his bribe is not being paid, invades again, picking up discontented mercenaries on his way.

409 Alaric besieges Rome, which begins to starve. Twice he is bought off but twice returns. Many barbarian slaves escape to his side.

The Vandals and their allies pour into Spain and plunder her rich cities.

410 (Aug.) A slave opens the gates of Rome and the Visigoths enter. Rome is taken and despoiled just 800 years after her previous fall to the Gauls; only the churches of St Peter and St Paul are spared. Alaric continues south to conquer Sicily, but only reaches Consentia in the toe of Italy, where he dies of a fever, being buried with an immolation of slaves.

411 Honorius tells the Britons that they must look to their own defences.

412/14 Alaric's brother-in-law Ataulf (Adolphus), having declared that he wishes to strengthen and not destroy the Empire, marries Honorius' half-sister Placidia and sets up a Visigoth kingdom in Gaul, theoretically subject to the Empire.

415 Ataulf is assassinated and Wallia becomes king of the Visigoths.

419/20 Wallia is bribed by Honorius to regain Spain for the Empire—which he does, the Vandals retiring into Andalusia (Vandalusia).

423 Honorius, Emperor of the West, dies, and there is a struggle for the throne.

A. Politics, Law and Economics

405 Fa Hsien (see 399 A) reaches India and reports on its prosperity and the social liberty that it is enjoying under the Guptas.

411 The Donatists (see C) besides being prone to violence and fanatical self-immolation, form a sect called the Circumcelliones or Prowlers—robbers with a social and egalitarian purpose, forerunners of Robin Hood.

425 A university is founded at Constantinople, as a counterpoise to Athens and concentrating on Latin and Greek rhetoric.

B. Science and Discovery

425 Flavius Vegetius *fl*. He is a founder of veterinary science, writing a book on the medical treatment of mules.

C. Religion and Philosophy

401 St Patrick, son of a Roman official living on the Severn Estuary, is captured by pirates and sold in Ireland as a slave.

404 St John Chrysostom offends the Empress at Constantinople by his open rebuke of profligacy and is banished. The result is a riot and the burning of the first church of St Sophia.

407 St Patrick, after 7 years as a swineherd, returns to his family in England—only to leave it after a few years to study on the continent for the priesthood.

410 Pelagius and Caelestius (see 380 C) leave Rome for Carthage.
Theodore of Mopsuestia *fl*; he makes intelligent assessment and criticism of the books of the Bible.

411 A council, called by Honorius, meets at Carthage and endeavours to curb the excesses of the Donatists (see A).

415 Orestes, pagan prefect of Alexandria, expels the Jews, and takes vengeance on some monks who stone him. Archbishop Cyril blames the philosopher Hypatia (see 400 B) as an evil female influence on Orestes; one of his staff leads a mob who tear Hypatia to pieces.

418 Pelagius, having caused great stir by his fight against the doctrine of original sin, is banished; later—probably after his death—his teaching is pronounced heretical.
Germanus, a lawyer, is elected bishop of Auxerre.

D. The Arts

420 The Japanese emperor Inkyo is said to have played the zither, while his wife danced, at the inauguration of a new palace (and see 500).

424 The Roman soldier Aëtius, who has spent some of his early years as a hostage amongst the Goths and Huns, invades Italy in support of a usurper, John, at the head of a large force of these barbarians.

425 John is defeated and the young Valentinian III becomes Emperor of the West, with the real power in the hands of his mother Placidia (one-time wife of the Goth Ataulf). Aëtius enters her service.

———————————

By the beginning of this century the Slavs, moving southwards, begin to appear in Western history in the shape of a confederation of tribes living between the Dnieper and Dniester and known as the Antae. (Up to this date, whereas the population of S. Russia has appeared, as Cimmerians, Scythians and Sarmatians, N. Russia, the home of the Slavs and deeply forested, has made no mark on the civilized world.)

415 At the time of the accession of Kumara Gupta to the throne India's threat of the Huns from the N.W. begins; he manages however to keep his kingdom intact.

425 At the end of this period the Ephthalites, sometimes known as the White Huns, spread into the region south of Lake Aral. The Persians, under their king Bahram V, for a while keep them at bay.

E. Literature

401 At the same time as Claudian (see 395 E), the Christian poet Prudentius *fl.* He writes on simpler themes: *The Crowns of the Martyrs* and *The Daily Round*.
Synesius of Cyrene, pupil of Hypatia, *fl.* He writes *In Praise of Baldness*.
Augustine writes his autobiography, his *Confessions*.

405 The Chinese poet Tao Chien *fl.* He retires to a simple life from a minor government post because he is tired of "crooking the hinges of his back", i.e. kow-towing, for his daily ration of rice.

413/26 Augustine writes his *City of God*, wherein he seeks to explain the fall of Rome and show that that fall cannot be attributed to the Christians.

425 Fastidius writes, in Britain, his book, *On the Christian Life*.

F. Births and Deaths

400 Attila b. (–453).
Leo I Emperor b. (–474).

401 Theodosius II b.

407 St John Chrysostom d. (60*c*).

408 Stilicho d.
Arcadius d. (31).

410 Symmachus d. (68).
Alaric d.

415 Hypatia d. (45).
Ataulf d.
Chandra Gupta II d.

420 St Jerome d. (89*c*).

423 Honorius d. (41).

426/8   Aëtius campaigns in Gaul against Goths and Franks.

429   Germanus (see 418 C), coming to Britain to combat Pelagianism, takes up the sword and wins the "Hallelujah" victory against the Saxons.
The Vandals, under their leader Genseric, invade Africa from Spain; they are said to have been invited by the Roman governor Boniface, out of jealousy for his rival at the western court of Ravenna, Aëtius.

430   The Vandals, helped by the local Moors and the Donastists, are successful. They besiege and take Hippo, Augustine dying during the siege.

431   Peace is made with the victorious Vandals and Governor Boniface retires to Ravenna —where he defeats Aëtius but dies.
Chlodio, the first known king of the Franks, prevented by Aëtius from taking Cologne, makes Tournai his capital.

433   Attila inherits the Hunnish kingdom with his brother, who however dies. For the first years of his reign Attila consolidates his power in his Hungarian capital, probably on the site of Buda. Both Emperors, Theodosius II of the East and Valentinian III of the West, bribe him to keep the peace.

435   The Burgundians, making peace with Aëtius, are attacked by the Huns.

438   Spain is overrun by the Suevi, a collection of German migratory tribes.

439   Genseric, breaking the peace with the Romans, seizes Carthage, despoiling it with much cruelty.

440   Genseric invades Sicily.
St Leo I, the Great, becomes Pope.

441   The Huns cross the Danube and spread over the Balkans, taking Belgrade and then Sofia. The Eastern Emperor trebles his tribute money.

446   The Britons, left virtually without Roman protection since 407 and suffering from Picts and Scots and Saxons, send an appeal for help to Aëtius. It is at about this time that the Saxons begin to arrive in numbers—to settle and not merely to raid.

447   The Huns have entered Thrace, Thessaly and Scythia, sacking towns with great cruelty as they go. Theodosius II buys them off again and they turn to the Western Empire.

449   Vortigern, a Welsh king who has authority as far east as Kent, invites the Saxons under their leaders Hengist and Horsa to settle in Kent, in order to help him against the Picts and Scots.

Two great Christians flourish– Nestorius and St Patrick; A.D. 426–450
Carthage is revived

A. Politics, Law and Economics

438 The Codex Theodosianus divides the East and West Empires administratively—and provides the barbarian inheritors of Rome with a code of laws.

439/50 Genseric, having won Carthage, builds it up to some prosperity again; he also uses it as a base for efficient piracy and coastal ravaging by sea-borne cavalry.

441 The invasions of the Huns across the Danube ruin the Balkans and also the great river itself as a carrier of commerce.

B. Science and Discovery

431 Persecuted Nestorians (see C) are welcomed in Persia for their medical and astronomical knowledge; they build an observatory with royal encouragement.

447 An earthquake and an eclipse of the sun increase the fear of the people of Constantinople.

C. Religion and Philosophy

428 Nestorius, a pupil of Theodore (see 410 C), Archbishop at Constantinople, disputes with Cyril of Alexandria on the nature of Christ and the Mother of God.

429 St Simeon Stylites sets himself up on his pillar in the Syrian desert.

431 Nestorius is excommunicated by the Council of Ephesus. Persecuted Nestorians spread into Persia (see B) and finally as far as China.

432 St Patrick is made a bishop at Auxerre, and then goes to convert the Irish to Christianity. The king at Tara (son of Niall—see 351) is not converted but allows St Patrick's mission to proceed—which it does, amidst dangers and difficulties, for 29 years.

447 Germanus again visits Britain to counter Pelagianism.

449 Another council at Ephesus finds in favour of the "Monophysite" heresy of Eutyches of Alexandria, to the effect that Christ's human and divine natures are one. (But see 451 C.)

450 Proclus *fl.*, one of the last of the philosophers of note at Plato's Academy at Athens.

D. The Arts

439 Cyrus, Egyptian poet and philosopher, becomes city and praetorian prefect at Constantinople; he repairs the city's buildings (and her protective sea wall).

450 Some Romano-Briton buries at Mildenhall in Suffolk a treasure of plate, including a dish decorated in classical style with gods and nymphs. (Discovered in 1942).
In Ravenna is built the mausoleum of Galla Placidia (sister of Honorius), richly decorated with mosaics.

450 Theodosius II, Eastern Emperor, dies and is followed by Marcian, who refuses to continue the tribute to Attila. Valentinian III of the West follows his example.

Honoria, sister of Valentinian III, having been banished for misconduct, sends a ring and a plea for help to Attila—who pretends to take the ring as a proposal of marriage and demands half the kingdom.

Valentinian III loses the wise guidance of his mother Placidia.

———————

The Franks are spreading in the Netherlands and as far as the Somme: Teutonic language and paganism go with them. Some time in this half century King Chlodio (see 431) is succeeded by Merovech ("Son of the Sea") about whom many legends grow up and who gives his name to the Merovingian Dynasty.

In these years the Slavs of northern Russia are being pushed by the Huns into the area of the Germanic tribes.

E. Literature

428   The Pope, appealed to in the Nestorian dispute (see C) is unable to read Nestorius' submission because it is in Greek: thus even by this date the Eastern and Western Churches have ceased to have a common language.

433   Attila comes to the throne an illiterate; he is an exponent however of propaganda, the propaganda of fear and terror c/f the Assyrians: Christians come to know him as the Scourge of God.

439   Cyrus (see D) is the first to publish the Eastern Empire's decrees in Greek.

448   Priscus, historian, is one of the ambassadors sent by Theodosius to parley with Attila.

450   The poem *Hero and Leander* by Musaeus, is written.

F. Births and Deaths

430   St Augustine of Hippo d. (76).

432   Sidonius, Gallic prose writer, b. (–526).

450   Emperor Theodosius II d.
       Placidia d.

451 Attila, having been refused half the kingdom (see 450), makes his grand attack on the Empire of the West. Burning Trier and Metz on the way, and at the head of an army of reputedly half a million, he approaches Paris and reaches Troyes. At the battle of the Catalaunian Fields (or Chalons, sometimes called the battle of Troyes) he is defeated. On his side are Franks and also Visigoths under Wallia (who is killed); the Roman general, and victor, is Aëtius.

452 Attila, who has retired in good order, recuperates and advances into Italy. Aquileia falls (and see D); Milan buys him off. Valentinian III flees from Ravenna to Rome and sends Pope Leo I to parley. Leo, his hand strengthened with news of reinforcements from Constantinople and by the fact of plague having broken out among the Huns, prevails upon Attila to return to his capital.

453 After a wedding feast, Attila is found dead in bed, with a burst blood vessel. His empire is divided between his sons, and the Hunnish threat to the West is ended.

454 In Rome Valentinian III, with no heir and jealous of the successful general for wanting to ally with his family matrimonially, murders Aëtius.
The Ostragoths settle in Pannonia.

455 Valentinian III is murdered and a puppet, Avitus, is put on the western throne. Genseric the Vandal, seeing an opportunity, attacks and loots Rome, Pope Leo being only able to obtain a promise not to massacre or set fire to the city. With his booty Genseric takes away the Empress Eudoxia and her two daughters.

455 The Saxons, having rebelled against Vortigern (see 449) fight the Britons. Horsa is said to have been slain at Aylesford.

456/7 Rome goes through a time of chaos and changing rulers with the Visigoth Ricimer as the power behind the throne.

457 Leo the Thracian succeeds to the Eastern Empire as Leo I, put there by Aspar the Alan, another such barbarian king-maker as Ricimer in the west. The Emperor Leo however is strong enough to stand on his own feet.

462 The Vandals capture Sardinia.
Theodoric the Great, aged 7, becomes a hostage at Constantinople.

466/70 Euric becomes king of the Visigoths and conquers Spain and Marseilles.

468 The western empire supports the eastern under Leo I in an attempt to invade N. Africa and to defeat Genseric the Vandal. The attempt fails.

471 Ricimer the Visigoth withdraws to Milan.
Aspar the Alan is murdered.

472 Ricimer captures Rome but dies.

473 Julius Nepos is appointed emperor in Rome by Leo I.

474 The Emperor Leo I dies and is followed by his grandson and then, in the same year by Zeno, his son-in-law.

A. **Politics, Law and Economics**
451   The Church protects itself from unruly monks by laying down rules at the Council of Chalcedon—e.g. that vows should be irrevocable (and see C).

455   Much of N. Italy is by this date devastated: towns are walled, farms are abandoned, population has shrunk—Rome's, it is estimated, from about a million and a half to a third of a million.

B. **Science and Discovery**
451   Persecuted Monophysites follow their Nestorian predecessors to Persia. They translate major Greek philosophical works into Syriac. Cultural and scientific advance continues in Persia and Syria from this Monophysite stimulus.

472   Vesuvius erupts and ash is said to have fallen as far afield as Constantinople.

C. **Religion and Philosophy**
451   Nestorius, long banished to the Libyan desert, dies; his followers withdraw to eastern Syria, there to establish a school at Edessa, to translate both the Bible and the Classics, and eventually to help pass on their learning to the Moslems.
        The Council of Chalcedon ends a long struggle for ecclesiastical supremacy between Constantinople and Alexandria—in the former's favour. It also condemns the Monophysite heresy (see 449 C), which however continues to flourish in Egypt (the Copts) and Ethiopia and elsewhere. (And see B.)

D. **The Arts**
452   Attila's destruction of Aquileia—from which its inhabitants escape to the Lagoons—leads eventually to the founding of Venice (see 568).

E. **Literature**
452   Sidonius, the Gallic writer, marries the daughter of Avitus (see 455) and for a while lives a life of Roman ease and refinement at his villa near Clermont.

455/61   St Patrick writes his *Confessions*, telling of his perils and difficulties in Ireland. Legends grow up around him after his death, Nennius, the 9th century historian, crediting him with raising nine persons from the dead and writing 365 books.

468   Sidonius, now in Rome as prefect of the city, describes in cultured prose its society life.

469/75   Sidonius returns to Clermont, there to be made bishop, and in 475 to be imprisoned (for 2 years only) by the Visigoths who besiege and take the city.

F. **Births and Deaths**
451   Wallia (Goth) d.

451   Nestorius d.

475 Julius Nepos (see 473) is deposed by a Pannonian general, Orestes, who puts his young son Romulus, nicknamed Little Augustus, on the throne.
Theodroic the Great succeeds to the throne of the Ostrogoths.
Britain in this period is falling apart into a pattern of warring local chiefs, sometimes fighting each other, sometimes the Saxons. Towns decay: but some hill forts—the Cissbury and South Cadbury—are re-occupied, whilst the Wansdyke, running from the Bristol Channel to the Marlborough Downs, is built. Ambrosius, the strongest chieftain apparently, is said by Gildas to have driven the Saxons back to the Isle of Thanet.

In India the Gupta kingdom falls to the White Huns (see 425 B). The last certain date for a Gupta king is 467.

F.   **Births and Deaths** (continued)

453   Attila d. (47c).

454   Aëtius d.

455   Theodoric the Gt. b. (–526).
      Valentinian III d.

457   Marcian Emperor d.

459   St Simeon Stylites d. (69)

461   St Patrick d. (76).
      Pope St Leo I d.

466   Clovis b. (–511).

471   Aspar (Alan) d.

472   Ricimer (Goth) d.

474   Leo I, Emperor, d.

475   Boëthius b. (–524).

476   Further Germanic tribes invade Italy; and in Rome Romulus Augustulus resigns his throne to their general, Odoacer. Odoacer agrees to become King of Italy whilst Zeno of Constantinople becomes Emperor of the re-combined Roman empires of East and West: the last person therefore who can fairly be called Emperor of Rome has come and gone.

477   Aelle lands with his three sons, probably near Pevensey, and founds the Saxon settlement of Sussex.

479   A revolt against Zeno in Constantinople is put down.

480   Julius Nepos, the ex-Emperor of the West, is assassinated.

481   Clovis becomes king of the Franks, at the age of 15.

483   Zeno invites Theodoric the Great of the Ostrogoths (see 475) to Constantinople and makes much of him.

484   King Balas of Persia is forced to pay tribute to the Ephthalites (see 425) who have formed a kingdom between the Caspian and the Indus with its capital at Gurgan.

486   Clovis defeats a Roman army at Soissons and begins to extend his Frankish kingdom (centred on modern Belgium).

488   Theodoric the Great, with the Emperor Zeno's blessing, advances over the Alps to win back Italy from Odoacer.

488   Hengist dies, having founded a Saxon kingdom in Kent.

489   Theodoric defeats Odoacer and takes Milan.

490   Odoacer retires into Ravenna.

491   Zeno dies after a troubled reign, and is followed by Anastasius, a man of ability and courage but already 61 years of age.

491   Aelle (see 477) storms and captures the fortress of Anderida.

493   Theodoric, after five years war, invites Odoacer and his son to a peace treaty and feast at Ravenna, and assassinates them. He extends his realm to the western Balkans and to Sicily and settles down as a king with nominal subordination to Constantinople. Cassiodorus, the historian, becomes his secretary (probably at a fairly early age, his date of birth being unknown).

495   A Saxon chief, Cerdic, lands in Dorset.

500   Clovis wins a battle over the Burgundians.

———————

During this period (and to an extent on each side of it) Celtic inhabitants of England migrate to Armorica (Brittany).

A. Politics, Law and Economics

493 Theodoric the Great, ruling from Ravenna as king of Italy, observes the Roman laws and institutions and is respectful to the Senate at Rome. He allots two-thirds of the land to the Romans and one third to the Goths. He redrains the Pontine Marshes; he issues an edict controlling prices and brings down the cost of food.

At about the same time Anastasius, Emperor at Constantinople, improves the eastern empire's finances and economy.

B. Science and Discovery

480 Constantinople suffers from earthquake, extending, it is said, over 40 days.

C. Religion and Philosophy

476 St Brigid of Ireland becomes a nun and begins her career of Christian education.

482 The Emperor Zeno causes a schism between the Churches of Rome and Constantinople by issuing a letter to bishops called his *Henoticon* or Union Scheme.

483 The Nestorian Christians, persecuted by Zeno, move into Persia, where they find tolerance and flourish (see 451 C).

490 In Persia a priest named Mazduk preaches a form of communism and is favoured by the King.

493 Clovis, married to a Christian, is baptized.

494/7 St Benedict, having come to Rome to study, leaves to live for three years as an anchorite.

495 Synods at Seleucia and elsewhere favour the marriage of Christian priests.

499 The Babylonian version of the Jewish Talmud (i.e. the "Study" of the Torah or Law, see 70 C) is completed, the other version, the Palestinian, being probably completed a hundred years or more earlier).

D. The Arts

493 Theodoric builds himself a modest palace at Ravenna and also two churches, He helps to preserve, and increase, the architectural splendour of other Italian cities.

500 On the re-occupied hill fort at South Cadbury in Somerset is built a large wooden hall, owned by a man rich and important enough to be able to import wine-jars from the continent: he could have been Arthur.

E. Literature

500 Böethius studies the Greek classics in Athens prior to making Latin translations of them.

To about this time may be attributed the books *On the Celestial Hierarchy* etc, seeking to reconcile Neo-Platonism and Christianity and attributed by medieval writers to "Dionysius the Areopagite".

500 At about this time "Arturus, Dux Bellorum" has taken up the struggle against the Saxons. In 12 battles he subdues the Saxons, the last battle being at Mons Badonicus (site unknown). This is the legendary King Arthur, probably not a king but a "war leader", a Christian Romano-Briton, who sees his chance to defeat the Saxons with a mobile field army of armoured cavalrymen, such army being at the service of the British chieftains. (And see D. The authenticity and provenance of Arthur are ever in dispute, but not his date.)

By the end of this century the Japanese have coalesced into one nation and culture.

F. **Births and Deaths**

477   Genseric d.

480   Julius Nepos d.

480   Cassiodorus b. (–568c).
       St Benedict b. (–547).

482   Justinian, emperor, b. (–565).

488   Hengist d.

490   Procopius, historian, b. (–570).

491   Zeno d.

493   Odoacer d.

501   The century begins in Constantinople with one of the many outbreaks of violence that are caused by the enmity of the circus factions, the Greens and the Blues each backing their favourite chariot drivers. On this occasion 3000 are said to have died.

502/6   The Emperor at Constantinople, Anastasius, having met trouble in both Egypt and Thrace, finds himself at war once again in Armenia with a revived Persia, After an inconclusive struggle a seven year peace is signed.

507/10   The Visigoth Alaric II is defeated and killed by Clovis at the battle of Vouglé, near Poitiers. Clovis puts an end to the old division between the Ripuarian and Sallic Franks, and moves his capital to Paris: Gaul may be said to have become France. Clovis is made a Roman consul and patrician by the Emperor Anastasius.

511   Clovis dies and leaves his Frankish kingdom to his four sons, who proceed to expand it.

515   There is a break through of Huns at the Caspian Gate into Cappadocia.

518   At Constantinople Anastasius is succeeded by a Senator, Justin, already old, who leaves the management of affairs to his nephew Justinian. Both uncle and nephew are of Illyrian stock.

521   The consulship of Justinian is observed with great pomp.

522   Boethius, serving Theodoric the Great, becomes finally his chief minister.

523   Theodoric, ageing and suspicious, hears of a senatorial conspiracy to depose him. Boethius is among three suspected and is imprisoned.

524   Boethius is executed.
       In England, after Arthur's successes, the aggressiveness of the Saxons collapses and changes to peaceful settlement.

A. Politics, Law and Economics

At the beginning of this century Constantinople is using Egypt as a granary to the extent of some 175,000 tons of wheat a year.

501   The Emperor Anastasius builds further fortifications around Constantinople, restores its finances, and puts a stop to its shows of wild beasts versus men.

During this period the Salic laws of the Franks are formulated, written it is said by "four venerable chieftains". The most important law is: "Of Salic land no portion of the inheritance shall go to a woman." The law of ordeal is still favoured: it is upheld by a Burgundian king, Gundobad, in the phrase, "Is it not true that the issue of wars and combats is directed by the judgement of God?"

B. Science and Discovery

516   The Indian astronomer and mathematician, Aryabhata, *fl.* He writes, in verse, on eclipses, quadratic equations, and the value of π.

525   A year of earthquakes in Asia Minor and Syria.

C. Religion and Philosophy

511   After the death of Clovis I in this year, his widow, who has helped to make the Christianity of the Franks orthodox and not Arian, retires to Tours, to serve in the church of St Martin.

518   Justinian, as Regent, revokes the *Henaticon* of Zeno (see 482 C), winning the support of the orthodox in Rome but not of the Monophysites in the East.

523   Justinian banishes all Manicheans from the Empire and denies civil or military office to all pagans and heretics.

Theodoric in Rome makes a present of silver chandeliers to the Pope. More tolerant than Justinian, he protects the Jews against the destroyers of their synagogues.

E. Literature

518   Justinian is favoured by his uncle Justin, the Emperor, because he can read and write whereas Justin cannot.

523   Boethius writes his *De Consolatione Philosophae*; also the shorter *De Musica*.

F. Births and Deaths

505   Belisarius b. (−565).

508   Theodora, wife of Justinian b. (−548c).

511   Clovis I d. (45).

516   Gildas b. (−570c).

518   Anastasius d.

F. **Births and Deaths** (continued)
521   St Columba b. (–599c).

524   Boethius d. (49c).

525   St Brigid d.
      Alexander of Tralles b. (–605c).

526   Theodoric the Great dies and is succeeded by his ten year old grandson Athalaric, with the boy's mother the real ruler.

In Constantinople Belisarius, with the historian Procopius as his secretary, is given by Justin his first task in combatting the renewed aggression of Persia.

527   Justin dies and his nephew Justinian succeeds as emperor. Justinian, who has married the actress Theodora, declares her Empress—which role she fills with greatness.

528   The White Hun king Mihirakula (sometimes called the Atilla of India) is deposed and the Hunnish invasion of India (which never produces a kingdom) begins to lose its force.

530   Belisarius wins a victory over the Persians at Dara or Darasin in N. Mesopotamia.

531   The greatest of the Sassanid kings, Chosroes or Khosru I comes to the Persian throne. Belisarius is recalled to Constantinople.

532   Justinian in an effort to put down the disorders consequent upon the Green and Blue factions (see 501) meets serious rebellion (the Nika rebellion). With the help of Belisarius and much slaughter it is put down.

Justinian patches up an expensive peace with Persia and plans to send Belisarius on the first campaign to fulfil his own great ambition of re-unifying the Roman Empire.

533   (June) Belisarius with his wife to support him and his secretary Procopius to write of his victories, sets sail to win back Vandal Africa to the Empire.

533/4   Belisarius takes Carthage easily, is recalled prematurely by Justinian, but returns and saves Carthage from the Moors: N. Africa remains Byzantine until the Moslems come.

534   Athalaric, young king of the Ostrogoths (see 526 above) dies: this Gothic kingdom is now waning.

535   Justinian, making himself safe from the Franks by an alliance, sets out on the recovery of Gothic Italy to the Empire. Belisarius captures Sicily.

536/40   Belisarius captures Naples and enters Rome unopposed. Witigis, new king of the Ostrogoths, besieges Belisarius in Rome but gives up after a year. Belisarius in turn besieges Ravenna, which finally capitulates.

539   King Chosroes of Persia declares war on Justinian.

540   Belisarius returns in triumph to Constantinople and earns Justinian's jealousy.

541   Chosroes retires, having despoiled Antioch and bathed in the Mediterranean.

542/3   Chosroes makes another raid into Roman Asia: Justinian buys him off with gold and negotiates a five years peace, extended for another 5 years.

543/6   Yet another Gothic king, Totila, is successful in Italy and, in spite of Belisarius' return, captures Rome, but spares the city. Totila moves to Ravenna and Belisarius retakes Rome.

548/9   Belisarius is recalled and Totila recaptures most of Italy.

550   The eunuch general Narses is sent, in place of Belisarius, to combat Totila.

A. Politics, Law and Economics

At this time Syria is experiencing a renaissance of learning, with schools of rhetoric and law, etc, at Antioch, Edessa, Beirut and Nisibis.

528 Justinian begins his codification of Roman law. He appoints a panel of ten jurists to systematize, reform and clarify the law, the chief protagonist being Tribonian.

529 The first *Codex Constitutionum* is issued.

531 King Chosroes I of Persia reorganizes his government and laws and taxes, much as Justinian does. He creates a standing army and improves his roads.

533 The *Digesta* or *Pandecta* (of Case Law) is issued; at the same time a handbook or guide to the Codex is issued, the *Institutionis*.

534 A revised *Codex* supplants the earlier one. (And see C.)

542/3 The Empire is scourged by Plague, a cause of one of Justinian's economic difficulties, shortage of man-power. Another difficulty is shortage of cash, leading to tax exactions, directed by his hated finance minister, John of Cappadocia. Wages and price regulations are attempted; trade with India is encouraged; new harbours are built on the Black Sea.

542/8 The Empress Theodora in her last years becomes an upholder of public morals, building a Convent of Repentance for fallen women.

B. Science and Discovery

545 The Indian astronomer Vahahamihira *fl.* He writes *Tne Complete System of Natural Astrology*.

547 Cosmas Indicopleustes, a flat-earth geographer, produces *Topographia Christiana*, a good example of an early illuminated manuscript.

550 Probably in this century the Chinese invent gunpowder—to use in fireworks. They also produce a treatise on animal husbandry, (which survives into the 11th century) and begin the practice of ecological control (of crops by means of insect culture).

C. Religion and Philosophy

527 The use of the chronological notation "A.D." is introduced by the monk Dionysius Exiguus.

529 St Benedict ends his career as an anchorite, owing to the jealousy of local priests, and founds his monastery of Monte Cassino.
Justinian finally closes the great Platonic Academy of Athens—see 385 B.C. C. Some professors move to a Persian university founded by Chosroes I (see 531).

530 The Alexandrian philosopher John Philoponos *fl.* He is converted to an active Christianity and wars against all forms of paganism (gaining his name of "trouble-lover"). He denies Aristotle's theory of motion.

C. Religion and Philosophy (continued)

531 King Chosroes I of Persia on his accession gathers round him scholars from India and Greece; he tolerates Christianity.

534 The Justinian *Codex* of Laws shows great influence from orthodox christianity; beginning by declaring for the Trinity, it establishes the emperor's dominion over the Church.

540/8 Theodora in her late years challenges her husband's religious orthodoxy and favours the Monophysites and the Eastern Church rather than the Western.

547 Justinian, a keen theologian and anxious to re-unite the Eastern and Western Churches, issues his tract known as the *Three Chapters*; he endeavours to make the Pope subscribe to it.

549 The Buddhist emperor of S. China, Kiang Wu Ti, has created a centre of culture at Nanking, which is destroyed at this date by a rebel invader.

D. The Arts

531/7 The great church of St Sophia is rebuilt in Constantinople. A dome has by now become a favourite architectural feature.

547 After Belisarius' capture of Ravenna the city is rebuilt and beautified. By this year the church of San Vitale is completed — later to inspire Charlemagne to copy it. Its mosaics reach to a height of genuine, though styled, portraiture, including likenesses of Justinian and Theodora.

550 The Mayan "classic" culture (see 325) produces magnificent buildings at Tikal, some 190 miles N. of Guatemala City.

E. Literature

526 Priscian, a professor at Constantinople University, compiles a Latin and Greek Grammar.

533 Procopius, in writing of his master's taking of Carthage describes the Vandals' African empire as thoroughly Romanized but rather effete.

537 Procopius enthuses over the dome of S. Sophia, whilst Justinian praises God that he has been able to outdo Solomon.

540 Cassiodorus (see 497 E) retires at last from public service to the Goths. He founds two monasteries in Calabria and lives there until the age of about 93 — he writes a *History of the Goths*, which is extant only in the shape of an epitome.

546 Gildas, a monk of Wales, writes *On the Destruction of Britain*, which mentions Arthur's battle of Mons Badonicus (see 500).

550 Agathias of Constantinople, writes a poem on the theme "leave but a kiss within the cup!".

F   **Births and Deaths**
526   Theodoric the Great d. (71).
       Sidonius d. (94).

527   Justin, Emperor, d.

538   Gregory of Tours b. (–594).

540   St Gregory the Gt. b. (–604).

543   St Columban b. (–614).

548   Theodora d. (40c).

551/3 Narses (successor to Belisarius) successfully ends Justinian's Gothic war, Totila being defeated and killed and the Goths expelled from Italy. Narses has used Lombard mercenaries.

556/8 Famine and plague come to Constantinople. Justinian is relaxing his hold on government and turning to theology.

558 The Avars, of Turkish origin, serve in Justinian's armies.

559 Another barbarian tribe, the Bulgars, having crossed the Danube (into modern Bulgaria) advance towards Constantinople. Justinian recalls the aged Belisarius from retirement and Belisarius, with a very small force, brilliantly saves the city.

561 The surviving son of the Frankish king Clovis, Chlotar I, has amassed a very considerable kingdom, which includes Burgundy, Provence and Swabia. He divides it into Austrasia (the Rhineland), Neustria (W. France) and Burgundy, and bequeathes a part to each of his three sons.

562 After further fighting Chosroes and Justinian at last sign a 50 year peace agreement: Chosroes, for 30,000 pieces of gold a year, renounces claims around the Black Sea and the Caucasus.

563 Belisarius is imprisoned by the ageing and suspicious Justinian on a charge of conspiracy, but is released after 6 months.

564 King Athanagild has established a strong Visigothic kingdom in Spain with its capital at Toledo.

565 Belisarius dies and Justinian confiscates half his property—and then himself dies, 8 months later (in November). Justin II, nephew, succeeds.

566 Sigebert, Frankish king of Austrasia, marries the Visigoth princess Brunhilda, daughter of Athanagild.

567 Chilperic, Frankish King of Neustria, follows his brother's example, but has his Gothic wife strangled. Sigebert declares war on Chilperic but is murdered; Brunhilda rules in her young son's name.

568 Lombards (see 551), pressed from behind by Avars (see below) and to the numbers of some 130,000, cross the Alps into the plains of the River Po, a land which will come to be called Lombardy. With Justinian and Belisarius dead and Narses deposed and disgraced, there is no one to stop them. Refugees flee, to join the earlier refugees from Aquileia (see 452); and the city of Venice is founded.

570 Chosroes I expels Abyssinians from Arabia.

572 Justin II renews war with Persia.

573 The Lombards having taken Verona, Milan and Florence, the Byzantine rule of Italy, achieved by Justinian, is ended almost as soon as it is begun.

A. Politics, Law and Economics

552 Justinian imports silkworms from the East: a silk industry begins to flourish in Syria and the Peloponnese (the latter coming to be known as Morea after the mulberry tree).

553 By the end of the Gothic war (see 551) Italy is economically ruined. Rome's population has dwindled to about 40,000 and with its aristocracy so depleted that the Senate peters out and is heard of no more. (And see D.)

570 Justin II endeavours to keep up to date the laws of Justinian by more *novellae*.

B. Science and Discovery

565 Alexander of Tralles, physician, *fl.* He writes a medical textbook that is later translated into Latin and Arabic and has a lasting influence.

C. Religion and Philosophy

550 A drift of monks and hermits seeking peace reaches Ireland in this year, a boatload landing at Cork.

552 Buddhism is introduced into Japan and gradually becomes the official religion.

553 Justinian calls an ecumenical council at Constantinople; few western bishops attend however and the schism between the E. and W. Churches is resumed.

563 St Columba flees from Ireland where his hot temper has got him into trouble and founds a monastery on the Hebridean island of Iona, whence he sends out missionaries to mainland Britain.

570 Mohammed is born in Mecca, a member of the Hashimite faction of the ruling merchant family, the Quraish.

575 St Columban (not to be confused with St Columba) leads a band of monks from Bangor to the Continent and founds a strict order at Luxeuil.
St Gregory the Gt. enters a monastery.

D. The Arts

553 The decay of Italy's aqueducts after the Gothic wars causes equally the decay of her splendid baths; also many statues have been melted down for war purposes.

564 The Visigoth kings (see opposite) build fine churches and palaces in Toledo—which however the Moslems later destroy, leaving only a description of them.

E. Literature

In the latter part of the 6th century the pre-Moslem Arabs, proud of their language, hold contests for their poets at the yearly Ukaz fair. The winning entries are written down in gold and silk and hung up in the mosque at Mecca—hence their name, "suspended" or *Muallaquat*.

573/5   King Chosroes I of Persia, old but taking the field in person, wins some success against Constantinople.

574   The Emperor Justin II, who is lapsing into insanity, appoints one Tiberius, head of the Palace Guard, as "Caesar".

In this period the Avars enter history, moving through S. Russia, enslaving the Slavs (see 401), raiding as far as the Elbe, driving the Lombards into Italy (see 568), and finally pouring down into the Balkans.

E. **Literature** (continued)

551 The Gothic historian Joruandes or Jordanes writes his summary of Roman history, the *Getica*, partly an epitome of Cassiodorus' book (see 568 below).

563 The founding of the monastery at Iona brings the art of book copying and illustration, practised by the Irish monks, to Britain: it thrives both at Ioan and Lindisfarne.

565 Venatius Fortunatus, poet, *fl*. He leaves Ravenna for the Frankish court, becomes a bishop and writes hymns.
Procopius' *Secret Histories*, attacking Justinian, are published about now, i.e. after Justinian's death.

568 The statesman and historian Cassiodorus dies, leaving his history of the Goths, *De Rebus Geticis*.

F. **Births and Deaths**

553 Totila, the Goth d.

561 Chlotar I (Frankish king) d.

565 Belisarius d.
Justinian d.

567 Sigebert, Frankish king, d.

568 Cassiodorus d. (88*c*).

570 Procopius d. (80).
Gildas d. (54*c*).

570 Mohammed b. (–632).

577 The Saxons in Britain, gradually gaining the upper hand since the victories of Arthur (see 500), win the battle of Deorham and become virtual masters of England (and see below).

578 The imperial forces under their general, Maurice, inflict a defeat upon the ageing Chosroes I, who retires to Ctesiphon.
Tiberius (see 474) is appointed Emperor by Justin II before he dies. The policy of this Emperor is to concentrate on the East and against Persia and to let the West take its chance against the barbarians.

579/81 Maurice continues his successful campaign against Persia, which has now lost its great king, Chosroes I.

582 Tiberius dies, having appointed Maurice his heir.

584 Chilperic, the Frankish king (see 567) is murdered. Brunhilda is still in power.

589 China approaches unity again under the warlike Yang Chien of the short-lived Sui dynasty (and see 618).
Persian dynastic trouble relieves the pressure upon Constantinople. An usurping general, Bahram, declares himself regent for the infant king, a second Chosroes.

590/1 Bahram seizes the Persian throne. The young Chosroes flees to Syria and seeks Roman protection. The Emperor Maurice is able to put him firmly on the throne as Chosroes II and to make a favourable peace with him.

592 Shotoku (or Kotoku) becomes ruler of Buddhist Japan (and see A and D).

592/3 The Emperor Maurice is able to turn against the Avars who are spreading over the Balkans under their king Baian. They are driven back across the Danube.

594 Maurice's brother Peter, put in command, renews war with the Avars. This continues for the rest of the century.
Mohammed enters the service of the rich widow Khadija.

595 Mohammed marries Khadija (40 years old to his 25).

596 Pope St Gregory sends St Augustine and 40 monks to convert the kingdom of Kent to Christianity (and see C).

597 Maurice draws up a will appointing one son to rule at his father's death in Rome and the other in Constantinople.

598/600 Maurice is finding it difficult to recruit enough troops to fight the Avars, who make inroads south and are guilty of killing Roman hostages.

In this period the Anglo-Saxons form a heptarchy of kingdoms in S. and E. England: the Jutes in Kent, the Angles in Mercia, Northumbria and East Anglia, and the Saxons in Essex, Sussex and Wessex.
A tide of Slavs (see 426) sweeps down through the Balkans into the Greek countryside (but not into the cities). (And see 640 C.)

A. Politics, Law and Economics

592 Shotoku (sometimes called the Asoka of Japan) gives his country a written constitution and decrees based on Buddhist ethics.

579 Chosroes I at his death leaves a strong Persia with a sound administration (which the Moslems will take over with little change).

594 The Emperor Maurice attempts to reduce his soldiers' pay, but desists on causing a mutiny.

594 The long period of a population-reducing Plague ends in Rome.

598 Canterbury's first school is believed to have been founded.

B. Science and Discovery

Towards the end of this century comes the use by Hindu mathematicians of a number-system with *place* notations and the use of the symbol *zero*. This makes addition etc on paper an infinitely easier matter than with Greek or Roman numerals—it democratizes arithmetic as iron had democratized warfare. (And see 662 B.)

594 St Gregory of Tours (see E) asserts that he has little faith in medicine but prefers the powers of religion and miracles.

C. Religion and Philosophy

589 King Recared of Visigoth Spain changes his faith from Arian to orthodox Christianity and the Church in Spain grows in power. The position of Spanish Jews henceforth worsens.

590 St Gregory becomes Pope, the first monk to do so. He enforces the celibacy of the clergy. He uses church funds for charity rather than in building programmes.

597 St Augustine, coming unwillingly to Kent, fails to ally himself with the native, Welsh, Christians but is well received by King Ethelbert and his Christian (and Frankish) wife Bertha. He is allowed to proseletize. The king and his daughter are in due course baptized, but not his son. Augustine is made first bishop of Canterbury.

D. The Arts

580 A cave shrine of the Sui Dynasty shows sculpture of pronounced Hellenized Buddhist influence.

591 Pope Gregory, anxious to wean the Lombards from Arianism, crowns their king Agilulf and his wife—who build a cathedral at Monza, N. of Milan.

592 The ruler of Japan, Shotoku, encourages the arts and sciences and imports artists from Korea and China.

600 A magnificent specimen of book-making, a Gospel with gold and jewelled cover, is given by Gregory to a Lombard queen.

E. **Literature**

By the time of this last quarter of the 6th century the Visigoth rulers of Spain and the Frankish rulers of France, using Latin, have each created their own distinctive corruptions of the language.

594 St Gregory of Tours, dying in this year, leaves behind his *History of the Franks*, the chief source of knowledge of the Merovingian kings.

596 Pope Gregory's puns become famous: the slave boys are angels not Angles; their land of origin Deira (Yorkshire) must be saved from *Dei ira*.

597 St Columba in dying blesses Iona and prophesies "great and unusual honour" for it.

600 Bishop Isodore of Seville *fl*. He produces a kind of encyclopaedia which is not always accurate or scientific but which has much influence in the Middle Ages: *Twenty Books of Etymologies or Origins*.

F. **Births and Deaths**

578 Justin II d.

579 King Chosroes I of Persia d.

582 Tiberius I d.

584 Chilperic, Frankish king, d.

585 Edwin, king of Northumbria b. (–633).

594 St Gregory of Tours d. (56c).

597 St Columba d.

600 Emperor T'ai Tsung b. (–649).

602 Maurice's soldiers south of the Danube, alarmed at the prospect of wintering there,
revolt under their leader Phocas, an uneducated ex-centurion. They return to
Constantinople—where Maurice's cure for unrest, more Games, has the opposite
of the desired effect. The "Greens" ally with the mutineers, and Maurice is forced
to flee with his family across the Bosphorus to Chalcedon, appealing for aid from
the young Persian king, Chosroes II (see 590) whom he has helped. Phocas moves
too rapidly however and Maurice is murdered.

603 Chosroes II seeks revenge upon Phocas for the murder of Maurice and declares war
on him.

605 Phocas as Emperor sickens the Byzantines by his cruelty, torturing and murdering
Maurice's widow and children.

606 In northern India a king of the old Gupta line, Harsha, brings a return of prosperity
during his ensuing reign of 40 years (and see 629 A).

606/7 The Persians conquer Mesopotamia and advance westwards across the Euphrates.
The Avars seize much of the agricultural hinterland of Constantinople.

609 The Byzantines appeal for deliverance from Phocas to the military governor of Roman
Africa, by name Heraclius. The governor sends his son, also named Heraclius.

610 The young Heraclius displaces the usurper Phocas and reigns in his stead.

612 The Irish abbot Columban reproves the Frankish court for its bloody dynastic quarrels, and has to flee for his life.

614 Chosroes II (sometimes called Parvez, the Victorious) now declares holy war on the
Christians and (with many Jews in his army) sacks Jerusalem, capturing the True
Cross.
The Frankish queen-mother, Brunhilda, is at last put to death (very cruelly) and the
young Chlotar II reigns over a reunited (Merovingian) Frankish kingdom.

616/19 Chosroes II continues his victorious career, conquering Egypt and Asia Minor and
occupying both Alexandria and also Chalcedon across the Bosphorus from Constantinople. He despoils as he goes (weakening these lands before the Arab invasions
soon to come).

618 The Avars march up to the gates of Constantinople and take many prisoners as slaves.
Heraclius is only prevailed upon by the people and the clergy from transferring his
capital to Carthage.
Heraclius is nearly captured by the perfidy of Chagan, king of the Avars.

620 Heraclius makes peace with the Avars.

621 Heraclius prepares to beat off the great threat of the belligerent Persian king.

622 Mohammed's flight from Mecca to Medina (see C) precipitates a war between the two
cities and the development of the prophet as a military leader.

A. Politics, Law and Economics

618/22 Constantinople, cut off from its hinterland and also from Egypt, is nearly starving; she is saved from defeat by her navy. The Patriarch at Constantinople lends Heraclius the funds of the Church in order to encourage him to declare a holy war on the Persians—who have been demanding excessive tribute (including 1000 horses and 1000 virgins).

C. Religion and Philosophy

604 Ethelbert builds the first church of St Paul in London.

610 Mohammed receives his vision wherein Gabriel tells him he is the messenger of Allah.

610/22 Mohammed slowly builds up his following, including six "companions" of whom the chief is Abu Bekr; he experiences his vision of a visit to Jerusalem, which thus becomes a holy city for him.

613 St Columban, turned out of the Frankish kingdom, is welcomed into Lombardy,

622 Mohammed, on invitation, flees to Medina—the *Hegira*—and establishes himself there as religious and political leader. His faith becomes known as *Islam*, the "surrender" to Allah, and his followers *Muslimin*, "surrendering ones" or Moslems.

624 After Mohammed has raided a Meccan caravan, outright war begins between Mecca and Medina.
The Emperor Heraclius avenges the Persians' despoiling of Jerusalem (see 614) by destroying the birthplace of Zoroaster.

625 In Britain the Christian Ethelburga, sister of king Ethelbert of Kent, marries King Edwin of Northumbria and brings with her one of Augustine's priests, Paulinus.

D. The Arts

604 Pope Gregory has told the Christian world: "Painting can do for the illiterate what writing does for those who can read." He has also systematized and improved the Church's *plainsong*, to become known as the Gregorian Chant.

616 Shotoku of Japan causes the Buddhist temples at Horiuji to be built.

E. Literature

604 Pope Gregory leaves behind fourteen books of *Epistles* (known later to Bede and Boniface).

624 In Medina Mohammed does not scruple to have those who write verses against him assassinated.

F. Births and Deaths

601 Ali (Mohammed's future son-in-law)b. (–661).

622/5   Heraclius sets out on a brilliant campaign against the Persians, penetrating as far as Ispahan. Chosroes II has retired from active campaigning and his generals are much less successful.

      Mohammed, having fled with his followers from Mecca to Medina (see C), sets in train the struggle between the two cities.

---

618   China, fertilized by Hunnish blood (see 311) and Buddhist ideas (see 549 C), begins a new era of greatness under its T'ang Dynasty at the capital city of Ch'ang-an.

F. **Births and Deaths** (continued)
602 Maurice, Emperor d.
      Theodore of Tarsus b. (–690).

604 Gregory the Gt. d.

605 Alexander of Tralles d. (80c).

610 Phocas d.

614 St Columban d. (73).
      Brunhilda d.

615 Agilulf, king of the Lombards, d.

616 Ethelbert, king of Kent, d.

624 Empress Wu b. (–705).

626   Medina (see 624 C) is unsuccessfully besieged by the Meccans. A truce between the two cities is arranged.

627   The Emperor Heraclius crowns his campaign against Chosroes and the Persians by a victory near to the ancient Nineveh.
The founder of China's T'ang Dynasty comes officially to the throne: the great T'ai Tsung.

628   Chosroes II is murdered by his son, and Heraclius makes an advantageous peace with the Persians (and see 630 C). This is the end of the greatness of the Sassanid dynasty, Persia now relapsing into a period of anarchy (aided by Plague).
The Merovingian king Chlotar II dies and is succeeded by Dagobert, who however finds that power is passing into the hands of the Mayor of the Palace, Pepin the Elder, the first of the Pepins who are later to found the Carolingian dynasty.

629/39   The warrior Srong-tsan establishes himself in Tibet, annexes Nepal and builds himself a capital at Lhasa. He reigns until about 650 and establishes the golden age of Tibet. (And see 639 C.)

630   Mohammed breaks the truce (see 626 above) and advances on Mecca—which he enters without opposition and makes his capital.

630   Edwin, King of Northumbria, builds himself a capital: Edinburgh.

632   Mohammed dies. His companion and disciple, Abu Bekr, is elected "Caliph" or Representative. Abu puts down incipient rebellion in Arabia with the aid of his general Khalid. A request by the Arabs in Syria for help against Byzantine persecution is responded to—and the era of Moslem conquest is, almost without intention, inaugurated.

633   Edwin, who has called himself Bretwalda, or Overlord, of Britain, is defeated and killed, at Hatfield Chase near Doncaster by the pagan king of Mercia, Penda, in alliance with the Welsh king, Cadwallon.
Khalid makes a profitable raid into Persian territory.

634   Khalid is called away from Persia to meet a Byzantine army under the Emperor Heraclius. Khalid crosses the desert and defeats Heraclius at a decisive engagement on the Yarmuk River near Damascus. The Byzantine name for the Moslems, the "Saracens", now comes into use.
The fierce and fanatical Omar succeeds Abu Bekr as Caliph.
The new king of Northumbria, Oswald, defeats the Welsh king, Cadwallon (and see 635 C).

635   The Saracens occupy Heliopolis and restore it to its original name of Baalbek.

637   The Persian general Rustam (presumably named after the mythical hero, father of Sohrab) is defeated, in a continuing campaign for the possession of Syria, at the battle of Kadisiya.

638   Jerusalem is captured by the Moslems (now to be called Saracens—see 634 above).

A. Politics, Law and Economics

628/35   China is visited by many missions: from Byzantium, from Mohammed, and from the Nestorian Christians of Persia. The Emperor T'ai Tsung codifies the law; he reintroduces the examination system and reissues the Chinese classics; he greatly increases his country's trade and prosperity.

629   Chinese traveller, by name Yuan Chwang, arrives at the Indian court of King Harsha (see 606) and reports on its prosperity and on the openhandedness of the king.

640/4   A wave of immigration into Syria and Persia follows Saracen conquest. At home the Saracens grow rich.

643   Rathari, Lombard king, issues a code of laws, a mixture of the primitive and the liberal: religious freedom of worship is accorded.

645   In its "great reform" Japan becomes a more closely knit state, with an autocratic monarchical government.

648   The Emperor T'ai Tsung sends a diplomatic mission to Tibet, accompanied by a Chinese princess.

B. Science and Discovery

634   The Moslem victories, beginning in this year, owe much to their skilful use of cavalry.

640   Brahmagupta, Indian astronomer and mathematician, *fl.*

650   Probably somewhere about this mid-century the Chinese invent the horse collar, enabling the animal to pull from the shoulders and not restrict its own wind-pipe.

C. Religion and Philosophy

627   Paulinus (see 625 C) converts to Christianity King Edwin of Northumbria.

628   In leading his exiled followers back to Mecca, Mohammed incorporates into his religion the ancient worship of the symbolic black stone, housed in the Kaaba, and makes Mecca into a holy city into which no unbeliever may enter.

630   The Emperor Heraclius journeys to Jerusalem to restore to that city the true cross which the Persians have surrendered.

633   Abu Bekr has Mohammed's revelations (which the prophet has been recording throughout his later life) made into the *Koran*.
In Visigoth Spain, a Council of Toledo rules that relapsed Christians shall be separated from their children and sold into slavery.
In N. Britain Christianity relapses temporarily as a result of Edwin's defeat (see A).

635   The new king of Northumbria, Oswald, invites Aidan, a monk of Iona, to preach Christianity in his kingdom. As a result the monastery at Lindisfarne is formed, a second Iona, and, in the North, Celtic Christianity replaces the Roman variant brought from Kent. (King Oswald is later made a saint, and on his death his head is kept as a relic.)

639　The Frankish king Dagobert dies, as does also his Mayor of the Palace, Pepin I or "the Elder". The power of these mayors continues to grow, whilst the nominal kings become insignificant and lazy, the so-called *rois fainéants*.

640　The Saracens, having subdued Persia and Syria, invade Egypt, the Monophysite Copts (see 451 C) having invited them.

641　The Emperor Heraclius dies, having prevented the Saracens from advancing beyond the Taurus Mts. He is followed, for a few months only, by Constantine III and then by Constans II.

642　After a reign of only 8 years the Christian King Oswald of Northumbria is defeated and killed by the pagan king Penda of Mercia. This battle, of Mansfield, marks the rise of Mercia at the expense of Northumbria.

644　The Caliph Omar is murdered by a Persian slave. He is succeeded by Othman, of the Umayyad clan, hostile to Mohammed in his lifetime: the result is internal dissension.

645　In Japan a palace revolution leads to political reform (see A).
　　　King Penda of Mercia conquers Wessex.

647　Alexandria finally falls to the Saracens.

648　The Chinese Emperor T'ai Tsung extends his empire as far as Bokhara and Samarkand.

649　He dies and is succeeded by Kao Tsung, who soon leaves his consort the Empress Wu, to direct affairs.

650　By the end of the half century, the conquering Saracen generals, under the Caliphate of Othman, have reached east to Kabul and north to the Black Sea.

———————

In China the T'ang rulers begin to change from a policy of war to one of diplomacy and peace.

In central India, in a shifting kaleidoscope of power, the Pallava kings achieve a temporary supremacy. Both here and in the north, after the demise of King Harsha, India is lapsing into a Dark Age—in which will slowly rise to power the warlike princes of Rajputana.

C. **Religion and Philosophy** (continued)

639 Srong-tsan (see 629), in founding Lhasa, invites Buddhist monks from India and is said to have retired from government for 4 years in order to learn to read and write. Lhasa becomes the great stronghold of Buddhism, and the building of monasteries in Tibet begins.

640 Slav tribes enter Pannonia and Illyria to become the Serbs and Croats and to adopt the Greek and Roman forms of Christianity respectively.

647 With Syria, Palestine and Egypt (all strongholds of various heresies) lost to the Byzantine Empire, the Eastern Church is free to become "Orthodox" and the heretics free from persecution.

648 The first church at Westminster is built.
The Emperor Constans II issues his model of faith, his "Type", and persecutes the Pope for not supporting him.

650 On the Saracens passing through Cappadocia the Christian inhabitants build underground cities (recently discovered, as at Kaymakli, S.E. of Ankara).

D. **The Arts**

627 T'ai Tsung of China spends great wealth in beautifying his capital Chang-an.

638 Omar chooses the site in Jerusalem for his mosque.

649 The Emperor T'ai Tsung has executed on his tomb, instead of the usual sculptured lion guardians, six spirited horses in bas relief.

E. **Literature**

642 The Library at Alexandria is destroyed at the command of the Caliph Omar.

648 The traveller Yuan Chwang returns to China and translates his Indian manuscripts.

650 The Anglo-Saxon epic poem about the dragon-slaying hero Beowulf is written, presumably in England.
Caedmon, a monk of Whitby, turns the Bible stories into verse.

F. **Births and Deaths**

628 Chosroes II d.
Chlotar II d.

632 Mohammed d. (62).

633 Edwin d. (48).

634 Abu Bekr d.

635 St Cuthbert b. (–687).

639 King Dagobert and Pepin the Elder d.

F.   **Births and Deaths** (continued)

641   Heraclius, emperor, d.

642   Oswald of Northumbria d.

644   Paulinus d.
Omar d.

649   Emperor T'ai Tsung d. (49).

650   St Aidan d.

651 King Penda of Mercia invades Northumbria, but retires after an abortive attempt to burn Bamborough. Northumbria, though unconquered by Mercia, retires from the race for political supremacy, which Mercia will later win.

653 Rhodes is taken by the Saracens (and see D).

654 There arises in Persia a movement supporting Mohammed's son-in-law, the Hashimite Ali, as the only legitimate heir to the caliphate.

655 Penda of Mercia is defeated and killed at the battle of the river Winwaed, near Doncaster: this marks the final decline of paganism in England.

656 The pro-Ali movement flourishes in Egypt—whence fanatics penetrate to Othman's palace and murder him. Ali becomes Caliph.
Myawiya, of the Umayyad clan (see 644) revolts. Ali, supported by the Arabs of Kufa (near ancient Babylon) meets Muawiya at Khoraiba in S. Iraq and temporarily defeats him. (Mohammed's widow Aisha is present on Ali's side and commands her contingent of troops from camel-back; the fight is called the Battle of the Camels.)

656 King Ethelhere of E. Anglia, having relapsed into paganism, is killed in battle, probably drowned and his body lost (see 660 C).

657 Muawiya renews the struggle for the caliphate. Ali is prevented from winning a battle by his enemy's appeal, under the Koran, for arbitration.

661 A fanatical sect, the *Khariji* or Seceders, breaks away from Ali, and finally murders him. Ali's son Hasan submits to Muawiya, who becomes Caliph, forming the Umayyad dynasty and making Damascus his capital.

663 Constans II pays a visit to Rome, the first emperor to be in the capital for 190 years.

667 The Saracens conquer Numidia and advance into Mauretania.

668 Constans II, despairing of saving the East, tries to expel the Lombards from S. Italy and to make this country and Sicily a bastion against the Saracens. In this year, in Sicily, he is murdered. His son Constantine IV succeeds him.

669 The Saracens take Syracuse. They make an abortive naval attack on Constantinople.

671 King Grimoald of the Lombards dies, having extended his kingdom in Italy and defied both the Emperor and the interfering Franks.

673 The Saracens renew their naval attacks on Constantinople, which they make yearly for five years; the Byzantines under Constantine IV however successfully fend them off (see B).

675 Muawiya, hoping to make the Caliphate hereditary, appoints his son Yezid his successor. A first and abortive Saracen attack on Spain is made.

A. Politics, Law and Economics

661   The first Umayyad Caliph, Muawiya, consolidates Saracen conquests and achieves a period of prosperity and cessation of internal strife. Trade increases under Saracen rule, that between East and West growing greater than at any time in the Roman Empire. From this expansion comes knowledge to the West of the manufacture of paper and porcelain and the secret of making steel blades.

664   The decision in favour of Roman Christianity at Whitby (see C) signifies also a movement in Britain away from tribalism and towards racial unity, feudal power and better administration and legislation.

673   Archbishop Theodore (see 669 C) imposes a stricter discipline on English monasteries and also on English husbands—who henceforth cannot divorce their wives so easily as in ancient Saxon days. A church hierarchy begins to appear in Britain.

B. Science and Discovery

662   Severus Sebockt, a Monophysite bishop of Syria, makes the first mention in the West of the Hindu "place notation" of numbers (see 576 B) known as the "Arabic" system.

673   "Greek Fire", a mixture of naphtha, quicklime, sulphur and pitch and said to have been invented by a Syrian named Callinicus, is used most effectively in the defence of Constantinople against the naval attacks of the Saracens.

C. Religion and Philosophy

651   A revised edition of the Koran is produced.
St Cuthbert, a shepherd, has a vision of St Aidan being borne to Heaven; he enters the monastery of Melrose.

660   A pagan king's memory (the body being absent) is afforded a spectacular ceremonial funeral, the king's boat and treasure being buried. The place is Sutton Hoo in Suffolk and the king is almost certainly Ethelhere (see 656 and 660 D).

661   The Moslem *Shia* sect is formed on the death of Ali (see opposite).
St Cuthbert moves to Lindisfarne.

664   King Oswy of Northumbria calls the Synod of Whitby, to decide ostensibly on the date for observing Easter but in reality on whether the Roman or the Celtic Church shall be supreme in Britain. The decision is for Rome (and see A).

665   The Northumbrian nobleman Wilfrid, champion of the Roman Church at Whitby, is consecrated bishop at York.

669   Britain benefits from the aegis of the Roman Church by having the Greek scholar Theodore of Tarsus appointed Archbishop of Canterbury. St Chad, a disciple of Aidan, becomes bishop at Lichfield (and see 785 C).

D. The Arts

653   The Saracens break down and take away what is left of the Colossus of Rhodes.

D. **The Arts** (continued)

660 The Sutton Hoo ship burial (see C) comprises much fine jewelry, mostly of Saxon origin and including a sceptre in the shape of a whetstone, but also a purse filled with gold coins coming from various mints in France, and a silver dish from Constantinople.

661 The Caliph Muawiya makes his court and capital at Damascus a centre of splendour in the Byzantine style.

G. **Literature**

665 A story of St Cuthbert (who accepts the Whitby decision) is that on returning from having waded out to sea to pray he has two sea otters coiled around his feet to keep them warm—a story much in line with the old Celtic tradition.

669 The Northumbrian Benedict Biscop, with the encouragement of the Archbishop Theodore, collects books from Rome and sets up a library at his monastery at Wearmouth and later at Jarrow.

F. **Births and Deaths**

651 St Aidan d.

655 Penda d.

656 The Caliph Othman d.

656 Ethelhere of E. Anglia d.

661 Ali d. (65).

668 Constans II d.

671 Grimoald (Lombard) d.

672 St Chad d.

673 Bede b. (–735).

677   Constantine IV (see 668), having successfully kept the Saracens out of his capital, makes an advantageous peace with them.

678   The Bulgars establish themselves in the N. of Thrace.

679   Theodore (see 678 C) interferes in the recurring wars between Mercia and Northumbria. The Mercian king wins a battle on the river Trent, but is dissuaded from invading his rival's territory. The ensuing peace agreement is in Mercia's favour, and is followed by the kingdom of Kent recognizing Mercian overlordship.

680   The Caliph Muawiya dies, and in spite of efforts in his lifetime (see 675) a war of succession breaks out amongst the Saracens again. Another son of Ali, Husein, responds to an appeal to regain the leadership but is defeated and killed at Kerbela.

683   On the death of Kao Tsung the Empress Wu openly assumes sovereignty in China.

683/5   The death of the Umayyad Yezid (see 675) results in two years' anarchy, ending in the comparatively mild and efficient reign of Abd-el-Malik.

684   The pagan king of Wessex, Caedwalla, embarks on a bloodthirsty career of conquest.

685   The Emperor Constantine IV dies of dysentry and is succeeded by his son, aged 16, Justinian II. Peace is renewed with the Saracens.

687   The second of the Frankish mayoral dynasty of the Pepins, Pepin le Gros, defeats his rivals at the battle of Testry (or Tertry) and becomes virtual ruler of all the Frankish empire (except Aquitaine). He gives himself the title, Dux et Princeps Francorum.

688   Caedwalla, having died in Rome (see C), is succeeded, as king of a revivified and Christian Wessex, by Ine.

688/90   The Emperor Justinian II, taking advantage of internal quarrels amongst the Saracens, wrests Armenia from them and makes a further advantageous peace with them. He has however been less successful in a war with the Bulgarians—during which he has settled a large number of Slavs in the N.W. of Asia Minor under the title of "The Abundant People".

691/3   Justinian picks a quarrel with the Saracens over Cyprus (removing many Cypriots to the Hellespont in continuance of his population-shifting policy), and, collecting an army largely composed of Slavs, advances to meet the Saracens. He loses the battle of Sebastopol, partly owing to the defection of the Slavs, on whom he takes vengeance in a massacre.

694/5   The Saracens are victorious in Armenia and Syria.

695   Leontius, a Byzantine general imprisoned for his failure in Armenia, is released by Justinian and given a fresh command. Leontius takes the opportunity to rebel, seizes the Emperor and, having cut off his nose, sends him into banishment and is himself crowned Emperor.

A. Politics, Law and Economics

680   The 6th Ecumenical Council (see C), seeking theological harmony, is also made aware that the Byzantine Church's rule is shrinking: the patriarchates of Antioch, Jerusalem and Alexandria can no longer be considered part of its world.

688   The Christian pilgrimage of the Wessex king to Rome (see C) illustrates the growing power of the clergy in Britain: virtually they alone can write (and can suggest wills made in the Church's favour); the bishop sits beside the sheriff in the lawcourts.

690   The laws of King Ine of Wessex are put into writing by the clergy. The fact that the area, which includes Dorset and Somerset, still contains many Celts is shown by a reference to a separate class called Welshmen. The Anglo-Saxon laws are still primitive, e.g. in regarding murder a personal matter and deserving only of a fine: 'If one man slay another, 100 shillings wergeld."

B. Science and Discovery

678   A comet is recorded at Constantinople as visible from August to October.

C. Religion and Philosophy

678/9   Archbishop Theodore, in his task of reorganizing the bishoprics in Britain, quarrels with Wilfred (see 655 C) who retires to the Continent, helps to convert the Frisians to Christianity, and then puts his case before the Pope and wins it.

680   The 6th Ecumenical Council is convened at Constantinople.
Theodore seals Church unity in England at the synod at Heathfield (declaring orthodoxy on the *Monothelete* question, an offshoot of Monophytism).
The Shia Moslems build a shrine at Kerbela where Husein has fallen (see opposite).
Bede comes under the tutelage of Benedict Biscop.

683   In the Saracen civil wars the Kaaba (see 628 C) is destroyed.

684   St Cuthbert leaves his hermit life on Farne Is. to become bishop of Hexham. After two years however he is back in his hermit's cell.

687   Pepin II protects the Christian missionaries in Frisia.

688   Caedwalla (see 684) having overrun Sussex, suddenly repents of his bloodthirstiness, makes a pilgrimage to Rome, is baptized by the Pope, and dies.

690   Willibrord, a Northumbrian monk educated in Ireland, travels to Utrecht with twelve disciples to convert the Frisians. He has the blessing of the Franks; but a Frisian king declines baptism when he learns that his ancestors are likely to be in Hell.

691   At another synod at Constantinople an abortive effort is made to agree upon Church laws or canons for East and West.

694   There is reference in China to Manicheism having arrived.

697/8 Leontius sends a fleet to recover Carthage and Roman Africa from the Saracens. After initial successes the sailors return for reinforcements, and on the way home, at Crete, mutiny and proclaim their admiral emperor. Proceeding to Constantinople (suffering from Plague) they in turn deprive Leontius of his nose, send him to a monastery, and set their admiral on the throne as Tiberius II. Carthage becomes Saracen.

699/700 Tiberius continues the war against the Saracens, restrengthens Constantinople's sea defences, and restores displaced Cypriots to their island.

D. **The Arts**

By the end of this century the Moslems are writing *mensurable* music; i.e. the notes show duration as well as pitch.

691   Caliph Abd-el-Malik (see 683) lavishes his revenues from Egypt on buildings in Jerusalem: the "Farther" Mosque and the Dome of the Rock (known later as the Mosque of Omar).

700   Wu Tao-tzŭ, most famous painter of the T'ang period, *fl.*

E. **Literature**

680   Adamnan, a successor to St Columba at Iona, writes the latter's *Life*.

682   Benedict Biscop (see 669 E) founds a monastery at Jarrow and stocks it well with books.

699   Arabic replaces Greek as the language of administration in Damascus.

F. **Births and Deaths**

680   Caliph Miawiya d.
Husein d.
St Boniface b. (–755).

680   Caedmon d.
Leo III Emperor b. (–741).

683   Yezid d. Kao Tsung d.

685   Constantine IV d.

687   St Cuthbert d. (52c).

688   Caedwalla, Wessex d.

689   Charles Martel b. (–741).

690   Theodore of Tarsus d. (88).

701/3   Dynastic troubles in Lombardy.

704/5   Justinian II returns from exile to Constantinople and to power; he does so with the help of barbarians, firstly the Khan of the Khazars in the Crimea (whose daughter he marries and calls Theodora) and secondly King Terbel of the Bulgars, whom he sets beside him, temporarily, on the throne of the Caesars. Both Leontius and Tiberius (see 697) and most of their followers are massacred (except Tiberius' son, who becomes a bishop).

705   Walid I succeeds his father Abd-el-Malik as Caliph, continuing his efficient rule and extending the Saracen empire.
The Empress Wu of China is compelled to resign her powers; she dies in the same year.

706/7   The Saracens cross the Taurus Mts. into Asia Minor.

708   Justinian II suffers a defeat by the Bulgars.

708   The Saracen governor in Africa, Musa, pacifies the Berbers (or Moors).

709   Bokhara becomes Saracen.

710/11   Justinian II takes cruel vengeance upon the people of Chreson (whose treatment of him in exile he deprecates). He is, however, deserted by his army and fleet, and killed.

711   The Moors are encouraged by Musa (see 708 above) to invade Spain, though the initial move is taken by the Christian governor of Deuta, who has a quarrel with Roderick, the last Visigoth king of Spain. Led by the Moorish chief Tariq, the Moorish army lands near Gibraltar (the Mountain of Tariq) and at the battle of Lake Janda (July) decisively defeats Roderick, who is probably killed in the battle.

711/13   Justinian II is succeeded by a soldier, Vardan (or Bardanes), who becomes Emperor as Philippicus; he is more interested in Church affairs than State.

712   The Lombard king, Liutprand, comes to the throne and begins to consolidate the loose-knit kingdom.
The Saracen conquest of Spain is taken in hand; Musa, following Tariq in person, captures Seville, but dies a year later.

713   The Emperor Philippicus is deposed in favour of the chief imperial secretary, who becomes the next Emperor, a capable but short-lived one, as Anastasius II.

713   Hsuan Tsung comes to the Tang throne of China (and see D).

714   Pepin II dies, and his illegitimate son Charles Martel in the next 3 years makes himself undisputed ruler of the Frankish kingdom, uniting Neustria and Austrasia. He still, however, avoids the title of king.

715   Walid I dies and is succeeded by three unimportant Caliphs in rapid succession.

716   Ethelbald becomes king of Mercia, to increase its power and to reign for 41 years.

A. Politics, Law and Economics

705 The Caliph Walid builds schools, roads, and lazar houses for the poor and diseased, especially lepers; his governor in Mesopotamia, Hajjaj, restores irrigation.

712 Spain is dealt with leniently by the conquering Saracens: taxes are not increased and the land only of resisters is confiscated.

B. Science and Discovery

Bede, who is teaching and writing throughout this period, covers science as well as history – mathematics and chronology, and grammar.

706 A hospital, the Bimaristan, is founded in Damascus; it also becomes a medical school.

C. Religion and Philosophy

703 Bede is ordained a priest.

704 King Ethelred of Mercia abdicates to become a monk.

710 St Boniface (a Devonian) is ordained.

711 Justinian II meets the reigning Pope, kisses his feet, and makes some sort of agreement on the findings of the Synod of 691.

718 After an unsuccessful attempt and then a blessing from Pope Gregory II, St Boniface returns to evangelize the Germans.

723 St Boniface is made a bishop.

D. The Arts

706/14 Under the Caliph Walid the great mosque of Damascus is built, to outdo Christian monuments. Walid also enlarges and beautifies mosques at Jerusalem and Mecca and Medina; he is himself a musician of ability.

713 Hsuan Tsung (see opposite) inaugurates a 'second blossoming' of Tang culture. He encourages poets, artists, and scholars and establishes a college of music.

E. Literature

703 Bede intensifies his great effort towards scholarship in his long, quiet career at Jarrow monastery as a writer and historian.

705 The Japanese poet Tahito *fl.* He writes an ode in praise of drinking *sake*.

712 The *Kojiki* or 'Record of Ancient Things' is published in Japan – more legend than history.

720 A more accurate history of Japan, the *Nihongi* or 'Record of Nippon' is published.

716/17   Anastasius II, in an attempt at disciplining his army, is deposed. He is followed, unwillingly, by Theodosius III, who abdicates in the following year in favour of the general of the Asia Minor army and a saviour of the Empire, Leo the Isaurian or Leo III.

717/18   The Saracens make their last and supreme effort, by land and sea, to take Constantinople. The city's walls and defenders both hold out through a winter's siege and the Saracens retire.

718   In S.W. Spain resistance to the Saracens has continued, and the Goth, Pelaya, wins a battle at Covadonga and makes himself king of Asturias.

719   Duke Eudo (or Eudas) of Aquitaine acknowledges the sovereignty of Charles Martel.

720   The Saracens cross the Pyrenees.

721   Duke Eudo checks the Saracens near Toulouse.

724   Hisham becomes Caliph.

725   Charles Martel is busy holding back an attack from the Allemanni and Saxons. The Saracens take Autun, but Duke Eudo stops their further advance.

    The Emperor Leo III, shocked at the amount of image worship in the Christian Church, prepares for his "iconoclastic" campaign, whilst Pope Gregory II prepares his campaign to liberate Italy from the influence of Constantinople.

    The Khazars, of Turkish origin (see 704), having spread N.W. over the Caucasus into S. Russia, form a prosperous kingdom with its capital at Itil at the mouth of the Volga. Merchants of various faiths gather at Itil and suffer no religious persecution.

724   Caliph Hisham's reign, beginning in this year, sees the decline of the Umayyad dynasty, as also of Saracen aggression.

E. **Literature** (continued)

721 The book of the Lindisfarne Gospels is produced in memory of St Cuthbert, the hermit Bifrith being the artist.

F. **Births and Deaths**

701 Li Po b. (-761).

705 The Empress Wu d. (81).
Leontius and Tiberius II d.

707 St Wilfrid d.

711 Justinian II d.

713 Musa, Saracen governor, d.
Tu Fu b. (-768).

714 Pepin II d.

715 Walid I, Caliph, d.

726   The Emperor Leo III issues his iconoclastic decree (see C). It arouses much opposition and a rival emperor is even proclaimed in Greece—he, and his fleet, being
defeated in an attempt to capture Constantinople.

727   Pope Gregory II resists the iconoclastic edict.

728/9   King Liutprand of the Lombards (see 712), Romanized but ambitious and having
allied himself with Pope Gregory II against the power and interference of Constantinople (see C), approaches too near to Rome in the extension of his kingdom,
and is rebuked and checked by the Pope. He captures Ravenna, but restores it. He
dares to attack Rome, but again desists, on Gregory's persuasion.

731   Duke Eudo of Aquitaine (see 725) suffers a defeat by the Saracens at Arles.

732   The fanatical Saracen general Abd-er-Rahman resumes the offensive against Duke
Eudo, who retires northwards through Poitiers and enlists the aid of Charles
Martel. The combined armies of these two leaders face the Saracens in front of
Tours (the holy place of France's St Martin). After a 7 day confrontation—and a
hundred years after the death of Mahomet—the battle of Tours (sometimes called
the battle of Poitiers) is fought. The Saracen general is slain, and the advance of the
Saracens into Europe is stopped. Charles earns his title of Martel, the Hammer.

733   Leo III sends a fleet to castigate the recalcitrant Pope Gregory II; but it is wrecked.

735   Duke Eudo dies after inflicting, with Charles Martel, further defeats on the Saracens.
Charles Martel takes over Aquitaine, allowing Eudo's son the title of Duke. His
own son is "adopted" by the ambitious Liutprand of Lombardy.

737   Charles Martel takes Avignon from the Saracens.

738   The German barbarians feel the power of Charles Martel, who campaigns against them
and exacts tribute.

739   The defeat of the Saracens at Tours gives the king of Asturias a chance to extend his
frontiers into Lusitania.
Charles Martel, with Liutprand to help him and having had to lay waste much of the
countryside (and fire the amphitheatre at Nimes), succeeds in driving the Saracens
out of Provence.

740   Leo III defeats the Saracens at Acronon.

741   This is a year of death and change of rulers. Pepin the Short and Carloman succeed,
in combination, to Charles Martel, Zacharias succeeds Gregory III as Pope, Walid
II succeeds Hisham as Caliph and Constantine V succeeds Leo III as Emperor.

743   Pope Zacharias prevails upon the Lombard King Liutprand to stop his expansionist
policy.

744   Walid II is assassinated; the Umayyad caliphate is sliding down to its end.
Liutprand dies. Lombardy has reached its apogee.

746   Plague is rife in Mesopotamia.

A. Politics, Law and Economics

726   Pope Gregory II is resisting the Emperor not only for his iconoclastic decree but on account of excessive taxation. He begins a process, continued by his successor Gregory III, of emancipating Italy and the Papacy from the control of the Byzantine Emperor.

748   Merchants of Venice are commanded by the Pope to stop selling African slaves to the Saracens.

749   Ethelbald of Mercia (see 716) frees his clergy from "burdens": i.e. the revenue from church lands will go to the church and not the king.

750   Alcuin, the Anglo-Saxon scholar, is being educated at the growing cathedral school at York.

B. Science and Discovery

742   The most famous alchemist, Gebir, *fl.* He practises also as a physician at Kufa.

748   A priest by the name of Vergilius is convicted of heresy for believing in the existence of the antipodes.

C. Religion and philosophy

726   Leo's iconoclastic decree, issued after a great meeting of bishops and senators, requires complete removal of icons from the churches and church murals to be covered, whilst all representations of Christ and the Virgin are forbidden; the decree however is not always strictly enforced. Pope Gregory II summons the western bishops and anathematizes the Iconoclasts.
Ine of Wessex follows Caedwalla's example and abdicates to end his days in Rome under the holy aura of the Pope.

730   The Patriarch of Constantinople joins the revolt against Leo and the iconoclasts, and is deposed.

741   Constantive V continues the Iconoclastic policy.

743   Caliph Walid II builds a winter palace at Mshatta in the Syrian desert, providing good examples of Moslem sculpture (which is forbidden to make "idolatrous" statues).

744   St Boniface becomes archbishop of Maine. He founds many schools and monasteries in Germany.

747   Under the encouragement of Ethelbald of Mercia the English clergy hold a synod to impose church discipline.

D. The Arts

740   Wang Wei, Chinese landscape painter, *fl.* He is also a poet.

747   A bronze *daibutsu* or colossus of Buddha is made in Japan, to propitiate the gods who are visiting the land with the scourge of smallpox.

747 Carloman (see 741) resigns his share of the Frankish kingdom to his brother Pepin the Short and retires to a monastery.

748 Abu-al-Abbas, a descendant of the Prophet, organizes a revolt against Merwan II the last of the Umayyad dynasty.

749 Abu proclaims himself Caliph at Kufa and defeats Merwan at the battle of the River Zab. Marwan flees to Egypt but is caught and killed and his head sent to Abu.

750 Abu-al-Abbas besieges and invests Damascus, massacres his opponents and becomes the founder of the dynasty of Abbasid caliphs. He calls himself The Bloodthirsty and even exhumes some of the recent Umayyad caliphs and has their corpses scourged, hanged and burnt.

E. Literature

730 John of Damascus writes against the Iconoclasts.

731 Bede's *Ecclesiastical History* is completed.

735 The legend is that Bede dies dictating a translation of St John's Gospel: "Take your pen and write quickly!"

740 Chinese poetry, shaking off all formalism, reaches its heights under the patronage of Hsuan Tsung: Li Po and Tu Fu are the great exponents.

748 Paul the Deacon, at Cassino, writes his *History of the Lombards*.

750 The *Manyoshu*, an anthology of four centuries of Japanese poetry, is published.

F. Births and Deaths

731 Pope Gregory II d.

732 Abd-er-Rahman (general) d.

735 Alcuin b. (–804).
The Venerable Bede d. (62).

735 Duke Eudo of Aquitaine d.

741 Charles Martel d. (52).
Pope Gregory III d.
Caliph Hisham d.
Emperor Leo III d. (61).

742 Charlemagne b. (–814).

744 Caliph Walid II d.
Liutprand of Lombardy d.

749 Caliph Mirwan II d.

750 Irene, Empress, b. (–803).
Cynewulf, Saxon poet, b.

751   The Saracens clash for the first time with the Chinese, defeating them at a battle near
Samarkand and, through prisoners, absorbing some far-eastern culture and
techniques.
Byzantine rule in N. and central Italy is at an end.

751   Java is taken over by a Buddhist dynasty of Sumatran origin, and Buddhism becomes
the official religion (and see F).

751/2   Pepin the Short has himself made king of the Franks, in name as he has already been
virtually in fact. The last of the Merovingian *rois fainéant* is put in a monastery and
St Boniface crowns Pepin at Soissons. Pepin also seeks the Pope's blessing on his
deeds.
King Aistulf of the Lombards, Liutprand's successor, takes Ravenna and demands
suzerainty over Rome as part of his enlarged dominion. The Pope asks for help
from the Emperor and gets no more than a letter of remonstrance sent to Aistulf; he
therefore makes the momentous move of appealing to the Franks.

753   Pope Stephen III travels to France and gives his blessing to Pepin's assumption of
royalty.

754   Abu the bloodthirsty dies of smallpox and is followed as Abbasid caliph by his half-
brother Mansur, a man of ability.

754/6   Pepin crosses the Alps with an army, and deprives the Lombard king of possession
of the Ravenna province and gives it—the so called "donation"—to the Pope, thus
fostering the Papacy's temporal power. Pepin puts a client-king, Desiderius, on the
Lombard throne and marries the man's daughter: the independent Lombard
kingdom is at an end.

755   The first revolt of a military governor against the Tang emperors occurs. An Lu-shan,
a Tartar and a court favourite promoted to generalship, leads a great rebellion
against Hsuan Tsung, who abdicates in favour of his son, who finally quells the
revolt—but see 766. Saracen troops are sent to the Chinese emperor's aid.

756   The Saracens in Spain break away from the caliphate and a dynasty is founded by a
refugee from the massacres at Damascus, Abd-er-Rahman I, a grandson of Hisham.
He makes Cordova his capital.

757   Offa succeeds Ethelbald as king of Mercia, to reign for 39 years and to bring about the
height of Mercian power. (He will be addressed by Popes as King of England
without qualification.)

759   Pepin finally expels the Saracens from their last holding in France, the coastline
between the Rhone and the Pyrenees peopled largely by Goths who have appealed
to him for help.

762   The Caliph Mansur founds a new capital for himself at Bagdad, near to the Persian
Ctesiphon (and see A). He appoints as his vizier Khalid of the Barmak family ("the
Barmecides").

A. Politics, Law and Economics

762   The Caliph Mansur, in creating an efficient administration at his new capital at Bagdad, makes great use of Persian officials—it is said in fact that Persia now conquers her conqueror. Mansur discourages speculation, and is financially efficient; he is also parsimonious and earns the name of "Father of Farthings".

B. Science and Discovery

762   On its foundation, men from the Persian, Greek and Jewish world flock to Bagdad. There begins the translation into Arabic of the books of classical Greek science. (and see 790 B).

764   The Bosphorus, in a severe winter, is crossed on ice.

C. Religion and Philosophy

754   The Emperor Constantine V, intensifying the iconoclastic movement, calls a council of Eastern bishops, who announce that "Satan has re-introduced idolatry". (The "Council of Hieria").

755   St Boniface is murdered by the Frisian barbarians whom he is trying to convert. Saracen mercenaries (see opposite) stay in China—the nucleus of a Moslem population.

757   The philosophic school of the Mutazilites is founded, criticizing the Koran and insisting that it should at times be interpreted allegorically.

758   Abd-er-Rahman I issues a letter giving protection to Christians in Spain.

760   The Mohammedan Ismaili sect is founded when the seventh Imam (or reincarnation), Ismail, being deposed from his status on the accusation of drunkenness, is held by his admirers to be the last and true Imam.

767   The Emperor Constantine continues his iconoclasm, with torture: this barbarism spreads to Rome.

768   Under Offa's patronage Alcuin teaches theology at York.

775   The Empress Irene moderates iconoclasm.

D. The Arts

751   The building of the great Buddhist temple of Borobudur in Java is begun.

760   The Hindu temple of Kailasha is carved out of the rock.

E. Literature

755   In legend the Chinese rebellion of this year centres round the Emperor's romantic concubine, Yang Kuei Fei.

763   The *Life* of Mohammed (revised and enlarged from that of Ibu Ishaq) is issued by Ibu Hisham.

763   The Senate and people of Rome send a letter of thanks to Pepin the Short, "patrician of Rome".
Tibetans sack the Chinese capital Ch'ang An only just recaptured from the rebels.

765   Pepin is busy trying to convert the Saxons to Christianity at the point of the sword.

766   In China the great rebellion is finally put down, having, it is said cost 36 million lives: an obvious exaggeration but irreparable damage has been done.

768   Pepin dies and divides his kingdom between his two sons, Charles (known to history as Charlemagne) and a second Carloman.

769   Charlemagne and Carloman quarrel. Constantine V's son, another Leo, marries Irene, later to become Empress and Regent.

770   Charlemagne and Carloman are reconciled by their mother, Bertha, who tries to arrange marriages for them with the daughters of King Desiderius of Lombardy. Only Charles' takes place—and he divorces the girl in the next year.

771   Carloman dies, leaving Charlemagne, aged 29, sole king of the Frankish dominions.

772   Charlemagne begins his long war against the Saxons.

773   The Lombard king Desiderius having invaded the Roman states, Pope Hadrian (or Adrian) I appeals to the Franks for help. Charlemagne besieges Desiderius in Pavia.

774   Pavia is taken and Desiderius dismissed to a monastery. Charlemagne promptly assumes the crown of Lombardy, confirms his father's "donation" (see 754) and accepts the rôle of protector of the Church.

775   Caliph Mansur dies on a pilgrimage to Mecca and is succeeded by his more open-handed son, al Mahdi.
The Emperor Constantine V dies and is succeeded by his son as Leo IV, with his empress, Irene.

---

766   With the rebellion against Hsuan Tsung the T'ang dynasty and culture deteriorates: a decline of 200 years until the emergence of the Sung Dynasty.

763   Tibetan expansion (see above) lasts for about a century only.

762   The effect of the foundation of Bagdad is profound: the Saracens change from military conquerors to liberal administrators.

E. **Literature** (continued)
768 Willibald, a disciple of St Boniface, writes the latter's *Life*.

F. **Births and Deaths**
754 Abu-al-Abbas d.

755 St Boniface d.

757 Ethelbald of Mercia d.

761 Li Po d. (60).

763 Haroun al-Rashid b. (–807).

768 Pepin the Short d.
     Tu Fu d. (65).

770 Einhard, Frankish historian, b. (–840).

771 Carloman II d.

774 Kobo Daishi, Japanese artist, b. (–835).

775 Mansur, Caliph, d.
     Constantine V, Emperor, d.

776 Charlemagne is successful against the Saxons, who, when defeated, face baptism or
death.

777 Charlemagne holds an assembly at Paderborn, Saxony being regarded by him as now
part of his kingdom.

778 Asked to inferfere in the quarrels of the Saracens in Spain, Charlemagne crosses the
Pyrenees and advances as far as Saragossa, when news comes of a Saxon revolt and
he turns back. Passing through a defile of the mountains at Roncesvalles, his rear-
guard, under his nephew, the paladin Roland, is cut to pieces by Basques (see E).

779 Charlemagne continues his Saxon campaigns.

780 The Emperor Leo IV dies and his widow Irene rules in the name of her ten year old
son Constantine VI.

781 An agreement is made between Charlemagne and the Pope on the one side and the
Byzantine regent Irene on the other, whereby the latter abandons all claim to
sovereignty over the Papal state.

782/4 The Caliph, al Mahdi, sends his son Prince Haroun into Asia Minor to combat an
invasion made by Byzantine troops sent there by the Empress Irene. Haroun is
successful and gains the title "al Rashid" (the Upright). Irene pays an indemnity.

783 The reconquest of Greece from the Slavs begins (see 576).

785 Charlemagne finally subdues the Saxons.
Irene reverses the iconoclastic edicts.
Al Mahdi makes Haroun his heir, at the expense of his elder son, al Hadi, and dies in
the ensuing revolt on the part of the latter. On the advice of the Barmecide Yahya,
Haroun acquiesces in the accession of his elder brother.

786 Al Hadi dies, said to have been murdered by his mother, who favours Haroun.
Haroun al-Rashid becomes Caliph, giving his Vizier Yahya and his four sons great
powers.

787 The first recorded Viking raid on England occurs, somewhere on the Wessex coasts,
the King's Reeve being murdered when he comes to demand the Norsemen's
business.

788/91 Charlemagne successfully campaigns against the Slavs and Avars.

790 Irene is compelled by the Army in Constantinople to retire from the regency.

791 Irene is restored to power by her son.

792 Charlemagne's natural son Pepin conspires against his father, and is sent to a monastery.
Offa annexes East Anglia to his kingdom (and see C).

793 The Vikings sack the monastery at Lindisfarne.

A. Politics, Law and Economics

782   Charlemagne's *Capitulatio de partibus Saxoniae* punishes by death a number of barbarian and anti-Christian habits, from murdering a bishop to contemptuously eating meat in Lent or burning the dead on a pagan pyre.

Paul the Deacon and Alcuin teach in Charlemagne's school at his palace at Aachen, the latter sent by King Offa and persuaded to stay.

787   By the time of the coming of the Vikings the Saxons have cleared much of England's forest and improved her farming. Except slightly in London, they have done nothing to create cities.

795   Theodulph, Bishop of Orleans, organizes free schools in the parishes of his diocese.

796   A commercial treaty is signed between Offa and Charlemagne.

797   Irene's usurpation of the Emperor's throne at Constantinople gives men a chance to argue that there is now *no* Roman Emperor—thus opening the way for Charlemagne.

799   Charlemagne, as he finds more time from his military campaigns, sees to the administration of his empire. He arranges military service on a feudal basis; he appoints a "Seneschal" or Head of his Administration, a "Count Palatine" or Chief Justice, and "Palgraves" or Judges. He issues capitularies, or chapters, of legislation. He institutes biennial assemblies of nobles, bishops etc. to consider and approve his edicts and to report on the state of affairs in their particular regions. He sends out *Missi dominici* to convey his wishes to local officials.

B. Science and Discovery

785   King Offa builds his dyke, between the rivers Severn and Dee, to keep out the Welsh.

790   Haroun and the Barmecide family increase their patronage of the sciences, particularly medicine, astronomy and chemistry, but not ruling out astrology and alchemy: the Arabian revival of science and learning, to blossom in the next two centuries, has begun.

792   Charlemagne plans a canal between the rivers Danube and Maine.

C. Religion and Philosophy

777   At Paderborn (see opposite) Saxony is divided into missionary districts and bishoprics. Under the Franks, monasteries are built.

785   With the intention of strengthening his authority, Offa creates a third archbishopric in England—in the middle of his own territory, at Lichfield.

787   At the Seventh Ecumenical Council, at Nicaea, Charlemagne puts pressure on the Pope to reject the doctrines of the Eastern, i.e. the Greek, Church.

792   In expiation of a crime committed in his conquest of East Anglia, Offa financially supports the school that King Ina has founded in Rome: this contribution becomes "Peter's pence".

795 Charlemagne sends an army across the Pyrenees, and the "Spanish March", a strip of Spain's N.E. coast, becomes part of the Carolingian empire.
Leo III becomes Pope—and proves unpopular in Rome.
The Vikings begin to raid the Irish coast.

796 Charlemagne completes the conquest of the Avars (with their so-called "rings" or fortified booty-dumps).
King Offa of Mercia dies, leaving Mercia at the height of its power but to give place to Wessex in the next century.

797 Irene deposes and blinds her own son, and reigns as Emperor.

799 Pope Leo III is maltreated and imprisoned in a monastery. He escapes to Charlemagne. Charlemagne sees his chance to exert his power over the world of classical Rome as well as over the barbarians. He returns Leo to Rome under escort and demands that both Leo and his accusers shall appear before him in Rome in the following year: the events have been set in train that lead to the crowning of Charlemagne in the following year as "Augustus", head of the Holy Roman Empire.

––––––––––

At the end of this century Japan's new "Capital of Peace" the city of Kyoto, is founded and will remain for the next four centuries (which are sometimes known as Japan's golden age).

The Khmers of Cambodia begin their rise to prosperity, leading to the building of their great Hindu temples at the end of the 9th century.

The Mayan civilization at about the end of this century begins an inexplicable exodus from its cities (in modern Gautemala and Honduras), its place being partly taken by the more warlike civilization of the Toltecs from Mexico (predecessors of the Aztecs).

The great migration by canoe and raft into the Polynesian islands of the Pacific probably starts at this time: certainly from the Indonesian peninsula and possibly also from Peru. The dates of the various Peruvian cultures prior to the Incas (outside the period of this book) are too uncertain to be usefully given.

C. Religion and Philosophy (continued)

799 Shankara, brahman philosopher, *fl.*

D. The Arts

776 The abbey church of St Denis in Paris is completed by Charlemagne.

780 Ceylon's city of Anuradhapura, with its great Buddhist stupas, is abandoned to the Tamils.

784 A copy of the Koran of this date, in the Cairo library, shows Moslem skill in calligraphy and illumination.

785 The mosque at Jerusalem is restored after damage by earthquake.

786 The Blue Mosque at Cordova is built.

793 Under King Offa of Mercia St Albans cathedral begins to be built.

E. Literature

778 The story of Roland at Roncesvalles, and of how he unavailingly blew his great horn, is attributed to the contemporary Archbishop of Rheims, Turpin.

786 Haroun al Rashid, on accession, proceeds to build up at Bagdhad his brilliant court. The poets Merwan and Abu Nuwas are his friends. He records stories in his state archives—thus giving rise to the legend of Scheherezade and the *Thousand and One Nights* (which is founded on an earlier Persian collection of tales).

787 Charlemagne issues a directive to his bishops, reproaching them for "uncouth language" and encouraging literary studies. He himself, though he greatly respects learning, never fully masters the art of writing.

790 Cynewulf, Northumbrian, *fl.* His chief poem is *Elene*, telling of Helena's finding of the true cross.

796 Alcuin retires from the school at Charlemagne's palace, to become Abbot at Tours and there to encourage his monks to copy out the Vulgate and many of the Latin classics; he writes himself, on Ethics and the lives of the saints.

799 At about this time the great illuminated Four Gospels, "the Book of Kells", is being produced, the last great work of the monastery of Iona.
Han Yu, Chinese essayist, *fl.*, representing the end of the vast T'ang literary output.

F. Births and Deaths

776 Rabanus Magnus (Abbot of Fulna) b. (–856).

778 Roland d.

780 Emperor Leo IV d.

F. **Births and Deaths** (continued)

785 Caliph Al Mahdi d.

786 Al Hadi d.

794 Turpin, bishop of Rheims, d.

795 Pope Adrian I d.

796 Offa of Mercia d.

INDEX

Notes for Use

All B.C. dates are in *italic* type and all A.D. dates in Roman.

References are to dates and paragraph letters and not to pages. Dates with no asterisk or paragraph letter refer to entries on the left-hand page. Those with an asterisk refer to entries on the left-hand page for which no specific date is shown and the index reference is to the opening date at the head of the page. Dates with a paragraph letter refer to entries on right-hand pages. When a multiple date, e.g. 401/9, is given in the index it indicates that there are several references to the subject within that time span. On the other hand when a multiple date is given in the text the first date only is given in the index. Similarly when no specific date is shown in the text the index reference is to the opening date at the head of the page. Dates in brackets signify only a reference to the event or person.

The subjects and persons under the following headings are indexed under those headings and not separately indexed under their names:

Arms, Weapons and military formations	Heresies
Battles	Laws and Legislation
Books	Plays
Books of the Bible	Saints
Churches	Temples
Gods	Wars

although Battles and Wars are also included in the entries for the countries or generals concerned. Otherwise Persons, Places and Subjects are listed in a single alphabetical sequence.

Such materials and objects as iron, tools and musical instruments, where their general or first use is of interest are separately indexed.

There are the following major general subject entries:

Agriculture	Hieroglyphics
Alphabets (and their equivalents)	Libraries
Aquaducts	Maps
Arms, weapons & military formations	Marriages
Assassinations	Mathematics
Astronomy	Medicine
Bridges	Monasteries & monasticism
Buddhism	Music
Boats & ships	Persecutions of Christians
Canals & waterworks	Plagues & epidemics
Coinage	Pottery
Drainage	Rebellions & revolutions
Earthquakes	Roads
Eclipses	Sculpture
Geography	Treaties

Kings, popes, emperors, pharaohs and caliphs are always listed under their names and not under a general heading. Not all of the ninety-six Popes who reigned between the death of St Peter and the year A.D. 799 are of historic interest and they have not therefore been listed; similarly neither are all the Pharaohs named nor all the Roman Emperors after Constantine.

Names are given in their most commonly used form and spelling, e.g. Mark Antony and not Marcus Antonius, Tutankamen and not the more orthodox Tutankhamun, the Koran and not Qur'an. Persons of the same name are distinguished by their titles; but on occasion, where there has been no simple distinction available, a number in brackets is given, e.g. Hannibal (II). When not obvious, the nationality of a person or the situation of a place—by modern reference rather than ancient if more helpful—is given.

Entries for persons considered important are treated in some detail, dates of less significance preceding the itemised entries. Dates of birth, and death where known, are shown by the first and last 'F' entries respectively. Where there are no 'F' entries the other references will show when the person flourished.

Countries with long histories such as Greece and Rome have their entries subdivided under Events and Other Topics, the first being in chronological order and the second in alphabetical.

The following abbreviations are used:

Alex.	Alexandrian	Eg.	Egyptian	math.	mathematician
Ass.	Assyrian	Gaul.	Gaulish	Mus.	Muslim
Ath.	Athenian	Ger.	German	Pers.	Persian
Bab.	Babylonian	Gk.	Greek	philos.	philosopher
Br.	British	Is.	Israelite	R.	Roman
Byz.	Byzantian	It.	Italian	Sax.	Saxon
Carth.	Carthaginian	Jap.	Japanese	Sp.	Spanish
Ch.	Chinese	Jew.	Jewish		

INDEX

A

Aaron, *1235* C
Abd-el-Malik, Caliph, 683, 691 D
Abd-er-Rahman, Saracen General, 732 and 732 F
Abd-er-Rahman I, ruler of Spain, 756, 758 C
Aberdeen, 208
abortion, *721* A, *200* A, *116* B
Abraham, *1800*
Absolam, *1000*
Abu-al-Abbas, Caliph, 748, 754, 754 F
Abu Bekr, Caliph, 632, 633 C, 634, 634 F
Abu Nuwas, Mus. poet, 786 E
Abu Simbel, Egypt, *1290* D, *589* E
Abyssinia, 329 C, 570. *See also* Ethiopia
Academy, Athens, *385* C, *450* C, *529* C
Achaea, Gk. state, *453, 446. See also under* Mycenae
Achaean League; founded *279* A; revived, *251*; frees
    Corinth, *245*; at war with Sparta, 222, *193, 188, 149*
Acragas, Sicily, *580, 570, 554, 488, 480, 475* D, *406.
    See also under* Agrigentum
Acropolis, Athens, *640, 448* D, *435* D, *407* D
Adad-idri, Syrian King, *859, 855*
Adad-nirari II, Ass. King, *911*
Adad-nirari III, *811, 802, 783, 783* F
Adamnan, Br. biographer, 680 E
Adrian I, Pope, 773 795 F
Adriatic sea, *387, 386* A
Aedile, R. office, *367* D
Aedui, Gaul tribe, 58
Aegean sea, *1600*, *1000**
Aegina, Gk. state and islands, *491, 491* A, *490* D, *487,
    459, 457 431,*
Aelia Capitolena (Jerusalem), 130 C, 132
Aelle, Sax. king, 477, 491
Aemilianus, R. emperor. 253, 253 F
Aemilius, Paullus, R. general, *195, 168/7, 167* A,
    160 F
Aequi, It. tribe, *500*, *431, 420**
Aeschines, Ath. orator, *389* F, *346* A
Aeschylus, Ath. dramatist, *525* F, *499* E, *484* E,
    472 E, *468/7* E, *458* E, *456* F
Aesop, *570* E
Aetius, Gk. medic, 356 B
Aetius, R. general; in Italy, 424; at Ravenna, 429; Br.
    appeal, 446; defeats Huns, 451; death, 454, 454 F
Aetolian League, *279* A, *193, 189*
Afghanistan, *180**
Africa, *6000* B, *610* B, *125* B
Africa, Roman, *146*; expansion, *101**; revolt, 117,
    160; Timgad, 117 A; Hadrian's visit, 128; under

Pertinax, 190; Severus' visit, 203; Gordian pro-
consul, 238; Vandals invade, 429; attempted in-
vasion, 468; Heracleus governor, 609; Byzantines
invade, 697; under Saracens, 708
Agag, Amalekite, king, *1025*
Agamemnon, Spartan king, *1400**
Agathias, Byz. poet, 550 E
Agathocles, Syracusan, *361* F, *304*; exiled, *325*;
    returns, *322*; becomes tyrant, *316*; beseiged, *312*;
    at Carthage, *310*; dies, *289, 289* F
Agathon, Ath. poet, *416* E
Ager gallicus, 232 A
Agesilaus, Spartan king, *441* F, *399, 399* A; fights
    Persia, *396, 395* A; invades Arcadia, *370*; in Egypt,
    363/1; dies, *360, 360* F
Agilulf, Lombard king, 591 D, 615 F
Agis, Spartan king, *415, 331* F
Agora, Athens, *465* D, *450*, *430* A
Agricola, R. general, 37 E, 74; governor of Britain,
    77; invades Scotland, 82/4; dies, 93, 93 F
agriculture, *8000* A, *7000* B, *4800, 4200, 4000*, *3100*,
    2500, 1800, 320 A, *170* E, *133* A
Agrigentum, Sicily, *278, and see* Acragas
Agrippa, Jew. king, 60 C and E
Agrippa, R. general, *63* F; supports Octavia, 33, *33* B;
    builds aquaduct, *33* B; geographer, *23* B; marries
    21 A; pacifies Spain, *19*; in the East, *16/13*; dies,
    12 F
Agrippina, wife of Claudius, 48, 54/9, 59 F
Agum III, Kassite king, *1560* C
Ahab, King of Is., *877, 870, 853, 853* F
Ahaz, *723* F
Ahhiyawa, (? Greeks), *1380**
Ainus, Jap. Tribe, *660**
Aistulf, Lombard king, 751
Akhneten, pharaoh, *1363/50, 1363* A, C, D and E,
    1350 F
Akheteten, Eg. city, *1363, 1363* D
Alaca Huyuk, Hittite site, *2400, 2400* C and D
Alalakh, Syrian site, *1700*, *1600* E, *1370, 1194*
Alalia, *see* Aleria
Alans, barbarian tribe, 136, 355
Alaric I, Gothic king, 396, 401/9, 410, 410 F
Alaric II, 507
Albinus, Clodius, R. pretender, 194/6, 197 F
Albinus, R. consul, *110*
Alcaeus, Gk. poet, *600* E
Alcibiades, Ath., *450* F, *430* D, *420* E, *410*; life saved
    by Socrates, *432* C, *424* C; leads war party, *422*;
    elected Strategos, *420*; has Melos destroyed, *416*;
    is recalled from Sicily, *415*; defects to Sparta, *413*;

467

I